AF352502

THEOLOGY NEEDS PHILOSOPHY

THEOLOGY NEEDS PHILOSOPHY

ACTING AGAINST REASON IS CONTRARY TO THE NATURE OF GOD

Edited by Matthew L. Lamb

THE CATHOLIC UNIVERSITY OF AMERICA PRESS

Washington, D.C.

Library of Congress Cataloging-in-Publication Data

Names: Lamb, Matthew L., editor.

Title: Theology needs philosophy : acting against reason is contrary
to the nature of God / edited by Matthew L. Lamb.

Description: Washington, D.C. : The Catholic University of America Press,
2016. |

Includes bibliographical references and indexes.

Identifiers: LCCN 2015038133 | ISBN 9780813228396 (cloth : alk. paper)

Subjects: LCSH: Catholic Church and philosophy. | Philosophical theology |
Faith and reason—Christianity.

Classification: LCC BX1795.P47 T44 2016 | DDC 230.01—dc23

LC record available at http://lccn.loc.gov/2015038133

Contents

Acknowledgments

This volume owes its excellence to the scholars who researched and wrote on the need of philosophy for good theological reflection. In a variety of ways they have shown the relevance of ancient wisdom and intelligence to meeting the problems the Church and cultures are facing in our times. I also owe a debt of gratitude to the administration, faculty, and staff of Ave Maria University who assisted in holding yearly conferences on theological questions. Some of the essays in this book originated at a conference in 2011, "Philosophy in Theological Education."

Special thanks are due to Mercedes Cox and Susan Nutt, as well as Dr. Michael Dauphinais, Dr. Matthew Levering, and Dr. Roger Nutt. Gratitude is also due to Trevor Lipscombe, Richard Lender, James C. Kruggel, Susan Needham, and Theresa Walker, along with their staff at the Catholic University of America Press, for invaluable assistance in bringing this work to publication. Gratitude is also due to Louise A. Mitchell for proofreading and for the index. The scholars chosen to review the manuscript provided helpful suggestions that have improved the book.

The Need for Reason in Theology

MATTHEW L. LAMB

The studies in this book indicate the influences of human reason throughout Christian theological reflections on the teachings of Christian faith. The universality of this faith—proclaiming salvation to all races and peoples—requires that reflection on it draw upon the universality of the God-given light of human reason. Pope Francis in his first encyclical, *Lumen Fidei*, has taken up the theme of his predecessors in stating that the light of faith heals and elevates the light of reason.[1] Saint John Paul II and Pope Emeritus Benedict XVI learned from great Catholic minds, like those of Augustine and Aquinas, how to articulate the universality of human reason across all times and cultures. This is the key to counteracting the distortions of nominalism/ voluntarism and meeting the intellectual challenges we face at the dawn of Catholicism's third millennium. St. John Paul II realized how St. Thomas Aquinas had provided this key.[2] *The key is that all human beings experience in their conscious living related and recurrent patterns of objects and acts. It*

1. Cf. Reinhard Hütter, "Reflections on *Lumen Fidei*," *Nova et Vetera* 12.1 (2014): 1–10; and Irene Alexander, "*Lumen Fidei* and Contemporary Errors on Faith," *Nova et Vetera* 12.1 (2014): 11–23.

2. Cf. the volume *John Paul II and St. Thomas Aquinas,* ed. Michael Dauphinais and Matthew Levering (Ave Maria, Fla.: Sapientia Press, 2006), especially the essays by Avery Dulles, Michael Sherwin, Reinhard Hütter, Guy Mansini, Thomas Weinandy, and Matthew Levering; also Matthew Lamb, "The Challenges Facing Catholic Intellectual Life," *Nova et Vetera* 11.4 (2013): 969–91.

was obvious to Karol Wojtyła and Joseph Ratzinger that the logos of human reason means that all human beings are endowed with God-given reason, and so human experience is structured by related and recurrent acts moved by experienced objects. As Wojtyła wrote in *The Acting Person*:

The expression "actus humanus" itself is not only derived from the verb *agere*—which establishes its direct relationship with action and acting because *agere* means to act or to do—but it also assumes, as it is traditionally used in Western philosophy, a specified interpretation of the action, namely, the interpretation found in the philosophies of Aristotle and St. Thomas Aquinas. This interpretation is realistic and objectivistic as well as metaphysical. It issues from the whole conception of being, and more directly from the conception of *potentia-actus,* which has been used by Aristotelians to explain the changeable and simultaneously dynamic nature of being.[3]

Following Church Fathers and medieval schoolmen Wojtyła knew that all human beings experience acts of sensing, of perceiving, of imagining, as well as acts of inquiring, understanding, conceiving, weighing the evidence, judging the truth of something understood, along with acts of deliberating what is good, of deciding, of acting, loving, etc. The acts are moved by all the sensible objects in the world around us, as well as by persons and realities that go beyond our senses. The universality of reason is oriented to the universality of being. Thus there is an implicit metaphysics in all human acting. Rendering metaphysics explicit requires a collaborative attuning of mind and heart to the whole of being and its causes down the ages. Vincent Potter has shown the similarities between Wojtyła and Bernard Lonergan, who transposed Aquinas's metaphysics into the worldview of emergent probability and a metaphysics that provides open and ongoing orderings of all the natural and human sciences.[4]

3. Cf. Karol Wojtyła, *The Acting Person,* trans. Andrzej Potocki (Boston: D. Reidel Publishing, 1997); see the better German translation from the Polish by Herbert Springer, *Person und Tat* (Freiburg: Herder, 1982), 33. Joseph P. Rice has drawn upon the Polish original and emphasizes, as I do, Wojtyła's transcendental approach that breaks through the dichotomies between subjectivity and objectivity; see his "Consciousness, Conscience, and Persons: A Reflection on Wojtyła's 'Trans-Phenomenological' Approach to Subjectivity and Intersubjectivity," at the 2012 Fellowship of Catholic Scholars Conference unpublished. Also Rocco Buttiglione, *Karol Wojtyła: The Thought of the Man Who Became Pope John Paul II,* trans. Paolo Guitti and Francesca Murphy (Grand Rapids, Mich.: Eerdmans, 1997); as Vincent Potter, SJ, points out, it would be futile to oppose Wojtyła to Thomas Aquinas. In this regard Potter sees that Bernard Lonergan, SJ, adopts a similar way of seeing a key to human experience in Aquinas; cf. *The Thought of Pope John Paul II*, ed. John McDermott, SJ (Rome: Gregoriana, 1993), 205–12.

4. Potter, "Philosophical Correlations," and Lonergan, *Insight: A Study of Human Understanding* (Toronto: University of Toronto Press, 1992), 93–162; 410–617. See also Matthew Lamb, "Lonergan's Transpositions of Augustine and Aquinas," in *The Importance of Insight,* ed. John and David Liptay (Toronto: University of Toronto Press, 2008), 4–21; and "Bernard Lonergan, S.J.: The Gregorian Years" to be published by the Gregorian University Press.

Wojtyła understood that the ancients realized human beings can attend to the objects and acts that are in the field of their conscious experience. Augustine had provided a narrative description of these, distinguishing the acts of judging as knowing, distinct from acts of thinking that may or may not be true. It was through judgment that reason guided the will to choose what is truly good rather than what only appears good to disordered human desires. Wojtyła saw that we must make attention to our personal identity explicit, and not simply speak of the soul with its powers or faculties. Personal identity transposes, that is, makes intelligible to contemporaries, what the Thomist theoretical metaphysics analyzes as the rational soul (animus) with its faculties of intellect and will. All men experience their own identity, who they are. Augustine had forged autobiographical narrative in his *Confessions*. Who one is involves an ongoing set of experiences of conscious questioning and desiring. This is universal in human beings. Wojtyła's *Acting Person* called attention to these conscious experiences as related and recurrent patterns of acting. Learning something at first is difficult but then becomes much easier as habits are acquired. While himself attending to Aquinas's metaphysical theory, Wojtyła conveys the experiential import, calling all men and women to attend to what they all share as rational beings.

By concentrating upon the related and recurrent acts in all human experiencing, understanding, knowing, deliberating and deciding, recent popes have shown that the intellectualism of an Augustine and Aquinas provides us with ways to correct the distortions caused by nominalism and voluntarism in modernity. In William of Ockham, metaphysics became dominated by a conceptualist logic that replaced potency-form-act with "mere possibilities" to be exploited by power calculations. Against the "intellectualism of Augustine and Aquinas" Benedict XVI traced nominalist a-rational voluntarism to "the image of a capricious God, … who is not even bound to truth and goodness." God's otherness is "so exalted that our reason, our sense of the true and good, are 'not found in God,' whose ungrounded possibilities are eternally unattainable and hidden behind His actual decisions."[5]

Benedict XVI sees the deepening rejection of the Hellenic discovery of logos and reason in successive nominalist philosophers and theologians through the Protestant Reformation and the Enlightenment.[6] Reason is

5. *Pope Benedict XVI*, "Regensburg Lecture," citing Manuel II Palaeologus, *Dialogue VII*, 3b–c, in Sources chrétiennes, vol. 115, ed. Theodore Khoury (Paris: Cerf, 1966) 144; see "Lecture of the Holy Father: Faith, Reason and the University; Memories and Reflections," (Libreria Editrice Vaticana; September 12, 2006), §2: "ungrounded possibilities" is a better translation of "abgründige Möglichkeiten," since it brings out the break between reason and will that allows the will to dominate reason and to subjugate it as a tool of the will to power.

6. "Regensburg Lecture" §25; see also James V. Schall, SJ, *The Regensburg Lecture* (South

bifurcated into sensations and concepts, so that we intuit only sensations or concepts rather than real beings. There was a massive eclipse of judgment as knowing the real. Universals are only "flatus vocis"—empty words used to arbitrarily label fragmented individual entities or, in Leibniz's terms, monads. Will as will-to-power dominates and controls any and all uses of reason, which is reduced to an instrument in the will's struggle for control and dominance. Eventually cultures become distorted by relativism, historicism, nihilism, and fundamentalism:

Looked at closely, nihilism and the fundamentalism of which we are speaking share an erroneous relationship to truth: the nihilist denies the very existence of truth, while the fundamentalist claims to be able to impose it by force. Despite their different origins and cultural backgrounds, both show a dangerous contempt for human beings and human life, and ultimately for God himself. Indeed, this shared tragic outcome results from a distortion of the full truth about God: nihilism denies God's existence and his provident presence in history, while fanatical fundamentalism disfigures his loving and merciful countenance, replacing him with idols made in its own image. In analyzing the causes of the contemporary phenomenon of terrorism, consideration should be given, not only to its political and social causes, but also to its deeper cultural, religious and ideological motivations.[7]

Nominalism, in exalting the will over reason, broke all living continuity with the great philosophical and theological traditions of the past. Doctrinal and theoretical traditions were devalued into purely "textual" and "verbal" matters. Reason as an instrument of the will to power simply slaps labels on objects, and the ones with more power do more labeling of objects and laws. Laws were not expressions of practical intelligence aimed at educating citizens in virtues, as classical traditions held; rather, laws became arbitrary exercises of will to enforce external behavior. How can Catholic intellectual life overcome the dualisms between mind and body,[8] between subjects and

---

Bend, Ind.: St. Augustine's Press, 2007), 90–124.; Etienne Gilson, *The Unity of Philosophical Experience* (San Francisco: Ignatius Press, 1999) 61–121; Brad S. Gregory, *The Unintended Reformation: How a Religious Revolution Secularized Society* (Cambridge, Mass.: Harvard University Press, 2012); and the writings of Alasdair MacIntyre.

7. "Regensburg Lecture," §10. Benedict sees the world of today threatened by those who deny the truth of human nature and reason. Foremost among such denials he singles out, citing Blessed Paul VI and St. John Paul II, are nihilism and fundamentalism that feed upon one another.

8. In his encyclical *Deus Caritas Est*, Benedict spells out how the infused love of the Triune God, *agape* or charity, in no way negates or minimizes the human forms of love such as *eros* and *philia*, married love and the love of friendship. The redemption of creation heals erotic love and friendship from the disorders that sin had introduced. Indeed, agapic love transforms erotic love into the holy mystery of Christ's love for his Church in the sacrament of marriage. The higher does not negate the lower; so also the light of faith in no way "blinds" or negates the light of reason.

objects, between empirical science and theoretical wisdom, to recover the unity of the God-given light of reason in its full breadth and depth?

Among philosophers seeking to recover the reach of reason, Ralph McInerny wrote a few months before his death:

The reach of reason must be defended, its capacity to know and to attain truth. This is of supreme philosophical importance. Why else did Plato and Aristotle devote so much attention to the Sophists? To the principle of contradiction? But it has the further importance that, if reason's ability to arrive at truth is questioned, faith, which builds on reason, will be undermined as well. It would be impious of us to permit such undermining.[9]

When Popes John Paul and Benedict emphasized the fundamental role reason must play in all human living, especially in living out religious faith, they were calling attention to a fundamental tenet of Catholic theology. Popes and scholars have long realized that the wisdom traditions of millennia to be found in Catholicism offer contemporary men and women invaluable resources to meet present and future challenges to the cultivation of reason in all spheres of human endeavor and living.

In this volume theologians and philosophers explore the importance of understanding that Christian faith builds on reason. Some of the presentations originated at a conference, "Philosophy in Theological Education" at Ave Maria University, February 10–12, 2011. An exceptional philosopher, Ralph McInerny, whom I had originally invited to attend the conference, died the previous year. Thus some of the presentations, and the conference in general, honored his valuable legacy. All the presentations, along with other essays, were submitted in writing after the conference for inclusion in this volume.

McInerny clearly understood the vital significance of philosophy and the reasoned demands of truth for theology. The light of faith, far from blinding the light of reason, should heal and elevate human intelligence and reason. His 1999–2000 Gifford Lectures, *Characters in Search of Their Author*, summed up well his dedication to the importance of human reason attaining the truth of God's existence in natural theology. While he might agree with Walker Percy that modern secularists try to live like "cosmic orphans," he nevertheless saw that all human beings are, in fact, characters in search of their divine author.[10]

---

9. Ralph McInerny, "Why I Am a Thomist," *American Catholic Philosophical Quarterly* 83.3 (2009): 330.

10. Cf. *Characters in Search of Their Author* (Notre Dame, Ind.: University of Notre Dame Press, 2001); also Walker Percy, *Lost in the Cosmos: The Last Self-Help Book* (New York: Picador, 1986).

The chapters in this work indicate some of the main areas wherein theology needs sound philosophy. The first part takes up the need for faith to build on reason. Bishop Charles Morerod demonstrates that even theologians who never advert to philosophy in their works, not unusual in the theologians he cites, are in fact making philosophical claims that can be adjudicated by reasoned philosophical arguments. Morerod shows how failure to attend to demonstrably wrong philosophical presuppositions undermines the validity of theological positions. A student, friend, and colleague of McInerny, Dr. John O'Callaghan, then raises a similar theme. He shows that full justice to the revelation of mankind made in the image of God is most adequately accomplished by the Aristotelian philosophy appropriated by St. Thomas Aquinas. O'Callaghan shows the importance of recovering a holistic Thomist philosophy of human nature to the overcoming of modern dualistic tendencies toward idealism or materialism. These tendencies spring from a neglect of Aquinas's achievements by philosophers after Ockham, Descartes, and Kant.

Part Two takes up the recovery of the metaphysics of nature and the natural knowledge of God as fundamental for theology. The Dominican Fr. Lawrence Dewan, who died February 12, 2015, spells out the metaphysics of creation in the light of the first question in Aquinas's *Summa theologiae*. Referring to a later work of McInerny,[11] Dewan shows what Aquinas meant by the preambles to the faith on the part of human reason, and why reasoned philosophical reflection in no way diminishes, but rather increases, the merit of believing sacred teachings of faith. Following Augustine's insight that we do not love the unknown but love to know the unknown, Dewan ends by quoting Aquinas that our very love for the revealed Triune God revealed in sacred doctrine encourages reasoned reflections on the mysteries.

Fr. Joseph Koterski then reflects on the philosophy of nature needed for an adequate theological anthropology. He carefully outlines key elements for an understanding of nature and how different kinds of natures have intrinsic orientations to diverse goods. Only then will the significant consequences for the *bodily, psychic, and spiritual dimensions of human nature* be seen in the divine plan for creation. Attention to human nature in this complex interplay of its dimensions will orient the freedom of personal choices toward the truly good. Koterski then shows that the elaboration of nature in a theological anthropology is decisive for a theological understanding of God's redemption of fallen human nature in recapitulating the whole of creation in Christ.

Dr. Steven Long provides a detailed argument that Aquinas correctly

---

11. Cf. Ralph McInerny, *Praeambula Fidei: Thomism and the God of the Philosophers* (Washington, D.C.: The Catholic University of America Press, 2006).

understood Aristotle as holding a natural theology in which God is first cause. Because he is Pure Act, God transcends the universe *a se*. God is not for Aristotle an outermost part of the universe, but is eternal and immutable, causing all finite beings but not being caused. Aquinas draws upon Aristotle to develop an analogy of proper proportionality since all created being is composed of potency and act. Long argues that this implies a divine immediacy, which other forms of analogy cannot provide. Aquinas will base his teachings on participation on the quintessentially Aristotelian teaching that all being is divided by potency and act. McInerny's insistence on the logical dimensions of analogy in Aquinas does not, for Long, exclude the metaphysical aspects of analogy. Metaphysicians have to articulate their field in grammatically and logically correct ways. Long also argues that both Aristotle and Aquinas acknowledged the real distinction of essence and existence.

The chapters in Part Three explore the foundational relevance of human reason in responding in faith to divine revelation. Jesuit Fr. Brian Daley takes up Pope Benedict's use, in his Regensburg Lecture, of logos as applied to both reason and Christ. Daley masterfully traces the interplay of reason and faith through the Greek Fathers Justin, Athanasius, Gregory Nazianzen, and John Damascene. He then shows it in Augustine and Aquinas, concluding with the need to recover it after Reformers and Enlightenment thinkers introduced the modern dichotomy between reason and faith in Christ. Echoing the Regensburg Lecture, Daley concludes: "If philosophy represents the best and most concentrated efforts of human reason … to connect and arrange our understanding of the world, philosophy and theology clearly need each other to reach their goal."

Dr. Roger Nutt, drawing upon McInerny's book *Praeambula Fidei*, develops a detailed argument against Kant, Locke, and Russell insofar as their rationalism dichotomized human reason and faith in Christ and his Revelation. Nutt bases his criticisms on a careful analysis of how for Aquinas philosophy ought to be used by the believer in order to demonstrate the preambles of faith, which we must necessarily know in the act of faith. Such are the truths about God that are proved by natural reason, for example, that God exists, that he is one, and other truths of this sort about God or creatures proved in philosophy and presupposed by faith. Far from blinding reason, the preambles show the credibility and connaturality of believing the Word of God as a call to an absolutely supernatural friendship with the Father in the Son through the Holy Spirit.

The next two chapters further a recovery of Aquinas's complementarity of reason and faith. McInerny founded Dumb Ox Press to publish translations of Aquinas's commentaries on Aristotle, to which he would write prefaces.

Dr. Kevin White takes up three of these commentaries in which Aquinas offers cogent theoretical reflections on human reason; reason's task is both to discover the order in nature and rightly to order genuinely human living. Introducing Aristotle's *Posterior Analytics,* Aquinas shows the order needed in the science of logic with its demonstrations and its relation to rhetoric and poetics. The introduction to the *De Caelo* takes up the proper order of the natural sciences; there, Aquinas distinguishes the four kinds of order in practical reason and the four analogous kinds of order in the works of speculative reason. Introducing his commentary on the *Nicomachean Ethics,* Aquinas distinguishes two kinds of order in things, the order of parts to the whole and a teleological order of things to an end. With these distinctions he goes on to show the ordered activities of reason (1) in natural philosophy, including mathematics and metaphysics; (2) in rational philosophy ordering principles to conclusions; (3) in moral philosophy, with which he deals in the commentary, the order of right reason in human living; and (4) in the mechanic arts that produce or make things. White deftly discusses reason discerning order in things while also ordering its own movements, as well as other human acts.

The Dominican Fr. Timothy Bellamah describes some medieval theologians using philosophical resources to know sacred Scripture in its causes. Bellamah discusses the work of Proclus, *Elements of Theology.* He shows that Aquinas correctly realized that the *Liber de Causis,* attributed to Aristotle, was in fact dependent upon Proclus. This work showed the interplay between God's governance and the freedom of secondary human causes. This attention to secondary causes led twelfth- and thirteenth-century commentators increasingly to attend to authorial intention. In Aquinas we see the centrality of the literal sense of Scripture as fundamental, while also acknowledging the spiritual senses. Bellamah shows that the four causes of Aristotle and the *Liber de Causis* provided the scope for thirteenth-century commentators on Scripture, and pre-eminently Aquinas, to give attention to the literal sense of the diverse human authors, without compromising the unity of revealed truth in the Bible.

The final two parts take up the role of philosophy in doctrinal-systematic and moral theology. Fr. Gilles Emery, well known for his books on Aquinas's Trinitarian theology, analyzes Aquinas's philosophy of relations. This is a topic crucial, not only in logic and metaphysics, but also in Trinitarian and Christological theology. Emery first sets out the category of relation and its constitutive elements; he then discusses the distinctions between real relations and relations of reason. After this he deals with the most significant properties of relations and concludes by contrasting Aquinas's account of the relationship between the world and God with that of Duns Scotus.

Dr. John Boyle begins his essay quoting McInerny to the effect that today a recovery of traditional philosophy is urgently needed. Turning to a treatment of the Holy Spirit in Thomas's Roman commentary on Book One of Peter Lombard's *Sentences*, Boyle gives us Aquinas clearly showing his students the place of philosophical analysis at the heart of theology. The procession of the Holy Spirit is understood differently from that of the Word, once the students grasp the difference between the key concepts or *rationes* of love and word. The defining intelligibility or *ratio* of a word is a natural likeness to that from which it proceeds, so fathers generate sons and true concepts generate true sentences in words. This is the proper analogue for the Father generating the Son. But the procession of the Holy Spirit has the *ratio* of love, and love makes the lover proceed to the beloved. So the proper analogue for the procession of the Holy Spirit is the love spirated as love and gift between Father and Son. Nature, Aquinas tells his students, is not univocal but analogical. So there is one Divine Nature with three equal Divine Persons. Boyle concludes that these analogs of the Triune mystery are needed today. If we ignore traditional philosophy, our theological reflections on the Trinity will be at best opaque and at worst erroneous. "Here too, as Professor McInerny would remind us, St. Thomas is a good teacher."

The Benedictine theologian Fr. Guy Mansini seeks to clarify the need of philosophy in theology by sketching Msgr. Robert Sokolowski's reflections on the topic relative to Christology. When commenting on Aristotle and Aquinas, McInerny frequently asserted that the speculative/theoretical activity is the highest natural activity aimed at knowing the truth. "In the speculative use of our mind we have in view no end beyond the perfection of the act of knowing itself, and perfection is truth, to be in conformity with the way things are."[12] Mansini's chapter first describes the need to acquire a habit of philosophical reflection; then he takes up Sokolowski's theology of disclosure. Knowing the truth of natural things, theologians will be able to disclose the contours of natural things with the true realities revealed by God and known in faith. There is a complementarity of natural truth and revealed truth. After he summarizes some of the disclosures in Sokolowski's books, Mansini concludes by pressing a Christology of disclosure in ways that reveal that Christ on the cross could take into his mind and heart the massive histories of suffering throughout history, and so dramatically present in the twentieth-century holocaust.

The next chapter takes up the role of philosophy for Mariology. Fr. Romanus Cessario introduces the reader to the Thomist reflections on the Blessed

12. Cf. McInerny, "The Division of Philosophy," in Thomas Aquinas, in *History of Western Philosophy*, vol. 2, http://www3.nd.edu/Departments/Maritain/etext/hwp220.htm

Virgin Mary of Charles De Koninck, in his work, *Ego Sapientia: The Wisdom That Is Mary*. After sketching De Koninck's concern as similar to the concerns of the River Forest Dominicans, Cessario wonderfully illustrates how *Ego Sapientia* provides an authentic Thomist undergirding of St. Louis de Montfort's true devotion to Mary, whose created wisdom manifests the dignity of creation and the redemption of creation in her son, Jesus Christ, who is also the Son of God. Cessario then takes up the need for a philosophically astute recovery of the sacramental theology of Aquinas. The wisdom of sacramental causality, Cessario shows, was eclipsed by a neglect of Thomist philosophy of efficient causality and now must be recovered in order to realize that the sacraments carry forward the redemptive visible and invisible missions of Christ and the Holy Spirit who graced the Blessed Virgin Mary, Mother of God.

Fr. Kevin Flannery then provides a moving set of reflections on the last book that Ralph McInerny published, *Dante and the Blessed Virgin*. Flannery takes us through the three levels of McInerny's meditations on Dante's masterpiece: hell, purgatory, and heaven. The truths that philosophers like Plato and Aristotle have proved are taken up among the truths about God revealed to the faithful. This is what McInerny, following Aquinas, calls the preambles. Not Virgil, but Beatrice—whom McInerny and others see as a "stand in" for Mary the Mother of God—is the Queen of Heaven and Earth leading the blessed into the beatific vision.

Chapters in the final section emphasize the need of philosophy for moral theology. Already in Part Two, the concern for natural law was established as fundamental for ethics and morality.[13] Dr. Marc Guerra takes up the problematic issue of Aristotle's notion of magnanimity and the fact that among his list of virtues humility is nowhere to be found. This is often used to criticize Aquinas's use of Aristotelian ethics. Guerra shows, however, that Aquinas incorporates magnanimity into his understanding of the natural virtue of justice, which he calls "the most excellent of all the moral virtues" informing, ennobling, and transcending the realm of human affairs. Guerra first carefully analyzes Aristotle's presentation of magnanimity in Book IV of his *Nicomachean Ethics*, showing that he developed it in ways not seen in his previous reflections on the virtue. Then he takes up Aquinas's commentary on the texts in the *Nicomachean Ethics* and shows how he grasped the nuances of Aristotle's thought. Then in the *Summa theologiae* Aquinas analyzes magnanimity as a part of fortitude or courage in ways Aristotle did not know. As Guerra remarks: "In sharp contrast to the great-souled man of

---

13. Cf. Ralph McInerny, Ethica Thomistica: *The Moral Philosophy of Thomas Aquinas* (Washington, D.C.: The Catholic University of America Press, 1982).

Book IV of the *Ethics*, St. Thomas's magnanimous man acknowledges not only a cosmos above himself, but a cosmos that is ordered by and to a Being infinitely greater than the magnanimous man himself."

Fr. Sebastian Walshe examines De Koninck's careful analysis of Aquinas's understanding of the common good. Walshe first discusses three of the difficulties a contemporary student has in regard to the common good: Aquinas did not write a treatise on the common good; its meaning depends upon the various contexts in which he uses the term; most of all, it requires the sapiential theoretical or contemplative way of understanding that the intelligible, while causing the sensible, requires the student to move from the descriptive "priora quoad nos" to the explanatory "priora quoad se." There are then three key distinctions that De Koninck clarifies to understand the common good in Aquinas: first are integral, universal, and potential wholes; second is the distinction between the good as efficient cause and the good as final cause; third is the distinction of the good perfecting the speculative intellect and that perfecting the practical intellect. Walshe concludes by showing how Aquinas's notion of the common good is important for understanding that God redeems creation in the missions of Christ and his Church, for the most exalted common good is God himself.

In his chapter Dr. Christopher Kaczor clearly and concisely refutes mistaken presentations of Aquinas's commentaries on Aristotle. Specifically he takes up an ongoing argument he has with Mark Jordan's claim that Aquinas's commentary on Aristotle's *Nicomachean Ethics* (the Latin is *Sententia libri Ethicorum*) has implicit "disclaimers" where Aquinas signals his disagreement with Aristotle. After presenting Jordan's views, he then presents his criticisms of these supposed disclaimers. Finally, he takes up Jordan's latest response to his criticisms and evaluates their adequacy. Kaczor has learned well the dialectical discernment taught so effectively by his mentor in philosophy, Ralph McInerny.

In the Afterword, Ambassador Michael Novak's "Remembering a Genuine Lover of Wisdom" is a delightful way to conclude this exploration of the need for philosophy in theology. Novak sketches the vast range of both scholarship and wit in McInerny's life and writings. As is clear from Novak's memoirs, Ralph McInerny wishes no honor to be bestowed on him. Rather the legacy of his work seeks to honor the Catholic legacy discerning the roles of our God-given reason in honoring the Triune God by continuing to cultivate in our lives genuine intellectual, moral, and theological virtues. Only then can we continue the collaborative task of building faith on reason to show that not acting in accord with reason is contrary to the very nature of God.

PART ONE

A NEED FOR PHILOSOPHY IN THEOLOGY

CHAPTER 1

All Theologians Are Philosophers, Whether Knowingly or Not

CHARLES MOREROD, OP

Papal Warnings

Theologians have many debts of gratitude owed to the life and prodigious work of Professor Ralph McInerny. He called attention to the need for a genuinely philosophical formation for any theologian committed to the truth of our Catholic faith and teaching. In this he was echoing many a papal warning.

Philosophers may live in their little world, but—as artists also do—they feel and influence their culture. Philosophy has some influence on what everybody thinks. Who would have suspected, at the beginning of the eighteenth century, how deeply the Enlightenment philosophers would change the world over the next decades?

Pope Leo XIII was vividly conscious of the impact of philosophy, as he explained in his encyclical *Aeterni Patris* (1879):

Who so turns his attention to the bitter strifes of these days and seeks a reason for the troubles that vex public and private life must come to the conclusion that a fruitful cause of the evils which now afflict, as well as those which threaten, us lies in this: that false conclusions concerning divine and human things, which originated in the schools of philosophy, have now crept into all the orders of the State, and have been accepted by the common consent of the masses. For, since it is in the very nature of man to follow the guide of reason in his actions, if his intellect sins at all his will soon follows.[1]

Leo then invites theologians to take seriously the natural use of our reason, thereby promoting Thomistic studies.

When Leo insisted on philosophy, a theological movement tried to exclude Greek philosophy from theology. As Pope Benedict XVI reminded us in his famous Regensburg Lecture of September 12, 2006, a call for the dehellenization of Christianity "first emerges in connection with the postulates of the Reformation in the sixteenth century" and "the liberal theology of the nineteenth and twentieth centuries ushered in a second stage in the process of dehellenization."[2] The basic idea common to the different forms of such a process is good: the gospel must not be submitted to a human culture or philosophy. But where do we find a submission of the gospel to a human culture? The specific charge against Greek philosophy is a problem in itself, because it underestimates the role of divine Providence in the early meeting of Christian faith with the Greek culture.[3] But the refusal of Greek philosophy just opens the door to other philosophies. The real question is whether any philosophy playing a role in theology undermines the gospel. St. John Paul II summarized this question very well: "Were theologians to refuse the help of philosophy, they would run the risk of doing philosophy unwittingly and locking themselves within thought-structures poorly adapted to the understanding of faith."[4]

This last papal warning introduces my topic: "All Theologians Are Philosophers Whether Knowingly or Not." Using some examples—different from the ones I have used on previous occasions (the Reformation, and contemporary interreligious dialogue)[5]—I will try to look for the reason

1. Leo XIII, *Aeterni Patris* (August 4, 1879), in Carla Carlen, IHM, *The Papal Encyclicals 1878–1903* (Raleigh, N.C.: The Pierian Press, 1990), 17–18.

2. *The Regensburg Lecture* §32 and §36.

3. See John Paul II, *Fides et Ratio* (September 14, 1998), §72: "The Church cannot abandon what she has gained from her enculturation in the world of Greco-Latin thought. To reject this heritage would be to deny the providential plan of God who guides his Church down the paths of time and history. This criterion is valid for the Church in every age, even for the Church of the future, who will judge herself enriched by all that comes from today's engagement with Eastern cultures and will find in this inheritance fresh cues for fruitful dialogue with the cultures which will emerge as humanity moves into the future."

4. Ibid., §77.

5. When theologians think that they approach the gospel under the presupposition of "sola scriptura," they usually depend on some unnoticed fashionable philosophy. I have already tried to show this feature of the thought in Martin Luther and later Protestant theology: See Charles Morerod, *Cajetan et Luther en 1518*, Edition, traduction et commentaire des opuscules d'Augsbourg de Cajetan, "Cahiers Œcuméniques" 26, 2 t., (Fribourg: Editions Universitaires, 1994); *Ecumenism and Philosophy: Philosophical Questions for a Renewal of Dialogue*, trans. Therese C.

why no theologian can ever avoid philosophy, and to suggest how we can avoid changing faith by our use of philosophy. In so doing, I keep in mind the example of St. Thomas Aquinas, about whom McInerny rightly said, "A first thing to notice about Thomas's comparison of theology and philosophy is that he clearly supposes that the study of the former presupposes that one has already studied the latter. That is, only someone trained in philosophy could profitably take up the study of theology."[6] The necessity of using philosophy in theology also raises the question of which philosophy can be on good terms with theology. I will also consider this question by indicating how philosophies do in fact influence theological opinions with reference to a few modern theologians; then, referring to the writings of Cornelio Fabro and the distinguished McInerny, whose work and memory we are rightly celebrating, I will take up the question of which philosophy can assist Catholic theology to overcome modern shortcomings.

When Modern Philosophy Changes Theology

One of the most famous leaders of last century's exegesis, Rudolf Bultmann, expresses in his own way the relationship between philosophy—in his case, the worldview of the time—and theology. There is a philosophy—a worldview—in the Bible, and we have another one nowadays: "To demythologize is to deny that the message of Scripture and of the Church is bound to an ancient world-view which is obsolete.... For the world-view of the Scripture is mythological and is therefore unacceptable to modern man whose thinking has been shaped by science and is therefore no longer mythological."[7] What matters is not the present state of scientific theories, which will certainly change, but a certain way of looking at things:

The science of today is no longer the same as it was in the nineteenth century, and to be sure, all the results of science are relative, and no world-view of yesterday or today or tomorrow is definitive. The main point, however, is not the concrete results of scientific research and the contents of a world-view, but the method of thinking from which world-views follow.... Modern man acknowledges as reality only such

---

Scarpelli (Ann Arbor, Mich.: Sapientia Press, 2006). I have also tried to show that John Hick, described by Cardinal Ratzinger as one of great lights of contemporary religious relativism, interpreted his interreligious experience within the framework of his previous Kantian epistemology: See Morerod, *La philosophie des religions de John Hick: La continuité des principes philosophiques de la période "chrétienne orthodoxe" à la période "pluraliste"* (Paris–Les Plans: Parole et silence, 2006). For those who have taken the time to go through some of my previous publications, I would rather not add to their boredom by suggesting other examples.

6. Ralph McInerny, *Aquinas* (Cambridge, UK: Polity Press, 2004), 30.

7. Rudolf Bultmann, *Jesus Christ and Mythology* (New York: Charles Scribner's Sons, 1958), 36.

phenomena or events as are comprehensible within the framework of the rational order of the universe. He does not acknowledge miracles, because they do not fit into this lawful order.[8]

Therefore, concludes Bultmann, the gospel must be explained in such a way that it is acceptable. Well, the gospel must certainly be explained in a way that is understandable, and philosophy must question the credibility of some theological statements: Bultmann took part in contemporary biblical critical renewal, which bore many good fruits for a better understanding of the Bible. But to say that the gospel can be acceptable only if it fits into certain contemporary categories can lead away from useful critique. For instance, must all miracles be demythologized? What about mysteries, generally speaking? Bultmann does not deny the dimension of mystery; he just limits it to a particular field of life:

The objection is raised by a mistake, namely, the objection that de-mythologizing means rationalizing the Christian message, that de-mythologizing dissolves the message into a product of human rational thinking, and that the mystery of God is destroyed by de-mythologizing. Not at all. On the contrary, de-mythologizing makes clear the true meaning of God's mystery. The incomprehensibility of God lies not in the sphere of theoretical thought but in the sphere of personal existence. Not what God is in Himself, but how he acts with men, is the mystery in which faith is interested.[9]

When Bultmann rejects the accusation of rationalism, he just expresses another philosophical presupposition: what matters are not theories about God but the personal-existential dimension. The reader recognizes here the influence of Kant, who had said nearly a century and a half before:[10]

Whether we are to worship three or ten persons in the Divinity makes no difference: the pupil will implicitly accept one as readily as the other because he has no concept at all of a number of persons in one God (hypostases), and still more so because this distinction can make no difference in his rules of conduct.... The same holds true of the doctrine that one person of the Godhead became man. For if we think of this God-man, not as the Idea of humanity in its full moral perfection, present in God from eternity and beloved by Him, but as the Divinity "dwelling incarnate" in a real man and working as a second nature in him, then we can draw nothing practical from this mystery ... Similar considerations can be raised about the stories of the Resurrection and Ascension of this God-man.[11]

---

8. Ibid., 37–38.

9. Ibid., 43.

10. Bultmann's *Jesus* was first published in 1926 (with a fourth edition in 1970), Kant's *Streit der Fakultäten* in 1798.

11. Immanuel Kant, *The Conflict of the Faculties (Der Streit der Fakultäten)*, trans. with an

More or less consciously, Bultmann is influenced by a Kantian view or, more generally, by modern anthropocentrism. Bultmann is clear: What matters is the human being, what *we* do, what *we* are. Not what God is in himself, but how he acts with *us*. *We* are at the center. Two questions arise: what Bultmann (influenced by Kant) says, and why he says it.

What he says is that we do not have to care about God in himself, but about the acts of God with us. But what if we love? Would a wife be delighted if her husband were to tell her: "I am not interested in who you are, but in the way you act with me"? As Aquinas says, quoting St. Augustine: "Love results from knowledge; for, nothing is loved except it be first known."[12] If we do not care about who God is, do we love him? I am not expressing a judgment about Bultmann's love of God, but I state that his philosophical background makes it difficult to avoid some indifference in regard to God. What reason leads him to say what he says? He does not deny any relation between theology and some "philosophy" (without the word itself), he just takes for granted that we must use the dominant philosophy of our time. He does not intend to change faith, and perhaps in his mind he does not. I hope that his personal faith led him to some happy incoherence, but the logic of his system can lead others to this unhappy, coherent conclusion. At any given time, part of the gospel should be left out, because it does not fit the contemporary culture. And some have moved even more decisively from Bultmann's premises to their radical consequences.

Bultmann wrote in the middle of the twentieth century. In 2008, the retired Episcopal bishop John Shelby Spong followed a very similar exegetical path:

I ... do not believe that the miracles described in the New Testament literally occurred in the life of Jesus of Nazareth or that of his disciples.... I insist that there must be a way to be both a believer and a citizen of the twenty-first century. I am convinced that a God the mind rejects will never be a God the heart can adore.... I do not wish to live in a world in which an intervening deity acts capriciously to accomplish the divine will by overriding the laws of nature established in creation.... My journey forces me to get beyond the literalism of a premodern world if I am to discover the reality of this Christ who continually transforms my life.[13]

In other words: My view of life will not change, and God must fit in my view of life, otherwise I will not worship him. Jesus must be reinterpreted:

---

introduction by Mary J. Gregor (Lincoln: University of Nebraska Press, 1992), 67. See Part I, Appendix II: "The Conflict between the Theology and Philosophy Faculties, as an Example to Clarify the Conflict of the Faculties."

12. Thomas Aquinas, *ST* I, q. 60, a. 1, sc.

13. John Shelby Spong, *Jesus for the Non-Religious* (New York: Harper One, 2008), 54–55.

Perhaps if we can break Jesus out of religion, free him from creeds, doctrines and dogmas, we can once again hear his invitation to enter the God experience known in the fullness of life. That is the Jesus I seek.[14]

No dogmas. Therefore no heresies any more? The retired bishop Spong adds that in view of past philosophical frameworks, there are heresies:

To literalize Easter, both the story of the resurrection and the story of the ascension, has become the defining heresy of traditional Protestant and Catholic Christianity. That transforming mystery has given way to propositional truths that no twenty-first-century mind can still embrace.[15]

Does Spong reject the resurrection? It seems that he does not:

I can, with absolute honesty and with deep conviction, say that I believe the resurrection of Jesus was real.[16]

Spong "only" reinterprets the gospel, in line with what his philosophy accepts, so that his religious experience can be possible:

Jesus was born in a perfectly normal way in Nazareth. His mother was not the icon of virgin purity. His earthly father, Joseph, was a literary creation. His family thought he was out of his mind. He probably did not have twelve male disciples. He had disciples who were both male and female. He did not command nature to obey him.... There was no resuscitated body that emerged from that tomb on the third day, no touching of the wounds of Jesus, no opening by him of the secrets of scripture. Finally, there was no ascension into a heaven that exists above the sky. All of these narrative details were the creation of a community of people who individually and corporately had an experience that they believed was of God in the human life of one Jesus of Nazareth. Their way of explaining their experience has now run its course. It makes assumptions we cannot make. It uses categories of thought we cannot use.... Every explanation dies when its time dies. The death of the explanation, however, does not mean the death of the experience.[17]

Not much of the creed is left, of course. But what is left is a gospel acceptable on Spong's planet, which is quite different from the planet of some past Christians:

I even went back to read anew such classics as the *Summa Theologica* by Thomas Aquinas and *The Institutes* by John Calvin. Even in those masterpieces of Christian history it was as if they did not inhabit the same planet on which I lived.[18]

The examples of Bultmann and Spong are striking. They suggest, at the very least, that it is not only past Greek philosophy that might lead us to

---

14. Ibid., 95.
16. Ibid., 117–18.
15. Ibid., 127.
17. Ibid., 128–29.
18. Spong, *Eternal Life: A New Vision* (New York: Harper One, 2009), 13–14.

lose part of the gospel. What is mainly interesting is the fact that these theologians adopted some presuppositions of modern philosophy, without wondering whether they were actually sound philosophically, and then applied them to theology without caring about their compatibility with Christian faith. While many believers would not accept their views, they must still make sure that they themselves avoid other philosophical traps harmful to Christian faith.

I have mentioned some rather liberal Protestants, who show that a paradoxical outcome of the *sola scriptura* principle submits the Bible to some philosophy. Does it have anything to do with the life of the Catholic Church? It would be interesting to see how many catechetical programs are built around a principle expressed by Bishop Spong, speaking about Aquinas and Calvin: "It was not that these people were not brilliant in their day; it was that they still operated out of assumptions that were no longer available to me."[19] If the faith we proclaim must be limited to what is available in the most common philosophical categories of the time, catechesis will not reach further than that philosophical framework. This is against the idea of Revelation. Bultmann and Spong still depend on modern philosophy. Perhaps postmodernity can change the picture.

Postmodernity and Christian Faith

So-called postmodernity is certainly more conscious than modern philosophy of the inescapability of presuppositions. It typically tries to avoid what Jean-François Lyotard calls "metanarrations,"[20] that is, global overviews that impose themselves upon our thinking, in all fields of life. But the cost for such a consciousness is a deep doubt about reason.

One of the most famous proponents of postmodernity, the Italian philosopher Gianni Vattimo, went back to some of his Catholic roots.[21] In a dialogue with Richard Rorty, Vattimo explains that he considers his reinterpretation of the Incarnation of the Son of God to be the key of history.[22] Rorty replies that he's "not really impressed by the B.C.–A.D. distinction."[23]

---

19. Ibid., 13.

20. See Jean-François Lyotard, *La condition postmoderne: Rapport sur le savoir* (Paris: Editions de Minuit, 1979), 7: "On tient pour 'postmoderne' l'incrédulité à l'égard des métarécits."

21. Even with the help of Nietzsche and Heidegger! See Gianni Vattimo, *Credere di credere: È possibile essere cristiani nonostante la Chiesa?* (Milan: Garzanti, 2007), 24.

22. See Gianni Vattimo, in Richard Rorty and Gianni Vattimo, *Il futuro della religione. Solidarietà, carità, ironia*, a cura di S. Zabala (Milan: Garzanti, 2005), 28.

23. Richard Rorty in Richard Rorty and Gianni Vattimo, *The Future of Religion*, ed. Santiago Zabala (New York: Columbia University Press, 2004), 65.

He considers that the philosophical bases of atheism have disappeared, but they disappeared because metaphysics disappeared in the first place.[24] (Here "metaphysics" means the possibility to know the nature of things.)

The limits imposed on theology by the presuppositions of modernity disappear. In this sense Bultmann and Spong, who wanted to speak the language of their time, are outdated. But is the postmodern situation better?

What might be seen by Christians as a philosophical triumph—an important contemporary philosopher turns from being an enemy of the Church and becomes a defender of Christianity—is rather ambiguous. The Christianity that Vattimo defends has lost its morals and its dogmas. It could hardly be otherwise, since interpretation has been substituted for truth: "Farewell to truth is the basis itself of democracy"[25] and "Salvation happens through interpretation."[26] For a similar reason, Rorty says that "Nietzsche or Loyola" must be seen as "mad," "because there is no way to see them as fellow citizens of our constitutional democracy, people whose life plans might, given ingenuity and good will, be fitted in with those of other citizens."[27] It is interesting to see how, in this general context, Vattimo understands the present state of religion in our world: "It seems paradoxical that the outcome of 'going beyond' metaphysics ... is just the legitimation of relativism and its 'shadow,' which is fundamentalism, and its 'democratic' version, communitarianism. Yet just that, judging by many indications, is what is happening."[28] Why are relativism and fundamentalism or communitarianism basically different faces of the same reality? Because truth has disappeared: this is postmodernity, where truth is more a danger than a value.[29]

Relativism and fundamentalism are basically similar. That reminds us of Vatican I, which condemned together rationalism and fideism. Although rationalism and fideism came to opposing conclusions, both started from

24. See Vattimo, *Dopo la cristianità: Per un cristianesimo non religioso* (Milan: Garzanti, 2002), 21.

25. "L'addio alla verità è l'inizio, e la base stessa, della democrazia." Vattimo, *Addio alla verità* (Rome: Meltemi, 2009), 16.

26. "La salvezza passa attraverso l'interpretazione" (Vattimo, *Credere di credere*, 57).

27. Rorty, *Objectivity, Relativism and Truth* (New York: Cambridge University Press, 1991), 187.

28. "Sembra paradossale che l'esito dell'oltrepassamento della metafisica ... sia solo la legittimazione del relativismo e della sua 'ombra', cioè del fondamentalismo e della versione 'democratica' di questo, il comunitarismo. Eppure proprio questo, a giudicare da molti segni, è quanto sta accadendo" (Vattimo, *Dopo la cristianità*, 23).

29. See Vattimo, *Addio alla verità*, 25: "La conclusione a cui voglio giungere è che la verità come assoluta, corrispondenza oggettiva, intesa come ultima istanza e valore di base, è un pericolo più che un valore."

the same basic premise. Since reason cannot tell us enough in religious matters, either we get rid of religion (rationalism) or we build a religion on a non-rational basis (fideism). In the present age, relativism and fundamentalism still share the same premise: a rational dialogue will never solve differences in the religious field. Contemporary theologians must beware of this contemporary presupposition: reason is weak (Vattimo's *ragione debole*), therefore our traditional enemies (Marxism, atheism, etc.) lose their claims, but so do we. Some defenders of Christian faith fall into that precise trap, as Francis Collins—the Evangelical Protestant scientist who used to be in charge of the human genome project—says about other Evangelicals: "Many believers in God have been drawn to Young Earth Creationism because they see scientific advances as threatening to God.... Is He honored or dishonored by those who would demand that His people ignore rigorous scientific conclusions about His creation? Can faith in a loving God be built on a foundation of lies about nature?"[30] In any age, believers run the risk of submitting their faith to contemporary philosophies; Christians in the postmodern age run the risk of sharing in postmodern skepticism even when they try to defend a pure faith. This contemporary fideism, like the nineteenth century's fideism, is much more similar to its enemies than it imagines: all take for granted that reason cannot achieve anything in the religious field.

Since the consequences of different philosophical presuppositions can be devastating for theology, two questions arise: (1) Is it possible to have a theology without philosophical presuppositions? and (2) How can one choose a good philosophy? The second question applies in any case, but above all if the answer to the first one is negative.

Can "*Sola Scriptura*" Transmit Any Revelation?

I have the good fortune to live in a community composed of Dominicans from more than twenty countries at any one time (through the years, perhaps about forty countries), and to teach students from about one hundred countries. In such a situation, one has to learn something sooner rather than later: people of different cultures do not always perceive jokes as jokes. People who come from different countries interpret news in widely different ways. To say this is not relativism, it is just basic realism.

Is theology exempted from the impact of the cultural background?

---

30. Francis S. Collins, *The Language of God: A Scientist Presents Evidence for Belief* (London: Pocket Books, Simon & Schuster, 2007), 176.

How could it be? It must use some words, after all. And as Aquinas said, the words that we use about God "are primarily applied by us to creatures which we know first."[31] Much has been said about that: here I just want to mention this particular aspect of our language about divine matters. Our words come from this world, and, because of earlier occurrences, when we use them we have in our mind certain connotations. This is why *sola scriptura,* beautiful program as it is in many ways, is simply impossible.

The early nineteenth-century German theologian Johann Adam Möhler has expressed the most concise question about *sola scriptura*:

If it is said that Scripture alone is enough for the Christian, one is justified in asking the meaning of this assertion. Scripture alone, apart from our apprehension, is nothing at all; it is a dead letter. Only the product, which comes into light by the direction of our spiritual activities from the Scripture, is something.[32]

This is a deep insight that actually applies to any text. The purpose of a text is not to be written. It is to transmit some knowledge. It can do so only if it is read and understood. And the reader first has to learn how to read, in a certain language from certain persons. He first has to use the same words in other situations. In short he must acquire a whole body of knowledge, which comes to his mind when he reads any text, even biblical texts. This very basic observation about reading is very much present in the Catholic insistence on the necessity of Tradition: the Bible cannot be correctly understood without Tradition, that is, the life of the community of the Church, the sacraments, the liturgy, past and present texts, and so on. And … philosophy. It is really naïve to think that anybody can read the Bible without having some more or less conscious philosophical ideas.

If any theology is due to be influenced by some philosophy (among other factors), how can we avoid a philosophical "contamination"? In other words: can we choose a good philosophy?

The Choice of a Philosophy

One sentence influenced me more than any other when I was a student of theology in Fribourg. Fr. Colman Eugene O'Neill said to us—his students: "There are many philosophies. You must choose one that is compatible with theology." This was said by a Thomist! Of course he knew what John Paul would summarize later on:

31. *ST* I, q. 13, a. 6.

32. Johann Adam Möhler, *Unity in the Church, or, The Principle of Catholicism: Presented in the Spirit of the Church Fathers of the First Three Centuries,* trans. Peter C. Erb (Washington, D.C.: The Catholic University of America Press, 1996), 117.

[W]hen it engages theology, philosophy must remain faithful to its own principles and methods.... A philosophy which did not proceed in the light of reason according to its own principles and methods would serve little purpose.[33]

Aquinas is very clear about the limits of the use of philosophy in theology: it can be used, but not as a proper theological argument;[34] even within theology, philosophy remains distinct. But using theological arguments in order to change philosophy would make philosophy become theology. This is no better than to make theology become philosophy: essentially, it is the same error. Fr. O'Neill certainly did not want to change the nature of philosophy by making it simply theology, not an *ancilla theologiae*. This would be against Aquinas's most central convictions.

Now though the aforesaid truth of the Christian faith surpasses the ability of human reason, nevertheless those things which are naturally instilled in human reason cannot be opposed to this truth.... The knowledge of naturally known principles is instilled into us by God, since God himself is the author of our nature. Therefore the divine wisdom also contains these principles. Consequently whatever is contrary to these principles, is contrary to the divine wisdom; wherefore it cannot be from God. Therefore those things, which are received by faith from divine revelation, cannot be contrary to our natural knowledge.[35]

This text makes a first distinction, which many do not notice: something can be over the power of our reason without being irrational. It is over, precisely, not against, and this is not because of a lack of intelligibility, but because of the weakness of our intellect: "In respect of the knowledge of that truth of which there is most to be known, the human intellect is as the bat's eye to the sun."[36] Aquinas then states that if our reason—a gift received from God—is used correctly, it cannot contradict divine revelation—another divine gift. Otherwise God would contradict God.

How is that related to the choice of a philosophy for theological purposes? If a philosophy contradicts faith, the believer knows that there is a mistake somewhere: either he has misunderstood Revelation, or there is a philosophical mistake. In a sense, we can apply to philosophy what St. Irenaeus said about theology. "Our opinion is in accordance with the Eucharist, and the Eucharist in turn establishes our opinion."[37]

If a philosopher stops going to Mass because of his philosophy, or denies the very possibility of miracles because of his philosophy, the believer knows that there is a mistake *in his philosophy*. Even though reason cannot

---

33. John Paul II, *Fides et Ratio*, §49.
34. See *ST* I, q. 1, a. 8, ad 2.
35. Aquinas, *SCG* Bk. 1, chap. 7.
36. Ibid., Bk. 3, chap. 25.
37. Irenaeus, *Adversus Haereses*, IV.18.5.

prove faith to be true, it can at least show that the arguments against faith are not conclusive.[38] And the reason for the mistake can be a tiny initial philosophical error, even within the system of a philosopher who is a convinced believer: "*Parvus error in principio magnus est in fine.*"[39] Philosophical errors are one of the reasons why theology uses philosophy. "Christian faith treats of creatures in so far as they reflect a certain likeness of God, and forasmuch as error concerning them leads to error about God."[40] For theology to be sound, philosophical errors must be avoided. A philosophy which is compatible with theology is simply philosophically true, and the compatibility is on account of philosophical reasons.

Philosophical errors are especially dangerous when they are used in defense of faith. Aquinas noticed that "when anyone in the endeavor to prove the faith brings forward reasons which are not cogent, he falls under the ridicule of the unbelievers: since they suppose that we stand upon such reasons, and that we believe on such grounds."[41] And this is a service modern philosophers tried to provide to Christianity. In their case the failure was not only that they did not provide the proofs they were looking for, but also that they actually achieved the opposite result, as I will now try to show.

The Danger of Christian Philosophers

Cornelio Fabro commented on the difference between the intention of modern philosophers and the impact of their thought: "The more or less explicit professions of theism of most modern philosophers, until the nineteenth century, belong only to the reign of good intentions, and reflect the subjective attitude of the individual philosophers, but they are inexorably washed away by the coherence of the principle."[42] Let's take an example. Descartes wanted to defend the main elements of Christian faith, and his conviction about his achievement was not weak: "There won't be anybody left in the world who will dare doubt the existence of God and the real distinction of the human soul and the body."[43]

---

38. See Aquinas, *Super De Trinitate*, pars I, q. 2, a. 1, ad 5.

39. Aquinas, *De ente et essentia*, prooemium.

40. *SCG*, Bk. 2, chap. 4. 41. *ST* I, q. 32, a. 1.

42. "Le professioni di teismo più o meno esplicito di buona parte dei filosofi moderni, fino al sec. XIX, appartengono unicamente al regno delle buone intenzioni e riguardano l'atteggiamento soggettivo dei singoli filosofi, ma vengono inesorabilmente travolte dalla coerenza del principio." (Cornelio Fabro, *Introduzione all'ateismo moderno*, seconda edizione riveduta e aumentata, 2 vol. [Rome: Editrice Studium, 1969], 81.)

43. "nemoque amplius erit in mundo, qui vel Dei existentiam, vel realem humanae animae & corpore distinctionem ausit in dubium revocare" (René Descartes, *Meditationes de prima*

Centuries later, Jean-Paul Sartre would show the real consequences of Descartes's arguments. Descartes wanted to find a solid foundation for our knowledge, and for our freedom. He speaks about God on the basis of what he wants to say about us. For Descartes, truth is not in the thing itself; rather, it is decided by divine freedom, and our own freedom is limited by the choices of divine freedom.[44] Sartre shows the historical consequences of the system of a philosopher who wanted to prove forever God's existence.

Descartes finally joins and makes explicit, in his description of divine freedom, his first intuition about his own freedom.... It does not matter that he hypostasized in God this original and constitutive freedom whose infinite existence he perceived by the *cogito* itself.... It will require two centuries of crisis—crisis of faith, crisis of science—before man recovers this creating freedom that Descartes had put into God, and for one to suspect this truth, the essential basis of humanism: man is the being whose appearance makes a world exist.[45]

The atheist Sartre sees in Descartes his precursor. Fabro shows that the problem of Descartes, in spite of all his explicit intentions, is his starting point, which will be accepted by modern philosophy as a whole: "Modern philosophy has ... turned around the perspective of being, making the most audacious and fascinating attempt of the human mind: the radical self-

---

philosophia, "Sapientissimis clarissimisque viris Sacrae Facultatis Theologiae Parisiensis Decano & Doctoribus," *Œuvres* [Adam-Tannery], t.VII, [Paris: Vrin, 1983], 6). My translation.

44. See the Introduction by Jean-Paul Sartre: "Introduction et choix par J.-P. Sartre," in *Descartes, 1596–1650* (Geneva-Paris: Traits, 1946), 48–50: "La racine de toute Raison, et à chercher dans les profondeurs de l'acte libre, c'est la liberté qui est le fondement du vrai, et la nécessité rigoureuse qui paraît dans l'ordre des vérités est elle-même soutenue par la contingence absolue d'un libre arbitre créateur.... En Dieu, le vouloir et l'intuition ne font qu'un, la conscience divine est à la fois constitutive et contemplative. Et, semblablement, Dieu a inventé le Bien. Il n'est point incliné par sa perfection à décider ce qui est le meilleur; mais c'est ce qu'il a décidé qui, par l'effet de sa décision même, est absolument bon. Une liberté absolue qui invente la Raison et le Bien et qui n'a d'autres limites qu'elle-même et sa fidélité à elle-même, telle est finalement pour Descartes la prérogative divine. Mais, d'un autre côté, il n'y a rien de plus en cette liberté qu'en la liberté humaine et il a conscience, en décrivant le libre arbitre de son Dieu, de n'avoir fait que développer le contenu implicite de l'idée de liberté. C'est pourquoi, à bien considérer les choses, la liberté humaine n'est pas limitée par un ordre de vérités et de valeurs qui s'offriraient à notre assentiment comme des choses éternelles, comme des structures nécessaires de l'être. C'est la volonté divine qui a posé ces valeurs et ces vérités, c'est elle qui les soutient: notre liberté n'est bornée que par la liberté divine."

45. "Descartes finit par rejoindre et par expliciter, dans sa description de la liberté divine, son intuition première de sa propre liberté.... Peu nous importe ait hypostasié en Dieu cette liberté originelle et constituante dont il saisissait l'existence infinie par le *cogito* même.... Il faudra deux siècles de crise—crise de la Foi, crise de la Science—pour que l'homme récupère cette liberté créatrice que Descartes a mise en Dieu et pour qu'on soupçonne enfin cette vérité, base essentielle de l'humanisme: l'homme est l'être dont l'apparition fait qu'un monde existe." (Introduction by Jean-Paul Sartre in: *Descartes, 1596–1650*, 50–51).

foundation of thinking in itself."[46] Fabro comments: "Whoever starts with human consciousness remains within the horizon of this world; only a philosophy that takes being (*ens*) as its starting point can reach the Absolute."[47] Until now it seems that I have been speaking only about philosophy itself, from Descartes to Sartre. This would at least be a reason for theologians to beware of Cartesian philosophy. But there is more to it.

Descartes's starting point has had an impact on the possibility of collaboration between philosophy and theology, as McInerny shows. As he says, the starting point of philosophy must be what all can know: "[Philosophy's] starting points or principles are available to all. Philosophy can become obscure, no doubt, but it must not start that way. Its initial task is to reflect on and clarify the truths that no one with standard cognitive equipment could fail to know."[48]

Such a view of philosophy is behind Aquinas's view of the collaboration between philosophy and theology. But another view of philosophy's starting point makes such collaboration more difficult. This view is the illusion that philosophy can and must be devoid of presuppositions (including of course the dangerous religious presuppositions). This is what I criticized above as an impossible situation for the theologian. The same applies to philosophy, with an impact on theology.

The ambience of faith within which the believer engages in philosophy has seemed to some to entail that the believer cannot truly engage in philosophy at all. This criticism is rooted in quite modern notions of how philosophy begins. Unlike the assumptions given above—that the philosopher begins with truths everyone already knows—since Descartes the initial task of the philosopher has been taken to be the rinsing from his mind of all prior knowledge claims. Various methods were devised to carry this out, such as methodic doubt, and the suggestion is that philosophizing is presuppositionless. The philosopher ideally is uninfluenced by his upbringing and culture; he is an isolated mind, and little else, to which somehow questions occur. Despite the continuing uncritical acceptance of this fantastic picture of the philosopher, it has been shown again and again to be impossible of realization. Of course, the only reason why one would seek to realize it is because he accepts the scarcely less fantastic assumption that everything one thought one knew prior to formal philosophizing may turn out to be false. For our purposes, it is enough to point out that many of the claims that Thomas could not be a real philosopher because he has

---

46. "La filosofia moderna ha ... capovolto la prospettiva dell'essere operando il più audace e affascinante tentativo dello spirito umano, quello dell'autofondazione radicale del pensiero in se stesso" (Fabro, *Introduzione all'ateismo moderno*, 1091).

47. See ibid., 1097: "Solo chi inizia con l'ente e fa leva sull'essere può arrivare all'Assoluto di essere chè Dio; chi parte dal fondamento della coscienza, deve finire per lasciarsi risucchiare dalla finitezza intrinseca del suo orizzonte ossia per perdersi nel nulla di essere."

48. McInerny, *Aquinas*, 30.

all those religious beliefs are grounded on a notion of real philosophy that has no foundation.[49]

A philosophy without presupposition would exclude its collaboration with theology. But such a philosophy is impossible, and is the philosophical form of the similar theological illusion. But McInerny points out that believers might actually be more conscious of this than non-believing philosophers. In any case, what matters is not the inescapable fact of having presuppositions, but the possibility of arguing.

One would think that the inescapability of antecedent convictions would be seen to be, well, inescapable. Everyone brings a lot of baggage with him as he climbs the purgatorial mountain of philosophy.... Is this a mere *tu quoque*? It is rather a reminder of something that is obvious in the case of the believer and somehow unnoticed in the case of the non-believing philosopher. Does this relativize philosophical argument, making it merely a function of our antecedent convictions? Not if there are common criteria for appraising arguments whatever their provenance in antecedent convictions.[50]

As I have already said, the point is not whether we are influenced by philosophy or not, but whether our philosophy argues well, whether it is true or not. This applies above all to the most radical presuppositions of a philosophy, to its starting point. Of course a biased starting point does not mean that everything said in that philosophy will be wrong—modern philosophy certainly made great contributions in some fields—for example, the development of human rights—but a biased starting point weakens even the good contributions of a philosophy and makes their reception more difficult. The long difficulty in the relationship between theology and even the good aspects of modern philosophy might be due not only to the personal weakness of Christians who struggled to defend a political view of their faith, but also to obstacles to dialogue that were built into the starting point of modern thought.

Conclusion

St. John Paul warned us: "Theologians [who] refuse the help of philosophy ... run the risk of doing philosophy unwittingly."[51] History shows that theologians have fallen into such a trap many a time. In the illusion of a liberation from the philosophical straitjacket of scholasticism, the Reformation actually unwittingly introduced some scholastic ideas within its own framework.

49. Ibid., 32.

50. Ibid., 116.

51. *Fides et Ratio*, §48.

Theologians like Bultmann or, more recently, Bishop Spong, "corrected" the Bible because of some unexamined modern philosophical presuppositions. Modern and postmodern thinkers reinterpret Christianity, and the result of even a benevolent reinterpretation is something other than Christian faith.

A theology without philosophy is impossible because theologians do not start thinking in a void. They have other ideas in their mind when they read Scripture, and they must check the result of the mixture of information in their mind. As modern Christians did, postmodern Christians run the risk of accepting the contemporary presuppositions within their defense of Christian truth; such a risk can be averted only through a conscious philosophical analysis of their own intellectual performance.

Theologians cannot avoid philosophy, but they can choose their philosophy, and not simply by choosing philosophers who *prima facie* are Christian. Aristotle was a pagan who held the eternity of the world: his philosophy was true enough to greatly help theology, after some corrections. Descartes was a convinced Catholic, but he—and with him modern philosophy—tried to establish a presuppositionless philosophy: on such a basis, collaboration with theology is made impossible from the start, however long it may take for that fact to be noticed.

A theologian's choice of a good philosophy is not in the first place a theological choice, although the suspicion of the incompatibility of a philosophy with Christian faith serves as a warning. The choice of a philosophy that theology can use is a philosophical choice. What can be used is what is true, because "*omne verum, a quocumque dicatur, est a spiritu sancto sicut ab infundente naturale lumen*" ("Every truth by whomsoever spoken is from the Holy Ghost as bestowing the natural light").[52] I have explored the importance of the human quest for truth and the Catholic Church, as well as the importance of philosophy in ecumenical dialogues. As St. John Paul II saw so clearly, the question of truth—"*An sit?*" "Is it so?" can be answered only by correct judgments either in the light of reason or in the light of faith. Our attention to the related and recurrent acts of understanding and judging shows the importance of recovering the wisdom of the ancients, with the importance it accords to reason, if we are to avoid the relativist loss of reasoned wisdom so widespread in modern and postmodern cultures due to nominalism and voluntarism.[53]

52. *ST* II-II, q. 109, a. 1, ad 1.

53. Cf. Charles Morerod, *Ecumenism and Philosophy* (Washington, D.C.: The Catholic University of America Press, 2006); also cf. my *The Church and the Human Quest for Truth* (Washington, D.C.: The Catholic University of America Press, 2008). For more on the relevance of St. John Paul II to these issues, cf. the Introduction to this volume, as well as Matthew Lamb's "The Millennial Challenges Facing Catholic Intellectual Life," *Nova et Vetera* 11.4 (Fall 2013): 969–91.

CHAPTER TWO

Videtur quod non sit necessarium, praeter theologicam disciplinam, aliam doctrinam haberi

Legitimacy of Philosophy as an Autonomous Discipline and Its Service to Theology in Aquinas and Ralph McInerny

JOHN P. O'CALLAGHAN

A volume on the importance of philosophy for faith and theology is certainly a legacy of my teacher and friend Ralph McInerny. I hope that I can do honor to him, not just as a friend or teacher, but as a colleague precisely on a topic of such great moment in McInerny's thought, the role of philosophy in the life of faith. One of his last books, *Praeambula Fidei*, was a spirited defense of philosophy and the good it achieves in the life of faith, and thus for theology as reasoned reflection upon God's revelation, what Aquinas called "*sacra doctrina.*" *Praeambula Fidei* was his second book to come out of his celebrated Gifford Lectures.

McInerny was such an inveterate writer that where some might write one book, he would write two or three or four. However, he was not the sort of author of whom he himself once said, "You know, Mr. Smith has never had an unpublished thought. And he's published *it* quite a bit." No, McInerny's two books from the Gifford Lectures expressed substantially different but related thoughts. I recall him saying to me when he was preparing to deliver them that Lord Gifford's endowment asked for lectures in natural theology. So he said he would honor the wishes of the dead, if the dead have wishes, and do just that. But the first volume, *Characters in Search of Their Author*, is devoted to defending the possibility of natural theology against secular philosophical movements in the modern period that would argue the impossibility of such natural theology. On the other hand, the second volume is devoted to addressing arguments from within the Christian church itself and its theological tradition that there is something questionable or untoward about Christians engaging in natural theology as a philosophical enterprise. So I think it is fitting to write an essay in McInerny's honor that discusses something so near to his philosophical, but also his Catholic theological, heart. What follows is for Ralph McInerny, may I do him justice, and may he rest in peace.

"*Videtur quod non sit necessarium, praeter theologicam disciplinam, aliam doctrinam haberi?*" "It seems that it is not necessary to have another doctrine, beyond the theological discipline." That is the title of this essay. Readers familiar with Aquinas's *Summa theologiae* will notice the similarity of my topic to the topic with which Aquinas opens his inquiry, "It seems that it is not necessary to have a discipline beyond the philosophical disciplines." As Aquinas approaches the question, it is theology or *sacra doctrina* that needs justification, at least theoretically. He seems to take it for granted that philosophy has a certain pride of place in human inquiry. Yes, he will go on to argue that *sacra doctrina* is necessary precisely because of the inadequacy of the philosophical disciplines to give us sufficient knowledge of our end in order that we may attain it. And even that knowledge of our end that philosophy does achieve is had only by a few, after a lifetime of study, and with a great admixture of error—hardly an encomium for philosophy. And yet, Aquinas's discussion makes sense only if we recognize that his attitude toward philosophical inquiry is a good deal more than a grudging acknowledgment of its meager success. Indeed, one way of understanding the first question of the *Summa* is as an extended argument that *sacra doctrina* is in fact the surpassing wisdom the Greeks were seeking in their inquiry—a philosophical inquiry that springs from human nature itself. *Sacra doctrina* surpasses Greek wisdom by the highest standards they themselves had set for *episteme* and *Sophia* as found in Aristotle's *Posterior Analytics*.

The background for the various questions Aquinas asks in the subsequent articles of the first question about the character of *sacra doctrina* is set by the various claims Aristotle had made mostly in the *Posterior Analytics*, but in other places within his corpus as well. Aquinas asks in article 2,

"Whether *sacra doctrina* is a science?" Yes, he replies, it is a science whose principles are known in the light of a higher science, namely the knowledge of God and the blessed in heaven. In article 3 he asks, "Whether *sacra doctrina* is one science?" Yes, under the formality of being revealed by God. In article 4, "Whether it is a practical science?" Anyone familiar with Aristotle will recognize the distinction implicit in the question between a speculative science and a practical science. And Aquinas notes that within the philosophical disciplines no particular science is both practical and speculative. And yet wisdom, as Plato had portrayed it in the *Republic*,[1] a work to which Aquinas did not have access, is supposed to be the science that in its knowledge of the highest causes of things allows those who possess it to govern themselves and others—a science that is speculative and yet has a practical bearing upon the living of one's life. Aristotle, however, speaks of two different sorts of wisdom. There is the wisdom discussed in the *Metaphysics*,[2] which is simply the knowledge of the highest causes of things pursued for its own sake and which approaches divine knowledge. And then there is practical wisdom as discussed in the *Nicomachean Ethics*,[3] the virtue by which a practical man devoted to a well-lived life puts order into his actions. Now Aquinas answers this question by saying *sacra doctrina* is primarily a speculative science concerned with divine things, and secondarily a practical science insofar as it treats of human acts as ordained toward eternal beatitude concerning these divine things. In that regard, one can think of it as expressing more closely the Platonic characterization of an integrated wisdom than the diversity of Aristotle's.

In article 5, "Whether *sacra doctrina* is nobler than other sciences?" Aquinas answers yes, it is nobler than all other sciences, and thus he argues in article 6 that it counts as what the Greeks called wisdom, the noblest of sciences, a wisdom beyond all human wisdom because it participates by revelation in God's own knowledge of himself. In article 7, "Whether God is the object of this science," St. Thomas answers "yes," and he establishes that *sacra doctrina* is not simply metaphysics, whose objects is the study of *ens in quantum ens* and which treats of God only as a principle of *ens*. Article 8, "Whether *sacra doctrina* is argumentative," establishes *sacra doctrina* as advancing from its revealed principles to the understanding of further truths and also establishes that difficulties raised for faith can be answered. Article 9, "Whether *sacra doctrina* appropriately uses metaphor," establishes that the use of metaphor may be the most appropriate way of speaking of

1. Cf. Plato's *Republic*, Books 6 and 7.   2. Cf. Aristotle, *Metaphysics*, Book XII.
3. Cf. Aristotle, *Nicomachean Ethics*, Book VI.

God. This is an important article precisely because Aquinas, in commenting on Aristotle's *Posterior Analytics*, includes poetics, as passing from one thing understood to another, within the realm of logic, which studies the various acts of reason. But poetics employs images, which is characteristic of metaphor "to lead to something virtuous by way of some pleasing representation."[4] Thus if *sacra doctrina* employs metaphor as the poets do, it risks being reduced to a practical science devoted to urging one on to virtue, whereas we have already seen that it is primarily a speculative science concerned with divine things, and that the metaphors it employs are for the purpose of revealing those divine things, not in the first instance urging virtue. And so, in response to the first objection, Aquinas argues *sacra doctrina* is not poetry, for the purpose of images in poetry is to produce something pleasing to the imagination, while in *sacra doctrina* that is not its purpose, but, rather, the images are both "useful and necessary" to the subject matter, which is God.

It is only in the tenth article that Aquinas turns to an identifiably Augustinian issue, and that is, "Whether in Holy Scripture words may have many senses?": yes. And of course, the second question begins just as an Aristotelian science is supposed to begin according to the *Posterior Analytics*, with the demonstration that the subject matter of this science, this highest of all wisdoms, does in fact exist, when it demonstrates by means of the "five ways" that there is a god.

Thus, the picture we get from Aquinas is that *sacra doctrina* is God's merciful response to the natural human love of wisdom. It answers our questions, questions that first arise naturally within us as to where we came from and where we are going. So even while arguing that *sacra doctrina* makes up for the inadequacies of the answers provided within the philosophical tradition to these human questions, Aquinas has no need to deny the legitimacy of the philosophical disciplines as if they are full of error from beginning to end and say nothing of the human end and the means to achieve it. Again, the *Summa* reads as if the legitimacy of the philosophical disciplines is a given, and the question is why we need anything other than them. And of course this attitude of Aquinas is not at all surprising in a historical context in which philosophical training, at least in university education, was a required precursor to theological studies, even if, as is likely the case, Aquinas was, in writing the *Summa*, working on ways in which theological studies might be reformed for the educational needs of the Dominican Order.[5]

4. "Nam poetae est inducere ad aliquod virtuosum per aliquam decentem repraesentationem." Sancti Thomae de Aquino, *Expositio libri Posteriorum Analyticorum*, Liber I, lectio 1, 6.

5. For a magisterial treatment of Aquinas's purpose in composing the *Summa*, see Leonard Boyle, *The Setting of the* Summa Theologiae *of Saint Thomas*, Etienne Gilson Series, Vol. 5

But we are in a situation very different from Aquinas's. We are in a historical and sociological context in which it is not at all odd to think one could pursue theological studies without any acknowledgment at all of the importance of philosophical studies as important for, even a necessary propaedeutic, to theological inquiry. So I want to start the reflection at the core of my inquiry with an anecdotal point. It often seems that in certain company when one is in a theological discussion, if someone contributes to the conversation a point that seems to come from Aristotelian philosophy, someone else will intone, "Well of course in its teaching and doctrinal statements the Church does not intend to affirm any particular philosophical system or philosopher." And this statement will often be greeted with various different signs of agreement from the assembled discussants. And yet, if in a theological discussion someone makes as a contribution to the conversation a point that in some way hints at a point of Platonic philosophy, no one seems to mention, "Of course in its teaching and doctrinal statements the Church does not intend to affirm any particular philosophical system or philosopher." On the contrary, in my experience, one is likely to receive knowing nods of comprehension. What should we make of this admittedly crude sociological generalization based upon anecdote about theological attitudes toward these two streams of philosophy? It would seem that if it really is the case that the Church does not pronounce on philosophical issues in its teaching, or provide teachings that imply positions on philosophical issues, the theological enterprise could go on without any sort of philosophical reflection at all.

But consider this statement from the Council of Vienne, 1311–12, promulgated by Pope Clement V: "With the approval of the aforesaid sacred council we condemn: defining, so that the truth of sincere faith may be known to all and access to all errors precluded and may not enter, that whoever hereafter stubbornly presumes to assert, defend, or hold that the rational or intellective soul is not the form of the human body per se and essentially is in that regard judged to be a heretic."[6] What are we to make of such a statement? Does it involve a teaching straightforwardly read out of the pages of

---

(Toronto: Pontifical Institute of Mediaeval Studies, 1982); and, for a more summary discussion, Jean-Pierre Torrell, OP, *L'Initiation à Saint Thomas d'Aquin: Sa personne et son oeuvre* (Paris: Editions Universitaires Fribourg Suisse and Editions Cerf, 1993), chap. 8.

6. "Praedicto sacro approbante Concilio reprobamus: definientes, ut cunctis nota sit fidei sincerae veritas ac praecludatur universis erroribus aditus, ne subintrent, quod quisquis deinceps asserere, defendere seu tenere pertinaciter praesumpserit, quod anima rationalis seu intellectiva non sit forma corporis humani per se et essentialiter, tamquam haereticus sit censendus." *Enchiridion symbolorum et definitionum quae in rebus fidei et morum*, ed. Henricus Denzinger (Wirceburgi, Sumptibus Stahelianis, 1854), 128, XLVIII.C. My translation.

Holy Scripture itself? No. Does it involve a teaching that results from the reflection of reason only upon the deposit of Revelation as found in Holy Scripture as its source, uninformed by any other sources of human thought? No. What could the statement possibly mean by "form," and "essentially" and "per se" or "in itself?" The words are not meaningless, and so like the words of Scripture they are subject to interpretation. What interpretation shall we give them?

There is of course a Platonic reading of the term "form." But to give that reading would quickly and straightforwardly lead right into another heresy, namely, that there is only one soul for all human beings. Oversimplifying a great deal, Plato's position, to the extent that we can discern it from his dialogues, seemed broadly to be that there is only one human form for all human beings, despite the plurality of individual souls associated with Socrates, Plato, Alcibiades, and Xanthippe. So in Plato it appears fairly incoherent to identify the human form with a human soul, since there are many souls but only one Platonic form of the human. But if we identity that one Platonic human form with the form of the human body and rational soul spoken of in the conciliar statement, it follows that there is numerically only one form of human bodies. So, inasmuch as the statement identifies the form with the rational soul, we must also conclude that, despite Plato's plurality of souls, there is only one rational human soul for all human beings. This of course is itself a heretical position as declared at the Fifth Lateran Council.[7] And in that latter declaration, Pope Leo X explicitly relates

7. See Fifth General Lateran Council, Session 8 (December 19, 1513). "Since then in our days (which we record with sorrow) the sower of cockle, the ancient enemy of humankind, has dared to sow and spread in the field of the Lord some most pernicious errors that have always been rejected by the faithful, concerning particularly the nature of the rational soul, namely that it is mortal or that it is one among all human beings, and some philosophizing rashly, profess it to be true at least according to philosophy; desiring to apply opportune remedies to a plague of this kind, with the approbation of this sacred council we condemn and reject any assertion that the intellectual soul is mortal or one in all human beings, and those turning this topic to doubt: since it is not only true that the soul exists per se and essentially as the form of the human body, as is in the canon of our predecessor Clement V of happy memory contained in the high (general) council of Vienne, but also true that it is immortal, and for the great number of bodies into which it is singularly poured it can be multiplied, is multiplied, and ought to be multiplied." "Cum itaque diebus nostris (quod dolenter referimus) zizaniae seminator, antiquus humani generis hostis, nonnullos perniciosissimos errores, a fidelibus semper explosos, in agro Domini superseminare et augere sit ausus, de natura praesertim animae rationalis, quod videlicet mortalis sit, aut unica in cunctis hominibus et nonnulli temere philosophantes, secundum saltem philosophiam verum id esse asseverent; contra huiusmodi pestem opportuna remedia adhibere cupientes, hoc sacro approbante Concilio damnamus et reprobamus omnes asserentes animam intellectivam mortalem esse, aut unicam in cunctis hominibus, et haec in dubium vertentes: cum illa non solum vere per se et essentialiter humani corporis forma existant, sicut in canone felicis recordationis Clementis Papae V praedecessoris nostri in

his declaration on the nature of the soul to Clement V's earlier declaration at the Council of Vienne, asserting that his, Leo's, is continuous with the teaching of his predecessor of "happy memory."

Let me be clear. The point is not that Plato himself held for only one soul for all human beings. The problem arises not for Plato, but for the teaching of the Council, if the term "form" in the conciliar teaching is given a Platonic reading. The term form here is indisputably drawn from a philosophical tradition. But which tradition? If drawn from the Platonic, such a reading of the term "form" leads to an incoherent teaching, since "form" and "soul" do not function as the same principle within broadly Platonic doctrine.

Still, the text speaks only of form, not of substantial form, which latter might more directly suggest an Aristotelian reading. And yet it is Aristotle's teaching that soul, which is the animating principle of living things, is the substantial form of the body. Soul and form of the body are the same principle in living things. Thus, at the very least, on a broadly Aristotelian reading of the term "form," the teaching of the Council is not rendered inherently incoherent, as it is on a Platonic reading. So on its face it looks like the teaching expresses something more like an Aristotelian account of the relation of soul to body than a Platonic account. And yet, even with Aristotle himself there are problems akin to those found in the Platonic account, since there are texts in which Aristotle seems to suggest that there is numerically but one form for any particular species of things, and others in which he seems to suggest there are multiple individual substantial forms corresponding to the multiple individual substances.[8]

In addition, Aristotle appears to distinguish in *De anima* III.5 the principle of *nous* as a separable part of the human soul that upon death departs, as the soul of the human animal corrupts with the animal. It is significant

---

(generali) Viennensi Concilio edito continetur; verum et immortalis, et pro corporum, quibus infunditur, multitudine singulariter multiplicabilis, et multiplicata, et multiplicanda sit." Denzinger, *Enchiridion Symbolorum*, LVII.A, p. 158. My translation.

8. Michael J. Loux pursues a reading of texts in Aristotle's *Metaphysics* that he thinks suggest (a) that primary *ousia* is substantial form, and (b) that primary *ousia* is a predicable and definable form, that is, a universal. See Michael J. Loux, *Primary* Ousia: *An Essay on Aristotle's Metaphysics Z and H* (Ithaca, N.Y.: Cornell University Press, 1991). From these positions it would seem to follow that everything of which a substantial predicable universal is said has numerically the same substantial form, since it has numerically the same predicable universal said of it. And inasmuch as the soul of a living thing is identified with its substantial form, it would further follow that every individual of a definable kind of living thing will have numerically one soul. Similarly it would seem that the only way out of this conclusion would be to deny that the soul of a particular animal is its substantial form. For a different reading of at least some of these texts, see Myles Burnyeat, *A Map of the Metaphysics Zeta* (Pittsburgh: Mathesis Publications, 2001). See also the parallel discussions in Aquinas's commentary on those passages in the *Metaphysics*.

that he calls this intellectual principle *nous* and not rational *soul*, since for him soul is the first principle of life in a body having life potentially. In distinguishing *nous* as a separable part of soul that departs upon death, Aristotle might be suggesting that *nous* as such ought not to be thought of as a soul informing a body and vivifying it. And such a reading of Aristotle's *De anima* was itself the source of an interpretation of Aristotle that led to the positing of numerically one human intellect for all human beings, in the reading of the Islamic philosopher Ibn Rush for example, a reading that Aquinas challenged in both his commentary on the *De anima* and his *De unitate intellectus contra Averroistas.*[9]

But if that reading of *nous* in the *De anima* as separable in being from the animal soul, and not just separable in definition, is adopted, then in that case Aristotle does not look any more amenable to the doctrinal statement than does Plato. On the strong reading of the separability of *nous*, the phrase "rational soul" would not pick out a genuine unity for Aristotle, but function more like the phrase "white man" does for him, picking out a merely per accidens unity signifying little or no relation between reason or *nous* and the embodied animal life of the substance in question. In fact Plato, even if he does not think of the soul as the form of a body, in several places suggests that soul on its own is a principle of both the living motions of a body and *nous*;[10] so in that respect one could see his position as closer to the doctrinal statement in speaking of the rational soul, but for the Platonic denial that the soul is the form of a body. So looking only at these two great philosophers and their "philosophical systems" it certainly appears to be true, or at least advisable, that the Church not advocate either when it speaks of the "rational soul" as the per se and essential "form" of the body. And so, we might say consistently with my anecdote above, that the absence of "substantial" to modify "form" suggests that the council fathers deliberately wanted to avoid advocating any particular philosophical system, especially the Aristotelian, in order to leave room for whatever reading one might wish to give the sense of "per se" and "essential form of the body," even perhaps a reverential Platonic reading.

I do not mean by this comparison of Plato and Aristotle to suggest that the council fathers of Vienne were confronting the texts of Plato and Aristotle directly; certainly they were not, particularly in the case of Plato. But Augustine and high medieval Augustinianism would be another matter. I simply want to point out for now two very broad philosophical positions

9. See *Summa theologiae* I, q. 76, aa. 1–2, as well as *Sententia libri de Anima*, and *De unitate intellectus contra Averroistas.*

10. See Plato, *Republic*, Book X.

as "in the air," in order to speak more specifically of a philosophical debate among figures in the century just prior to the Council of Vienne. We might say that according to the platonic (now small "p") position the soul is principle of motion and reason or *nous*; but the problem for platonic position is that the soul is not the per se form of the body. On the other hand, the aristotelian (now small "a") position is that the soul is the form of the body and so is the first principle of motion in the body; but the problem for the aristotelian position is that *nous* looks so different from the soul as form of the body that it is not clear that the phrase "rational soul" has any definite philosophical substance or unity to it.

The problem we face in understanding the doctrinal statement and these two great streams of philosophical thought is one of historical context. Insofar as theology needs to concern itself with history—not just the history of the writing of the biblical texts, but the history of the development of doctrine as working out the understanding of what has been revealed in what Aquinas calls *sacra doctrina*, considered in its historical context—we can not avoid identifying this teaching of Vienne as a condemnation of the position on the soul enunciated by, among others, Peter Olivi, a certain very strong version of medieval and Franciscan Augustinianism.[11] It would be a mistake to claim that the Council of Vienne was mostly concerned with doctrinal matters like the constitution of the human soul and its relation to the human body. Mostly it dealt with disciplinary and juridical matters. And, as was often the case in a condemnation, even in the part dealing with the soul it does not mention Olivi by name. And yet, Olivi had in fact said that the rational soul ought not to be thought to be the per se and essential form of the body.

Here Olivi was enunciating a version of the pluralist position on the number of substantial principles to be found in a human being, in the so-called "plurality of forms" debate. Others who in the thirteenth and early fourteenth centuries enunciated similar plurality positions were figures like St. Bonaventure, Henry of Ghent, Bl. Duns Scotus, and Ockham, many of them Franciscans. All of these figures writing before the council and just up to it adopted some form of plurality position on the rational soul and the substantial form of the human body.[12] The plurality position was compli-

11. Mauro Vincenzo, "La disputata de anima tra Vitale du Four e Pietro di Giovanni Olivi," *Studi Medievali* 38 (1997): 89–139. Also Robert Pasnau, "Olivi on the Metaphysics of Soul," *Medieval Philosophy and Theology* 6 (1997): 109–32; and Tonna Ivo, "La 'pars intellectiva' dell'anima rationale non é la forma del corpo (Dottrina di Pierre Jean Olieu sull'unione tra anima e corpo)," *Antonianum* 65 (1990): 277–89.

12. For historical discussions of the problem see Daniel Callus, "The Origins of the Problem

cated by those who held that there is a form of corporeity that makes matter to be a body to which a soul may come as the form that makes the material body to be the specific "kind" of body that it is. So if by "form of the body" one means the so-called form of corporeity, then these pluralists would deny that the intellectual soul is the per se form of the body. But they might still claim to affirm the doctrine later enunciated by the council, were it presented to them, by suggesting that the intellectual soul is the per se form of the body, if by body we mean the already formed body, the body formed already by the distinct form of corporeity. So they would just deny that the intellectual soul is the form of corporeity. One can see in such positions a kind of resonance with Augustine's position in his *De Trinitate*. But Olivi's denial of the doctrine is clear by contrast with such complications in others.

And apart from any inclinations one might have to provide a platonic reading of the doctrine oneself, in that historical context it is nearly impossible not to understand Olivi and perhaps others to be denying the medieval aristotelian understanding of the rational soul as substantial form of the body (that is, they are denying, not Aristotle himself, but medieval aristotelianism). If anything, Olivi's position on the soul looks not vaguely or ambiguously but rather substantially platonic in denying that the soul is the form of the body. The medieval aristotelian position was a philosophical understanding of human nature that had been a hard won *theological* victory in the thirteenth century. It was a victory of figures such as Aquinas as they wrestled with understanding the revelation that human beings are made in the image and likeness of God; they are *imago Dei*, and yet they are animals into whose face God breathes the breath of life.

As a matter of history, the medieval figures were confronted with the two broad philosophical accounts of what it is to be human: the platonic, in which human beings are fundamentally souls imprisoned or at least tethered to a body that is metaphysically speaking foreign to the nature of soul, and an aristotelian, in which human beings are fundamentally a certain sort of animal and in which soul, far from being utterly foreign to the body, is

---

of the Unity of Form," *The Thomist* 24 (1961): 257–85. Emily Michael, "Averroes and the Plurality of Forms," *Franciscan Studies* 52 (1992): 155–83. See also Paul Vincent Spade, "*Binarium Famosissimum*," in *The Stanford Encyclopedia of Philosophy*, ed. Edward N. Zalta (Fall 2008), available at http://plato.stanford.edu/ archives/fall2008/entries/binarium/. For an exhaustive discussion of the conceptual moves concerning the distinct positions, see John F. Wippel, *The Metaphysical Thought of Thomas Aquinas* (Washington D.C.: The Catholic University of America Press, 2000), chap. 9. And for its importance to Aquinas's discussion of the Augustinian theme of the *imago Dei*, see my "*Imago Dei*: A Test Case for St. Thomas's Augustinianism," in *Aquinas the Augustinian*, ed. M. Dauphinais, D. Barry, and M. Levering (Washington, D.C.: The Catholic University of America Press, 2007).

the fundamental intelligibility of the animal body in its living manifestation. In the case of Aquinas, despite any ambiguity in Aristotle himself, as seen for instance in the *De anima*, Aquinas's medieval aristotelianism decisively rejects the position of only one substantial form for all substances of a kind in favor of multiple substantial forms for the multiplicity of substances within a kind, and so he can coherently hold that the soul is the per se and essential form of the body without falling into heresy. Indeed the heart of question 76 of the first part of the *Summa theologiae* is precisely an argument for that per se and essential character of the soul as form of the human body. So as a matter of history it is hard to push the line that of course the Church was not weighing in here on a philosophical matter, not advocating one philosophical position over another as bearing on the proper understanding of *sacra doctrina*, as later it would again in the Fifth Lateran Council on the plurality and individual immorality of human souls.

But we should not see this discussion of conciliar teachings and condemnations as purely negative, and a case study in why it was a mistake in the first place to get into the business of using philosophical inquiry and various theses in the context of *sacra doctrina*. On the contrary, the background of the conciliar acts is precisely a positive movement of *sacra doctrina* to inquire into the meaning of Revelation. In this case, what could Genesis possibly mean in claiming that human beings, male and female, are made in the image and likeness of God? The victory for medieval aristotelianism took place against the background of the Augustinian tradition in which Aquinas himself was firmly planted, a tradition stemming from Augustine's treatise *De Trinitate,* in which the *imago Dei* was understood to be found only in the mind of the human being, the mind, which is the "essence or substance" of the rational soul, and strictly excluded from that part of the soul that "quickens the body," as well as, as Augustine puts it, any activity we share in common with the animals. This was a teaching in Augustine that hints very strongly at Platonic or neo-Platonic conceptions of soul, mind, and body. And yet if we use "soul" for that quickening principle of which Augustine speaks, then we have a picture of the soul that also looks rather much more like Aristotle of *De anima* 3.4 and 3.5, with "*mens*" doing duty for "*nous*," than like Plato, for whom the soul itself could both be the principle of the motions of the body and be the principle of *nous* in human life.[13]

In historical context, the statement from the Council of Vienne cannot be taken to be an isolated philosophical statement, but a statement about the philosophical presuppositions involved in a theological attempt to un-

13. See my "*Imago Dei*: A Test Case for St. Thomas's Augustinianism."

derstand Genesis and the doctrine of the *imago Dei*. In short we can think of Olivi as a sort of reactionary Augustinian and Aquinas as a kind of liberal Augustinian, with the Church weighing in on an explicitly philosophical issue on the side of the liberal Augustinian because of the high theological stakes of the *imago Dei*.

As Bl. John Henry Newman pointed out,[14] the historical development of doctrine takes place in the context of conflict, and we have to keep in mind that just a few decades earlier some in the Church had weighed in rather strongly against the liberal Augustinian on precisely his view of the unity of the human soul as substantial form of the body, condemning Aquinas's position or condemning him through those closely allied with him.[15] Given that context, should we still react negatively to the idea that at the Council of Vienne the Church was asserting a broadly medieval aristotelian and particularly Thomistic understanding of the soul against a broadly platonic and narrowly Augustinian inspired rejection of such aristotelianism? Should we be tempted to say that the Church in adopting language for its teachings never means to assert or even presuppose any philosophical truth?

How many Catholic Christians, including ourselves, do we think will react negatively to the following statement: "[The] image of God in man, is not *in the body*, but *in the soul*; which is a spiritual substance, endued with understanding and free will?" Do we not rather suspect that many if not all Catholic Christians will take that statement to be a rather concise statement of what we believe? And yet Aquinas's position on the unity of soul as substantial form of the body allows him to see the image of God in the human being, the living human body, even, contra Augustine, in a certain way in the animal activity of reproduction, an activity of the human body.[16] So the statement above seems to be in conflict with Aquinas's position. And as a matter of history the statement just quoted is from Bishop Richard Challoner's (1691–1781) notes accompanying the text of Genesis 1:26—"Let us make man to our image"—of the eighteenth-century Douay-Rheims edition of the Bible.[17] As in the battle four centuries earlier culminating in Vienne, it is a note to Genesis that concerns the theological topic of the *imago Dei*. But is it any less innocent of philosophical content than the statement from

14. See John Henry Newman, *An Essay on the Development of Christian Doctrine*, chaps. I through V.

15. See Torrell, *L'Initiation à Saint Thomas d'Aquin*, chap. 15, for a discussion of the controversies after Aquinas's death prompted by, among other things, the condemnations apparently aimed at his teaching on the soul by Stephen Tempier, Robert Kilwardby, and John Pecham.

16. See *ST* I-II, q. 93, a. 4, as well as my "*Imago Dei*: A Test Case for St. Thomas's Augustinianism."

17. The Challoner version of the Douay-Rheims is available on the CCEL website, ccel.org.

the Council of Vienne? Does it express that earlier teaching of Vienne, or conflict with it? If it conflicts with it, is the conflict only a theological one or does it presuppose an underlying philosophical conflict on the nature of the human being?

In what I have called the reactionary Augustinian tradition, the *imago Dei* is to be found in the mind alone of man, that is, insofar as human beings are distinct from and rise above animals, and not at all in the embodied animal life of human beings. Descartes too represents that reactionary Augustinian tradition in his *Meditations* centuries after Vienne, although he excludes the intellect from the *imago Dei*, restricting the image solely to the indifference of the will as a faculty of mind, where Challoner includes intellect with will in the image.[18] Now if we are to consider the historical conditions within which that image of the image of God that we see in Challoner and Descartes enters into the life and belief of the Church, might we find a good deal more of Plato and a good deal less, not just of Aristotle, but of Genesis itself? Do Genesis and the rest of Scripture provide us with an understanding of the human soul and human being more in tune with a broadly Platonic or a broadly Aristotelian understanding of what it is to be human?

Both Plato and Aristotle, for their parts, suggest that there are features of human life that bear the mark or image of the divine, a mark that both in their own ways think goes uneasily with bodily reality. And Genesis in the second account says that the body of the man was formed from the dust of the Earth, and God breathed into his face. But only animals have faces. In the first account, just after saying that man, male and female, are made to the image and likeness of God, the text relates that they are blessed by God and commanded to be fruitful and multiply. Does that mark a new passage, or is it

18. It is now a commonplace to recognize Descartes's debt to Augustine on crucial arguments within the *Meditations* in particular. See, for example, Stephen Menn, *Descartes and Augustine* (Cambridge: Cambridge University Press, 2002). In the Augustinian tradition, *Meditation* 4 explicitly raises the question of the *imago Dei* in the human mind. But it does so only to deny Augustine's thesis that the *imago Dei* is found in the mind as the unity of memory, intellect, and will. At this point Descartes has no use for memory, as it is a clear source of doubt and lack of certitude. And he denies the role of intellect in the *imago* because the human intellect is finite, whereas the divine is infinite. The *imago Dei* is found only in the human will, even though it too is finite in power, because it is considered formally indifferent to any and all possible alternatives present to it—in short, the image of God is found, according to Descartes, in the indifferent and thus absolutely free will. Against what I have written here, Menn on the contrary takes the position that this is not a "liberty of indifference" but a freedom from "irrational constraint," and that "the right use of this freedom is negative" (see p. 321). But it is difficult see how this negative freedom from irrational constraint could function as *imago Dei* even as Descartes wants it to. Certainly if it does, it is far afield of Augustine, for whom the will as *imago Dei* functions as a positive movement toward the beloved apprehended.

rather continuous with the *imago Dei* passage? But only living bodies can be fruitful and multiply. And yet it is Aquinas who, with his medieval aristotelianism on the unity and per se character of the soul as form of the body, and what I have dubbed his liberal Augustinianism, can read the Genesis passage in the first account as continuous and not disconnected into two separate pieces, the *imago Dei* with its blessing and the subsequent command to be fruitful and multiply.

Now we know that we cannot just read off of the text in the second account what we are to make of this "breathing into the face," as if from the plain meaning of the words in ordinary use. Surely it involves an image. Still, it is an image more closely related to the thought that we are animals than that we are spiritual substances, or that the *imago Dei* ought to be most easily seen in the mind, consisting of intellect and will, or, as in Descartes, the indifferent will alone. Indeed the second account in Genesis does not refer to the *imago Dei* at all, as the first account does. So to apply the *imago Dei* from the first account to this "breathing into the face" of the second account is already to be engaged in interpretation. So where do this interpretation and these latter thoughts come from? We know from Augustine that any interpretation of Scripture has to pass at least four tests to be considered legitimate. It must be in accord with the rule of faith. It must be internally consistent with the rest of the text of Scripture—a kind of biblical holism. It must build the kingdom of love according to charity, not do damage to it. And it must be consistent with what we know about the world.[19] It is that latter that is relevant to us now. What we learn from Revelation about God and the destiny of human beings is surely not confined to what we know about the world, as if knowledge of the world is a gatekeeper or a foundation upon which faith is built.[20] Still, no student comes into a classroom utterly ignorant. If the student truly knows nothing, he or she cannot learn anything. No doubt what is learned will go beyond, even well beyond, what is already known, and perhaps it will even correct some of what is thought to be known. But it is philosophically arguable that by and large we must be correct in most of what we claim to know about the world for language to work. And the key to Augustine's principles of interpretation is that God reveals salvation to us in a human—or better, humane—way through language, in such a way that we are to seek to understand and pursue. So the effort to understand *sacra doctrina*, as Aquinas calls it, and what we may call theology, cannot help but take place against the background of an effort to understand the preconditions of Revelation

19. See Augustine, *On Christian Doctrine*, trans. D. W. Robertson (New York: Liberal Arts Press, 1958), Bk. III.

20. On the contrary, cf. *ST* I, q. 1, a. 1.

in our knowledge of the world. One way of understanding the task of philosophy, beyond simply raising the natural human questions, is to provide a kind of unified perspective on all the different sorts of worldly inquiry. And one area of worldly inquiry is precisely the question, "What is man that you are mindful of him," or as another author put it, "What a piece of work is a man, how noble in reason, how infinite in faculties, in form and moving how express and admirable, in action how like an angel, in apprehension how like a god! the beauty of the world, the paragon of animals."

My point here is not to bury Plato, or to praise Aristotle. It is good to keep in mind, as the neo-Platonists did, that we ought not to consider Platonism and Aristotelianism as two utterly distinct philosophical traditions. After all, in criticizing positions of his teacher Plato in the first book of the *Metaphysics*, Aristotle referred to himself and his friends as "we Platonists." Still it is undeniable that on the question of the soul and human being, their positions are in deep conflict. So we may ask, do the philosophical differences between these two great *arche* of Greek thought actually matter to the theological enterprise of understanding Holy Scripture? This question is particularly important when we reflect upon the fact that the beginning of the Gospel of John illuminates the beginning of Genesis in order to place the *Logos* of John—who was with God and was God and who dwelt among us—as the primeval principle of Genesis, in which we are to understand human beings made to the image and likeness of God.

Aquinas certainly thought the philosophical differences matter. One way to think of the structure of the *Summa* is in terms of the question of what it means to be made in the image and likeness of God. The first part begins with God, then moves to the discussion of creation and a running commentary on the six days of Genesis, and culminates in a discussion of human nature and the *imago Dei*. The second part then proceeds to discuss human moral character. If the first part ended by discussing what Aristotle would call our first nature, the second part consists of a discussion of what he would call our second nature. But first and second nature do not mark out two distinct things. Rather, second nature is what first nature is born to be. To have a nature is to be born by first nature to an end, a *telos*, a second nature—it is not really two natures, but one that develops. Developed second nature is what we become if we pursue what we are born to be in first nature. And what we were to learn in the *Summa*'s third part, had it been finished, is how humanity can become what it was born to be only by returning to God through Christ. Why? Because it is Christ, the perfect image of the Father, who through the Incarnation is the perfect human image of God, and thus for us the model and means of what we are called by birth to be. Now philosophers will say that it is analytically true that only bodies are incarnate. So it turns out that the perfect human image of God is found in the Incarnation.

For all the complexity and scholastic rigor that now seems so foreign to us, as well as the at times mind numbing order of the *Summa*, what could be of greater theological import for all Christians than the subject of God and the *imago Dei*? It goes back to Aquinas's argument in the very first question of the *Summa* that *sacra doctrina* is primarily a speculative science about God, but secondarily a practical science instructing us on the practical conditions of achieving our natural union with God—through the perfect human image of God who is at once and identically the perfect image of the Father. We are made in the image and likeness of Christ both God and man.

And yet, we must ask what is man that thou art mindful of him? In the first part of the *Summa* in questions 75 and 76, Aquinas wrestles with the tension between a broadly platonic conception of the soul in question 75 and a broadly aristotelian conception in 76. Were one to read only 75, despite the occasional hints at an Aristotelian notion of soul here and there, one would come away with the idea that Aquinas was broadly a platonist. In fact, Thomas tells us that the order of questions is dictated by theological concerns which must concentrate upon the soul, and consider the body only insofar as it relates to the soul. So question 75 might suggest to us that the very nature of theology concerned with the soul, as if it is a distinct thing related in some way to the body, pushes us toward a platonic conception of the soul. And we could see here a way in which Challoner might take comfort in the *Summa* in his commentary on Genesis, if he looked only to question 75. But in 76 Aquinas pushes back, and pushes back hard, against the platonic conception of the soul, as he argues conclusively on philosophical grounds for his understanding of the aristotelian position on the human soul, the intellectual principle, that it is at once and identically the substantial form of the body. Soul and body are not two things. They are two principles of the one thing which is the human being. And so theology is in fact concerned with the living human animal, and with the soul because it is the principle of intelligibility of that living human animal. What is question 76 other than a philosophical corrective to a theological temptation toward platonism that found philosophical expression in question 75? And Aquinas's discussion of the *imago Dei* in question 93, the culmination of the commentary on the sixth day here in the first part of the *Summa*, is unintelligible without question 76 as a corrective to 75, or if not a corrective, the fully adequate account of the soul required by the *aporiae* left open and unanswered by 75.

So the entire discussion of human nature is itself ordered toward question 93, in which Aquinas explicitly takes up the Augustinian theme of the *imago*

Dei, in which the vast majority of authoritative sources are taken from Augustine's *De Trinitate*. Yes, it is "according to" the rational soul, but not "in" the rational soul, that the *imago Dei* exists in human beings.[21] That is why dogs are vestiges but not images of God. But the *imago* cannot be confined to the mind alone; it must be seen in the entire reality of the human being who is an animal, a rational animal, not distinguished *from* animals but distinguished *as* an animal, so much so that the *imago* must be seen even where Augustine feared to tread, in the reproductive capacity of human beings who, unlike the angels, produce in Aquinas's words "man from man as God from God." So too dogs produce dog from dog, but not as an embodied manifestation of, and according to, reason. The entire shape of that discussion expresses the earlier philosophical resolution concerning the nature of human beings that Aquinas had come to in the dialectical back and forth of questions 75 and 76.

This is but one snapshot of a brief moment of the concrete historical condition of the expression of *sacra doctrina* in the life of the Church. So, perhaps now with all of this talk of medieval aristotelianism versus Platonism and Neo-Platonism, with Cartesianism thrown in, the thing to do, to avoid the thought that the Church in *sacra doctrina* commits herself to philosophical positions, is to become devotees of a certain kind of Kantian, neo-Kantian, or post-Kantian epistemological turn that expresses skepticism about such weighty issues. We know that there has been throughout history a temptation to use philosophical categories to understand Revelation, a temptation even expressed in recent Church teaching. But it is a temptation that ought not to be pursued. Truth is, like the thing in itself, transcendent, by which we mean it is beyond all of our human categories of systematization. We cannot avoid thinking in categorical terms; that is our fault. Plato knew this in his myth of a forgetful fall from the transcendent realm of the forms. What he did not know is that there is no anamnesis, no purified return to that transcendent realm. The tragic human condition is to be saddled with categories that deform and warp the transcendent truth. Philosophy can at most assist theology by a kind of therapy that helps us to come to terms with our alienated-aletheitic condition. We may dream of Avalon, but it will remain always already forever over the horizon of human experience.

And with a certain sort of historical consciousness, we might add that even our categories of systematization shift and change over time—they are

---

21. Aquinas's discussion of the *imago Dei* palpably shifts from the language of "*in mente*" of his earlier discussion of it in question 10 of the *Quaestiones Disputatae De Veritate* to the language of "*secundum mentem*" in question 93 of the *Summa*, the latter being influenced and determined by the ways in which he had sorted through the issues of soul and body in questions 75 and 76. See my "*Imago Dei*: A Test Case for St. Thomas's Augustinianism."

contingent products of historical cultural contexts. We are yoked to some one or another set of immanent categories, but not these particular ones. In that respect the sorts of doctrinal and theological statements that we make are, to a sufficiently critical mind, more statements about us and our needs at any particular historical epoch than about the transcendent truth that is God and our transcendent destiny in Him. As our needs change, so also must we abandon outmoded ways of thinking. Case in point: the whole of both the Platonic and the Aristotelian—indeed, the broadly Greek philosophical—framework, yoked as it is to geocentrism, has been decisively undercut by the Copernican-Newtonian-Daltonian-Darwininian-Einsteinian revolution. This revolution in historical consciousness has taught us how *sacra doctrina* cannot afford to be yoked to the contingent categories of human experience. The Church cannot be bound to any particular set of philosophical categories, because such categories must render the transcendent truth of God immanent in our contingent historical experience and thus deform and do violence to that transcendence. So we must learn to live with the shifting historical categories of experience. Or better, to take up arms against them and banish all philosophy from theological understanding in an effort to retrieve the purity of Gospel truth unblemished by Greek metaphysical categories or any other categories for that matter—but, truth be told, especially the Greek ones. Banish all philosophy, that is, except that philosophical position that holds that all experience is conditioned by historically contingent categories that are in some sense wholly dependent upon the immanent mind, not any transcendent reality.

Those last two paragraphs, besides being extraordinarily simplistic, also sound more polemical than philosophical; and they are grounded in the sorts of simple anecdotal encounters with which this paper began. But the polemical feel of them has a non-polemical point. I do not intend to argue that the Church makes a definitive choice for this or that philosophical system. In fact, for philosophical reasons I think it is very difficult to make sense of the idea of a philosophical system. Traditions, yes. Systems? I am not so sure. What after all are the identity and boundary conditions of philosophical systems? How do such philosophical systems relate to the presupposed language and noetic setting in which they are framed, and so on? If they are embedded in larger linguistic frameworks, then that makes it all the more difficult to isolate them as distinct "systems" that one adopts as if they were distinct options for Descartes's indifferent will to choose between. No one expects definitive or final criteria for a "tradition," but a "system" lends itself to such questions of definitive criteria.

Still, it does not follow from the difficulty of isolating "systems" that might be chosen by the indifferent will that the Church does not adopt identifiably philosophical claims about the world and human nature, even if it does not adopt systems. Indeed, this is a point acknowledged by the Church on this most important of theological topics, upon which I have chosen to focus, the *imago Dei*.

Present-day theology is striving to overcome the influence of dualistic anthropologies that locate the *imago Dei* exclusively with reference to the spiritual aspect of human nature. Partly under the influence first of Platonic and later of Cartesian dualistic anthropologies, Christian theology itself tended to identify the *imago Dei* in human beings with what is the most specific characteristic of human nature, viz., mind or spirit. The recovery both of elements of biblical anthropology and of aspects of the Thomistic synthesis has contributed to the effort in important ways.[22]

For good or ill, the tradition of faith that seeks understanding draws within itself philosophical claims to better advance the understanding of the sacred deposit of Revelation. The attitude expressed in this passage, however, is not a rejection of philosophical assertions as such. It is no doubt critical of certain philosophical claims, and yet its criticism is itself informed by philosophical claims about human nature such as are found in what it refers to as the "Thomistic synthesis," the philosophical discussion in Aquinas and his contemporaries that I discussed briefly above, and have discussed at much greater length elsewhere.[23] The errors of philosophy are not simply addressed by "biblical anthropology," but are addressed philosophically in the pursuit of understanding *sacra doctrina*.

In any case, we could not do justice to the complicated history I so polemically simplified in anything less than a large book. But my point in being polemical was not actually to be polemical. It was to irritate, and by that irritation perhaps to inculcate that sense of wonder that Aristotle tells us is the beginning of philosophy. My point was to suggest that even theological skepticism about philosophical categories and their importance expresses philosophical presuppositions, if not a philosophical system, as much as the great metaphysical tradition of the Greeks that preceded it. Epistemological skepticism or Kantian and post-Kantian epistemological critique are no more immediately biblically grounded than are Greek metaphysical categories, and they are no less innocent of philosophical presuppositions generally than is Aquinas's medieval aristotelian anthropology. Instead of theology employing philosophical metaphysics of a Greek sort, it employs philosophical epistemology of a more modern and broadly European sort. And it

22. International Theological Commission, "Communion and Stewardship: Human Persons Created in the Image of God" (2004, §27; available on the Vatican website).

23. See my "*Imago Dei*: A Test Case for St. Thomas's Augustinianism."

tacitly affirms as the presupposition of doing theology the very prioritizing of epistemology over metaphysics that is distinctive of one dominant way of telling the history of the modern tradition of philosophy. The point of my medieval example and this polemical example is that it seems that philosophy is unavoidable in the exercise of theology, even if only to argue for the uselessness to theology of a more metaphysically robust philosophy—but to make that argument is to rely upon what appears to be an equally epistemologically robust philosophy in service to theology. We should come to terms with that reality, and ask why it is so.

Even if one's attitude toward philosophy in theology is that it represents a kind of Fall, an original sin in thinking of the divine, the problem is that no one escapes the sin. On the other hand, if one thinks of philosophical inquiry as part of the natural human condition created by God, there is no need to think of that inquiry as thoroughly corrupted by original sin and thus to be avoided. Mistakes are made in all natural human endeavors, even in the human participation in *sacra doctrina*, but the mistakes do not utterly destroy the good of those endeavors. It is worth keeping in mind that one of the specific reasons Augustine enunciated his exegetical principles concerning Scripture was precisely to avoid the Gnostic spiritualizing of Revelation that would divorce it utterly from worldly learning.[24]

Aquinas in his own peculiar way recapitulates the Augustinian spirit at

24. "Usually, even a non-Christian knows something about the earth, the heavens, and the other elements of this world, about the motion and orbit of the stars and even their size and relative positions, about the predictable eclipses of the sun and moon, the cycles of the years and the seasons, about the kinds of animals, shrubs, stones, and so forth, and this knowledge he holds to as being certain from reason and experience. Now, it is a disgraceful and dangerous thing for an infidel to hear a Christian, presumably giving the meaning of Holy Scripture, talking nonsense on these topics; and we should take all means to prevent such an embarrassing situation, in which people show up vast ignorance in a Christian and laugh it to scorn. The shame is not so much that an ignorant individual is derided, but that people outside the household of faith think our sacred writers held such opinions, and, to the great loss of those for whose salvation we toil, the writers of our Scripture are criticized and rejected as unlearned men. If they find a Christian mistaken in a field which they themselves know well and hear him maintaining his foolish opinions about our books, how are they going to believe those books in matters concerning the resurrection of the dead, the hope of eternal life, and the kingdom of heaven, when they think their pages are full of falsehoods and on facts which they themselves have learnt from experience and the light of reason? Reckless and incompetent expounders of Holy Scripture bring untold trouble and sorrow on their wiser brethren when they are caught in one of their mischievous false opinions and are taken to task by those who are not bound by the authority of our sacred books. For then, to defend their utterly foolish and obviously untrue statements, they will try to call upon Holy Scripture for proof and even recite from memory many passages which they think support their position, although *they understand neither what they say nor the things about which they make assertion* [1 Tm 1:7]." J. H. Taylor, "The Literal Meaning of Genesis" ("De Genesi ad litteram libri duodecim") in *Ancient Christian Writers*, vol. 41 (New York: Newman Press, 1982), 43.

the beginning of the *Summa*. Earlier I mentioned his position that *sacra doctrina* is both a speculative science about God and a practical science about our way to God. If human beings, intelligent agents capable of acting to achieve their end, are to succeed in achieving their end, they must know that end. The knowledge they can achieve of that end in this life apart from *sacra doctrina* is "nasty, brutish, and short." Aquinas says that the knowledge is meager, takes most of a life to acquire, and is filled with error. So God in his mercy, willing that we achieve our end, instructs through *sacra doctrina* how to know and love that end. But notice the presupposition of Aquinas's account of God's mercy. We have an end that is set for us by nature. As Augustine had said, we have a natural desire to know that end, and love it. From that desire there arise specifically human questions that have only the most meager of human answers. But they remain human questions, and meager human answers. And the answers that God puts to us in *sacra doctrina* are his merciful response to those human questions, and they thus presuppose those questions and their meager answers. Unless there was something true in our understanding of the world around us and ourselves in it, we could not even begin to fathom the adequate answers God proposes to us for our human questions.

Aquinas tells us that God's Revelation comes to us in a way suited to our human nature. It comes to us in human language. Its most appropriate linguistic form is to use metaphors, because it is through those metaphors or images that the literal truth concerning God and us is communicated. Metaphors serve a double purpose: concerning the divine, they are tailored to our human minds, which are by nature mostly occupied with the material world; also, they confute the proud, who think they know the transcendent God by their own efforts. But you cannot even recognize, much less understand, a metaphor without a prior knowledge of its non-metaphorical use. Language use by and large presupposes a great deal of knowledge of the world, not perfect or exhaustive knowledge of the world, but knowledge nonetheless. It is in that knowledge of the world, knowledge that Augustine and Aquinas maintain is presupposed to the hearing of God's word, that Aristotle saw the source of the wonder that is the beginning of all philosophy.

In the seventh book of the *Republic,* Plato had provided a picture of wisdom as a knowledge of the highest causes of things that allows one to put order into one's own life and the life of the world around one. So it follows that philosophy, the love of wisdom, is the love of the highest causes of things and the order attendant upon them. His student Aristotle distinguishes this wisdom into its speculative form and its practical form. By the Platonic criterion, *sacra doctrina* is the philosophy that far exceeds the efforts of the

Greeks. And Aquinas's argument in the first question—that *sacra doctrina* is both speculative and practical and still one *scientia*—amounts to an argument for Plato against Aristotle's separation of the two, even though Aquinas had no direct encounter with the *Republic*. In any case, *sacra doctrina* is a philosophy that addresses the questions of the Greeks, which questions often manage to be more than just questions for the Greeks, but questions for all human beings. Wonder is expressed in questions, spoken or unspoken. I often tell my students that the first task of education is to learn how to ask the right questions. And any process of education will return to the questions we began with to reshape them, and make them better. So theological education may well educate us in the appropriate questions to put to God, begging and pleading as Augustine did at the beginning of the *Confessions* that God give us not just the words but the questions as well. But God already gave us those questions when he created us as human beings capable of knowing at least some of his invisible things from the visible things of this world. Theological education may well help to reshape the philosophical questions we have; but it would be inhuman, inhumane to eliminate those philosophical questions. In that respect, like grace and nature, theology perfects philosophy, it does not destroy it. The usefulness of philosophy within theological education may well be that it helps us to sort through our human questions so that we may be better prepared to hear God's merciful answer, with the result that theology might actually have something to perfect.

A theology that would ignore philosophy, as well as both the questions philosophy raises about the human condition and the admittedly meager answers it may at its best provide, could not be a participation in and reasoned reflection upon *sacra doctrina*, since *sacra doctrina* is God's answer to those questions. So the answer to the question of this paper is, *necessarium est, praeter theologicam disciplinam, aliam doctrinam haberi*. Perhaps the purpose of philosophy within theological education is to make sure that theology remains merciful and humane.[25]

In conclusion, may we all one day join Ralph McInerny, who now knows an infinitely more adequate answer to the questions he so cheerfully inquired into when he walked amongst us, a better answer to his philosophical questions than even the most merciful if not meager theology could give him in this life.

---

25. I want to thank Alasdair MacIntyre for reminding me in conversation of the central role played by the notion of philosophy as raising human questions, particularly in the thought of St. John Paul II. I also want to thank Alfred Freddoso who, as a teacher in graduate school, first put me onto the idea of Aquinas's *Summa* as being in continuity with the earlier Church's *apologia* for *sacra doctrina* as *Philosophia*.

PART TWO

A NEED FOR A METAPHYSICS OF NATURE IN THEOLOGY

CHAPTER THREE

Theology and the Metaphysics of Creation

LAWRENCE DEWAN, OP

This book has for its general theme: the need of philosophy in theology.[1] My article invokes the legacy of a recently deceased colleague and friend, Ralph McInerny, one of whose last books was, in his own words, "a defense of a robust understanding of the teaching of St. Thomas Aquinas and of the Magisterium on *Praeambula Fidei*."[2] By the "*praeambula fidei*" he means those truths concerning God, and first of all the truth of his very existence, which can be demonstrated by philosophy, and which are essential for the life of supernatural faith.

In proposing to speak about the importance of the metaphysics of creation in educating theologians, I see myself as very much involved in this domain of the preambles to the articles of faith. It certainly is the doctrine of Aquinas (and I present myself as a disciple of Aquinas) that creation, as the mode of production of all things other than God, is a truth of the Cath-

---

1. Translations of Aquinas's texts are my own unless otherwise indicated.

2. Cf. Ralph McInerny, *Praeambula Fidei: Thomism and the God of the Philosophers* (Washington, D.C.: The Catholic University of America Press, 2006), ix. In the Preface, McInerny says that he means "to treat the negative attitude towards natural theology that is found among those one would have expected to be defenders of it" (ix). And he tells us, "This book is a defense of a robust understanding of the teaching of St. Thomas Aquinas and of the Magisterium on *praeambula fidei*" (ix).

olic faith and a philosophically demonstrable truth. As he says, "Not only does the Faith hold that there is creation, but reason also demonstrates it."[3]

And we recall such texts as *De potentia* 3.5. After speaking of the limitations of the Pre-Socratic philosophers, Aquinas concludes, "Later philosophers, such as Plato, Aristotle, and their followers, arrived at a consideration of universal being itself; and therefore they alone affirmed the existence of some universal cause of things, from which all others proceeded forth into being, as Augustine makes clear. And to this doctrine the Catholic Faith likewise consents. And it can be *demonstrated* by three arguments."[4]

And he goes on to sketch the arguments that he assigns to Plato, Aristotle, and Avicenna.

Still, I must qualify what I have said. Aquinas notes that the word "creation" is used by us Christians as including a note of newness.[5] So taken, it cannot be demonstrated. Thus, Aquinas tells us, "It is to be said that 'that the world has not always been' is held by Faith alone, and cannot be demonstratively proved; just as was said above (*ST* 1.32.1) concerning the mystery of the Trinity."[6]

3. Aquinas, *Scriptum Super Sententiis,* 2.1.1.2, ed. P. Mandonnet (Paris: Lethielleux, 1929), 17: "Respondeo quod creationem esse, non tantum fides tenet, sed etiam ratio demonstrat." Notice, however, that Aquinas goes on, on p. 18, at the end of the body of the article, to distinguish between "creation" as the philosophers admit it and "creation" as including the note of temporal beginning, in which case it cannot be demonstrated, but is held on faith.

4. Aquinas, *Quest. Disp. de potentia Dei,* 3.5: "Posteriores vero philosophi, ut Plato, Aristoteles et eorum sequaces, pervenerunt ad considerationem ipsius esse universalis; et ideo ipsi soli posuerunt aliquam universalem causam rerum, a qua omnia alia in esse prodirent, ut patet per Augustinum. Cui quidem sententiae etiam catholica fides consentit. Et hoc triplici *ratione demonstrari potest.*" The *De potentia* article, however, is on the universality of the divine causality of being, not on "creation." The reference to Augustine is given as *De civ. Dei,* 8.4 in the 1953 Marietti edition made by Paul M. Pession, OP. Augustine there presents Plato as seeing in natural or contemplative philosophy that God is the universal cause of existence.

5. *Summa theologiae (ST)* I, q. 45, a. 3, ad 3: "'Creation' signifies the stance (or relation) of the creature towards the Creator, together with a certain newness or beginning." And cf. especially *ST* I, q. 46, a. 2, ad 2, in the context of the argument about the eternity of the world, where we read: "Those who held that the world is eternal, held that the world was made by God from nothing, not that it was made *after* nothing, *as with what we understand by the word 'creation,'* but that it was not made from anything. And so it is that some of them did not refuse to use the word 'creation,' as is clear in the case of Avicenna in his *Metaph.*" (my emphasis).

6. *ST* I, q. 46, a. 2; And he continues, "And the reason for this is that the newness of the world cannot receive demonstration from the side of the world itself.... Similarly, also, neither [can the newness of the world receive demonstration] from the side of the efficient cause, which acts by will.... But the divine will can be manifested to man through revelation, on which Faith leans. Hence, that the world began is believable, but not demonstrable or scientifically knowable [*scibile*]. And this is something important to consider, lest someone, presuming to demonstrate what pertains to Faith, introduce non-necessary arguments [i.e., which do not conclude with absolute necessity], which provide a subject of ridicule for unbelievers, judging that we believe on the basis of such arguments the things of Faith."

In that sense of the word, creation is strictly an article of faith, and not a preamble to the articles. That is why I call my topic "the *metaphysics of* creation" and not simply "creation."

As regards "the metaphysics of creation" I am going to rely almost exclusively on what I find in the *Summa theologiae, prima pars* (*ST* I). The *ST* is presented by Aquinas as alive to the needs of pedagogy, and though it speaks of "beginners" and of the teaching contained therein as "milk, not meat," I dare say that graduate students will benefit greatly by camping at its door.

Before going on to the relevant texts in *ST* I, however, I want to say a word about "theology," since that word, too, is in my title and in the title of this book. While Aquinas calls what he is presenting in the *ST* "*sacra doctrina*," he also refers to it as "theology"[7] and to himself in the act of presenting it as a "theologian."[8] Thus, I am taking "theology" to mean the discourse about God as meant in the *ST*.

First, though, let us speak about the *place* of these "*praeambula* to the articles of faith" in our conception of what I will call "integral Christian mind." The first article of the first question of the *ST* teaches us that in their regard we *need divine Revelation*! They are introduced to us as truths to be *believed*, as truths *necessarily* revealed to us by God himself and held by supernatural *faith*.[9]

The *need* for the human being to know the doctrine contained in the *ST*, that is, the doctrine Aquinas is calling "the Holy Teaching," is explained in the very first article of the work. And we should notice how this issue is put. He asks, "Is there need for a teaching *beyond* [Latin: *praeter*] the *philosophical* disciplines?"

That first article of the *ST* affirms our *need* for a teaching that *transcends* the teaching of the philosophers. Aquinas says, "It is to be said that it was necessary for human well-being [human salvation] that there be a teaching by divine revelation, beyond the philosophical disciplines which are worked out by human reason."[10]

---

7. Thus, in *ST* I, q. 1, a. 1, ad 2, he refers to "the theology which pertains to the holy teaching" in contrast to "that theology that is presented as a part of philosophy"; and in *ST* I, q. 1, a. 7, sc, he argues that the subject of the science and wisdom that is "*sacra doctrina*" is God, on the basis of its being called "*theologia*," that is, discourse about God.

8. Cf. *ST* I, q. 75, prologue (Ottawa ed., 438b19).

9. This is why I deliberately use the expression: "preambles to the articles of faith" (cf. *ST* I, q. 2, a. 2, ad 1) and not the one used by McInerny, "praeambula fidei." In the *Summa theologiae* Aquinas does not use the expression "praeambula fidei," but it does occur in an earlier work, i.e., his lectures on Boethius's *De Trinitate* q. 2, a. 3.

10. *ST* I, q. 1, a. 1: "dicendum quod necessarium fuit ad humanam salutem, esse doctrinam quandam secundum revelationem divinam, praeter philosophicas disciplinas, quae ratione humana investigantur."

The primary reason for such a need is the nature of the goal that God has assigned for the human being, a goal that surpasses our natural knowing powers; what is the human being for?[11]

Let us not rush through this first article of the first question of the *ST*. It merits much reflection. Aquinas says, "The human being is ordered towards God as towards a goal that exceeds reason's comprehension; in accordance with the text of Isaiah 64.4: 'Eye has not seen, O God, without you, what you have prepared for those who love you.'"[12] And he goes on, "But the goal is supposed to be known in advance by human beings, who are supposed to order their intentions and their actions towards the goal. Hence, it was necessary, for the well-being of the human being, that some things be made known to him by divine revelation, things that surpass human reason."[13] That is, the human being, *as a kind of thing*, is meant to seek *known* goals: thus, it was necessary that God make known to us, *reveal* to us, the goal he has decided upon.[14] Our benefiting from that revelation must be through an act of supernatural *faith*.[15]

Still, there is more to the human situation, to your and my situation, than that. As Aquinas continues in the same first article, even as regards the truths concerning God that the human mind can know by its natural powers, there is need for a divine revelation, and so for faith. We read:

11. The magnitude of human dignity is properly grasped only in the light of that destiny. Cf. e.g., *ST* III, q. 57, a. 6, ad 3: "Christ, by ascending once into heaven, obtained for himself and for us the perpetual right and dignity [*ius et dignitatem*] of the heavenly dwelling." Cf. also ibid., q. 58, a. 4, ad 1 and 2; *ST* I, q. 12, and I-II, qq. 1–5, on beatitude; and *ST* I, q. 93, a. 4, on the three levels of man's being "in the image of God."

12. *ST* I, q. 1, a. 1, resp.: "homo ordinatur ad Deum sicut ad quendam finem qui comprehensionem rationis excedit, secundum illud Isaiae LXIV, oculus non vidit Deus absque te, quae praeparasti diligentibus te." Aquinas's text of Isaiah seems to be influenced by 1 Cor 2:9.

13. Ibid. "Finem autem oportet esse praecognitum hominibus, qui suas intentiones et actiones debent ordinare in finem. Unde necessarium fuit homini ad salutem, quod ei nota fierent quaedam per revelationem divinam, quae rationem humanam excedunt."

14. The necessity here pertains to God's justice and his wisdom; cf. *ST* I, q. 21, a. 1; cf. also my paper "Death in the Setting of Divine Wisdom: The Doctrine of St. Thomas Aquinas," which is chap. 19 in my book *Wisdom, Law, and Virtue: Essays in Thomistic Ethics* (New York: Fordham University Press, 2008), 327–29.

15. The role of faith is mentioned for the first time in the article's ad 1. The objector had used the biblical authority of Ecclesiasticus 3:22 to argue that we should not seek things that are above us; Aquinas replies, "Though those things which are above human knowledge are not to be inquired into by means of reason, they are, nevertheless, as revealed by God, *to be accepted through faith*." Thus, in the very same passage it is added, "Many things beyond the scope of humans have been shown to you. And the Holy Teaching is about such things." ("Licet ea quae sunt altiora hominis cognitione, non sint ab homine per rationem inquirenda, sunt tamen, a Deo revelata, *suscipienda per fidem*. Unde et ibidem subditur, plurima supra sensum hominum ostensa sunt tibi. Et in huiusmodi sacra doctrina consistit.")

Furthermore, regarding those things about God that can be investigated by human reason, *it was necessary that man be instructed by divine revelation*; because the truth about God, as investigated by reason, would have come only to a few people and after a long time and with an admixture of many errors; and yet on knowledge of this truth depends the entire ultimate well-being of the human being, which is [to be found] in God.[16]

This presentation here by Aquinas is crucial for our sound conception of ourselves and our own situation in reality. While there are things about God that human reason can discover, that sort of human knowledge is arrived at *with certainty* only by a few.

This brings Aquinas to the conclusion of his article, based on the two just seen reasons: "Thus, therefore, so that ultimate well-being[17] might come about for human beings both more suitably and *more certainly*, it was necessary that they be instructed concerning divine things through divine revelation."[18] I aim to stress that this article, with its two reasons, is meant for *all* of us and for most, if not all, of our lives.

The very terminology, "preambles to the articles of faith," is first introduced in the *ST* to characterize the truth that God exists. In *ST* I, q. 2, a. 2, ad 1, we read:

It is to be said that "*a god is*," and the other such [truths] which can be known through natural reason concerning a god, as is said in Romans 1.19, are not articles of faith, but *preambles to the articles*; for faith presupposes natural knowledge, in the way that grace [presupposes] nature, and as the perfection [presupposes] the perfectible. Nevertheless nothing prohibits that what is in itself demonstrable and scientifically knowable be accepted by someone as *believable*, [by someone, i.e.,] who does not grasp the demonstration.[19]

I am insisting on this because I have actually met people who thought that Aquinas did not mean to include among the needed *revealed* truths the truth of *the very existence* of a God. Surely, they thought, he means *other*

---

16. *ST* I, q. 1, a. 1: "Ad ea etiam quae de Deo ratione humana investigari possunt, necessarium fuit hominem instrui revelatione divina. Quia veritas de Deo, per rationem investigata, a paucis, et per longum tempus, et cum admixtione multorum errorum, homini proveniret, a cuius tamen veritatis cognitione dependet tota hominis salus, quae in Deo est."

17. I have so translated "*salus*" because "salvation" might be too much associated with "the usual sermon" to make its point.

18. *ST* I, q. 1, a. 1: "Ut igitur salus hominibus et convenientius et certius proveniat, necessarium fuit quod de divinis per divinam revelationem instruantur."

19. *ST* I, q. 2, a. 2, ad 1: "Ad primum ergo dicendum quod *Deum esse*, et alia huiusmodi quae per rationem naturalem nota possunt esse de Deo, ut dicitur Rom. 1, non sunt articuli fidei, sed *praeambula ad articulos*: sic enim fides praesupponit cognitionem naturalem, sicut gratia naturam, et ut perfectio perfectibile. Nihil tamen prohibet illud quod secundum se demonstrabile est et scibile, ab aliquo accipi ut credibile, qui demonstrationem non capit."

further philosophically demonstrable points. I accordingly stress that, when discussing later in detail the range of supernatural faith, Aquinas explicitly speaks of *the need to believe by supernatural faith the truth that a God exists*; this is the case until one truly understands the power of the philosophical demonstration.

We read:

It is necessary for the human being to accept *at the level of faith* [*per modum fidei*] not only those things which are above reason, but also those which can be known by reason. And this for three reasons, the first of which is so that the human being come *more quickly* to a knowledge of the divine truth: for the science to which it pertains to prove *that God exists*, and other such things about God, is proposed lastly to be learned by the human being, many other sciences being presupposed. And thus the human being would come only after much of his lifetime to a knowledge of God.[20]

I must prolong that quotation to cite the third reason, the issue of *certitude*. We read:

Thirdly, *for the sake of certitude*. For human reason, as regards divine things, is *exceedingly deficient*; the sign of this is that the philosophers, inquiring about *human* things by natural investigation, have erred in many ways, and judged in ways contrary to each other. Therefore, in order that there be among humans *undoubted and certain knowledge concerning God*, it was necessary that divine things be communicated to them on the level of faith, *as said by God*, who cannot deceive.[21]

---

20. *ST* II-II, q. 2, a. 4 (1416b45–1417a2): "necessarium est homini accipere *per modum fidei* non solum ea quae sunt supra rationem, sed etiam ea quae per rationem cognosci possunt. Et hoc propter tria. Primo quidem, ut citius homo ad veritatis divinae cognitionem perveniat. Scientia enim ad quam pertinet probare *deum esse* et alia huiusmodi de deo, ultimo hominibus addiscenda proponitur, praesuppositis multis aliis scientiis. Et sic non nisi post multum tempus vitae suae homo ad dei cognitionem perveniret" (my emphasis.) All three reasons are relevant, but I omit the second one for the sake of brevity. It deals with the small number of people who would know God because of limited intelligence or the practical limits of human existence, and even mentions the problem of the lazy student! Note also that later in the same question of the *ST* II-II, viz. at q. 2, a. 10, ad 1, Aquinas uses "the existence of a God" as the *example* of something pertaining to the faith that one can first believe and may subsequently *demonstrate*. We read, "Quando autem homo habet voluntatem credendi *ea quae sunt fidei* ex sola auctoritate divina, etiam si habeat rationem demonstrativam *ad aliquid eorum, puta* ad hoc quod est *deum esse*, non propter hoc tollitur vel minuitur meritum fidei." ("When a man has the will to believe solely on divine authority those things that pertain to faith, then even if he has a demonstrative argument for something among them, e.g., that a God exists, the merit of faith is not done away with or diminished because of that.")

21. *ST* II-II, q. 2, a. 4 (1417a10–19): "Tertio modo, propter *certitudinem*. Ratio enim humana in rebus divinis est multum deficiens, cuius signum est quia philosophi, de rebus humanis naturali investigatione perscrutantes, in multis erraverunt et sibi ipsis contraria senserunt. Ut ergo esset indubitata et certa cognitio apud homines de Deo, oportuit quod divina eis per modum fidei traderentur, quasi a Deo dicta, qui mentiri non potest" (my emphasis).

Why am I insisting on this point about ourselves relative to knowledge of God? It is because in our rather secularist culture, our rationalist culture, we are likely to see our faith as bearing solely upon those things that transcend reason, and see the very existence of God as *readily available* to what we might call "our natural selves." Aquinas explicitly speaks of the need to believe by supernatural faith the truth that God exists; this is the case until one truly understands the power of the philosophical demonstration.

This caution of Aquinas, a line of discussion he found in the writings of the twelfth-century Jewish theologian Moses Maimonides,[22] is quite in accord with the stress that Aristotle put on the *difficulty* of metaphysical knowledge, the philosophical knowledge that attains to some truths about God. It is the knowledge that is most difficult for the human being. It is "divine" knowledge, because God alone can have it, says Aristotle, or God above all others.[23]

22. Cf. Aquinas, *Expositio Super Librum Boethii de Trinitate* 3.1, trans. Armand Maurer (Faith, Reason and Theology) (Toronto: Pontifical Institute of Mediaeval Studies, 1987), 66–67, where Aquinas explicitly refers to five reasons given by Rabbi Moses why faith is needed even for things which some can demonstrate concerning God.

23. About the difficulties of metaphysics, Aristotle tells us that "these things, the most universal, are on the whole the hardest for men to know; for they are farthest from the senses" (*Metaph.* 1.2, 982a23–25 [Oxford trans.]). Again, in the same place (*Metaph.* 1.2, 982b25–32), it having been argued that wisdom is non-utilitarian but rather sought for its own intrinsic worth, the suggestion is made that it is perhaps not a suitable pursuit for human beings, whose nature is servile, that is, who must in large part be absorbed in the pursuit of the useful. Aristotle rejects this view, but he goes on to admit that one of the reasons wisdom should be regarded as "most divine" is that "God alone can have it, or God above all others" (*Metaph.* 1.2, 983a9–10).

In the *Nicomachean Ethics*, in the discussion of human happiness, the life of contemplation of truth is proposed as the most appropriate candidate to qualify as human happiness. An objection is raised, precisely on the grounds that "such a life would be too high for man; for it is not insofar as he is man that he will live so, but insofar as something divine is present in him" (*EN* 10.7, 1177b25–27 [Oxford trans.]). To this, it is countered that we "must, so far as we can, make ourselves immortal, and strain every nerve to live in accordance with the best thing in us" (*EN* 10.7, 1177b35). But Aristotle does not leave the matter there. He goes on: "This would seem, too, to be each man himself, since it is the authoritative and better part of him. It would be strange, then, if he were to choose not the life of his self but that of something else … for man, the life according to reason is best and pleasantest, since *reason more than anything else is man*" (*EN* 10.7, 1178a2–8). That is, in this argument, human nature itself is seen as something akin to divine nature. Still, and this is my constant point, the activity in question is viewed as requiring *extraordinary effort*.

It is not presented as easy. Nor should it be thought that Aristotle's gods care nothing for the human being, or that the human being's happiness involves no social relation to the gods. Thus, in the same *EN* context, we are told:

> He who exercises his reason and cultivates it seems to be both in the best state of mind and most dear to the gods. For if the gods have any care for human affairs, as they are thought to have, it would be reasonable both that they should delight in that which was best and most akin to them, i.e., their intellect, and that they should reward those who love and honour this most, as caring for the things that are dear to them and acting both rightly and nobly. And that all these attributes belong most of all to the wise man is manifest. He therefore is the

All of this is really preliminary to what I wish to say about the important place of the metaphysics of creation within theology. My main point is the *appreciation* of the divine magnitude, the divine transcendence relative to all created reality, that results from consideration of the truth concerning the mode of production that is creation.

The importance of creation for the believer is already indicated in the Creeds by the primacy they give to God as creator, but I would like to call attention to the role of the metaphysics of creation in the presentation of the virtue of religion (which of course exists both as natural and as infused virtue).[24]

By "the metaphysics of creation" I mean the doctrine of being as a scientific field, the doctrine that concludes to God as the subsisting act of being,[25] and thus understands the production by God of all beings other than God himself, the production, as Aquinas says, of "being as a whole" (*totius entis*, cf. *ST* I, q. 45, a. 1 [ed. Ottawa 284a2]). This metaphysics is sketched in the fourth way in *ST* I, q. 2, a. 3. On the basis of the God whose existence is concluded to there, namely, "a maximal being, … that is the cause for all *beings*

---

dearest to the gods. And he who is that will presumably be also the happiest; so that in this way too the wise man will more than any other be happy. (*EN* 10.8, 1179a22–33)

It should be added that in the *Nicomachean Ethics* Aristotle is not going into such matters in the deepest way possible, but only as far as is needed for practical agreement. Cf., for example, *EN* 10.8, 1178a2024.

24. I stress the importance of appreciation of it for spirituality, that is, religion. Cf. *ST* II-II, q. 81, a. 1, ad 3: "Ad tertium dicendum quod cum servus dicatur ad dominum, necesse est quod ubi est *propria et specialis ratio dominii*, ibi sit specialis et propria ratio servitutis. Manifestum est autem quod *dominium convenit deo secundum propriam et singularem quandam rationem, quia scilicet* IPSE OMNIA FECIT, et quia summum in omnibus rebus obtinet principatum. Et ideo specialis ratio servitutis ei debetur. Et talis servitus nomine *latriae* designatur apud Graecos. Et ideo *ad religionem* proprie pertinet." ("To the third it is to be said that since 'servant' is said relative to 'lord,' necessarily where there is a proper and special type of lordship, there one finds a special and proper role of service. But it is evident that lordship befits God according to a proper and singular role, i.e. because he has made all things, and because he has sovereign primacy regarding all things. And therefore a special type of service is due to him. And this service is signified among the Greeks by the word *latria*. And thus it pertains properly *to religion*.") And also *ST* II-II, q. 81, q. 3, c: "Respondeo dicendum quod, sicut supra habitum est, habitus distinguuntur secundum diversam rationem obiecti. *Ad religionem autem pertinet exhibere reverentiam uni deo secundum unam rationem, inquantum scilicet est primum principium creationis et gubernationis rerum*, unde ipse dicit, *Malach.* I, si ego pater, ubi honor meus? *patris enim est et producere et gubernare*. Et ideo manifestum est quod religio est una virtus." ("Habits are distinguished in accordance with the diverse character of the object. Now, it pertains to religion to exhibit reverence to the one God as regards one character, viz. inasmuch as He is the first principle as to the creation and governing of things, as He himself says, Malachi 1.6: 'If I am a father, where is my honor?' for it pertains to a father to produce and to govern.") On the two modes of moral virtues, the acquired and the infused, cf. *ST* I-II, q. 63, aa. 3 and 4.

25. An early version is at *In Sent.* 1.3.divisio primae partis textus, ed. P. Mandonnet, (Paris: Lethielleux, 1929), t. I, p. 89. On this text as a prelude to the *ST* fourth way, see my paper "St. Thomas and Creation: Does God Create 'Reality'?" *Science et Esprit* 51 (1999): 5–25, at p. 22.

of being and goodness and of every perfection," it is seen that it is essentially form (I, q. 3, a. 2), that it is subsisting form (a. 3), and that it is the very act of being subsisting as a form (a. 4). From this it follows that it (now called "*Ipsum esse subsistens*": I, q. 4, a. 2 [ed. Ottawa, 25a11]) contains eminently the perfections of all things. The doctrine of goodness and divine goodness, and of the unique infinity of God (I, q. 7, a. 1), stems immediately from this doctrine of God as *Ipsum esse subsistens*. It follows, too, from the infinity of perfection of being of *Ipsum esse subsistens*, that it must be unique: there can be only one such being (I, q. 11, a. 3, second reason). This uniqueness as to infinite being leads to the conclusion of I, q. 44, a. 1, that every being other than God is a being by participation, caused efficiently by the God who is *Ipsum esse subsistens*. This is the fourth way again, but from the top down.

This is what Aquinas derives from his reading of Aristotle, *Metaph.* 2.1 993b19–31. He tells us this in his very presentation of the fourth way, and we see him appeal to it in such decisive moments as when he accuses Averroes of having opposed the doctrine of Aristotle as to creative causality.[26]

I have said enough to indicate the unity of the doctrine of the *ST* I as it moves from the fourth way to I, q. 44, aa. 1–2, and the whole of I, qq. 45–46.[27]

I would like to call attention, as well, to what this line of thought implies about the power of the divine causality. Here I have in mind the doctrine that the cause of being as being (i.e., being as a nature) is cause of the proper differences of being as being. These are the necessary and the contingent. I have elsewhere focused on the implications of this for the doctrine of human freedom of choice, and for the explanation of the presence of the bad (*malum*) in the product of the infinitely good God.[28]

26. Cf. Aquinas, *In octo libros Physicorum Aristotelis expositio*, ed. M. Maggiòlo, OP (Rome: Marietti, 1954), bk. 8, lect. 2, 974 (4). He shows why he thinks Averroes is straying from the thought of Aristotle, namely that elsewhere, in *Metaphysics* 2, Aristotle proves that that which is maximally true and maximally a being is the cause of being for all existing things (*id quod est maxime verum et maxime ens, est cause essendi omnibus existentibus*). Thus, Aquinas argues, it follows that the very *being in potency* (*hoc ipsum esse in potentia*) which primary matter has is derived from the first principle of being (*a primo essendi principio*), which is the maximal being (*maxime ens*). Thus, it is not necessary (and here Aquinas is putting it mildly) to presuppose something to its action, something not produced by it.

27. Did time permit, I would indicate a seeming evolution in Aquinas's texts as to the origin of this doctrine. In the Commentary on the *Sentences* and in the *De potentia* it is associated with Avicenna. In the *ST* I, q. 2, a. 3, and in the Commentary on the *Physics* 8.2, Aristotle's *Metaph.* 2.1 is referred to. In the *De substantiis separatis*, cap. 9 both Plato and Aristotle are present (and already in *ST* I, q. 44, a. 1); it is interesting to see that in his *Commentary on St. John's Gospel* "the Platonists" are given credit, a work presenting Aquinas's teaching in his second Parisian sojourn. (Cf. James Weisheipl, OP, *Friar Thomas D'Aquino* [Garden City, N.Y.: Doubleday, 1974], 247, 1269–72.)

28. Cf. my "Thomas Aquinas and Being as a Nature," *Acta Philosophica* 12 (2003): 123–35. Aquinas can speak of contingent necessity—if Socrates sits, he necessarily sits—since the

I would like to finish by considering briefly the difficulty of the doctrine. I have already mentioned Aquinas's critique of Averroes's rejection of creation. One sees it also in the judgment of Aquinas concerning the creative mode of production as missed by Avicenna in essential respects such as the freedom of God in creating, and Avicenna's attributing to beings lesser than the first the ability to create.[29]

One sees it especially also in the quarrels over whether created reality could have existed always. St. Albert the Great, when Aquinas's teacher, maintained that if by "creation" is meant the production of the matter as well as of the form, then such production necessarily involves a beginning of duration: that is, it could not always have existed. Aquinas immediately rejected this view in his own commentary on the *Sentences*. Teaching on the *Sentences* at about the same time as Aquinas, Bonaventure ridiculed the doctrine of Aquinas as to the possibility of an eternal creature produced as to its total substance, matter and form. (We have Aquinas's sarcastic rejoinder in the *De Aeternitate Mundi*.)[30]

It is symptomatic of the problem that in our own time Prof. Gilson titled his chapter on creation in his Gifford Lectures (*L'Esprit de la philosophie médiévale*, delivered in 1931–32) "Beings and *Their Contingency*." This is a conception that obliges one to envision the *coming into being* as well as the ceasing to be of a creature. The remedy for such error is precisely the doctrine that the creator is the cause of both the necessary and the contingent. Later (1939–40), in *God and Philosophy*,[31] Gilson ruled out appreciation on Aristotle's part of the universe as created, on the grounds that Aristotle saw the universe as always having existed. In other words, Gilson associated the doctrine of creation with the "coming into being" of the creature. Aquinas himself had underlined the importance of Aristotle's doctrine that a thing's having necessary being did not rule out its having been caused.[32] Such error on the part

divine causality embraces all things and events in the one divine willing to create and to redeem intelligent creatures. Evil is a privation, and so when intelligent creatures sin, they alone cause the evil by taking a created good and trying to remove it from the God created order of the universe; hence all evil is doing violence to the created goods.

29. Cf. especially the *De substantiis separatis* criticism of those who came after Plato and Aristotle. Avicenna is criticized in chap. 10. Cf. my paper "Thomas Aquinas, Creation, and Two Historians," *Laval théologique et philosophique* 50 (1994): 363–87, at nn. 62 and 63.

30. Cf. my paper "St. Thomas Aquinas as an Example of the Importance of the Hellenistic Legacy," *Doctor Communis* (2008): 88–118, where I speak of Albert, Bonaventure, and Aquinas on this issue.

31. Cf. E. Gilson, *God and Philosophy* (New Haven, Conn.: Yale University Press, 1941), 33; Gilson in his Introduction, p. xvii, indicates that the lectures were delivered at Indiana University in the academic year 1939–40.

32. See my previously mentioned *Doctor Communis* (2008) paper for a critique of Gilson in this regard.

of such zealous searchers is a sign of the difficulty of a demonstration of God as creator. In the above I have not mentioned other readers of Aquinas in our time, such as A. Kenny, P. Geach, N. Kretzmann, and so forth, none of whom were able to cope with Aquinas's doctrine of God as *Ipsum esse subsistens*.[33]

There is one last point I wish to raise. Why bother to work toward the demonstration of the doctrine, if it has already been revealed? There is the reason that one is supposed to work to oppose those who deny the truths that have been revealed.[34] However, there is another doctrine of St. Thomas that I wish to stress as part of our view of ourselves as students of theology. It is our love for the believed truths that should be considered. As Aquinas teaches:

When a man has a prompt will to believe, he *loves* the believed truth, and he thinks about it and looks at it from every angle, to see if some *reasons* for it can be found. And in that respect human reason does not exclude the merit of faith, but rather is a sign of greater merit, just as the passion following (reason) in the realm of moral virtues is a sign of a more prompt will, as was said earlier.[35]

The world of faith is a world of participation in eternal life,[36] a life of contemplation of the divine. And metaphysics, in the natural order, is an approach to this life. Thus, it is supreme among the natural intellectual virtues, which themselves are a beginning of beatitude.[37]

33. See my papers "St. Thomas, Norman Kretzmann, and Divine Freedom in Creating," *Nova et Vetera* 4.3 (2006): 495–514; also "Discussion: On Anthony Kenny's *Aquinas on Being*," *Nova et Vetera* 3.2 (2005): 335–400.

34. As Aquinas quotes Titus 1:9 in the sed contra of *ST* I, q. 1, a. 8 (which asks: "Is the Sacred Teaching argumentative?") Paul, speaking of the bishop, says, "He must hold firm to the sure word as taught, so that he may be able to give instruction in sound doctrine and also to confute those who contradict it" (RSV trans.).

35. Cf. *ST* II-II, q. 2, a. 10: "Cum enim homo habet promptam voluntatem ad credendum, diligit veritatem creditam, et super ea excogitat et amplectitur si quas rationes ad hoc invenire potest. Et quantum ad hoc ratio humana non excludit meritum fidei, sed est signum maioris meriti, sicut etiam passio consequens in virtutibus moralibus est signum promptioris voluntatis, ut supra dictum est."

36. If we ask Aquinas for a definition of the virtue of faith, he proposes the following: "a habit of mind by which *eternal life is begun in us*, bringing it about that the intellect assent to *things that are not apparent*." *ST* II-II, q. 4, a. 1: "fides est habitus mentis, qua inchoatur vita aeterna in nobis, faciens intellectum assentire non apparentibus." In the context Aquinas is defending the appropriateness of the teaching of Hebrews 11:1 as a definition of faith: that faith is "that which gives substance to our hopes, which convinces us of things we cannot see" (trans. Ronald Knox). It is not in the technical form of a definition, and so after explaining its perfection, Aquinas adds what I have quoted, as the same thing presented in the form of a definition.

37. Cf. *ST* I-II, q. 66, a. 3, ad 1, and q. 66, a. 5.

CHAPTER FOUR

The Concept of Nature

Philosophical Reflections in Service of Theology

JOSEPH KOTERSKI, SJ

There are numerous ways in which philosophy can be of service to theological education. There is something invaluable, for instance, in the art of making distinctions, and among the many ways of acquiring such facility, this skill is especially promoted by training in logic, philosophy of nature, and metaphysics. It is not just a matter of avoiding arbitrary distinctions without a basis in real differences but of devising distinctions that make their cuts between diverse natural kinds. Crucial to the theoretical justification for this activity is the notion that things have real natures that can be discovered by human inquiry. The notion of "nature" that is intended here is the internal principle of a thing's structure, development, and typical patterns of operation as a member of some real kind.

In a similar way, there is something methodologically crucial for theology as for any field in being able to articulate definitions that are clear and unambiguous and that can, if we are careful, allow us to grasp the forms that make things what they are. Likewise, it is indispensable for intellectual progress in theology as in any other discipline to be able to craft logically valid arguments and to spot problems that render an argument invalid or a conclusion doubtful. In theology, such definitions, arguments, and conclusions concern not only the truths about God that come from Revelation but also the truths about creatures of various kinds, and thus theological progress depends, in part, on having an adequate concept of nature in general as well as on having reliable knowledge of the nature of various kinds of being. And, of course, there is something of great benefit in being able to distinguish among the degrees of certitude with which a given claim ought to be credited. This is particularly important for a discipline like theology, which needs to work at determining the kind of assent required for various types of theological proposition. In all these cases, it is not that philosophical instruments like the tools of logic and epistemology can by themselves decide theological questions. But these tools can be incredibly helpful in countless ways—if for nothing else, at least to sharpen our grasp of the paradoxes that faith seeking understanding cannot avoid pondering.

Thus, besides the contributions that come from the realm of logic and epistemology, there are various substantive notions that a realist metaphysics and natural philosophy proffer for the use of theology. The concept of nature is of special importance here. Although scorned nowadays by some as a notion that is outmoded and needing to be replaced by a probabilistic perspective like that used in some of the empirical sciences,[1] the concept of nature, in my view, remains a valid tool of philosophical analysis and one that is indispensable to a sound theological education. It has perennial importance for probing such mysteries as the hypostatic union of two natures in one person that results from the Incarnation of the Word, the role of grace in healing and perfecting human nature, the relationship of the natural moral law to divine law and eternal law, the interplay of the supernatural and natural virtues that helps human beings to meet the obligations of their condition, and even the inspiration that the Church has received over time about the need for such material mediations as art, symbols, and sacraments, in light of the psycho-physical structure of human nature. Hence, the kinds of assistance that we, because of that nature, need to receive for our sanctification and salvation. The present essay will attempt to exemplify this general point by reflecting on the role of the concept of nature in just one area of inquiry, the human person.

---

1. There is a vast literature on this topic, but see, e.g., Bernard J. F. Lonergan, *Insight: A Study of Human Understanding*, in *Collected Works*, vol. 3., ed. Frederick E. Crowe and Robert M. Doran (Toronto: University of Toronto, 1992); Richard M. Rorty, *Philosophy and the Mirror of Nature* (Princeton, N.J.: Princeton University Press, 1979).

Philosophical Anthropology

Catholic views on personhood and human nature take shape on the basis of insights from both Revelation and reason.[2] Revelation, of course, refers not only to the written record of what God has revealed that is to be found in the sacred scriptures that constitute the Bible, but also to the sacred tradition of God's self-disclosure, a tradition that the Church has faithfully handed down, beginning with creation and culminating in the person of Jesus Christ and the ongoing mission of the Holy Spirit. To speak here of reason is to refer especially to the record of philosophical reflection that the Church has long embraced, but also to the breadth of lessons about human nature discovered and communicated in art and poetry, in history and the social sciences, and in countless other disciplines. For such a vast subject, it will be necessary to choose a small number of points for greater elaboration, while sketching out the rest of the subject in only a very general way. For this reason, I will try to lay out what I take to be the general lines of Christian anthropology as that subject tends to be understood within Catholic theology, while pointing especially to the use of philosophical insights about human nature in this first section. In the second section I will turn toward more specifically theological perspectives on human nature, by adverting to its use in the doctrine of recapitulation by, in, and through Christ.

The human being is a creature of God, with a nature that is distinct in kind.[3] It is, however, not simply that humanity is one species among others, but that each human being as a person has an immaterial and spiritual dimension that is of a wholly different sort than that found in any of the other types of material beings. While it is true that every single being of every species is a unique individual, that sort of uniqueness is almost trivial in comparison to the brand of uniqueness that belongs to each member of the set of human beings, precisely because the uniqueness arises from the personal character of human nature.[4] Paradoxically, what the members of this set have in common—a rational nature that makes each one a person— is the very thing that makes each one irreducibly unique in its dignity and intrinsic importance. And yet, like everything else in the entire universe, human beings owe their existence and their common nature not to them-

2. For an account of this topic by the Magisterium, see the encyclical letter of St. John Paul II, *Fides et Ratio* (September 15, 1998).

3. On the claim that human nature is different in kind and not just in degree, see especially Mortimer J. Adler, *The Difference of Man and the Difference It Makes* (Bronx, N.Y.: Fordham University Press, 1993 [1967]).

4. See John F. Crosby, *The Selfhood of the Human Person* (Washington, D.C.: The Catholic University of America Press, 1996).

selves or even just to their forebears but to the divine plan for creation, a plan recognized to have been operating for millions of years before human beings came upon the scene and to have important consequences for the bodily and psychic condition of human nature. By virtue of its commitment to both reason and Revelation as reliable sources of knowledge, Catholicism can readily acknowledge the work of contemporary science in having traced the emergence of the cosmos back at least as far as the "Big Bang" and at the same time can hold that the entire universe is God's creation.[5] The Catholic understanding here is not some deist picture of a God who designed the universe and then stepped back to watch it all unfold mechanically, but rather the picture of a creator who actively sustains the universe at every moment of its being, who not only designed the physical and moral laws of nature but who is present to every part of the universe at once and who is exercising providential care for what he loves.

The human being is thus not only a creature of God and thus an effect owing to its cause, but that particularly important kind of creature that was made in God's image and likeness. For this reason, every human being has the type of dignity that sets each member of humanity apart from the rest of creatures, and all human beings risk dishonoring that dignity if they fail to live up to the demands of this nature.[6] Among the creatures that are animals, human beings are distinct from the rest by their possession of the powers of intellect and will. These are the power of understanding (conceived broadly so as to include the many ways in which thinking and knowing take place) and the power to make free choices and to love. The rational powers of human nature must be conceived broadly to include the various operations of deliberation, affection, consent, choice, and so on. It is by virtue of these powers that human beings possess various (and changing) degrees of freedom in the course of their lives, depending in important ways on diverse factors that can constrain their freedom, to the point of diminishing or even eliminating their responsibility in some cases. There is much more to say about the topic of image and likeness—particularly about the shattering of the image and likeness at the time of the Fall (original sin) and about its restoration in Christ—and I will return to this material in the section on recapitulation in Christ. But for the purposes of this general

5. See Robert J. Spitzer, SJ, *New Proofs for the Existence of God: Contributions of Contemporary Physics and Philosophy* (Grand Rapids, Mich.: Wm. B. Eerdmans, 2010).

6. For an excellent account of the distinction between the natural dignity of every human person and the moral dignity in accordance with which human beings must conduct their lives, see J. Brian Benestad, *Church, State, and Society: An Introduction to Catholic Social Doctrine* (Washington, D.C.: The Catholic University of America Press, 2011), esp. chap. 1: "The Dignity of the Human Person, Human Rights, and Natural Law."

sketch, it is also important to offer some broad observations on such questions as human development in time, the relation of intellect and will to the emotions and the flesh, and the question of providing appropriate sorts of definitions and demarcation-criteria. In the course of commenting on questions like this, it will be possible to comment on many of the important issues that invariably need to be part of any systematic treatment of the Catholic understanding of personhood, and by this review one can more readily see the indispensability of making reference to the concept of nature if one is to give a proper account.

While there have been Catholic theorists in the course of history who were inclined to treat the subject of human personhood by using some kind of philosophical dualism in the general tradition of Plato and who have held that the person is really the soul that needs to use a body in this life, the mainstream position is that the human person is truly a unity of body and soul and that the condition, after bodily death, of the separately existing soul as the bearer of personality is a temporary situation that will eventually be rectified, for God has promised the eventual resurrection of the body. Most Christian theologians in the first millennium were, in effect, Christian Platonists, but to characterize them in this way is not yet to say enough. The question in any given case is whether the thinker was a committed Platonist who also wanted to be Christian, or (more commonly) a Christian who saw in Platonism a philosophy helpful to articulating the faith.[7] It also seems clear that Aquinas and many others who embraced Aristotelianism after the recovery of Aristotelian texts in the thirteenth century, saw themselves primarily as Christians but that the new Aristotelian categories, especially in his philosophy of nature, could be even more useful for articulating and defending tenets of the faith than was the traditional Platonism. There were, of course, some who seem to have seen themselves primarily as Aristotelians, such as Siger of Brabant and others who make up the school known now as the Radical Aristotelians, whatever the compromises this position required with Christian doctrine.[8] Without trying here to settle all the disputes about the unicity of substantial forms and thus the unity of the human person, whether among medieval scholastics or among contemporary bioethicists,[9]

7. See, e.g., the discussion of Augustine's Christian Platonism in Peter Burnell, *Augustinian Person* (Washington, D.C.: The Catholic University of America Press, 2005).

8. See Ralph McInerny, *Aquinas against the Averroists: On There Being Only One Intellect* (West Lafayette, Ind.: Purdue University Press, 1993).

9. For an interesting (but, in my opinion, flawed) article at the intersection of debates in medieval scholasticism and contemporary bioethics, see Allan Wolter, "Mediate Animation: A Reinterpretation of Some Texts," *Proceedings of the American Catholic Philosophical Association* 72 (1998): 25–39.

it is relatively easy to see why the Thomistic version of Aristotelian hylomorphism has had so many adherents. Aristotle's vision of individual beings as substances, each one of which is a unified composite of matter and form, and his definition of human nature in terms of "rational animality" were easily taken up by Aquinas and accepted by many others after him as reliable philosophical insights into human nature that could be put into the service of the faith.[10]

As noted above, it is also of great philosophical significance that human life takes place in time. By virtue of having a bodily life that arises at a certain moment in time from the gametes provided by one's parents and that needs to develop over the course of long years, human beings likewise tend to experience both the growth and the retardation of their spiritual powers of intellect and will over the course of time in a manner that is correlated with the status of their biological life. If one were a Platonist, one might try to think of these powers as always fully developed in the soul but invariably hindered in their operations by the body that the soul is inhabiting. Notwithstanding those Christian Platonists and later the Cartesians who took an approach of this sort,[11] Catholic theology has generally found more helpful a philosophy that takes its start from the Aristotelian position, once that position has been suitably modified so as to make the immortality of the soul more intelligible. In that general approach, the powers of the mind are regarded as truly spiritual (that is, immaterial) powers of the soul, but the soul that is the seat of those powers serves during this life as the substantial form that animates the material body. By virtue of their genuine dependence on various bodily organs, these spiritual powers themselves unfold and grow in the course of time, and their operations can be hampered or curtailed over the course of time by injury, disease, and senility. The chief modification in the basic Aristotelian position here is the development of an understanding of the nature of the soul that permits one to hold for its subsistent existence after death and before the resurrection, and this view thus makes an argument for immortality that is not found in any text of Aristotle that is still extant today. For Aquinas,[12] the rational soul of a human

10. For a rigorous and insightful use of the basic Aristotelian-Thomistic paradigm to discuss contemporary questions of recent bioethical questions by virtue of its references to current understandings of embryology, see Dianne N. Irving, "Scientific and Philosophical Expertise: An Evaluation of the Arguments on 'Personhood,'" *Linacre Quarterly* 60, no. 1 (Feb. 1993): 18–46, http://www.uffl.org/irving/irvsci.htm.

11. See the discussion of the Cartesian position in Patrick Lee and Robert P. George, *Body-Self Dualism in Contemporary Ethics and Politics* (New York: Cambridge University Press, 2008).

12. I do not at all mean to suggest that all Catholic thinkers are Thomists, but simply that

being is capable of separate existence after death and serves as the bearer of personal subjectivity and selfhood, even though the separated soul in this state is incomplete by reason of a lack of a body to animate.[13] For Catholics, the resurrection of Christ and the promise of the resurrection of the dead, which are essential parts of the Christian faith, speak to this question by assuring us of eventual re-embodiment in glorified bodies as part of the new heavens and new earth.

The necessity of a prolonged process of development for our human powers and the inescapability of their being subject to the vicissitudes of injury, disease, senility, and death show the intrinsic importance of discussing this matter in terms of time, maturation, and human nature. The genetic endowments of individuals, the prenatal environment of our gestation, the families that nurture us, the education that we receive, and all the other factors of nature and nurture that one might care to mention—all of these contribute to the process by which the natural powers of any individual person's intellect and will develop. And yet, for all of the material and social factors that condition their emergence and experience, these powers remain spiritual powers, immaterial in their very nature, and irreducible to any physicalist explanation, notwithstanding the dependence of these spiritual powers on various material factors for their operation. This position is the heart of hylomorphic philosophy, and it is the basis for the Thomistic development of that position.

Without trying to provide here the full argument for the immaterial or spiritual character of intellect and will, it may be helpful to our consideration of the importance of the concept of nature to sketch the basic position briefly. Even though only individual beings and not their kinds (that is, species) have independent existence within the world of our earthly experience, the intellect by virtue of its nature grasps things by recognizing their kinds (that is, by noting the differences that are common to individuals of any one group but that differentiate the members of this smaller group from the rest of the individuals in some larger group). In short, the intellect

Thomism has long been recognized as a particularly helpful theological and philosophical approach for articulating and defending any number of important positions within the Catholic faith. There is a long history to papal recommendations of Thomism, and in my judgment it is linked in an interesting way to the modern papal articulation of Catholic social teaching, as discussed later in this paper. Its most recent expression can be found in the encyclical *Fides et Ratio* (Faith and Reason).

13. The commonly held view among Thomists is that human personhood ceases at death, requiring the resurrection of the body to be regained. A few hold that human personhood perdures after death. I hold that the soul is a "bearer" of personhood. See Patrick Toner, "Personhood and Death in St. Thomas Aquinas," *History of Philosophy Quarterly* 26, no. 2 (April 2009): 121ff.

grasps things by noticing what things are and what they are like. Utterly dependent on a physical brain, an animal organ, the intellect nevertheless does things that are not just physical actions. Its abilities include the capacity to grasp kinds, to make connections and assertions, to make distinctions and negations, and all the other activities of this sort, whether one is thinking about immaterial beings like God or angels, whether thinking about abstractions like numbers or theories, or whether thinking about things that are entirely material, like pipes and plumbing. Even when we are thinking about material things and have recourse to thoroughly material images as providing crucial data for our abstractive process, we are nonetheless making use of immaterial concepts and judgments and patterns of reasoning that transcend the material. We know by grasping "kinds" even though the "kinds" do not as such have material existence, but only the individuals that together make up the kind.[14] It is possible, for instance, to know timelessly true propositions (in mathematics, for instance) even though our statements and our thinking up of those statements will always take place in time. Even though human persons necessarily exist in time, our mental powers let us transcend time just as our power of will lets us rise above the patterns of material determination to self-determination.

Our will's power of free choice is also something that transcends materiality, for we can choose against even the strongest desire that rises up in us, as anyone knows who has ever tried to lose weight, quit smoking, deal with sexual arousal, or conquer fear. If we were entirely material beings, then all of the instances of apparently free choice would turn out to be operations of our bodies that were fully determined by various material causes acting in or upon them; these actions would only appear to be free because we did not know in advance what these various causal lines would produce. It is not even clear what "to know" would mean in this case if it did not entail that the knower had at least a relative independence of those causes and thus the possibility of acting for or against those causal lines. But even if we were to overlook that point for the sake of argument, the need for assuming the reality of freedom in the sense of self-determination is indispensable in our account of our selves and the responsibility that we bear for our actions. Life in society would be impossible without this assumption.

The point here is not that we are always perfectly free, but that free

14. At issue here, of course, is the famous problem of universals. My point in bringing it up here is not to insist on any one particular solution to the philosophical problem of universals, but merely to suggest that whatever solution one advances to this problem requires that the knower be recognized to be using an immaterial or spiritual power and thus to have an immaterial or spiritual dimension.

choice is something quite real in us, something that we can gain or lose, and something that can be measured by degree—we can be more or less free in various respects. In the language of Catholic theology, there comes a time when we reach the age of reason, and what that claim means is that we can arrive at the point when we can be quite conscious and aware of what we are doing. We are then considered responsible for what we choose to do or not do. But developing virtuous habits, avoiding (or, more likely, trying to eradicate) bad ones, and growing in will-power are lifelong tasks, never complete and always challenging; all this speaks to the reality of freedom in our choices. But freedom of choice cannot mean merely the absence of a cause—if it did our freedom would only amount to randomness or be as fickle as the breeze. Freedom in the sense required here has to mean something in relation to the specific sort of nature that human beings have, namely, to the capacity for self-determination understood in terms of the power of the self to control one's own actions and even (at least to some extent) to control the direction of one's thinking. Metaphysically, this entails the position that there is some real but immaterial power of the soul—the will and its ability to make free choices. In a sense, this pair of powers (intellect and will) is at the deep core of the person, but it is crucial always to bear in mind that the authentic Catholic sense of these powers insists that the person is a whole, a unity of body and soul, and that our bodily actions are the expression of the person as a whole.

For an adequate theological anthropology, there is also need to remain attentive to the fleshly realities of human existence—to such facts as our embodiment, the life of feeling and emotions, and the relations of family and society as important constituents in our account of personhood and human nature. In saying, for instance, that it is by virtue of having an intellect and a will that we bear a special resemblance to God, we need to add that intellect and will must always be thought about in relation to our embodiment. Our way of sensing with our eyes, for example, or hearing with our ears is like—but also decisively unlike—the way in which any other seeing creature sees or the way any other hearing creature hears. Because the power of understanding permeates the operation of our sense organs, we see in a way that is correlated with our understanding—for us it is a matter not just of reacting to stimuli but of constantly asking ourselves what we are seeing.[15] Likewise, our way of feeling fear or boldness, hunger or thirst, pleasure or pain is, in some respects like that of any other sentient creature,

---

15. There is an excellent account of this topic in David Braine, *The Human Person: Animal and Spirit* (Notre Dame, Ind.: University of Notre Dame Press, 1992).

but it is also unlike the experience of any other such creature, because of the way that intellect and will pervade all these other operations of our nature as well.

Since any effect shows forth something of its cause, all creatures may claim some likeness to God, but our possession of these powers makes for a unique kind of resemblance to God, and with the power of deliberate choice and self-determination come all the responsibilities for their use. I think that this is true and crucially important simply for the proper description of our experience of emotion, feeling, appetite, and countless other features of conscious and embodied existence, let alone for the elaboration of a suitable notion of morality, that is, the prescriptive account of what we minimally may or may not do, and more broadly, what we should or should not do in order to be virtuous, to live in a way that is truly praiseworthy and more likely to bring happiness. As a short example for this point, we might consider the way in which Catholic moralists have regularly understood moral virtues as dispositions by which a person chooses the mean between the extremes of excess and deficiency in regard to action and feeling, in accord with right reason.[16] In this understanding, a virtue such as courage or fortitude involves our becoming accustomed not only to choose to act appropriately but also to acquire a disposition to feel the degree of boldness or fear that is proportionate to the danger of the situation, to the good to be accomplished, and to the resources at our disposal. In this respect the theological anthropology of Catholicism tends to differ from, say, the views of moralists in the Kantian tradition, who tend to exclude natural inclination from their accounts of virtue, on the reasoning that such inclination runs in the direction of heteronomy and derogates from reason's autonomy. This is a position that tends to put greater emphasis on practical reason than on nature in its account of the human condition.

To speak more generally, in my view any particular theory of morality tends to be correlated rather directly with that theory's vision of the human person; further, one's account of human personhood tends to be correlated in turn with one's stance in metaphysics. A strictly materialist metaphysics, for instance, entails that the human person must be regarded as entirely material and without any spiritual dimension, and the corresponding theory of ethics will need to take this into account by holding for some form

---

16. Catholic moralists have regularly distinguished the *supernatural virtues* of faith, hope, and charity (sometimes called the *theological virtues*), which can come about only by the gift of divine grace, from the various *moral virtues* (such as justice, temperance, or fortitude) that can arise by virtue of our own efforts (and are then called the *natural virtues*) or can be given to us by divine grace (and are then called *infused virtues*).

of utilitarian calculation of values in terms of pleasure and pain (however sophisticated one's description of these matters), with the faculty of human reason described in instrumental terms. Metaphysical dualism in any form will likewise have implications for one's view of the person and for what will make sense in ethics. The hylomorphic metaphysics being articulating here also has various direct correlations with the picture of the human person as well as for the view of ethics. It is not my position that Catholicism conforms its view of the person to philosophical hylomorphism, but rather that Catholic theology's respect for the truths about the human person that God has chosen to reveal, as well as its experience of actual human beings, provides a number of reasons why Catholic theorists have tended to prefer a hylomorphic philosophy.

Let me conclude this first portion of the essay with some remarks about the definition of the term "person" and the proper demarcation of the set of human persons. In order to determine the type of definition that one ought to seek, it is crucial to identify the purposes for which that definition is being offered. A definition that is designed, for instance, to differentiate one species from another will do well to focus on features that are distinctive of one group and that are totally lacking in another. Such a definition might be called a functional definition, by reason of the emphasis that it places on the identification of certain functions as a way to differentiate one species from another. But it is important to note that this approach does not imply that the distinctive features are wholly developed or even minimally present and operative in every member of the set (e.g., in the very young, the very old, or those impaired by disease, injury, or accident). This approach takes its bearing by considering mature healthy individuals of the species in question for the purpose of making a comparison with other species. Precisely because it takes as its focus the mature healthy member of the species, this definition abstracts to some degree from the process of development and is not well suited to provide easy-to-use membership criteria. Other approaches to definition can do a better job of demarcating a given species in ways that will be helpful to indicate which beings are and which beings are not members of the species by pointing to things like parentage or genetic make-up. Those approaches do not put so much emphasis on the typical traits of mature individuals within the species as on specific tests designed to help make judgment calls at the borders.

The problem of definition is, in a way, like the problem of mapmaking. Should we use a globe or a flat map? Should we distort the size of certain areas of the earth (near the poles, for instance) for the sake of allowing the map user to figure out more easily the proper direction for travel, or should we make figuring out direction more difficult but determining area much easier? So long as one knows the type of distortion that is being introduced in a given map for the sake of representing some other real feature of the world, we can use the map well, provided that the map does conform to the reality that we are trying to capture in this mode of representation.

When choosing a strategy for giving definitions and demarcation-lines we need to bear a similar point in mind. For the comparison of one species of animal to another and the articulation of what is distinctive about human beings, Aristotle's famous definition of human nature as "rational animality" does fine work. Its utility diminishes, however, if it were used as a demarcation-tool for trying to determine whether the unborn, the mentally retarded, the emotionally disturbed, the senile afflicted with dementia, or those damaged by serious disease, accident, or injury are still human. For the work of demarcating the group that is the human species and determining the question of an individual's membership in that group, what one needs is the identification of non-arbitrary criteria of group membership. One needs to look to things like parentage and the chromosome patterns of our genetic make-up.

One can see the relevance of this sort of distinction to some of the highly controversial questions of the present day. The abhorrence of Catholic theology for induced abortion, for infanticide, for euthanasia, for physician-assisted suicide, and so on comes from a sense that all human beings are by their nature persons, regardless of the stage of their development or the state of their ability to perform the operations typical of the species. The reason why we must include them in the set of human persons and thus in the set of those with an inviolable dignity is that they meet the group-membership criterion and thus they are human being "made in the image and likeness of God."

Likewise, Catholic social teaching on questions of the rights and duties of parents to educate their own children, the importance of a family wage, the duty of a society to respect human rights and to promote human development as well as to work for a system of ordered liberty and economic prosperity—all this flows from the importance of persons and the need to understand beings with a human nature as morally requiring appropriate conditions for even their biological conception within a family, for their education and maturation and growth within appropriate circumstances, for the use of their abilities and talents within a setting that makes it possible for them to profit from their labors and to be held responsible for their decisions.

Some of the most interesting and most disputed questions of our time tend to be couched in terms of our definitions and demarcation points.

Many questions about animal rights, for instance, involve the use of functional definitions and inappropriate attempts to compare members of various animal species at the highest levels of their potentiality with very young or even disabled members of the human species. Questions about euthanasia, to take another case, are often framed in terms of the inability of some individuals to function at certain levels, but this approach also tends to misuse a definition designed for distinguishing one species as a whole from another, as if that definition also warranted dismissing individuals from the rights of species-membership when they slip below a certain threshold of functionality. It is a use that the definition is not designed to handle.

It goes without saying that one need not be a Catholic in order to answer the question of animal rights or to know what to think about euthanasia. But it is important to note that the position of sound Catholic theology on personhood and dignity necessarily has recourse to the concept of human nature, precisely in order to bring out the full scope of the class that needs to be protected. There may be some strong rhetorical advantage gained in the contemporary debates by focusing on personhood, especially because of the widespread popularity of the Kantian paradigm and the personalist character of the categorical imperative. But if one were to try to delimit the class of those who are to be regarded as protected by the mantle of human dignity to those whose distinctively personal functions are presently active or capable of operation, one would risk missing those whose functions are not yet developed or are impaired (perhaps beyond the present possibilities of repair and recovery). In this way, even the best personalist arguments require a throughgoing account of human nature,[17] and thus it is no surprise that sound Catholic theology has regularly made use of certain types of philosophical models in preference to others in order to understand and present its positions on disputed as well as on merely descriptive questions. Catholicism has used such philosophical models because of their philosophical realism and their epistemic reliability. These insights and these models have become deeply engrained in Catholic culture, and so Catholicism as a social institution within American society needs to communicate not only the fact of its moral positions (e.g., opposition to abortion and euthanasia, support for immigrant groups, the concept of a family-wage within economic policy) but also some of the philosophical argumentation that supports these positions (e.g., the continuity argument that tries to make the case for opposition to abortion by showing the continuity in being of

17. I argue for this position at greater length in my essay "The Status of Personalism in Catholic Moral Thinking Today," *The Dunwoodie Review* 32 (2009): 241–59.

the child after birth with the unborn child all the way back to the moment of conception, or the use of the principles of distributive justice and of solidarity in the effort to resolve various problems about tax structures).

To summarize, the position on personhood and human nature, in a well-developed theological anthropology, invariably includes an emphasis on the inherent dignity of each human person by virtue of that person's having a human nature. The claims made for this inviolable dignity invariably stem from the recognition that all human beings, regardless of their state of dependency, are made in the image of God and thus are the bearers of certain moral rights. The philosophical accounts used to articulate the concept of human nature and to defend human dignity may be various, but there is a clear reason for the decided preference of many theorists for some form of hylomorphism of a generally Aristotelian sort, primarily because of the ways in which this approach seems favorable to a deep appreciation of human embodiment and of bodily and psychological development while at the same time allowing for an appreciation of the spiritual and immaterial aspects of the person associated with intellect and will. Finally, in Catholic views on personhood and human nature there tends to be great respect for stressing the intrinsically social character of human life. This dimension includes both the familial character of human origins and development and the variety of voluntary associations into which individuals will find it helpful to enter, ranging from marriage and friendship through politics and economics. For an appreciation of some other aspects of the role played by the concept of nature in Catholic theology, let us turn briefly to the doctrine of recapitulation in Christ as an example.

Following Christ as Contributing to the Recapitulation in Him

The human being is made in the image and likeness of God. Sometimes one hears it said that "we are all children of God." While the sentiment that this phrase expresses is clear enough, this is not an accurate reflection of Catholic understanding on this point. Strictly speaking, only the eternal Word is by his nature the Son of God—in the words of the Nicene Creed, "begotten, not made." We can become the children of God by adoption, and this adoption is supernaturally effected by Christian baptism. With this act we are made the brothers and sisters of Jesus, with all the duties as well as the benefits of entering into the family of God. To say this is still to affirm philosophically that all human beings are members of the human species, and by this fact endowed with whatever natural rights are inherent in human nature, such as the right to life, and obligated by whatever duties fall to us by the natural law and by our state, such as the universal negative duty never to murder or the positive duties that may arise from our circumstances, such as to care for our dependents. But to say this is also to make the stronger claim that not all human beings are the children of God in the strict sense. What Catholics believe that baptism does is to begin the restoration of God's image and likeness in us by the gift of sanctifying grace—God's own life—within us. This gift of grace makes us the adopted children of God and thus makes us members of the Church. It brings forgiveness of any actual sins committed up to that point, and it begins the process of regeneration (being born "again"—"born from above"—in the language of the story about Jesus's conversation with Nicodemus in the Gospel of John) that needs to continue all our lives, both by our participation in the sacraments and by the imitation of Christ in all our choices and actions.

A crucial dimension of the Catholic understanding of the human person is the doctrine of original sin, the impairment of our human nature, and the correlative doctrine of our need for sanctification in Christ. For present purposes, we may presume a familiarity with the scriptural origins of the doctrine of the Fall in Genesis, and we may pass over the history of the development of the doctrine by such theologians as Augustine (including the contested questions about how to understand the transmission of original sin from one generation to the next). Instead, for present purposes, I would like to present a sense of the way in which we might understand how original sin affects our human nature and how we believe divine grace to be at work to heal it. This treatment requires us to consider the following points: all human beings are made in the image of God (whom we understand to be a Trinity of Divine Persons in One God), but the Fall has badly damaged our resemblance to the triune God by bringing about certain defects and wounds in us; our sanctification must include the repair of these wounds.

While we cannot claim to understand all the mysteries of divine life, reflection on the ways of God's self-disclosure has made clear that God is both One and Three. In the language of the ecumenical councils of the Church, there are three Persons in the One God: the Father, the Son, and the Holy Spirit. Their very names are relational: the Father is the Father who has from all eternity begotten the Son; the Son is from all eternity the Son of the Father; the Spirit is the Love between them who from all eternity proceeds forth from the Father and the Son.[18] While they are always one and always act in unison, it is possible to identify a type of love that is specially charac-

18. Let me here acknowledge, without entering into further discussion, the important question of the *Filioque* that still divides Catholic theology from Orthodox theology.

teristic of each of the Persons of the Trinity. The love especially associated with the Father is the love of gift and generosity, for he gives all of himself (except the relation of Fatherhood) to the Son, and does so freely and without condition or reserve. The Son is particularly characterized by the love of receptivity and gratitude, for with the same freedom he receives what the Father bestows without condition or reserve, from all eternity. The love of the Holy Spirit is often designated in terms of joy and glory—that is, delight at the communion of perfect giving and the perfect receiving.[19]

As the one type of being that is made in God's own image and likeness, human beings also have by their very nature a triadic structure, and concomitantly, a tri-partite pattern of how they ought to love. But human nature as we know it is fallen. It is not some pure nature that is still unaffected by the Fall.[20] One traditional way of describing the effects of the Fall has been to say that our minds are darkened, our wills weakened, and our desires disordered. The advantages of this way of speaking are considerable. But for present purposes let me try to put the matter in terms of the damage to the types of love that ought to characterize human beings considered precisely as made in the image and likeness of the Trinity and the characteristic loves of each member of the Trinity.

Where there ought to be a love of generosity within us that is like that of the Father, human beings in their fallen state tend by nature to love only what strikes them as good and thus what seems to them as love-worthy. At any given time, or over the course of time, there can often be many apparent goods before us, and hence we need to choose among them. As noted earlier in this essay, our freedom in choice can be increased by growing in the power to discern true and genuine goods from among the apparent goods. As such, the tendency within our nature is to seek and pursue what appears to us as good, and especially those things that pass our tests for being genuinely good. But, curiously, our inclination to love what strikes us as good and thus in some way love-worthy is not the fullness of generosity to which charity would direct us, for we do not tend to give our love to what does not strike us as love-worthy. Growth in virtue can help us to become gener-

19. For the deeper understanding of these points, and detailed documentation, see Paul M. Quay, SJ, *The Mystery Hidden for Ages in God* (New York: Peter Lang, 1995), esp. chap. 3.

20. Here too there is an enormous literature on the vexing problem of how to think about "pure nature." Was there ever actually such a state (as Bonaventure held), or is this idea to be considered more in the fashion of a helpful hypothesis (as Aquinas held), or is it an unhelpful notion that we should no longer employ (as various figures within twentieth-century neo-scholasticism have maintained). I will not enter into this problem here, but see Steven A. Long, *Natura Pura: On the Recovery of Nature in the Doctrine of Grace* (Bronx, N.Y.: Fordham University Press, 2010).

ous more often and more deeply, but the development of such a trait takes time and training. Secular understandings of generosity and even altruism in this regard are historically dependent on Christian understandings of the virtue of charity—that is, learning how to love as God loves, for God loves not just what is already love-worthy but with an abundance of generosity that can be readily seen in the two greatest acts of divine charity: (1) creation—in which God brought the universe into being from nothing, and (2) redemption—in which God the Father sent his Son to redeem a world of sinners. In neither case is it a matter of God being attracted to what already seems good, but rather a matter of rendering good what was not good, either because it did not even exist or because it was sinful and disordered.

Second, while there ought to be a likeness between our own form of receptivity and the receptivity of the Son, the Fall has also damaged this resemblance. There seems to be a kind of psychic inversion that takes place in us that is correlative to the defect in our love of generosity. If spontaneously and by nature we tend to give our love only to what strikes us as love-worthy, we fear that we will not receive love unless we appear love-worthy. So, instead of trusting with confidence that we will be loved and thereby receiving what is given freely and without condition, there is a tendency to manipulate our situations and to make ourselves appear more love-worthy, so that we will be the object of the love of others. This defect in us is quite likely that aspect of original sin that is especially responsible for much actual sin in our lives.

Thirdly, there ought to be within us a love of joy and delight in being witnesses to giving and receiving as our analog to the love of glory that is the characteristic love of the Holy Spirit. But, given the defects already noticed in us as the result of the Fall, we find ourselves afflicted by damage in this third aspect of our likeness to God as well, namely, that we easily become envious and jealous of love given and love received when we are not ourselves the subject or object of this love.[21] The point is not that any of these defects are yet actual sins, for "actual sin" according to the Catholic understanding of this matter requires that there be deliberate choice of something that is wrong. One would have to know right from wrong, one would have to choose to do what one knew to be wrong, and the relative gravity of the sin would also depend on how serious the nature of the wrong was. Rather, the point here is to take note of the difference between any actual sins that anyone may commit and the fallen condition in which we find ourselves, that is, the fact of various defects in our inclinations with respect to love.

21. See Quay, *Mystery Hidden*, esp. chap. 6.

This account of the matter, to be sure, is only a brief outline of what needs much amplification. But perhaps by sketching out even this much it will be possible for us to see the Catholic understanding of our human need for Christ, for our redemption, for our sanctification, and for the repair of our wounded human nature. Catholic understanding has rightly focused on the person of Christ as the Incarnate Word in terms of the mission received by the Son as the Second Person of the Trinity from the Father to take on a complete human nature and to sacrifice himself for us. Within this mystery the Church has rightly emphasized both redemption and sanctification. Redemption, strictly speaking, refers to the act by which God himself generously paid the debt that we human beings have incurred by sin and thus the act by which God has saved us. Sanctification, by contrast, refers to the process by which the shattered image and likeness of God in us is restored and by which we are healed, that is, by which we are made to be like God again, made holy, or (to use the terminology that I have been emphasizing here), made to love once again according to the pattern of loves that God intends that we freely choose for our actions and our loves.

The process of sanctification in the Catholic understanding has two main components: the life of the sacraments and the life of morality. For Catholics, baptism is the sacrament by which sanctifying grace and thus the very life of God return to us. The other sacraments that we come to receive in the course of our lives continue the work of God in us. The sacrament of Reconciliation is a way to receive forgiveness for our sins and to be restored to friendship with God. The sacrament of the Eucharist gives us a way to receive the body and blood of Christ within us and thus to be nourished for our daily lives with his divine life. The sacrament of Confirmation seals us with the gifts of the Holy Spirit that first came to us in Baptism and strengthens the presence of those gifts within us for the duration of our lives. The sacrament of the Anointing of the Sick provides a medicine for body and for soul, not just in immediate preparation for death but at various times of sickness. The sacraments of Matrimony and Holy Orders provide divine graces needed for particular forms of life, that is, for marriage and for priestly life. Without God's grace, we cannot be healed. Without these sacraments, we would be left on our own, to do as best we can, perhaps with the aid of our human culture, and we would simply be at the mercy of God with respect to our salvation.[22] The Church understands the sacraments that Christ gave to the

22. Here too there are various important questions about why Christians often still live so badly despite these gifts, as well as about the possibility of salvation outside the Church and the sacraments. By this note I mean to acknowledge the importance of these questions, without trying to resolve them here. See *Catechism of the Catholic Church*, §846–48.

Church as the great gift of God by which his image and likeness are restored and strengthened within us. All of this theological discussion necessarily takes place in terms of our human nature as well as our personal state and condition.

The other important aspect in the process of sanctification concerns the moral life, that is, our response to God's initiative to restore us to himself by the proper use of our powers of understanding and free choice. We discussed some of this material in the first section of this essay when we were concentrating on such topics as the natural moral law and the other philosophical resources that are important for the Catholic understanding of the human person. Precisely by virtue of its employment of the category of human nature and its use of the natural moral law, many aspects of the Catholic understanding of the moral life are accessible to every human person and every culture. The Church's understanding of the possibilities of achieving various degrees of understanding about the moral life, even by the use of reason apart from Revelation or faith, goes hand-in-hand with the philosophical approach to the concept of nature discussed in the first part of this essay. When thinkers in the Thomistic tradition, for instance, say that grace builds on nature, they are affirming not only our need for grace to do something that we cannot do by nature, but also a certain basic goodness that remains in nature even after the Fall. The Thomistic view of nature, for instance, does not think of us as utterly helpless or without recourse, but as having a nature that is genuinely wounded and suffering from some defects and can be restored by grace.

It is absolutely vital to emphasize here the need for imitating the life of Christ, that is, for modeling not just individual actions but our whole lives on the pattern of Christ's life, especially as his life involves the taking on of our nature and the healing of that nature. We understand the Son of God to have become incarnate in Christ, that is, to have taken upon himself the fullness of our nature, from the moment of his conception in the womb of Mary by the power of the Holy Spirit. In his human life he shows us what our human lives and loves should be. Notwithstanding other relevant aspects of this mystery that might profitably be considered, let me concentrate for our present purposes on just one: the stages of his life and the order of his loves present to us a pattern for our own. The Christian needs to learn to recapitulate the life of Christ in our own lives by growing through the stages of human life according to the model that he presents to us, for in his own life he has perfected what was imperfect, he has completed what was incomplete, and he has sanctified what was sinful.[23]

23. For a fine account of this point, see Quay, *Mystery Hidden*, esp. chaps. 17–19.

A more complete account of this process and its challenges is beyond the scope of this essay but would involve meditation on the life of Christ as recounted in the Gospel, both to grasp how the life of Christ recapitulates the life of Israel that is narrated throughout the whole of the Old Testament and how we need to recapitulate the life of Christ in our lives and families and cultures. What this example has tried to show is the relevance of the concept of nature for a particularly important and fruitful area of advanced work in theology, the doctrine of recapitulation in, by, and through Christ. In this area, as frequently elsewhere, the concept of nature is indispensable for a theology that recognizes the way in which grace builds on nature and perfects it.

CHAPTER FIVE

On Natural Knowledge of God

Aquinas's Debt to Aristotle

STEVEN A. LONG

Here I will elaborate the Aristotelian foundations of the metaphysics and natural theology of St. Thomas Aquinas. In any consideration of the debt owed by Aquinas to Aristotle, the controverted question must necessarily arise as to what Aristotle himself accomplished. This has not infrequently been answered in the negative. That is, those who do not consider metaphysics to be a naturally knowable discipline with conclusions regarding God and the soul subject to demonstrative reason as such, apart from advertence to any revealed premise, will find it impossible to credit Aristotle as having so much as adverted to God rather than to a merely intraterrestrial principle. Indeed it is not uncommonly said that Aristotle did not affirm God as Creator, and that for Aristotle it is the universe, and not God, that is fundamental. *So the first objection to Aquinas's dependence on Aristotle with respect to the doctrine of God is the global denial that Aristotle so much as affirmed God rather than a merely intra-terrestrial principle.*

Beyond this objection, many are inclined to deny that Aristotle's thought "could have" provided the foundation for Aquinas's metaphysics, given the latter's strong affirmations regarding *esse*—certainly not found in any developed fashion in Aristotle's text—and particularly given Aquinas's stress upon the *analogy of participation*. With respect to the latter, Aristotle's rejection of Platonic participation is contradistinguished with Aquinas's insistence upon finite being as nothing other than participated being. How, then, could Aquinas's metaphysics be thought to be founded in any essential way upon the metaphysics of Aristotle, given these crucial differences? Especially when (so it is said) Aristotle did not even rise to the level of understanding the distinction between God and the created universe as such? My purpose in this lecture is to provide reasons for thinking that these general objections involve certain misunderstandings of the teaching of Aristotle as well as that of Aquinas. Accordingly I will say a few words about both these objections.

For Aristotle Is God Merely a "Part of the Whole" and Not the Cause of the Being of Things?

First is the question as to whether, for Aristotle, God is merely a part of the whole terrestrial universe. Fr. Robert Sokolowski, in his well-known and profoundly instructive work *The God of Faith and Reason*, famously argues that according to Aristotle, and to pagan thought generally speaking, God is and could be thought of merely as the noblest of causes and the highest part of the universe, rather than as transcendent creator. As he puts it, "Aristotle's god is so clearly a 'first substance' within the world that the distance between his teaching and Christianity is obvious to almost every reader."[1] As he puts it about pagan thought most generally—and, as he makes clear later, extending to the teaching both of Plato and Aristotle:

The pagan sense of the divine is that of the best, highest, greatest, most powerful and most necessary beings within the whole or within the world. There are bound to be many different conceptions of the highest and first substance, depending on what approach is used to come to it. It can be described as the pervasive life-force of the world, as the Stoics described it; or as pure thinking; or as a cause of motion; or as a comprehensive and final architectonic force; or as some sort of ultimately necessary being in the world.[2]

Sokolowski is very clear that Aristotle did not and could not have thought of the world as created, or of the very *existence* of things as opposed to nothingness, rather than the quite different consideration of the way that things emerge in the world as differentiated against the world itself as ultimate horizon.[3] He goes so far as to argue that:

1. Robert Sokolowski, *The God of Faith and Reason* (Washington, D.C.: The Catholic University of America Press, 1995), 50.
2. Ibid., 46–47.
3. See, for example, ibid., 42–43.

Furthermore, if "being" is the term that philosophers use to name that which is articulated in the sameness and otherness that reason can register, if "being" is used for the world as last horizon, it is appropriate that another term, like "*esse*," be introduced for us in the "whole" made up of God and the world, as a name for what is articulated in the identities and differences occurring in this new context.[4]

It does not appear that, for Sokolowski, the "Christian distinction"—understood as the distinction between God and the world such that God exhibits no dependence upon the world, that "God plus the creature" does not signify *more perfection of being* than "God minus the world"—is accessible to reason outside of its tutoring by Revelation and grace.

Yet, as he surely is aware, others have thought differently. Certainly not the least of these is Aquinas himself, who expressly attributes the doctrine of creation—*not creation in time*, but creation, that is, the doctrine that the sum total of the being of things in the world is an *effect* received from God—to Aristotle. To quote Aquinas, who expresses himself on this matter unequivocally in several places, from his *Treatise on Separated Substances*:

For there are certain necessary things which have a cause of their necessity, as Aristotle himself says in the fifth book of the *Metaphysics* and in the eighth book of the *Physics*. Therefore, although Plato and Aristotle did posit that immaterial substances or even heavenly bodies always existed, we must not suppose on that account that they denied to them a cause of their being. For they did not depart from the position of the Catholic faith by holding such substances to be uncreated, but because they held them to have always existed—of which the Catholic faith holds the contrary.[5]

Aquinas, then, considers that Aristotle erred not in denying the doctrine of creation as such, but rather in denying that there is a temporal first moment of creation.

However, given that Aristotle held the universe always to have existed, one might consider it very difficult to find in his words signs of the divine causality of being, and of God's transcendence of the world. Certainly there is no strong sense manifest in Aristotle's text—given the error regarding the eternity of the world—that the universe might not have been. The question is this: given Aristotle's teaching of the eternity of the world, does this necessarily imply the denial that God is utterly perfect wholly apart from

4. Ibid., 33.

5. St. Thomas Aquinas, *Treatise on Separate Substances*, trans. Francis J. Lescoe (West Hartford, Conn.: St. Joseph College, 1963), 90. "Sunt enim quaedam necessaria quae suae necessitatis causam habent, ut etiam Aristoteles dicit in quinto metaphysicae, et in octavo physicorum. Non ergo aestimandum est quod Plato et Aristoteles, propter hoc quod posuerunt substantias immateriales seu etiam caelestia corpora semper fuisse, eis subtraxerunt causam essendi. Non enim in hoc a sententia Catholicae fidei deviarunt, quod huiusmodi posuerunt increata, sed quia posuerunt ea semper fuisse, cuius contrarium fides Catholica tenet."

all other things? Does it of itself imply the lack of divine transcendence? Aquinas thought that the transcendent God could conceivably always have sustained the world in being, and that the eternity or non-eternity of the world was not a provable philosophic truth but made known to us exclusively through revelation. St. Bonaventure famously thought the contrary, framing careful philosophic arguments against the thesis of the eternity of the world. Aquinas also held that it was clear from their general accounts of being that Plato and Aristotle considered the being of created things to be derived from God. As he put it earlier in the same chapter of his work on separate substances already quoted above:

But beyond this mode of becoming, it is necessary according to the teaching of Plato and Aristotle, to posit a higher one. For, since it is necessary that the First Principle be most simple, this must of necessity be said to be not as participating in "to be" but as itself being "to be." But because subsistent "to be" can be only one, as was pointed out above, then necessarily all other things under it must be as participating in "to be." Therefore there must take place a certain common resolution in all such things according as each of them is reduced by the intellect into that which is and its "to be." Therefore, above the mode of coming to be, by which something becomes when form comes to matter, we must presuppose another origin for things according as "to be" is bestowed upon the whole universe of things by the First Being that is its own "to be."[6]

Yet to many minds the view of the teaching of Aristotle expressed in the above-quoted passage from St. Thomas Aquinas is unthinkable, as it seems to imply that for Aristotle there is some insight into the real distinction of essence and existence, a distinction which in any case Aristotle did not develop extensively as did Aquinas. Yet, surely, Aristotle was not unaware that the substance "man" is not imperishable. Further, one may note that in the *Sophistical Refutations* and the *Posterior Analytics* Aristotle expressly teaches that to be this or that is not the same as simply to be (*Sophistical Refutations*, 167a2; *Posterior Analytics*, II, 1, 89a23–24; or, at 32–35: "e.g., if a centaur or a god is or is not [I mean if one is or not simpliciter and not if it is white or not]. And knowing that it is, we seek what it is [e.g., What is a god? What

6. Ibid., 86. "Sed ultra hunc modum fiendi necesse est, secundum sententiam Platonis et Aristotelis, ponere alium altiorem. Cum enim necesse sit primum principium simplicissimum esse, necesse est quod non hoc modo esse ponatur quasi esse participans, sed quasi ipsum esse existens. Quia vero esse subsistens non potest esse nisi unum, sicut supra habitum est, necesse est omnia alia quae sub ipso sunt, sic esse quasi esse participantia. Oportet igitur communem quamdam resolutionem in omnibus huiusmodi fieri, secundum quod unumquodque eorum intellectu resolvitur in id quod est, et in suum esse. Oportet igitur supra modum fiendi quo aliquid fit, forma materiae adveniente, praeintelligere aliam rerum originem, secundum quod esse attribuitur toti universitati rerum a primo ente, quod est suum esse."

is a man?"]). I am happy to say that I owe my reference to and understanding of these texts on this precise point to Ralph McInerny.

Nonetheless, it is true that Aristotle does not make real distinction of essence and existence central in the development of much of his thought. Thus many view the matter as manifesting not alone Aristotle's failure to achieve the truth of the doctrine of creation, but as manifesting the impossibility of unaided natural reason attaining this truth: contrary to Aquinas, who famously argues that "not only does faith hold that there is creation but reason also demonstrates it"[7] while also holding, as already quoted, that Aristotle did in fact demonstrate it. *Fides et Ratio* in its official Vatican translation into English states that "Revelation clearly proposes certain truths which might never have been discovered by reason unaided, although they are not of themselves inaccessible to reason. Among these truths is the notion of a free and personal God who is the Creator of the world."[8] By contrast, Anthony Meredith and Laurence Paul Hemming, in their translation of *Fides et Ratio*, render this as follows: "Revelation brings into clear focus certain truths, which, though available to reason, *would never* have been discovered by it were it left to its own resources. In this general area certain questions are asked about the concept of a personal God who is both free and creator"[9] (my emphasis). One sees that, for them, "might" never have been discovered becomes a rather more decided "would" never have been discovered.

Did Aristotle, then, truly view God as merely the highest "part of the whole"? I believe there are two decisive considerations militating against this. The first is that *if* for Aristotle God is merely the noblest or highest cause *within* the world-system of causes, *then* for Aristotle God should clearly be subject to reciprocal causality by other beings. However, it is clear that this is not what Aristotle held. For Aristotle the First Cause is Pure Act, and wholly incapable of being affected by any other causality. Inasmuch as God can be affected by no other causality whatsoever, God is *a se* and transcendent of the world. To say that something is part of the whole, but subject to no reciprocal causality on the part of any or all of the other parts of the whole, seems a contradiction in terms. That God is subject to no causality from any other being is a function of what Aristotle clearly and

7. Cf. Aquinas, *In Sent.* 2.1.2 sol.

8. Cf. the Latin text: "lucide quasdam exhibit veritates Revelatio, quas tametsi attingere potest ratio, nunquam tamen easdem repperisset si suis unis viribus innixa essent. Hoc in rerum prospectu quaestiones ponuntur, veluti notio Dei personalis, liberi et creatoris."

9. *Restoring Faith in Reason: A New Translation of the Encyclical Letter Faith and Reason of Pope John Paul II: Together with a Commentary and Discussion*, ed. Laurence Paul Hemming and Susan Frank Parsons (Notre Dame, Ind.: University of Notre Dame Press, 2002), 124.

incontrovertibly holds regarding the perfect actuality of God, as contrasted with hypothetically unmoved movers.

Many scholars argue that for Aristotle God causes exclusively with final causality. One passage in particular is often used to illustrate the point, the line of Aristotle from Book Lambda of the *Metaphysics* that God "produces motion as being loved" (1072b3). But as Enrico Berti argued in a recent essay,[10] this passage affirms that God, like objects of knowledge and love, does not change in causing; that, like the objects of knowledge and love, God moves without being moved; that God can be a genuinely final cause; that "A final cause may be found among unchangeable entities" and that since "there is something which moves while itself unmoved, existing actually, this can in no way be otherwise than as it is." But this does not imply that God exerts only final causality, nor that God does not efficiently bring about motion. As already noted, the term commonly used in translation is "produces," which is precisely what an efficient cause does, namely, produces its effect.

Just as God as final end escapes the limits of other, subordinated ends, God as first efficient cause escapes the limits of other, subordinated efficient causes. It is also an important observation that throughout Aristotle's account efficiency is always coupled with finality, so that for God to be last final cause without being first efficient cause would seem to introduce disproportion and—much worse from the point of consistency with Aristotle's general teaching— *self-actuating* potencies. These points all should be considered in the light of the truth that *a real Cause which cannot in any way be affected by or subject to the causality of any other reality absolutely transcends all other being and so exerts a transcendent causality.* Thus, without changing, God moves subordinate beings, inclines them, *produces* motion as being loved—the emphasis is on why God need not change in causing motion in others, and on God as both efficient and final principle (produces motion as being loved). This is simply to say that the sense in which Aristotle's God is "within" the world is merely the predicative logical sense in which the absolutely transcendent God is said to be numbered among real things—but this affects all theistic speech about God, since Christians themselves admit that the existence of creatures augments being in *extension or quantity.*

10. Cf. Enrico Berti, "Unmoved mover(s) as efficient cause(s) in Metaphysics Λ 6," in *Aristotle's Metaphysics Lambda, Symposium Aristotelicum,* ed. Michael Frede and David Charles (Oxford: Clarendon Press, 2007), 181–206. Since the publication of this essay he seems to have altered his view of the matter, but his earlier point retains its validity howsoever much wider arguments are also needed—arguments that I am inclined to believe are well founded and which I try to suggest in the text above.

As for the idea that the proposition Christians know to be erroneous owing to Revelation—the eternity of the world—derogates God, arguably in Aristotle the *motive* for holding this teaching to be true (as distinct from the demonstrative arguments brought to establish it, and justly criticized by Aquinas) was the sense that it is more fitting for the effects of the eternal God to be brought about with eternal duration. That is, its motive seems to be to retain distinctly the supereminent, absolute eternity of God, in relation to which it may seem more fitting that God bring forth effects without limit in duration. There is arguably no sufficient metaphysical ground for holding that God could not have created in this way: it is a question of fact, to be known through divine Revelation if Aquinas is correct in arguing that the question is indemonstrable. Further, it was natural for Aristotle—given his error about the eternity of the world—at times to speak in a way that might seem to imply that God exists "in" the world. But how does God exist? In section 10 of Book XII or Lambda, Aristotle speaks of the way in which the nature of the universe contains the good, and argues:

We must consider also in which of two ways the nature of the universe contains the good, and the highest good, whether as something separate and by itself, or as the order of the parts. Probably in both ways, as an army does; for its good is found both in its order and in its leader, and more in the latter; for he does not depend on the order but it depends on him.

God "does not depend on the order, but it depends on him." That is quite literally a theistic affirmation of the divine transcendence vis à vis all other realities. Granted, the universe is said to "contain"—but, that this is the universe merely extensively considered is sufficiently indicated by the fact that for Aristotle God is subject to no reciprocal causality from the world. Aristotle argues in Book Lambda of the *Metaphysics* that God exists as "separate" and "by itself," for, with respect to the world, "he does not depend on the order but it depends on him." This is of course if anything a weak observation, since perfect act cannot be otherwise—and so Aristotle likewise affirms in Book Lambda that God is *eternal and immoveable; impassive and unalterable.*[11] Thus, from the vantage of Christian belief, even Aristotle's metaphysical errors—the judgment that the eternity of the world is demonstrable; the refusal unequivocally rather than merely obliquely to affirm divine knowledge of the world—flow from the desire to preserve the divine aseity, transcendence, and immutability. The semantics of the ways in which the universe "contains" good cannot alter the datum that this is the universe of the real, of all that is, and that God is separate from and ab-

11. Cf. the end of section 7 of Lambda/Book XII.

solutely transcendent of this world as its principle, independent of all other things inasmuch as no other thing exerts the least causal power upon God. Indeed, Christians too must work out the metaphysics and semantics of divine transcendence. Bl. Scotus seems to have held that the being affirmed of God and creature is univocal, yet he is not for this reason supposed not to have held the Christian distinction—even though, it is true, this great mind does seem to have lacked the distinction of being a Thomist. In any case, affirming the divine aseity and so transcendence in principle is immeasurably helpful in developing a correct understanding of the relation of creature to God. Contrary to the view of the matter that today seems most common, this affirmation of the divine aseity is one that Aristotle clearly made (which is precisely why Aquinas could so well develop his natural theology from the most central Aristotelian judgments and analyses).

Aquinas's Formal Metaphysical Dependence on Aristotle

With respect to the formal dependence of Aquinas's metaphysics on Aristotle, I will make two points. The first is that Aquinas shares Aristotle's response to the metaphysical arguments of Parmenides (in *On Nature*). This response of Aristotle's is worked out in the *Physics*, but it is a response to a metaphysical argument and actually and implicitly of metaphysical value. As everyone knows, Parmenides argued that being is unitary, unlimited, and immobile. It is unitary because wholly identical with itself; it is unlimited because outside being there is nothing which could limit it; and it is immobile because being cannot become nonbeing nor derive from it, and so being is unchangeable. Aristotle, of course, looked up and saw birds flying, and knew that the Parmenidean account denying manyness, limit, and change of being must be incorrect. If we were merely analytic philosophers we could stop here. But Aristotle realized that the distinction between being and nonbeing is a metaphysical and real distinction, although the *relation* of being and nonbeing is purely notional. Nonbeing is of course conceptual, and any putative "relation" of being and nonbeing would be conceptual, since what does not exist does not have real relations. But the *distinction* between being and nonbeing *is founded on the real character of being.* Just as one might say that, even had creation never occurred, God's nature is not a created nature—by virtue of the reality of the divine nature itself—or that one's sister is by virtue of her real humanity not a square root—so one may say that being is, by virtue of its real character, not nonbeing. So construed, the principle articulates a real distinction. But this means that one must reconcile the first principle—that being is not nonbeing—with the intelligible perception of manyness, limit, and change. Aristotle of course argues that there is a principle of being which is not act, but which is not merely nonbeing or negation, but rather potency or capacity that is always founded upon act. Thus, being is understood as act as limited by potency; and the analogy of being is that of the likeness of diverse acts as limited by potency. Indeed, for Aristotle potency and act divide every order of being.[12] And the language of this division of being by potency and act is the *analogy of proper proportionality*. As Aristotle argued:

Our meaning can be seen in the particular cases by induction, and we must not seek a definition of everything but be content to grasp the analogy, that it is as that which is building is to that which is capable of building, and the waking to the sleeping, and that which is seeing to that which has its eyes shut but has sight, and that which has been shaped out of the matter to the matter, and that which has been wrought up to the unwrought. Let actuality be defined by one member of this antithesis, and the potential by the other. But all things are not said in the same sense to exist actually, but only by analogy—as A is in B or to B, C is in D or to D; for some are as movement to potency, and the others as substance to some sort of matter.[13]

As he argues in the *Metaphysics* (Book XI, 1065b15–16), "Now since every kind of thing is divided into the potential and the real, I call the actualization of the potential as such, motion."[14] "There being a distinction in each class of things between the potential and the completely real, I call the actuality of the potential as such, movement." Being—indeed, "every kind of thing"—is divided by act and potency. In short, the language of being is

---

12. Thus Aristotle's words from *Metaphysics* Book XI, chapter 9, the first paragraph (or, sometimes translated as two paragraphs), from St. Thomas's *Commentary on the Metaphysics*, trans. Richard J. Blackwell, Richard J. Spath, and W. Edmund Thirlkel (Notre Dame, Ind.: Dumb Ox Books, 1995): "One thing is actual only, another potential, and others both actual and potential; and of these one is a being, another a quantity, and another one of the other categories. Motion is not something apart from things themselves; for a thing is always changed according to the categories of being, and there is nothing that is common to these and in no one category. And each belongs to all its members in a twofold way, for example, this particular thing; for sometimes this is the form of a thing and sometimes its privation. And with regard to quality, one thing is white and another black; and with regard to quantity, one is perfect and another imperfect; and with regard to motion in space, one thing tends upwards and another downwards, or one is light and another heavy. Hence there are as many kinds of motion and change as there are of being. Now since each class of things is divided by potentiality and actuality, I call motion the actualization of what is potential as such."

13. *Metaphysics*, Book 9, section 6 (1048a32–1048b12), trans. W. D. Ross, from Internet Classics Archive of MIT, http://classics.mit.edu/Aristotle/metaphysics.html.

14. Aristotle, *Metaphysics*, trans. Hugh Tredennick (Cambridge, Mass.: Harvard University Press, 1933, 1989); it is also available online at the Perseus Project. Compare with W. D. Ross's translation cited above.

that of the likeness of diverse *rationes* of act as limited by potency. Aquinas famously took this up in his Commentary on the *Sentences* and, more fully and clearly, in *De veritate*. But it has become popular to argue that he dropped this account of the analogy of being, of which he held in *De veritate* that "to this kind belong all attributes which include no defect nor depend on matter for their act of existence, for example, being, the good, and similar things."[15] There are many profound issues here, and to argue all the sed contras that have been issued to the idea that the fundamental analogy of being is that of proper proportionality would require a book.[16] However, I will provide one essential argument that I believe invalidates the argument of Fr. Bernard Montagnes, OP,[17] that the analogy of being is simply the analogy of participation.

One of the essential reasons why Aquinas in *De veritate* affirms the need for analogy of proper proportionality, is that there is no determined relation of God to the creature. The distance from the nickel to the dime is the distance from the dime to the nickel; but the distance from the creature to God is measured in a determined relation, whereas God has no determined relation to the creature but wholly transcends the creature: God is not in his essence "Cause of Steve," as though I were a divine hypostasis naturally emanating from the Godhead. Now, the argument that the analogy of being *is* the analogy of participation, is the argument that the fundamental analogy of being is that of a *causal relation*, because participation is a causal relation. However, because God has no real determined relation to the creature, prior to the being of the creature, the divine cause exists, but the *causal relation as such* does not exist. It sounds very fine to say that the causal relation of the creature to God constitutes the being of the creature: but that is false. It is not the causal relation to God that constitutes the creature, it is

15. Aquinas, *De veritate*, q. 2, a. 11, resp., unequivocally referring by context to the analogy of proper proportionality: "Quandoque vero nomen quod de Deo et creatura dicitur, nihil importat ex principali significato secundum quod non possit attendi praedictus convenientiae modus inter creaturam et Deum; sicut sunt omnia in quorum definitione non clauditur defectus, nec dependent a materia secundum esse, ut ens, bonum, et alia huiusmodi." ("At other times, however, a term predicated of God and creature implies nothing in its principal meaning which would prevent our finding between a creature and God an agreement of the type described above. To this kind belong all attributes which include no defect nor depend on matter for their act of existence, for example, being, the good, and similar things.")

16. Since giving this lecture, I have published such a book: *Analogia Entis: On the Analogy of Being, Metaphyscis, and the Act of Faith* (South Bend, Ind.: Notre Dame University Press, 2011).

17. Bernard Montagnes, *The Doctrine of the Analogy of Being According to Thomas Aquinas*, trans. E. M. Macierowski, ed. Andrew Tallon (Milwaukee, Wis.: Marquette University Press, 2004).

God who constitutes the creature. Since the causal relation as such does not exist in God, its foundation can be found only in the gift of being received by the creature.

Because nonexistent beings cannot have real causal relations; and given that the causal relation is not God; it follows that for the creature to be really related to God *it must first exist.* Hence *whatever* the analogy of being is, it *cannot* be a causal relation, because being—and, accordingly, the analogy of being—is a prior and necessary condition for the causal relation of participation to obtain. *Pari passu* or temporally (but not ontologically) simultaneous with the being of the creature is its causal relation of dependence on God and of participation in being, but the *ground of this relation* is the ontologically prior gift of being, which enables the creature to be so related. The analogy of causal participation, then, is discriminated on the basis of the ontologically prior analogy of being. *But the analogy of being is understood in terms of the likeness of diverse* rationes *of act as limited by potency, and it is on the basis of this analogy of being that causal wisdom discriminates and infers the dependence of finite being on God.*

In fact, as Klubertanz notes,[18] after the Commentary on the *Sentences,* Aquinas never articulates the doctrine of participation save in relation to act as limited by potency, explaining the reason why participated perfections are necessarily limited by referring to potency as the ground of manyness, limitation, and change in created being. Although in the early *Scriptum on the Sentences* Aquinas's adversion to the division of being by act and potency is not fully developed, from *De potentia Dei* onward, Aquinas founds his metaphysical account of created participation on the analogical division of being by act and potency. That is to say, the reason why any participated perfection is received in a limited manner, is held by Aquinas to be owing to its contraction to potency, inasmuch as act is not self-limiting. The hierarchy of participated being thus is understood in terms of diverse degrees of the intensive perfection of act as limited in relation to potency. This analogical division of being by act and potency—from which Aquinas will causally derive his argumentation for God, and which is essential to his account of creation—is a doctrine that Aquinas to be sure perfects and develops, but which he receives from Aristotle.

Of course, the analogy of being does not substitute for causal reasoning—but it is that upon which such causal reasoning supervenes and which is the evidentiary foundation of the reasoning that concludes with the affir-

---

18. See George P. Klubertanz, SJ, *St. Thomas Aquinas on Analogy: A Textual Analysis and Systematic Synthesis* (Chicago: Loyola University Press, 1960), 27–29.

mation of the truth of the proposition that God exists. There is much more to be said on this score—in particular, regarding the consistency of this teaching with respect to the analogy of being throughout Aquinas's later work, which is often denied. But, suffice it to say that in the *Summa theologiae*, as well as earlier, Aquinas denies any strict proportion of creature and Creator, since God has no determined real relation to the creature. The creature is really related to God, but God is not really related to the creature. Hence the language of analogy of attribution of effect to cause, or of what Aquinas in *De veritate* called "transferred proportion"[19] of one to another, must always be retranslated back into the analogy of proper proportionality, because God has no real determined relation to the creature, and because the dependence of the creature upon God is not essential to God, although of course it is real in the creature (everything predicated of God is said by way of identity with his simple substance,[20] but being Creator of the world is not essential to God, who necessarily wills only his own infinite good).

Conclusion

Aristotle held that God transcends the world, existing wholly separate and causally independent of it. With Aquinas, I confess that it seems to me that Aristotle teaches that God is not only the final but the efficient cause of the world. That the principles of efficiency and finality are divorced, and that sublunary act is not dependent upon *Actus Purus*, seems to me, as it did to Aquinas, contrary to Aristotle's teaching. Aristotle held that the world is upheld by God with eternal duration, and this is incorrect; but he did not hold it to be independent in being from God, but rather to be wholly dependent in being on God. Further, Aristotle articulates the division of being by act and potency, a distinction which is the foundation of the further development of the real distinction of essence and existence by Aquinas. And he held that the analogy of being is that of proper proportionality, a teaching expressly held by Aquinas in *De veritate*, which he never expressly renounced, and which I believe to be a teaching that can be reconciled in detail with Aquinas's later work. It is upon the analogy of being understood as an analogy of proper proportionality of diverse *rationes* of act as limited by potency that the further analogy of participation is founded; and it is from the analogy of being so understood that the reality of the First Cause is inferred.

19. *De veritate*, q. 23, a. 7, ad 9, "proportionis translatum."
20. Aquinas, *Summa theologiae* I, q. 22, a. 2, ad 1.

Hence Aristotle should be seen as contributing to Aquinas the very foundations of his metaphysics and natural theology, which are perfected in the maximal articulation of the distinction of potency and act in Aquinas's doctrine of the real distinction of essence and existence. Of course, if Aristotle had done none of this, it would still be true that certain truths lie within the orbit of natural reason. We do not say that the ice cube maker, anesthesia, nuclear fission, or Mozart's 40th symphony were not developed in Athens and therefore were impossible to all but the recipients of Christian Revelation. There are valid and sound arguments containing no premise knowable by Revelation alone that conclude to the reality of God as transcendent cause of all things that are—we can know this, because we are familiar with the philosophic demonstrations—*and this would be true if no one prior to Christianity had discovered them.* Happily, however, as St. Thomas Aquinas discovered to his delight in the work of Aristotle—as Dr. McInerny celebrated in many works, and as one likes to imagine he now delectates in the infinitely superior light of beatific vision—*that is not the case.* Or, as he put it at the end of his masterful work *Praeambula fidei: Thomism and the God of the Philosophers*:

Let's reestablish Aristotelico-Thomism as the norm. Let us proceed, as Thomas does, on the assumption that Aristotle has adequately set forth the subject matter of metaphysics once and for all. Of course, if it were true that Aristotle identified essence and existence, his views on substance would be incompatible with Thomas and with the truth of the matter. But the consequences of making such an assumption about Aristotle render the interpretation untenable. One cannot say that for Aristotle natural substance necessarily exists, that its essence is its existence, and that such a conception of the natural substance is taken over by Thomas Aquinas. Aristotle simply was not an essentialist if that is what the term means. If there is but the one metaphysics with its specific subject matter for both Aristotle and Thomas, we then have the discipline to which St. Thomas, in his commentary and elsewhere, made such remarkable contributions. That he incorporated Neoplatonist doctrines into that same metaphysics is another way in which the discipline grew in his hands. It is a very different thing to say that we have much more with Thomas Aquinas and quite another to suggest that that "more" is not a development of the science of being as being established by Aristotle.

And, given the telos of metaphysics, that is, such knowledge as we can attain of God from things more knowable by us, we are better able to see the continuity of the theology of the *Metaphysics* and Thomas's development of what he called the *praeambula fidei*. The Renaissance Aristotelian Antonio Cittadini once wrote that *Thomam aufer, mutus fiet Aristoteles.* The reverse is also true. *Aristotelem aufer, mutus fiet Thoma: apart from Aristotle, Thomas cannot speak to us.*[21]

To this the present author can only add that it is also demonstrable that the Neo-platonically inspired doctrine of participation was developed by St.Thomas Aquinas only on the scientific foundation of that quintessentially Aristotelian teaching: that being is divided by act and potency.

21. Ralph McInerny, *Praeambula Fidei: Thomism and the God of the Philosophers* (Washington, D.C.: The Catholic University of America Press, 2006), 305–6.

PART THREE

HUMAN REASON AND REVELATION

CHAPTER SIX

Logos as Reason and *Logos* Incarnate

Philosophy, Theology, and the Voices of Tradition

BRIAN DALEY, SJ

One of Pope Benedict XVI's first serious clashes with the "chattering classes" represented by today's media was his now-famous lecture to academic faculties of the University of Regensburg, in September of 2006. As you doubtless remember, that lecture was widely interpreted as a strong critique of Islam on religious grounds, and it inspired heated reactions—against him and against Christian institutions in general—all over the Muslim world. Actually, though, it was not a lecture on Islam and Christianity at all, but a subtle and carefully constructed discussion of faith and human reason. More explicitly, Benedict was really talking about the role of rational thought—of the faculty for argued, ordered thinking, which the Greeks called *logos*—in our understanding of the God who is, by definition, infinitely beyond reason's ability to conceive in rational terms, or to set within the rational boundaries of moral obligation.

In spite of God's ontological and moral transcendence, Benedict apparently wanted to say, the Christian tradition has always, somewhat paradoxically, taken it for granted that God is most closely approached by creatures through the exercise of their reason, and their love of what reason approves. Being an academic, he chose to begin his lecture with a fascinating, slightly off-beat example of this ancient assumption: a passage in one of the Byzantine Emperor Manuel II Palaeologus's learned *Dialogues* on Christianity and Islam; composed in the last decade of the fourteenth century, it compares the presentations of God, humanity, and behavioral ideals in the Scriptures of those two traditions. There, in the seventh of the *Dialogues*, Emperor Manuel comments on the ancient Islamic tradition of holy war— of spreading the faith by force of arms—with what Benedict rightly calls "a brusqueness that *we* find unacceptable," but with perceptive depth nonetheless: "God," the emperor straightforwardly says, "is not pleased by blood— and not acting reasonably (σὺν λόγῳ) is contrary to God's nature."[1] Thus the kind of activities that our moral reasoning would reject as repugnant to human goodness, because they contradict our nature at its best, must also be rejected as contrary to what we can know of how God acts in the world, and so of what God is.

Benedict's point, of course, was not to offer a criticism of the Islamic idea of the sovereignty of the divine will, or to summarize the foundational assumptions of late Byzantine theology, but to underline the role that reasoning and our criteria for reasonable behavior have played in development of the thought and life of the Church. Against the suggestion of Harnack and other liberal Protestants of the late nineteenth century that the "Hellenization of Christianity" has been, from the beginnings of the Church, a kind of corruption of the limpidly simple teachings of the rabbi Jesus about "the fatherhood of God and the brotherhood of man," Benedict asks:

Is the conviction that acting unreasonably contradicts God's nature merely a Greek idea, or is it always and intrinsically true? I believe that here we can see the profound harmony between what is Greek, in the best sense of the word, and the biblical understanding of faith in God.... The Faith of the Church has always insisted that between God and us, between his eternal Creator Spirit and our created reason there exists a real analogy, in which—as the Fourth Lateran Council in 1215 stated— unlikeness remains infinitely greater than likeness, yet not to the point of abolishing analogy and its language. God does not become more divine when we push him away from us in a sheer, impenetrable voluntarism; rather, the truly divine God is the God who has revealed himself as *logos* and, as *logos*, has acted and continues to act lovingly on our behalf.[2]

---

1. Pope Benedict XVI, "Regensburg Lecture of the Holy Father: Faith, Reason and the University; Memories and Reflections" (University of Regensburg, September 12, 2006), citing Manuel II Palaeologus, *Dialogue VII*, 3b–c, ed. Theodore Khoury, in Sources Chrétiennes, vol. 115 (Paris: Les Éditions du Cerf, 1966), 144.

2. "Regensburg Lecture," 2–3. Reasoning on the implications of the gospel, and on the person and origin of Jesus, has been central to Christian discipleship from the beginning, despite the contention of some post-Enlightenment critics that Christian theology is a deformation of Jesus's message. Benedict clearly has in mind such passages as this in Harnack's famous Berlin

To talk about *logos*, the human faculty and process of rational thought in all its manifold aspects and uses, is of course to talk—in the most general terms, at least—about *philosophy*: that collection of strategies and practices by which human beings since ancient times have tried to help each other become wise. Philosophy, more than any other branch of human thought, is ancient Greece's contribution to human culture: it began with the questions Greek poets and pundits asked of each other, especially of the young, about what is most truly real in our world of experience, what goals are most worth pursuing, what beauty and goodness and the well-ordered human society really might be like. Benedict's argument—surely not new to anyone who takes the Catholic tradition seriously—is that philosophy has played a distinctive, at times even normative role in the Church's elaboration of what Scripture and the teaching of the disciples of Jesus have to say about these things: that our Christian theology, in other words—our language and thought about God in God's deepest reality—have not and really cannot be elaborated meaningfully without the intentional use of what philosophy, since the pre-Socratics, has clarified for us. Philosophy and theology, surely, have distinctively different sources, methods, and goals. If theology, in the Anselmian truism, is "faith seeking understanding," the faith with which the search begins is something quite different from *logos* as analysis: trust in the words of historical persons within a historical community; committed membership in a community which hears the word of God as something strange and totally reorienting, and keeps it.

Theology, then, when seen in this light, bears in itself a certain degree of tension, even of paradox. One might think of it as philosophical discipleship, a self-questioning and world-questioning participation in the openhearted faith of a group of friends—a life lived in the space between *logos* and love. What I would like to do here is simply to reflect a bit further on that tension, as it has developed through twenty centuries of Christian thought about the person and meaning of Jesus Christ, by singling out a handful of key figures, especially in the early development of the Church's theology, and to ask how this history of reflection—reflection by *logos* as

---

lectures on the "essence of Christianity": "[Jesus's] message is simpler than the churches would like to think it; simpler, but for that very reason sterner and endowed with a greater claim to universality. A man cannot evade it by the subterfuge of saying that as he can make nothing of this 'Christology' the message is not for him. Jesus directed men's attention to great questions.... The individual is called upon to listen to the glad message of mercy and the Fatherhood of God, and to make up his mind whether he will be on God's side and the Eternal's, or on the side of the world and of time. The Gospel, as Jesus proclaimed it, has to do with the Father only, and not with the Son." Adolf von Harnack, *What Is Christianity?* trans. Thomas Bailey Saunders (Philadelphia: Fortress Press, 1937), 143–44.

reason on *Logos* as Word made flesh, God's own *Logos* in person—has invited us to live faithful Christian lives today.

Figures from History

One of the most influential achievements of Pierre Hadot, the distinguished French historian of later Greek philosophy, in recent years has been to remind us of the essentially practical, "pastoral" character of most of what we would characterize as philosophical activity in the ancient world. Although philosophy in ancient Greece, even in its earliest known stages, certainly focused on asking ultimate questions about the nature of reality and the ultimate values human action and human society strive to realize, Hadot insists that most of its ancient practitioners—from the Sophists and Socrates to the Peripatetics, the Stoics, and the Cynics—saw it above all as a way of raising unsettling questions in the minds of their contemporaries: moving ordinary people, especially young people, to develop a critical understanding of their inherited cultural and religious and ethical assumptions, by suggesting a habit of reflective thought—"spiritual exercises," as Hadot calls them—that led to deeper awareness of the truth and to greater personal freedom. Far from being the highly specialized, esoterically cerebral form of discourse that we identify as philosophy in the post-Enlightenment West, philosophy in late Hellenistic times—claiming in its name to be the "love of wisdom"— used a variety of strategies to help people develop focus and self-mastery in day-to-day life.[3] So it was perfectly understandable that early Christian ascetical practice, at least from the early fourth century, was usually called the *bios philosophikos*, even when those who practiced it had little formal education.[4] If one thoughtfully prayed over a selection of memorized Psalms and Gospel sayings, lived a life as free as possible from sensual distraction, and was under the guidance of an experienced spiritual director, one was—in the ancient sense—living as a philosopher.

Justin, writing in the mid-second century, was the first Christian writer

---

3. See, for example, Pierre Hadot, *What Is Ancient Philosophy?* trans. Michael Chase (Cambridge, Mass.: Harvard University Press, 2002), esp. 2–4. Hadot writes (p. 3): "In the first place, at least since the time of Socrates, the choice of a way of life has not been located at the end of the process of philosophical activity, like a kind of accessory or appendix. On the contrary, it stands at the beginning, in a complex interrelation with critical reaction to other existential attitudes, with global vision of a certain way of living and of seeing the world, and with voluntary decision itself. Thus, to some extent, this option determines the specific doctrine and the way this doctrine is taught. Philosophical discourse, then, originates in a choice of life and an existential option, not vice versa."

4. See ibid., 237–52.

to be generally styled "a philosopher" by profession. Originally from Flavia Neapolis in Samaria (present-day Nablus), Justin spent the last few decades of his life as a teacher of the Christian way of life in Rome, and was put to death for it, with a few of his pupils, around the year 165. The first eight chapters of his *Dialogue with Trypho* give us a glimpse—unusual in ancient documents—of his early intellectual formation, which he describes as a continuing, if somewhat circuitous, search for the unitary vision of truth on which a "happy life" is founded.[5] "Philosophy," he says at the start of his narrative, "is in fact the greatest possession, and most honorable before God, to whom it leads us and who alone commends us; and they are truly holy men who have bestowed attention on philosophy."[6]

Philosophy, as Justin understands it, is in itself a pursuit of holiness, a way to God; what disturbed him in his early years was not its secularity, but the variety of schools and competition of theories by which ancient philosophy was characterized. He tells us that, after brief but unsatisfying stints as a pupil of Stoic, Peripatetic, and Pythagorean teachers, he made greater progress toward what he was seeking when he became a Platonist and discovered that the only worthwhile object of contemplation is immaterial reality.[7] Then, however, he says, while walking by the sea he encountered a "venerable old man" who apparently was himself a Christian teacher. Justin recounts their conversation—stylized, probably, to reflect a living genre of philosophical conversion stories[8]—as itself a kind of Socratic dialogue. The old man leads him to clarify his conception of philosophy, as "the knowledge of that which really exists, and a clear perception of the truth"— knowledge that leads to happiness and is rooted in the conviction of a transcendent God.[9] Further, Justin and his teacher agree that such a God *can* be known by the human mind, which has an affinity with God because it is itself "divine and immortal."[10] They also agree that a just life is the prerequisite for the happy survival of the human soul. Finally, Justin's companion leads him to reject Plato's theory of reincarnation and to affirm that our hope for everlasting life is founded not on some primordial identification of the soul with life (as the *Phaedo* suggests), but on the soul's participation in the life of God.[11] Gradually, through these steps, their conversation leads

5. Justin, *Dialogue with Trypho*, Ante-Nicene Fathers, vol. 1, ed. Archibald Roberts and James Donaldson (repr. Grand Rapids, Mich.: Wm. B. Eerdmans, 1981), chaps. 2, 8.

6. Ibid., chap. 2.

7. Ibid.

8. See Arthur J. Droge, "Justin Martyr and the Restoration of Philosophy," *Church History* 56 (1987): 304.

9. Justin, *Dialogue*, chap. 3 (ANF 196). 10. Ibid., chap. 4.

11. Ibid., chaps. 5–6.

Justin to ask where one might turn to find a reliable teacher for such a path to life with God, and his partner points to the Christian Bible as the source of a philosophy which "alone is safe and profitable":

There existed, long ago, certain men more ancient than all those who are thought of as philosophers, blessed and righteous and beloved by God, who spoke by the Divine Spirit and foretold events which would take place, and which are now happening. They are called prophets.... They did not use demonstration in their treatises back then, seeing that they were trustworthy witnesses to the truth that is above all demonstration.... They both glorified the Creator, the God and Father of all things, and proclaimed his Son, the Christ sent by him.[12]

It is the Hebrew prophets, in their Spirit-led witness to Christ who was to come, who are presented here as the teachers of a philosophy that can be relied on, purveyors of a wisdom that alone brings its practitioners to the happy life.

Behind Justin's identification of the biblical prophets as the most trustworthy teachers of the "truth that makes us free" lies the notion, found in a variety of ancient pagan and Christian sources, that Plato, the most religious of Hellenic teachers, had traveled to Egypt on his own quest for wisdom and had learned there from sources more ancient and more venerable than his own Greek contemporaries.[13] Philo and other Hellenistic Jewish thinkers identified this Egyptian source of classical wisdom with the Hebrew Bible, especially the books of Moses—by their time widely available in Egypt in Greek translation. Early Christian writers readily picked up the story. For Justin, the central point is not simply that Plato borrowed from Moses, but that the fullness of the divine wisdom, guiding the world and offering itself to us as a norm for right living, is to be found in the one to whom Moses and the prophets pointed in the Scriptures, Jesus Christ.[14] So a key argument in all of Justin's works is that Old Testament prophecy has been fulfilled in the words and deeds of Jesus;[15] in Jesus, in fact, God's own providential wisdom, previously offered to the human race in a variety of forms, has taken human shape, lived a human life, and died a human death on the cross. Interpreting a long series of passages from the Hebrew Bible

12. Ibid., chap. 7 (ANF 198; translation altered).

13. For this idea, suggested by Poseidonius, Numenius, and others, that Plato had made contact with an *Urphilosophie* among the Egyptians, see Droge, "Justin Martyr and Restoration of Philosophy," 311, 317.

14. This is especially a Lucan theme; see Lk. 24:25–27, 32, 45–48; Acts 10:43.

15. See, for instance, Justin Martyr, "First Apology," trans. Edward R. Hardy, in *Early Christian Fathers* (Library of Christian Classics, vol. 1) (Philadelphia: Westminster John Knox Press, 1953), 1.47–53 (hereafter "Apology"); *Dialogue*, chaps. 13–14, 28–30, 32–34, 36–38, 43–45, 49, 53, 66, 68, 77–78, 98, 125.

as prophecies of Christ, Justin insists that "he was 'before the morning star' (Ps 109:3) and the moon, and, when he was made flesh, submitted to be born of this virgin, of the family of David."[16] Assigning the details of human distress and abandonment mentioned in Psalm 22 to Jesus in his passion, Justin asserts: "I have already proved that this man was the unique offspring of the Father of all things, being begotten from him in a distinctive manner, as Word and Power, and afterwards becoming man through the Virgin."[17] That divine "Word and Power," for Justin, is precisely the rational presence of God in creation.[18]

Justin's boldest, most famous statement of Christ's eternal identity as the eternal reason or *Logos* of God, the guiding force in creation and the object of every human search for wisdom, appears in his *First Apology*. Countering the pagan charge that Jesus cannot be a genuinely divine figure of transcendent import, because he lived only a century or so before Justin's own time, the Christian philosopher affirms:

We have been taught that Christ is the first-begotten of God, and have previously testified that he is the reason (λόγος) of which every race of humanity partakes. Those who lived in accordance with reason are Christians, even though they were called atheists—such as, among the Greeks, Socrates and Heraclitus and others like them; among the barbarians, Abraham, Ananiah, Azariah and Misael,[19] and Elijah, and many others, whose deeds and names I forbear to list for now, knowing that this would be lengthy. So also those who lived without reason (λόγος) were ungracious,[20] enemies to Christ, and murderers of those who lived by reason; and those who live by reason (λόγος) now are Christians, fearless and unperturbed.[21]

In a single stroke, Justin here identifies the Jesus of the gospels both with the object of Old Testament prophecy and the content of Old Testament types, on the one hand, and with the divine reason guiding the cosmos, on the other—a divine mind in whose activities and knowledge the searching human mind, at its best, is able to share. The implications, though hardly worked out here with any sophistication, are staggering: philosophical ethics are essentially the same as biblical teaching, for Justin, and are summed

16. Justin, *Dialogue*, chap. 45 (translation altered). See also chaps. 48, 63, 68, 75.

17. Ibid., chap. 105 (ANF 251; translation altered).

18. Justin, "Apology," 1.10.

19. These last three names refer to the "three young men" thrown in the furnace by Nebuchadnezzar, in Dn 1:7 (LXX).

20. Greek: ἄχρηστοι. Justin is playing on the title "Christ," which, though unrelated, is similar in sound to the Greek word χρηστός: "good," "honest," "upright." So those who live according to reason, he argues a few lines later, are by the very fact of being *chrēstoi*—"upright people"—also *Christianoi*.

21. Justin, "Apology," 1.46.272 (translation altered).

up most perfectly in the moral teachings and parables of Jesus; the divine Wisdom by which God shaped and still guides the world,[22] is a universal presence, which has become embodied, personified, in the carpenter of Nazareth. Christ has implicitly become for Justin the norm for an adequate philosophical quest for truth and moral righteousness, the implied content of the philosopher's attempts to lead others to freedom and personal integration. On the other hand, the language and concepts of Platonism and Stoicism, which we would call "philosophical" in the more usual sense, are now available to Justin and his colleagues not as religious alternatives, but as tools for deepening their own grasp on biblical images and narratives, and for making them intelligible as religious teachings of universal significance.

For Harnack and other liberal Protestant scholars, at the end of the nineteenth century, this identification of philosophical laws and cosmic teachings with the historical kerygma of Jesus was the first major step in the alienation of the Christian message from its Jewish beginnings: the distancing of the simple, essentially ethical gospel, free from ontological claims, from the person of the rabbi Jesus, and the beginning of a clerical "intellectualism" that even the Reformation—with its presumed emphasis on *sola Scriptura*—was not completely successful in purging from Christian faith.[23] For the Orthodox and Catholic traditions, on the other hand, it marked the beginning of theology in the full sense, as the engagement of faith by reason and the transformation of reason by faith. The *logos* of the philosophers had become flesh for the Church, tangible and immediately nourishing, because it was embodied in the Church's Lord.

A second phase to which we might fruitfully point, in this challenging

22. See, for example, Prv 8:22–36; Ps 104:24.

23. Harnack writes wistfully, in the fourth chapter of Book II of his *History of Dogma*: "In the dogmas of the Apologists … we find nothing more than traces of the fusion of the philosophical and historical elements; in the main, both exist separately side by side. It was not till long after this that intellectualism gained the victory in a Christianity represented by the clergy. What we here chiefly understand by 'intellectualism' is the placing of the scientific conception of the world behind the commandments of Christian morality and behind the hopes and faith of the Christian religion, and the connecting of the two things in such a way that this conception appeared as the foundation of these commandments and hopes. Thus was created the future dogmatic in the form which still prevails in the churches and which presupposes the Platonic and Stoic conception of the world long ago overthrown by science. The attempt made at the beginning of the Reformation to free the Christian faith from this amalgamation remained at first without success" (*History of Dogma* II, trans. Neil Buchanan [London: Constable & Robinson, 1900], 229). For Harnack, it would presumably be only in the less institutional, non-clerical form of liberal Protestantism in the late nineteenth and early twentieth centuries that dogma and Hellenistic "intellectualism" would finally come to an end, being replaced by a Christianity of high-minded, middle-class religious and moral sentiment within a culture of scientific enlightenment.

yet fruitful dialogue between philosophy and faith, began to unroll toward the end of the fourth century, as worldly and educated Greek Christians—now free and honored citizens in an at least nominally Christian empire—argued earnestly and sometimes heatedly about the proper way to understand the apostolic confession that Jesus is truly the divine savior of the world. What modern historians of theology usually refer to as the "Arian controversy" began in Alexandria, at the end of the second decade of the fourth century, with the reaction of Alexander, the local archbishop, to the preaching and pamphleteering of Arius, a respected local pastor. Arius's position, as far as we can determine it from this distance, was apparently only a somewhat oversimplified—and so radicalized—form of a way of thinking about Christ, the divine *Logos* made flesh, that had been widely accepted since at least Origen, a century earlier. Jesus, as Christian tradition made clear, was the mediator between an utterly transcendent God, about whom the human mind and human speech must remain silent, and this world of limited, intelligible, vulnerable beings. The world was created by the *Logos*, at the behest of his divine Father, and was brought back into a good relationship with the Father through him, after some intellectual creatures had turned away. This *Logos* or Son, as mediator between God and the world, was unquestionably a *divine* figure, for Arius and his forebears; but he was just as clearly *not* divine in the full, unlimited, primordial sense in which God his Father is. As "begotten," generated by God to be the minister of God's will, Arius argued, the Son belonged fundamentally to the realm of creatures: a pre-cosmic mediator created precisely to bring creation into being and to redeem it, "a creature—yet not like one of the creatures; an offspring, yet not like things begotten."[24]

The response of most bishops and theologians, in the early 320s, was to resist this highly structured way of conceiving the position of Christ, the Son of God and redeemer, within the cosmos, even though acceptable alternatives were not immediately clear. Gathered in council at Nicaea in Asia Minor, in the late summer of 325, they approved as normative for faith a

24. So Arius and his early colleagues, in a common profession of faith sent to Bishop Alexander, sometime around 321, present their position this way: "Before everlasting ages [God] begot his unique Son, through whom he made the ages and all things. He begot him not in appearance, but in truth, constituting him by his own will, unalterable and unchangeable, a perfect creature of God, but not as one of the creatures—an offspring, but not as one of things begotten.... But as we said, by the will of God he was created before times and before ages and received life and being and glories from the Father, the Father so constituting him" (Hans-Georg Opitz, *Athanasius Werke* III/1 [Berlin: De Gruyter, 1934], Urkunde 6.3, pp. 12–13; translation from *Christology of the Later Fathers,* trans. Edward R. Hardy [Philadelphia: Westminster Press, 1954], 332–33).

revised version of a traditional baptismal creed, which now affirmed that Christ, the Son of God and our Lord, the one who died and rose for us, was "begotten of the Father uniquely: that is, of the substance (οὐσία) of the Father; God of God, light of light, true God of true God; begotten, not made; of the same substance (ὁμοούσιος) as the Father." Language straight from Aristotle's *Categories* had suddenly been introduced into the Church's liturgical profession of faith; and the main subject of theological debate and Church-political wrangling for the next fifty years was precisely how to interpret and apply these terms to the rest of the Christian understanding of God and human history.

In his treatise *In Defense of the Nicene Definition*, written around 356 and usually referred to simply as *De Decretis,* Athanasius—successor to Alexander as bishop of Alexandria and a stalwart, if politically savvy, defender of the Council of Nicaea's doctrinal position on the person of Christ—felt compelled to deal with one of the main criticisms that had been raised against the Nicene formula in the intervening thirty years: that its language, in this crucial point of expressing the original identity of the Son of God, was taken from philosophical discourse rather than from Scripture, and could therefore not be normative for Christian faith in the same way that Scripture is. Athanasius's response to this challenge is to concede, implicitly, that the first choice of theological terms and concepts should normally make use of words taken from the Bible, yet also to affirm that maintaining the central religious understanding of the Christian community, drawn from Scripture—what he calls "reverence" (εὐσέβεια)—must be the Church's first priority, and that this sometimes requires using non-scriptural terminology to clarify Scripture's traditional meaning: "Reverent speech (τὸ δὲ εὐσεβεῖν) is acknowledged by everyone as a holy thing, even if someone should use terms of foreign origin, as long as the one speaking preserves a reverent intention, and wishes to make a reverent statement by what he has in mind."[25] Athanasius then goes on to describe the intention of the Fathers at Nicaea as precisely this: to make the Church's understanding of the biblical portrait of Christ unmistakably clear, by the use of secular philosophical language.

The Synod wanted to annihilate the impious interpretations of the Arians and to write in the recognized language of the Scriptures, that the Son does not come from what is not but is from God, and is *Logos* and Wisdom, but not a creature or something made, and that he is from the Father as his proper offspring. But those associated with Eusebius [of Nicomedia—one of Arius's main episcopal backers], drawing from their long-standing bad intentions, wanted to say that being "from God" is

25. Athanasius, *De Decretis*, 18.4 (Opitz II/1 [Berlin: De Gruyter, 1935], 15); my translation.

common to us and to the Word of God, and that in this respect he does not differ from us—since Scripture says, "There is one God *from whom* are all things" (1 Cor 8:6), and again, "What is old has passed away; behold, all has become new—and all is *from God!*" (2 Cor 5:17–18). But the Fathers, recognizing their trickiness and the evil intent of irreverent thinking (ἀσέβεια) were now forced (!) to say more plainly that he is "from God" and so to write that the Son is "from the essence of the Father," for the reason that being from God is not common and equivalent when understood of the Son and of creatures. . . .

And again, the bishops said that the Word is the true Power and Image of the Father, invariably like the Father in every way, unchanging and always in him without division—for the Word never *was not*, but exists always alongside the Father as a ray of his light. Those associated with Eusebius held back, not daring to contradict this out of sheer shame over what had been charged against them, but they were caught again, whispering to each other and rolling their eyes, to the effect that being "like" and being "always" and the language of "power" and being "in him" is common, once again, to us and to the Son; "No harm [they said] for us to agree with these things!" . . . But since the begetting of the Son from the Father is something different when compared to human nature, and he is not simply like but also inseparable from the substance of the Father, and since "he and the Father are one," as he himself says (Jn 10:30), and the Word is always in the Father and the Father in the Word, just as the ray is related to the light—for this is what the text indicates—therefore the Synod, with this in mind, made the excellent decision to write "of the same substance" (ὁμοούσιον), in order to defeat the bad intentions of the heretics and to indicate that the Word is different from created things.[26]

In this passage, with deep implications for Christian hermeneutics, Athanasius is clearly suggesting that while biblical terminology ought to remain the primary vehicle for the language in which Christian faith is expressed, there are situations in which non-biblical language—specifically, technical language taken from the realm of philosophy—is necessary simply to make clear how the community of faith has, through its history, come to understand the Bible's real meaning.

This same sense of the possible tension between the language of reverence or faith and the (often) more precise language of philosophical analysis emerged again, in an opposite direction, over the next two decades of continuing controversy on the faith of Nicaea. In the late 350s, a new group of anti-Nicene theologians began to form around Eudoxius, the bishop of Antioch (358–60) and later of Constantinople (360–70), who had been promoted to his offices by the Emperor Constantius II because of his steadfast rejection of Nicaea. The intellectual leader of the group around Eudoxius

26. Ibid., 19.1–2; 20.1, 5 (Opitz II/1, 15–17); my translation.

was Aetius, a skilled Antiochene grammarian and dialectician of humble origin. In his brief compendium or *Syntagmation*, Aetius argued on the basis of a developed theory of language, and through a chain of tightly constructed syllogisms, that God, if he is real at all, must also be intelligible to us, in terms of the most precise language used of him. So if it is agreed, by Scripture and by the philosophical tradition, that God is the first of causes, the being who simply *is* and who is the cause of all else, then all beings who are in any way caused by God are, by definition, *not* God but creatures. The consequences for understanding Christ, the Son and Word of God, are obvious: if he is truly the offspring of God, he is *produced* or caused; but if God is the Uncaused One (ὁ ἀγένητος), then the Son cannot be God in any true sense, and should not be called so. And if God's *substance* is defined as his being unbegotten, then the Son also cannot be "of the same substance" as the Father, or even *like* the Father in any significant sense. He is simply the first and noblest of creatures.

Aetius's more celebrated and influential pupil was Eunomius of Cyzicus, a Cappadocian also of humble origins, born around 330; he eventually came to Antioch and became a pupil of Aetius and a follower of Bishop Eudoxius, who eventually ordained him bishop of Cyzicus, across the Sea of Marmara from Constantinople. As an outspoken critic of Nicene theology, Eunomius eventually became involved in heated written controversies with Basil of Caesaraea, with Basil's younger brother Gregory of Nyssa, and (in more personal encounters) with their friend and colleague Gregory of Nazianzus (after this Gregory was made bishop of the Nicene party in the imperial capital in 378). One of the handful of works of Eunomius that have survived is his *Liber Apologeticus*, probably composed in the winter of 360–61 as part of his defense against charges of heresy that appear to have been brought before a local synod in Constantinople at that time.[27] Here Eunomius presents the central arguments proposed by Aetius in a somewhat less terse form. Arguing from the absolute simplicity and primacy of the divine nature, Eunomius concludes: "If it has now been demonstrated that God neither existed before himself nor did anything else exist before him, but that he *is* before all things, then what follows from this is the title Unbegotten—or rather, he is himself unbegotten substance."[28] Eunomius goes on to draw his principal conclusion: "If God is unbegotten in the sense shown by the foregoing demonstration, he could never undergo a generation which

27. For the dating of this treatise, see the introduction to the edition and translation by Richard P. Vaggione, *Eunomius: The Extant Works* (Oxford: Oxford University Press, 1987), 5–8.

28. Eunomius, *Liber Apologeticus* 7 (Vaggione 40–41; translation altered).

involved the sharing of his own distinctive nature with the offspring of that generation, and could never admit of any comparison or association with the thing begotten."[29] Later on in the treatise, Eunomius declares himself ready to accept the fact that the Son is in a genuine sense divine—genuinely the savior of humanity, genuinely the mirror of God's infinite perfections—provided these are understood as *derived* from the Father as his source, and provided we do *not* assert his unity in actual substance with the Father, or even an ontological likeness and parity of ontological status with him.

> We have not used these expressions in order to take away the godhead of the Only-begotten, or his wisdom, or his immortality, or his goodness, but rather to distinguish them with respect to the pre-eminence of the Father. For we confess that the Lord Jesus is himself "Only-begotten God," immortal and deathless, wise, good; but we say too that the Father is the cause of his actual existence and of all that he is, for the Father, being unbegotten, has no cause of his essence or goodness.... Rejecting, therefore, any "similarity of essence" and accepting the similarity of the Son to the Father in accordance with his own words, we must mount up in very truth to the one and only font and source of all things, clearly having subordinated the Son to the Father.[30]

Although all three of the "Cappadocian Fathers" were outspoken critics of Eunomius and his "Neo-Arian" colleagues, it was Gregory of Nazianzus who extended his critique not only to their conclusions about the divine status of Christ, but to the philosophical assumptions and methods in which they steadfastly trusted. A highly educated man of letters himself, Gregory was not only a prolific poet and rhetorician, but considered himself a "philosopher," both in the sense of a single-minded ascetic and in that of a speculative thinker.[31] Yet his main critique of the Neo-Arians, as he had come to know them in Constantinople in the debates of the late 370s,

---

29. Ibid., 9 (Vaggione, 42–43).

30. Ibid., 21–22 (Vaggione, 60–63).

31. For a fuller treatment of the ways in which Gregory considered himself a "philosopher," and for further bibliography, see my *Gregory of Nazianzus* (London: Routledge, 2006), 34–41. And see especially Gregory's own descriptions of the "philososphic life," in passages such as Oration (Or.) 26.8–17 or Epistle (Ep.) 178. The portrait which emerges is that of a person who has attained a remarkable degree of freedom from anxiety and unbalanced desire by his practice of the Christian virtues. "Let me put it in a nutshell," he writes: "two things stand beyond our control—God and an angel; and in third place comes the philosopher! He is an immaterial being in matter, uncircumscribed while in a body, a citizen of heaven on earth, impassible in the midst of vulnerability, beaten in all things except his thoughts, a conqueror of those who think they have subdued him—simply by letting himself be conquered" (Or. 26.13; ibid., 113). Gregory (who always saw himself as persecuted by his enemies) does not claim to have reached perfection in this way, but presents himself as a committed seeker of genuine philosophic enlightenment.

was that they prized cleverness of thought and speech, dialectical adroit-
ness, over faithful adherence to the faith of the gospel: they sought to be
intelligent, in a flashy and polemical way, rather than to be religious. In the
first of his celebrated *Five Theological Orations*, a five-part treatise on the
Trinity probably composed as an anti-Eunomian manifesto in the summer
of 379, Gregory calls his opponents "acrobats of words," and compares them
to professional wrestlers (who, even in fourth-century Byzantium, were apparently long on display and short on athletic substance!).[32] He cautions:

> Not to everyone, my friends, does it belong to philosophize about God; not to every-
> one—the subject is not so cheap and so low-flying! And, I will add, not everywhere,
> nor before every audience, nor on all subjects; but on certain occasions, and before
> certain persons, and up to certain limits.[33]

To "philosophize about God," was, of course, to carry on the kind of speculative reflection about God's being that we continue to call "theology;"[34] but
like all philosophy in the ancient understanding, this reflection had to be
carried on by people whose human passions had at least begun to be tamed
and integrated, whose mind was broadly educated, and whose desires had
matured; and it had to be done in a setting of serious, reverent dialogue. So
he continues:

> I am not saying that one should not remember God at all times—lest these swift
> and eager people fasten on me again like dogs! For we ought to remember God
> even more often than we draw our breath; indeed, if I may be allowed to say so, we
> ought to do nothing else but this.... It is not the continual remembrance of God that
> I would hinder, but only talking about God (θεολογία); nor would I prevent talk
> about God, as something irreverent, but only when it is out of place; nor teaching
> itself, but only a lack of moderation.[35]

Gregory then proceeds, in the rest of these five extraordinary "orations"
or essays, to sketch out the possibility of our finding indications of God's
reality in the natural world, as well as in the world of Scripture (Or. 28),
and then (in Ors. 29 to 31) to consider the uniquely Christian conception
of God—based on Scripture, especially on the New Testament, and on the
present life of the Church, but surely "messy" philosophically: that God is
both radically simple and single, and eternally three in his archetypally per-

---

32. See Or 27.1–2.

33. Ibid., 4. See Edward R. Hardy, ed., *Christology of the Later Fathers*, trans. Charles Gor-
don Browne and James Edward Swallow (Philadelphia: Westminster Press, 1954), 129; translation altered.

34. On the relation of "philosophy" and "theology" in ancient Greek thought and in Gregory's work, see my *Gregory of Nazianzus*, 42–43.

35. Or. 27.4 (Hardy, 130; translation altered).

sonal relationships of giving and receiving—the very conception of radically unified divine plurality that the Neo-Arians were bent on denying. At the start of the third "Theological Oration," he writes:

The three most ancient opinions concerning God are *anarchia* [there are no ultimate causes], *polyarchia* [there are multiple ultimate causes], and *monarchia* [there can be only one ultimate cause]. The first two are the sport of the children of the Greeks [atheists and polytheists].... But monarchy is what we hold in honor. It is, however, not a monarchy that is limited to one acting person, for it is possible for unity—if in a state of tension with itself—to come to be established as many; but a monarchy that is made of an equal dignity of nature, and a harmony of mind, and an identity of motion, and a convergence of its elements to unity [a thing which is impossible to created nature], so that though [the many are] numerically distinct, there is no separation of substance. Therefore that which is One from the beginning, being set in motion toward a Dyad, has come to its steady state as a Triad. This is what we mean by Father and Son and Holy Spirit![36]

Gregory is here bending the language of substance and individual, of identity and plurality, in a way that moves freely beyond the traditionally understood limits of philosophical analysis of divine simplicity, and even hovers on the edge of self-contradiction. Yet it is rooted, as he will go on to show, both in a long array of biblical texts, as they have come to be understood within the community of Christian faith and worship, and in the continuing experience of the Church, where the living presence of the Holy Spirit as the divine sanctifier is revealed in daily action. He writes in the final Oration, on the Holy Spirit:

To us there is one God, for the Godhead is one, and all that proceeds from God is predicated of one, even if we profess faith in three. For one is not more God, and the other less; nor is one before and another after; nor are they divided in will or parted in power; nor can you find here any of the qualities that exist in divisible things; but the Godhead is, to speak concisely, undivided in its division; and there is one mingling of lights, as it were of three suns joined to each other.[37]

Philosophical discourse is needed, Gregory seems to assume, to identify the scope and implications of Christian faith, to specify what faith does and does not embrace; but philosophical discourse also meets its limits in the paradoxical affirmations of Christian Scripture. So, after a long and painstaking discussion of the passages in the New Testament that present the main paradoxes implied in Christian faith in Jesus—passages that for fifty-

---

36. Or. 29.2. (Hardy, 161; translation altered). Gregory seems here to be deliberately evoking the classic Middle Platonic and Neo-Pythagorean language of a primordial Monad which, in its activities outside itself, develops into a Dyad and a Triad.

37. Or. 31.14 (Hardy, 202; translation altered).

some years had been at the heart of the dispute between Arian and Nicene Christians—Gregory boldly affirms this mutual limitation of the concepts of philosophy and faith:

This, then, is our reply to those who would throw riddles at us ... that they may be led to see that they are not wise in every respect, nor invincible in those superfluous arguments which empty out the Gospel. For when we give first place to what is attainable by reason alone, and let go of faith, and destroy by our investigations what the Spirit makes credible, and when then our argument is overwhelmed by the sheer size of the subject (and surely it *must* be overwhelmed, since it starts off from the weak instrument of our own reason), what is the result? The weakness of the argument seems to be a weakness in the Mystery, and so elegance in reasoning "makes void the cross," as Paul also thought (1 Cor. 1:17). For faith is that which brings our own human reasoning to its fulfillment.[38]

Philosophical dialectics, in Gregory's view, must find their context in the thought and worship of the community of faith, if they are to complement Christian faith in its articulation and not to become an alternative, ultimately a non-Christian, form of theology in themselves.

A third period to which one might point, as significant for the developing relationship between classical philosophy and Christian theology, is the seventh and eighth centuries: a time, in the Greek-speaking world especially, when the portrait of Christ enunciated at the Council of Chalcedon in 451, and reaffirmed in slightly different terms at the Second Council of Constantinople in 553, continued to be analyzed and discussed in what by then was primarily philosophical language. It seems fair to say, in general terms, that what we think of as "scholastic" theology began in earnest in the Eastern Christian world, in the wake of Chalcedon, and that the bitter debates which followed, about the adequacy of that council's dogmatic definition as an expression of the Church's faith, were carried on almost exclusively in the language of the classroom rather than that of the pulpit: in definitions and syllogisms, well-constructed theses and highly technical sets of questions and answers, rather than in the more homiletic and biblical theological style of the third, fourth, and early fifth centuries.[39] By the late fifth century, too, what we understand as philosophy had become more identifiably academic. In the established schools in Athens and Alexandria, for instance, imperially salaried professors lectured on the classical sources of the Greek philosophical tradition: the major dialogues of Plato, Aristotle's *Ethics*, *Physics*, and *Metaphysics*, as well as the *Organon*, and Porphyry's

38. Or. 29.21 (my translation).

39. See my article, "Boethius' Theological Tracts and Early Byzantine Scholasticism," *Mediaeval Studies* 46 (1984): 158–91.

Eisagoge—his introduction to Aristotelian logic. The texts being commented on were mainly familiar representatives of Hellenistic philosophy, reaching back a millennium; but the perspective in which they were construed was, in general terms, Neoplatonic—that more inward-turned, even mystical style of philosophical thought that drew inspiration from both Aristotle and Plato, as well as from the eclectic traditions of the second century.

One might point to the work of a number of sixth- and seventh-century Christian theologians to show the growing influence of Neoplatonic philosophical commentaries on Aristotle within the language and style of theology: to the work of Leontius of Byzantium and Leontius of Jerusalem, to that of the theologian-emperor Justinian I, and especially to the dense and original essays and letters on the ascetical life and the Mystery of Christ by Maximus the Confessor, in the seventh century. Here, however, it might be more helpful simply to consider the relation of school philosophy and the patristic theological tradition to each other in the work of one of the great synthesizers of antique Christian thought, John of Damascus (c. 680–750).

Like the majority of influential Christian writers since Chalcedon, John was not a bishop, but a monk and priest who devoted most of his energies, it seems, to study and writing. A member of the Palestinian monastic community of Mar Saba for almost fifty years, John was a prolific poet, an accomplished and profound preacher, and above all a philosophically acute theologian who saw his work as one of retrospective synthesis: "I will say nothing of my own," he insists in the preface of his ambitious compendium of philosophical and theological learning, the *Spring of Knowledge* (Πηγὴ γνώσεως), "but will collect into one place the labors of the most respected of our teachers, … and keep my language as brief as possible."[40] Like the Western scholastics of the thirteenth century and later, John saw his work, on the surface at least, as one of systematization and integration.

The Damascene begins this monumental treatise with a section usually called the *Dialectica*: a summary of the key concepts and logical rules of late antique reasoning and analysis, largely drawn from Aristotle's *Categories* and Porphyry's *Eisagoge*, and presented here conveniently in 68 terse chapters.[41] He then offers us, in Part II, 101 chapters outlining the key "heresies" or sects of the early Christian centuries, each focused on a particular mis-

---

40. John Damascene, *Spring of Knowledge,* in *Die Schriften des Johannes von Damaskos,* vol. 1, ed. Bonifatius Kotter (Berlin: De Gruyter, 1969), Prooemium, 53.

41. Since the second and third parts of the *Spring of Knowledge* consist each of 100 chapters, it is possible that John planned to offer 100 preparatory philosophical chapters, as well. This part of the project may not have been finished—a possibility suggested by the somewhat disorganized and repetitive character of the last three chapters of the longer version of the *Dialectica*—or John may simply have run out of suitable material.

construal of the Church's tradition of understanding biblical faith; significantly, the final, "bonus" chapter of the work is a description of Islam—the dominant religious system in John's native Damascus while he was growing up, which John took to be a Judaeo-Christian heresy. Part III—subtitled "On the Orthodox Faith"—contains a further 100 chapters, outlining in contrast the main recognized teachings of mainstream Christianity; Christian doctrine is expressed here in terms that often draw on Hellenistic philosophy, and that stands in contrast to the beliefs of quasi-Christian sects, but its guiding norm is the Scriptures and their interpretation within the Church.[42]

The guiding theme of the whole *Spring of Knowledge* is the unsurpassable importance of knowledge, our access to the truth; this knowledge is grounded in God's being, and is revealed to us both in the historical events and teachings of Scripture and in the operation of human reason. John begins the first chapter of the *Dialectica*:

Nothing is more precious than knowledge (γνῶσις). For if knowledge is the light of the rational soul, ignorance, on the other hand, must be darkness. And as the deprivation of light is darkness, so the deprivation of knowledge is a darkness of our reason. But ignorance is proper to irrational beings, knowledge to rational ones. If someone, then, does not possess knowledge, when he is naturally able to know and to give reasons for things, this person—being rational by nature—is, because of indifference and laziness of soul, worse than irrational beasts![43]

Knowledge is the intellectual creature's contact with reality; but it is always precarious and halting for the human mind, because the mind is "covered, as it were, with the veil of the flesh,"[44] and so can mistakenly embrace ignorance rather than real knowledge. As a result, the mind needs to be purified from passionate attachments, and patient in its search; more important still, John points out, it needs a Teacher. He continues:

Let us draw near to the Truth, the Teacher who does not deceive. But Christ is Wisdom and Truth personified; in him "all the treasures of knowledge are hidden,"[45] and he is "the Wisdom and Power of God" the Father.[46] Let us listen to his voice speaking through the divine Scriptures, and let us learn the true knowledge of all things that are.[47]

42. This final section of the *Spring of Knowledge* was translated several times into Latin in the early Middle Ages, most famously by Burgundio of Pisa in the second half of the twelfth century, and was known in the West as *De fide orthodoxa*. This translation, in which the numbering of chapters is altered to turn the treatise into four "books," corresponding to the parts of Peter Lombard's *Sentences*, was the vehicle through which St. Thomas Aquinas came to know it and to use it so widely as a guide for his own arguments.

43. *Dialectica* 1, ed. Kotter, in *Schriften*, vol. 1, p. 53; translation mine.

44. Ibid.

45. Col 2:3.

46. 1 Cor 1:24.

47. *Dialectica* 1, p. 53; translation mine.

To know Christ, who is divine Wisdom in person, and through contact with him to be able to use human reason as a reliable instrument for discovering truth, John is convinced—as Origen and Augustine had been before him—that we need to undertake the laborious task of "knocking at the door" of Scripture, as it points to Christ in figures and discloses his presence in our midst.

And as we move forward, let us not be satisfied with simply arriving at the gate, but let us knock vigorously, so that the door to the bridal chamber might be opened to us and we might see the beauties within it. The gate, after all, is the letter; but the bridal chamber within the gate is the beauty of the thoughts which it hides, or the spirit of truth. Let us knock vigorously; let us read the scriptural text once, twice, many times, and so—by opening the treasury of knowledge—we shall find it and feast on its riches.[48]

Knowledge of the truth of things, in other words, engages the human mind in the hard labor of analysis and argument—in what we have come to call philosophy—as well as in the equally hard labor of seeking for the real meaning of scriptural revelation, the story of God's unpredictable actions in human history. In the end, knowledge of the truth is an encounter with Christ, the Wisdom of God and the foundation of the truth of all else that is; it depends both on human shrewdness and effort and on God's gratuitous self-disclosure. "If we love to learn," he writes, "we shall learn much! All things can naturally be grasped by concentration and labor, and before and after all else by the grace of God, who has given them all to us."[49]

With this as his presupposition, John then goes on to sketch an outline of what reason can achieve by engaging the world around us; he gives brief definitions of what the Greek world has come to understand by being, substance and accident, genus and species and differentiating characteristic, of what an individual is and how it is related to universals—essentially the kind of philosophical terminology one would need to know, to understand classic Christian discussions of the Trinity and the person of Christ. Yet the focus, even in this essentially philosophical treatise about terminology, is on what the mind can do with Revelation. So in chapter 3, where he offers several definitions of philosophy itself, John begins with a definition one can find in the Neoplatonic commentators on Aristotle: "Philosophy is knowledge of the things that are, insofar as they are—that is, knowledge of the nature of what is."[50] But he concludes, six definitions later, with a characterization of philosophy that is not found in the commentators but may

---

48. Ibid., 54; translation mine.   49. Ibid.; translation mine.
50. Ibid., 3, p. 56; translation mine.

well have grown from his own experience as scholar and monk: "Philosophy, once again, is love of Wisdom. But true Wisdom is God. Therefore the love of God is true philosophy."[51]

Christ as the Reason

One might, of course, offer many other examples to illustrate how deeply intertwined Christian theologians, since the second century at least, have seen reason and Revelation to be in God's long history of engagement with the human race. Although he often acknowledged that faith—trust in the word of another, on the basis of the other's known credibility—is essential for all human knowledge, Augustine, for instance, insisted that faith is only a provisional form of knowledge (*scientia*); knowledge of truth in its fullness is to be looked for in the unitive, participative contemplation of God, and of all things in God, which is reserved for the life to come, beyond time, and which Augustine calls wisdom (*sapientia*).[52] He writes in Book 13 of *De Trinitate*:

Our *knowledge* therefore is Christ, and our *wisdom* is the same Christ. It is he who plants faith in us about temporal things, he who presents us with the Truth about eternal things. Through him we go straight towards him—through knowledge towards wisdom—without ever turning aside from the same Christ, "in whom are hidden all the treasures of wisdom and knowledge" (Col. 2:3).[53]

Augustine was always ready, of course, to make use of the best available strategies for reasoning critically and truthfully about the world; for him, this normally involved making limited use of the philosophical strategies of Latin Neoplatonism. He describes at some length, in Book 7 of his *Confessions*, how his engagement with "books of the Platonists" during his time teaching in Milan solved a number of the intellectual problems with orthodox Christianity that had led him to become a Manichee some thirteen years earlier.[54] Yet it was not until he was able to recognize Christ, as God humbling himself out of love for our sakes[55]—a notion that philosophical speculation would doubtless find bizarre—and to discover for himself the

51. Ibid.; translation mine.

52. This distinction runs throughout his works. On faith as a form of *scientia* based on trusting the credibility of another, see, for instance, *De vera religione* 25.46–47 (written in 390); *De utilitate credendi* 10.23–16.34 (written in 391–92). For the distinction of *scientia* and *sapientia* in a broader sense, see *De Trinitate* 12.15.22–16.25; 13.1.2 (written in 417–19?).

53. *De Trinitate* 13.19.24 (trans. Edmund Hill, O.P. [Brooklyn, N.Y.: New City Press, 1990], 363–64).

54. See *Confessions* 7.9.13–17.23.

55. Ibid., 7.20.26.

equally non-philosophical humility to accept the grace of Christ, by reading Paul,[56] that he was able to move beyond his questions and accept baptism. Philosophy could take him only so far toward knowing truth in its fullness.

St. Thomas Aquinas, too, is clearly aware both of the importance of the newly rediscovered, Aristotelian philosophical system for ordering and balancing our theological knowledge and of philosophy's limitations for helping us know God, since philosophy is simply an articulation of human reason. In the classic presentation of article 8 of question 1 of the *Summa theologiae*, for instance, he insists that *sacra doctrina*—our knowledge of God, and all things in their relation to God, arranged as a "science" in terms of ordered explanation from first principles—is certainly a realm of human knowing that is open to argument: a place where people of good will and sound mental powers must labor and can plausibly disagree. But because the first principles of the science of theology are affirmed in the Scriptures, and are thus "articulations of faith" (*articuli fidei*) rather than affirmations to be proved by reasoning, one can argue about theological statements only with a person who is able to concede as true at least something of what the Scriptures present of God. Aquinas writes in his famous response to the second objection of this article:

Arguing on the basis of authority is especially characteristic of this body of knowledge (*doctrina*), for the reason that the principles of this knowledge are possessed through revelation, and thus it is appropriate that the authority of those people is to be believed to whom revelation was made.... Sacred doctrine, however, makes use also of human reason: not to prove the content of faith, since through that the merit of believing would be taken away, but to make clear some of the other points that are communicated in this doctrine.... That is why sacred doctrine even makes use of the authority of the philosophers, when, by the use of natural reason, they have succeeded in knowing truth.... But sacred doctrine makes use of authorities of this kind as extrinsic evidence, forming part of probable arguments; whereas it uses the authorities of canonical Scripture in the full sense, arguing to necessary conclusions.[57]

Clearly, the understanding of religious knowledge that Aquinas shows here, and that is evident in the patristic examples we discussed earlier, leads in a very different direction from the conception of knowledge, on the one hand, and of religious faith, on the other, that has characterized the modern West since the seventeenth century. In the wake of the Enlightenment, as has often been observed, religious faith came more and more to be considered as part of the realm of interior assumptions, moral convictions, or

56. Ibid., 7.21.27.

57. St. Thomas Aquinas, *ST* I, q. 1, a. 8, ad 2 (translation mine).

personal feelings, in contrast to that of empirical, "scientific" knowledge of the objective world. For Harnack and his colleagues, as we have seen, Christianity itself was not originally a set of doctrines at all; it was essentially a moral stance, a trusting benevolence toward one's fellow human beings, grounded in a sense of being creatures of a benevolent God, that was rooted in the teaching and practice of Jesus, but that nineteen centuries of philosophical speculation had simply alienated from its source.

In response to Enlightenment critique, and to the liberal Protestant rejection of historical dogma, much of the effort of nineteenth- and early twentieth-century Catholic scholasticism was to reaffirm the reasonableness and philosophical coherence of faith as officially formulated, and to present Church doctrine as an abstract, tightly reasoned system of principles and conclusions. As the Belgian Dominican M. M. Tuyaerts argued in his work *L'Évolution du dogme: étude théologique* (1919), "The nature of dogma, and of our mind, make possible only one single process in the evolution of dogma: the dialectical process, which is reasoning."[58] Faced with the range of propositions one can identify in Scripture and in the Church's official teachings through the centuries, the theologian's task was simply to draw out their implications in a logically consistent way.

Much of the energy of Catholic theology since the 1930s has come from a reaction against both of these approaches to conceiving the role of philosophical reason in the articulation of the Church's faith: the anti-dogmatic moralism of liberal Protestant historians, and the stiff and exclusive rationalism of some scholastic handbooks. In the writings that represent what came to be called—first disparagingly, then approvingly—*la nouvelle théologie*, an important group of mid-twentieth-century European theologians, mainly French Dominicans and Jesuits, began to raise serious questions about both of these theological styles and to emphasize once again both the importance of historical and cultural context and the possibility of genuine development of new issues and ideas in the articulation of faith, based on the concrete reality of Jesus, the Word made flesh.[59] In an influential article

58. M. M. Tuyaerts, *L'Évolution du dogme: étude théologique* (Louvain: Nova et Vetera, 1919), 236; cited by Henri de Lubac, "Le problème du développement du dogme," *Théologie dans l'histoire*, vol. 2 (Paris: Desclée, 1990), 38–39.

59. For a fuller treatment of the importance of this movement for the revival of patristic and liturgical studies in the Catholic Church, see my article "The *Nouvelle Théologie* and the Patristic Revival: Sources, Symbols, and the Science of Theology," *International Journal of Systematic Theology* 7 (2005): 362–82; also "Knowing God in History and in the Church: *Dei Verbum* and 'Nouvelle Théologie'," in *Ressourcement: A Movement for Renewal in Twentieth-Century Catholic Theology,* ed. Gabriel Flynn and Paul D. Murray (Oxford: Oxford University Press, 2012), 333–51.

published in 1935, for instance, the French Dominican scholar of twelfth- and thirteenth-century theology, Marie-Dominique Chenu, insisted that, unlike the philosopher,

the theologian works with a history. His "data" are not the natures of things, or the timeless forms; they are events, corresponding to an *economy*, whose realization is bound to time, just as extension is bound to the body—beneath the order of essences. The *real* world is this one, not the abstraction of the philosopher. The believer, the believing theologian, enters by his faith into this plan of God; what he seeks to understand, *quaerens intellectum*, is a divine initiative, a series of absolute divine initiatives, whose essential trait is to be without a reason—both the general initiatives of creation, the incarnation, redemption, grace, and the particular initiatives of the gracious predestination of individuals: the sweet and terrible contingency of a love which needs give no account of his benefits or his refusal to benefit. This world is the true world of contemplation, and of theological understanding.[60]

So the work of the theologian, however shaped in its articulated form by philosophical discipline and pastoral urgency, is always inseparable from a contemplation of the presence and the saving acts of God in history, as narrated in the Scriptures and as interpreted in the continuing, time-bound tradition of the community of faith. When theology turns from ideas, it turns from Christ, the Word and Wisdom of God; but when it becomes so preoccupied with building a coherent intellectual system of ideas that it loses conscious contact with either Scripture or tradition, it loses its identifying focus on the work of God. As Chenu writes in the same article:

The philosopher can ignore the history of philosophy—in theory, at least—without suffering any disadvantage; because it is not the historians [of thought] who give him his material, but things in themselves. The theologian, on the other hand, has no object apart from the *auditus fidei*, of which the historian, working in the light of faith, gives him the content—not simply a catalogue of propositions arranged by some Denzinger or other, but living material, in its full abundance, always active in the treasury of the Church, laden with divine intelligibility.[61]

A product of this same movement, arguably, is the Second Vatican Council's *Dogmatic Constitution on Divine Revelation* (November 18, 1965), which attempted to present the whole vexed question of the sources of faith, the "first principles" of the Church's theology, in the light of the historical reality of God's presence in the history of Israel and the Church. So the constitution declares at the outset its distinctive conception of what Revelation is:

60. Marie-Dominique Chenu, "Position de la théologie," *Revue des sciences philosophiques et théologiques* 25 (1935): 247; my translation.
61. Ibid., 245.

It has pleased God, in his goodness and wisdom, to reveal himself and to make known the secret purpose of his will (see Eph 1:9). This brings it about that through Christ, God's Word made flesh, and in his Holy Spirit, human beings can draw near to the Father and become sharers in the divine nature (I Pt 2:4). By thus revealing himself, God, who is invisible, in his great love speaks to humankind as friends, and enters into their life, so as to invite and receive them into relationship with himself. The pattern of this revelation unfolds through deeds and words bound together by an inner dynamism, in such a way that God's works, effected during the course of the history of salvation, show forth and confirm the doctrine and the realities signified by the words, while the words in turn proclaim the works and throw light on the meaning hidden in them. By this revelation the truth, both about God and about the salvation of humankind, inwardly dawns on us in Christ, who is in himself both the mediator and the fullness of all revelation.[62]

It is hard here not to be reminded of John of Damascus's insistence that it is Christ, made known to us in the challenging yet rich text of Scripture, who is the heart of the wisdom that reason so eagerly seeks, or of Gregory Nazianzen's astonishing affirmation that "faith"—faith in Jesus, the incarnate Word, expressed in the historical and culturally limited words of human speech—"is what brings our own human reasoning to its fulfillment."

Christian faith, as Pope Benedict reminded his scientist colleagues at Regensburg, has always cherished the assumption that God acts reasonably and that our created reason is grounded in the very reality of God. Hence Christian faith, since Paul's speech on the Areopagus, has attempted to connect the proclamation of God's work in history, which has reached its peak in the death and resurrection of Jesus, with the best instincts of secular literary and intellectual culture, and to see in Christ the embodiment of divine reason, the *Logos* who has become flesh. Christ is, for Christianity, not simply the one on whose identity revelation casts its light, the one about whom theology reasons in often philosophical terms. He is rather, in his own historical human person, the fullness of Revelation, the source of our ideas and understanding about God, the promise of a full share in eschatological wisdom, which will be no more and no less than a share of Christ in his fullness. If philosophy represents the best and most concentrated efforts of human reason, relying on its own powers, to connect and arrange our understanding of the world, philosophy and theology clearly need each other to reach their goals. But philosophy, as Christian theology uses it, can never be left to function on its own, an analytical or deductive system engaging experience as an independent intellectual discipline; it must be, in some

62. *Dei Verbum*, §2, in *Decrees of the Ecumenical Councils*, vol. 2, ed. Norman P. Tanner (Washington, D.C.: Georgetown University Press, 1990), 972.

sense, a philosophy aimed at making sense of the mystery of Christ's person and work. Without the Word in his flesh, philosophical reasoning struggles on without a reliable teacher, gropes in the dark of language games and rival schools, lacks substance and hope. As St. Paul wrote to the Colossians, "The Mystery hidden for ages and generations"—the lost key to the world's intelligibility, for which philosophers continue to search—"but [which is] now made manifest to the saints … is Christ in you, your hope of glory" (Col 1:26–27). What Christian faith has to offer the world—even the world of philosophy—is the challenge and the promise of sharing in that Mystery.

CHAPTER SEVEN

Are Aristotelian-Thomists Rationalists?

On Thomism, the *Praeambula Fidei*, and Theological Faith

ROGER NUTT

I came to know Ralph McInerny through my participation in the conferences of the American Maritain Association. I always enjoyed the filial piety with which he spoke of his great teacher, Charles De Koninck. So I will move into my topic by considering some foundational insights from both De Koninck and McInerny. De Koninck begins an essay (translated into English by McInerny) with the words of an unnamed modern author who "wrote that he could not understand how some of the most intelligent people of his acquaintance could still believe the most *afflicting foolishness* they are taught by the Catholic Church."[1] The point that De Koninck wishes to draw out is not merely rhetorical, but strikes at the very touchstone of the faith-reason relationship. "Some philosophers," he explains, "have thought that the relation of properly divine truth to natural truth can be compared to a series converging at its limit."[2]

This approach, De Koninck warns, is inadequate because it tends to "confuse" the "otherness" of the natural and supernatural, making the former a kind of probabilistic or demonstrative stepping stone to the latter. On the

---

1. Charles De Koninck, "This Is a Hard Saying," in *The Writings of Charles De Koninck*, vol. 2, trans. Ralph McInerny (Notre Dame, Ind.: University of Notre Dame Press, 2009), 393–98, 393.

2. Ibid.

other extreme are those who maintain "that divine truths are so different that natural reason can teach contrary to the faith."[3] Following St. Thomas Aquinas, De Koninck explains the error of these positions: "If it is absolutely impossible for natural reason to arrive at knowledge of truths which are of pure divine faith, it is equally impossible for reason to call them impossible." "If natural reason," De Koninck continues, "can determinately know that there are truths that it cannot conceive, it cannot say determinately what those truths are." He concludes: "We cannot call possible that whose impossibility we cannot see. That is the limit point of philosophical knowledge."[4]

McInerny confronts this same problem in one of his last book-length projects. Following his two great teachers, Aquinas and De Koninck, McInerny situates theological faith "between knowledge and opinion."[5] What differentiates faith, knowledge, and opinion is that with demonstrative knowledge "assent is elicited by things relevant to the content of the proposition. The evidence for S is P is either conclusive or only probable."[6] The contrast between the religious believer, the possessor of demonstrative knowledge, and the person of opinion is that the believer assents to the truthfulness of faith without being moved to do so by the mere demonstrative veracity of the proof, while the "opinionator" withholds assent due to a lack of a firm motive. This does not mean, however, that the believer's assent is arbitrarily or blindly commanded. Rather, McInerny explains, "In faith assent and cogitation are equally balanced, for the assent is not caused by cogitation, but by will."[7] This means, necessarily, that the truthfulness, rationality, and credibility of faith cannot be assessed simply by means of unaided human judgment. "For the mind to be moved by the will to accept something as true," McInerny argues, "is not its proper or natural way to claim something to be true. The believer's mind is rendered captive and his faith must seem a scandal and folly to unbelievers."[8]

Both De Koninck and McInerny underscore a common point that is central to differentiating the richly philosophical approach to faith and theology so proper to Aquinas from the approach of thinkers of the Enlightenment: namely, that although faith is rational, intelligible, and cognitional, Aquinas and the authentic Christian tradition do not—ever—make assent to the truths of faith the result of the judgment of unaided reason.

---

3. Ibid. 4. Ibid.

5. Ralph McInerny, *Praeambula Fidei: Thomism and the God of the Philosophers* (Washington, D.C.: The Catholic University of America Press, 2006), 12.

6. Ibid., 13. 7. Ibid., 21.

8. Ibid., 24.

I will argue that although the *praeambula* do not function as probabilistic steppingstones to faith (as the figures of the Enlightenment often characterize them), they do nevertheless retain a necessary role and function within the life of theological faith.

I will not include in my presentation the place of Romans 1:20, cited in support of the doctrine, as Vatican I puts it, that "God, the source and end of all things, can be known with certainty from the consideration of created things."[9] The same council points to this Pauline text as one of the bases for its teaching, as does Vatican II.[10] I will focus on Aquinas's understanding of faith with particular attention to the near omnipresent place that the eleventh chapter of the Letter to the Hebrews has in his presentation of the matter. Hebrews 11 affirms two things that inform Aquinas's thinking on faith and reason. First, the text offers the classic definition of faith as "the substance of things to be hoped for, the argument [or assurance] of things that appear not [not seen] (v. 1)." Faith is assuring or firm, but of things not seen. Secondly, a few verses later we learn that "without faith it is impossible to please God. For he that cometh to God, must believe that He is, and is a rewarder to them that seek him (v. 6)." These two truths—that God is and that God cares for those who seek him—bring together the relationship between the diverse modes of knowing God and the truths of Revelation assented to in faith. These truths also help forge Aquinas's understanding of the progressive development of revealed truth as perfective of man's natural knowledge.

Kant, Locke, and Russell on Faith and Reason

I will commence these reflections with some comments of Immanuel Kant, John Locke, and Bertrand Russell pertinent to the faith-reason question, for the sake of establishing the particular insight and contribution that Aquinas makes to this question. This list of commentators could certainly be expanded, but Locke, Kant, and Russell provide a representative sample of the sentiments of modern thinkers who subordinate the certainty and

9. *The Decrees of the Ecumenical Councils*, vol. 2, ed. Norman Tanner, SJ (Washington D.C.: Georgetown University Press, 1990), 806. For a helpful presentation of the *praeambula fidei* see McInerny, *Praeambula Fidei*, especially 3–32.

10. See the Dogmatic Constitution on Divine Revelation, *Dei Verbum*, §6. "Confitetur Sacra Synodus, "Deum, rerum omnium principium et finem, naturali humanae rationis lumine e rebus creatis certo cognosci posse" (Rom 1:20); eius vero revelationi tribuendum esse docet, "ut ea, quae in rebus divinis humanae rationi per se impervia non sunt, in praesenti quoque generis humani conditione ab omnibus expedite, firma certitudine et nullo admixto errore cognosci possint."

credibility of faith to the judgment of reason, situating the whole conversation within the parameters of their psychology and epistemology.[11]

John Locke, writing with a keen awareness of the difficulties raised by Descartes's methodological doubt, proposes an understanding of the relationship between faith and reason that is rooted in empiricist epistemology. Locke argues that the existence of God is naturally demonstrable, yet the nature of the demonstration is deduced from one's own existence. God's existence, in Locke's argument, issues from the intuitive idea of one's own existence, which is not derived from (empirical) experience. "The knowledge of our own being," Locke grants, "we have by intuition. The existence of a God, reason clearly makes known." Knowledge of all other created entities "is to be had only by actual sensation."[12] Locke's understanding of the natural knowledge of God's existence is therefore based not on the adequation of the mind with extra-mental reality, but on the deduction of God from the mind. In consequence, the role of a probablistic judgment of reason stands paramount in Locke's understanding of the credibility of faith. "For whatsoever truth we come to the clear discovery of, from the knowledge and contemplation of our own ideas," Locke holds, "will always be certainer to us than those which are conveyed to us by *traditional revelation.*"[13] Because of the putative limited certainty of Revelation, Locke affirms that "the knowledge we have that this revelation came at first from God can never be so sure as the knowledge we have from the clear and distinct perception of the agreement or disagreement of our own ideas."[14] Speaking of the certitude that can be known only through Revelation, such as the story of Noah and the Flood or the Mosaic authorship of Genesis, Locke asserts "that the assurance of its being a revelation is still less than the assurance of [the] senses."[15] Likewise, when addressing the question of the certitude of revealed truth vis-à-vis the very truthfulness of God himself who is the author of Revelation, Locke maintains that "it still belongs to reason to judge of the truth of its being a revelation, and of the signification of the words wherein it is delivered."[16]

Locke's epistemology of faith accordingly leaves the believer in a circular situation. While he does not rule out natural knowledge of God's existence, nor is he opposed to the existence of divine Revelation, there is no natural continuity between what is known via these two diverse orders. Knowledge

---

11. For a presentation of the problem of the relationship between faith, reason, and certitude see Avery Dulles, SJ, *The Assurance of Things Hoped For: A Theology of Christian Faith* (New York: Oxford University Press, 1997).

12. Locke, *An Essay Concerning Human Understanding*, book IV, chapter 11, 1.

13. Ibid., book IV, chapter 11, 4.   14. Ibid., IV, 18, 4.

15. Ibid.   16. Ibid., 18, 8.

that is certain is placed within the parameters of empiricism, whereas the credibility of faith is subject to the empirically bound judgment of reason.

Kant, for his part, in his essay *What Is Enlightenment?* declares the following:

Enlightenment is man's release from his self-incurred tutelage. Tutelage is man's inability to make use of his understanding without direction from another. Self-incurred is this tutelage when its cause lies not in lack of reason but in lack of resolution and courage to use it without direction from another. *Sapere aude!* "Have courage to use your own reason!"—that is the motto of enlightenment.[17]

This famous statement, which is the opening salvo of the essay, has manifest implications for the credibility of faith: theological faith obviously proposes truths that are beyond the natural demonstrative power of reason, truths that must be communicated by another. It is clear, at least by deduction, that the epistemological value of faith, especially regarding truths of the speculative order, is accordingly reduced by Kant to the unenlightened use of reason under the direction of another.[18] It is true that Kant allowed for what Dulles terms "a certain type of faith" within the practical-moral order, but reducing faith to the moral realm necessarily founds it on "personal motives that are subjectively compelling though objectively insufficient."[19]

Bertrand Russell stands as an articulate ancestor of the Kantian and Lockean assessment of the epistemological value of faith. As the setup to his presentation—and ultimate rejection—of arguments in favor of God's existence in his famous essay, *Why I Am Not a Christian*, Russell makes the following observation about the teaching of the Catholic Church on the natural knowability of God's existence: "You know, of course, that the Catholic Church has laid it down as a dogma," he quips, "that the existence of God can be proved by unaided reason. That is a somewhat curious dogma, but it is one of their dogmas." He continues by further offering what he deems to be the reason for this dogma: "They had to introduce it because at one time the freethinkers adopted the habit of saying that there were such and such arguments which mere reason might urge against the existence of God, but of course they knew as a matter of faith that God did exist." As a result of

17. Kant, *Foundation of the Metaphysics of Morals*, 2d ed., trans. Lewis Whitebeck (New Jersey: Prentice-Hall, Inc., 1997), 83.

18. In *The Assurance of Things Hoped For*, 206, Dulles summarizes Kant's position in this way: "Immanuel Kant, although he owed much to the rational critique of Christianity, limited the scope of speculative reason and thereby made room for faith as sovereign in the realm of moral values. In this he was followed by Protestant liberal theologians, who erected a dichotomy between speculative truth, which falls within the competence of reason alone, and practical truth, which is based on the axioms of faith."

19. Dulles, *A History of Apologetics* (San Francisco: Ignatius Press, 2005), 209–10.

the challenge of these "freethinkers," Russell surmises that "the Catholic Church felt that they must stop it. Therefore they laid it down that the existence of God can be proved by the unaided reason and they had to set up what they considered were arguments to prove it."[20]

Proceeding without the Christian a priori commitment to faith and accentuating what he deems to be the shortcomings of the rational arguments for God's existence and other philosophic inconsistencies intrinsic to the faith claims of Christianity, Russell makes the following conclusion: "I see no reason, therefore, to believe in any sort of God, however vague and however attenuated."[21]

There is obviously a great deal lacking in Russell's understanding of the Church's teaching on man's natural ability to come to know God. Perhaps, however, what is more worthy of comment is the relationship that Russell, Kant, and Locke assume to exist between what Christians claim to know by faith and the power of reason to naturally know such truths as the existence of God.

The arguments of these notable philosophers seem to fall directly within the scope of one of Jacques Maritain's musings about how modern philosophers understand the relationship between faith and philosophy. "Some modern philosophers who disbelieve in Christian revelation," Maritain observes, "presume to judge in terms of their own particular assumptions concerning this revelation the relationship established in the Christian system between philosophy and faith."[22] Speaking about himself as a believing philosopher, Maritain then quickly adds this additional clarification, "Surely, if I did not believe that the primordial Truth itself is my teacher in the tenets of faith, if I believed that faith presents me with a mere code binding me to a human tradition, I would not accept the subordination of philosophy to faith."[23]

Conversely, Russell seems to be working from the all-too-common premise—and this is where I think his assessment is farthest from the mark— that the assent to the truths of faith flows from the demonstrative veracity of philosophical arguments such as the ones for God's existence. Russell insinuates that the Church maintains the natural knowability of the so-called preambles of faith, not because of their truthfulness or her long-standing

20. Bertrand Russell, *Why I Am Not a Christian and Other Essays on Religion and Related Subjects*, ed. P. Edwards (New York: Simon and Schuster, 1963), 5–6.

21. Ibid., 33.

22. Jacques Maritain, *An Essay on Christian Philosophy*, trans. Edward Flannery (New York: Philosophical Library, Inc., 1955), 35.

23. Ibid., 36.

recognition of the harmony between the orders of faith and reason, but as a preemptive strike against opposing philosophical arguments.

Having in mind the example of Russell and the foundations laid by his Enlightenment ancestors,[24] in the remaining sections of this chapter I examine Aquinas's teaching on the relationship between faith and reason in the specific area of which the modern treatments seem wholly unaware—namely, faith and its epistemological value.

Science, Faith, and Opinion

In the *prima pars* of the *Summa theologiae* Aquinas introduces the *praeambula fidei* in the second question on God's existence. Here he first affirms that "the existence of God and other like truths about God, which can be known by natural reason, are not articles of faith, but are preambles to the articles." Aquinas develops this position because of the relationship between the natural and supernatural orders, "for faith presupposes natural knowledge, even as grace presupposes nature, and perfection supposes something that can be perfected." However, he immediately adds the following caveat, "Nevertheless, there is nothing to prevent a man, who cannot grasp a proof, accepting, as a matter of faith, something which in itself is capable of being scientifically known and demonstrated."[25]

24. The position adopted by Russell, carved out in large part by the parameters set by Locke and Kant, is not unlike the approach of many others who take up the question within the philosophy of religion. For example, see Peter van Inwagen, "It Is Wrong, Everywhere, Always, and for Anyone, to Believe Anything upon Insufficient Evidence," in *Philosophy of Religion: The Big Questions*, ed. Eleonore Stump and Michael Murray (Oxford: Blackwell Publishers, 1999), 273–84. In this article van Inwagen responds to William Clifford's famous anti-religious axiom which holds that "it is wrong always, everywhere, and for any one, to believe anything upon insufficient evidence." Van Inwagen rightly points out that Clifford's principle creates an epistemic standard that is scarcely followed even outside of religion, thus implicating many who hold no religious belief at all. However, van Inwagen's response is limited to moral culpability and offers no speculative explanation for the motive or nature of assent in matters of religious faith, nor is there any differentiation between the assent given to naturally demonstrable truths and truths proposed in faith. To some minimal degree everyone may live by faith or trust, but establishing this says little about the relationship between reason and religious faith.

25. Thomas Aquinas, *Summa theologiae* (hereafter *ST*) I, q. 2, a. 2, ad 1. "Deum esse, et alia huiusmodi quae per rationem naturalem nota possunt esse de Deo, ut dicitur Rom. I non sunt articuli fidei, sed praeambula ad articulos, sic enim fides praesupponit cognitionem naturalem, sicut gratia naturam, et ut perfectio perfectibile. Nihil tamen prohibet illud quod secundum se demonstrabile est et scibile, ab aliquo accipi ut credibile, qui demonstrationem non capit."

All English citations from the *Summa theologiae*, unless otherwise noted, are taken from the translation of the Fathers of the English Dominican Province originally published in 1911 and reprinted in five volumes as *The Summa Theologica of St. Thomas Aquinas* (Allen, Tex.: Christian Classics, 1981). The Latin texts, unless otherwise noted, are taken from E. Alarcón's posting of the *corpus Thomisticum* at www.corpusthomisticum.org.

This distinction between knowing by faith and knowing through scientific demonstration constitutes a foundational aspect of Aquinas's understanding of the relationship between faith and reason.[26] It is important to call to mind here, in light of the initial insights drawn from De Koninck and McInerny and the positions of Locke, Kant, and Russell noted above, that Aquinas did not approach epistemology with the same preoccupations that occupy modern philosophers.[27] This does not mean, of course, that Aquinas has nothing to say to us—he does indeed. Aquinas has different answers to these questions, in large part, because of his different conceptual framework, and we can learn something from this framework as well.

When Aquinas identifies the object of faith in the *secunda secundae*, he notes that the object of every cognitive habit has two aspects, the formal and the material. The material aspect is nothing other than "that which is known materially," and the formal aspect is "that whereby it is known."[28] The formal aspect, or that whereby the object of faith is known, is held by Aquinas to be "nothing else than the First Truth." "For the faith of which we are speaking," he says, "does not assent to anything, except because it is revealed by God." The mind assents in faith on account of the things of faith being disclosed by God Himself. Following this distinction, Aquinas identifies the difference between knowing God through faith and by *scientia*.[29]

The difference between what is known scientifically by reason through demonstration and by faith is presented by Aquinas in terms of seeing. The assent of the intellect to what is known (seen) happens in different ways. In the first way the intellect assents to the object because it is known or seen by the knower either in itself, as is the case with first principles, "or through something already known,"[30] as happens in demonstration. Nonetheless, it

26. For a thorough and rigorous treatment of *scientia* in Aquinas see John I. Jenkins, *Knowledge and Faith in Thomas Aquinas* (Cambridge: Cambridge University Press, 1997).

27. "The questions of Thomas Aquinas about knowledge and faith are not ours," John Jenkins reminds us. "When Aquinas raises broadly epistemic questions," Jenkins continues, "he does so in a different conceptual framework" (ibid, 1).

28. *ST* II-II, q. 1, a. 1, c. "cuiuslibet cognoscitivi habitus obiectum duo habet, scilicet id quod materialiter cognoscitur, quod est sicut materiale obiectum; et id per quod cognoscitur, quod est formalis ratio obiecti."

29. Ibid., a. 2, c. "cognita sunt in cognoscente secundum modum cognoscentis. Est autem modus proprius humani intellectus ut componendo et dividendo veritatem cognoscat, sicut in primo dictum est. Et ideo ea quae sunt secundum se simplicia intellectus humanus cognoscit secundum quandam complexionem, sicut e converso intellectus divinus incomplexe cognoscit ea quae sunt secundum se complexa. Sic igitur obiectum fidei dupliciter considerari potest. Uno modo, ex parte ipsius rei creditae, et sic obiectum fidei est aliquid incomplexum, scilicet res ipsa de qua fides habetur. Alio modo, ex parte credentis, et secundum hoc obiectum fidei est aliquid complexum per modum enuntiabilis. Et ideo utrumque vere opinatum fuit apud antiquos, et secundum aliquid utrumque est verum."

30. Ibid., a. 4, c. "Uno modo, quia ad hoc movetur ab ipso obiecto, quod est vel per seipsum

may be that the intellect is not "moved to this assent by its proper object, but through an act of choice, whereby it turns voluntarily to one side rather than to the other." If this turning to one side rather than the other be, according to Aquinas, "accompanied by doubt and fear of the opposite side, there will be opinion." Conversely, "if there be certainty and no fear of the other side, there will be faith."[31] As a result, Aquinas maintains that "all science is derived from self-evident and therefore seen principles; wherefore all objects of science must needs be, in a fashion, seen."[32] By contrast, when speaking of the assent of the intellect in faith he explains, "faith implies assent of the intellect to that which is believed."[33] "Wherefore it is evident," he concludes, "that neither faith nor opinion can be of things seen either by the senses or by the intellect."[34]

This does not mean that Aquinas does not deem faith to be a form of knowing or seeing in any sense whatsoever. To the contrary, faith can indeed be referred to as a form of seeing, but a seeing that virtuously—as an infused habit—inclines one to believe rightly, not a form of seeing in which the object itself is held by the intellect. "The light of faith," Aquinas teaches, "makes us see what we believe. For just as, by the habits of the other virtues, man sees what is becoming to him in respect of that habit, so, by the habit of faith, the human mind is directed to assent to such things as are becoming to a right faith, and not to assent to others."[35]

While Aquinas is ready to admit that the object of faith, First Truth, is above the natural light of reason, it does not follow for him that the assent of faith has no rational basis. Drawing on the distinction between faith, science, and opinion, Aquinas holds: "Those things which come under faith can be considered in two ways. First, in particular; and thus they cannot be seen and believed at the same time."[36] That is, knowledge understood

<hr>

cognitum, sicut patet in principiis primis, quorum est intellectus; vel est per aliud cognitum, sicut patet de conclusionibus, quarum est scientia."

31. Ibid. "Alio modo intellectus assentit alicui non quia sufficienter moveatur ab obiecto proprio, sed per quandam electionem voluntarie declinans in unam partem magis quam in aliam. Et si quidem hoc fit cum dubitatione et formidine alterius partis, erit opinio, si autem fit cum certitudine absque tali formidine, erit fides."

32. Ibid., a. 5, c. "omnis scientia habetur per aliqua principia per se nota, et per consequens visa. Et ideo oportet quaecumque sunt scita aliquo modo esse visa."

33. Ibid., a. 4, c. "fides importat assensum intellectus ad id quod creditur."

34. Ibid. "Unde manifestum est quod nec fides nec opinio potest esse de visis aut secundum sensum aut secundum intellectum."

35. Ibid., ad 3. "lumen fidei facit videre ea quae creduntur. Sicut enim per alios habitus virtutum homo videt illud quod est sibi conveniens secundum habitum illum, ita etiam per habitum fidei inclinatur mens hominis ad assentiendum his quae conveniunt rectae fidei et non aliis."

36. Ibid., ad 2. "ea quae subsunt fidei dupliciter considerari possunt. Uno modo, in speciali, et sic non possunt esse simul visa et credita, sicut dictum est."

as seeing cannot coexist with either faith or opinion in respect of the same object. However, Aquinas does not simply leave us without any connection between faith and natural knowledge. He adds (besides) the particular aspect in which the things of faith cannot be seen: "Secondly, in general … under the common aspect of credibility; and in this way" the things of faith "are seen by the believer. For he would not believe unless, on the evidence of signs, or of something similar, he saw that they ought to be believed."[37]

In his *Expositio* on the *De Trinitate* of Boethius, Aquinas situates the life of faith squarely within the healthy use of reason. "Living according to reason," Aquinas admits, "is our good insofar as we are human. Living apart from reason in one sense can be taken as a defect, as in the case of those who live sensually; and this is an evil for us."[38] However, when considering the life of faith in relation to reason, he then adds:

In another sense it [living apart from reason] can mean an excess, as when a person is led by divine grace to what is above reason. In the latter sense living apart from reason is not an evil for us but a good that is above us. Knowledge of the truths of faith is of this sort, though faith itself is not entirely apart from reason, for natural reason maintains that we should assent to the words of God.[39]

In other words, reason may not be able to see the truths of faith with the clarity of demonstrative science, but this does not mean that faith's act of assent itself is contrary to reason. Faith as such never claims scientific demonstration as its motive for assent.

Aquinas's position on the assent of faith, stands, therefore, on premises that are not determined by the epistemic problems encountered by Locke, Kant, and Russell. His understanding of the assent of faith is rooted in the

37. Ibid. "Alio modo, in generali, scilicet sub communi ratione credibilis. Et sic sunt visa ab eo qui credit, non enim crederet nisi videret ea esse credenda, vel propter evidentiam signorum vel propter aliquid huiusmodi."

It should be noted, however, that the existence of signs does not negate the unseen nature of faith. "Aquinas holds that miracles," Bruce Marshall points out, "are in fact epistemically dispensable for Christian faith. We would have to believe what Christ teaches even if it were accompanied by no visible signs." Marshall, "*Quod Scit Una Uetula*: Aquinas on the Nature of Theology," in *The Theology of Thomas Aquinas*, ed. Rik Van Nieuwenhove and Joseph Wawrykow (Notre Dame, Ind.: University of Notre Dame Press, 2005), 12–13.

38. *In Boeth. De Trin.*, q. 3, a. 1., ad 5, in Aquinas, *Faith, Reason and Theology*, trans. Armand Maurer (Toronto: Pontifical Institute of Mediaeval Studies, 1987), 69. "vivere secundum rationem est bonum hominis in quantum est homo, vivere autem praeter rationem potest uno modo sonare in defectum, sicut est in illis qui vivunt secundum sensum, et hoc est hominis malum."

39. Ibid., 69–70. "Alio modo potest sonare in excessum, ut cum homo divina gratia adducitur in id quod est supra rationem; et sic praeter rationem vivere non est hominis malum, sed bonum supra hominem. Et talis est cognitio eorum quae sunt fidei, quamvis et ipsa fides non omnibus modis sit praeter rationem; hoc enim naturalis ratio habet, quod assentiendum est his quae a Deo dicuntur."

fact of creaturely finitude relative to the infinity of God. In Thomas's understanding of the cosmos, the human mind acknowledges that even the height of metaphysics does not exhaust the frontiers of possible knowledge.[40] "Aquinas firmly insists, however," Bruce Marshall observes, "that believing what we cannot see would only be a mistake if we could see everything—if we 'could know perfectly all things visible and invisible.'"[41] With God as its object, faith, therefore, will always be in the unseen, not because of any epistemic weakness, but, on the contrary, because of the majesty of its object.

Faith and Merit

Aquinas's systemization of this issue is heavily influenced by his understanding of the irreplaceable role that faith has within the economy of salvation. Faith's assent to the unseen on the authority of God is meritorious in the order of salvation.

Aquinas identifies the relation of reason to merit from two different perspectives: the perspective of one who does not have faith and the perspective of one who does. Reason may, Aquinas acknowledges, come before the assent of the will, "as, for instance, when a man either has not the will, or not a prompt will, to believe, unless he be moved by human reasons."[42] If this is actually the case, "human reason," Aquinas maintains, "diminishes the merit of faith." This is so, he explains, because man "ought ... to believe matters of faith, not on account of human reason, but on account of the Divine authority."[43] Human reason, however, may also interact with faith consequent to a man's coming to believe. "For when a man's will is ready to believe," Aquinas explains, "he loves the truth he believes, he thinks out and takes to heart whatever reasons he can find in support thereof; and in this way human reason does not exclude the merit of faith but is a sign of greater merit."[44]

40. Maritain explains: "That, then, is the poverty of metaphysics (and yet its majesty, too). It awakens a desire for supreme union, for spiritual possession completed in the order of reality and not only in the concept. It cannot satisfy that desire." *The Degrees of Knowledge*, trans. Gerald Phelan (Notre Dame, Ind.: University of Notre Dame Press, 1995), 7.

41. Marshall, "*Quod Scit Una Uetula*," 2.

42. *ST* II-II, q. 2, a. 10, c. "Uno quidem modo, sicut praecedens, puta cum quis aut non haberet voluntatem, aut non haberet promptam voluntatem ad credendum, nisi ratio humana induceretur."

43. Ibid. "Et sic ratio humana inducta diminuit meritum fidei, sicut etiam supra dictum est quod passio praecedens electionem in virtutibus moralibus diminuit laudem virtuosi actus. Sicut enim homo actus virtutum moralium debet exercere propter iudicium rationis, non propter passionem; ita credere debet homo ea quae sunt fidei non propter rationem humanam, sed propter auctoritatem divinam."

44. Ibid. "Cum enim homo habet promptam voluntatem ad credendum, diligit veritatem

Aquinas continues this line of reasoning by discussing explicitly the place of the preambles within the act of faith and the impact that they have on the merit of faith. Speaking directly to arguments in favor of revealed doctrines, such as the Trinity or the Incarnation, Aquinas holds: "The reasons which are brought forward in support of the authority of faith are not demonstrations which can bring intellectual vision to the human intellect, wherefore they do not cease to be unseen."[45] Such reasons on behalf of the authority of faith are important because "they remove obstacles to faith, by showing that what faith proposes is not impossible; wherefore such reasons do not diminish the merit or the measure of faith."[46] In short, those arguments which negate objections to revealed doctrines do not diminish the soteriological value of faith, because they do not positively demonstrate the doctrine in question but negatively refute challenges to it.

This does not mean that, in order to protect the merit of faith, Aquinas prefers the believer to remain in the dark about philosophical demonstrations in support of the preambles. "On the other hand," Aquinas adds, "though demonstrative reasons in support of the preambles of faith [the Leonine Edition reads: "in support of matters of faith which are however, preambles to the articles of faith, diminish," etc.], but not of the articles of faith, diminish the measure of faith, since they make the thing believed to be seen, yet they do not diminish the measure of charity, which makes the will ready to believe them, even if they were unseen; and so the measure of merit is not diminished."[47] Rational demonstration can lower the range of faith by bringing the object into sight, but for the docile believer, not the merit of charity, which continues to love and seek out that which is known.[48]

---

creditam, et super ea excogitat et amplectitur si quas rationes ad hoc invenire potest. Et quantum ad hoc ratio humana non excludit meritum fidei, sed est signum maioris meriti ..."

45. Ibid., ad 2. "rationes quae inducuntur ad auctoritatem fidei non sunt demonstrationes quae in visionem intelligibilem intellectum humanum reducere possunt. Et ideo non desinunt esse non apparentia."

46. Ibid. "Sed removent impedimenta fidei, ostendendo non esse impossibile quod in fide proponitur. Unde per tales rationes non diminuitur meritum fidei nec ratio fidei."

47. Ibid. "Sed rationes demonstrativae inductae ad ea quae sunt fidei, praeambula tamen ad articulos, etsi diminuant rationem fidei, quia faciunt esse apparens id quod proponitur; non tamen diminuunt rationem caritatis, per quam voluntas est prompta ad ea credendum etiam si non apparerent. Et ideo non diminuitur ratio meriti."

48. Faith's ongoing search for deeper understanding leads Maritain to draw the following conclusion about faith and mysticism: "An essentially superhuman formal object; a human mode of knowing: here lies ... the reason why faith will perpetually strive to exceed its own way of knowing. That is why faith, as distinct from metaphysics, will of itself place in the soul, at least radically, an unconditional desire for mystical contemplation properly so called, which, although it is contained within its own proper sphere, faith is nevertheless not adequate to procure all by itself." *The Degrees of Knowledge*, 268.

The presence of charity within the life of faith adds an epistemic note that is lacking in the modern thinkers examined above. Charity impresses onto the believer a certain familiarity or likeness of its unseen object such that the unseen object is, in a way, participated in by the creature.

In as much as charity seeks union with the good that is outside of oneself, it unites the believer with the object of faith in a firm way. Speaking of the credibility of faith in conjunction with the firmness of the assent of the believer, Aquinas argues:

The believer has sufficient motive for believing, for he is moved by the authority of Divine teaching confirmed by miracles, and, what is more, by the inward instinct of the Divine invitation: hence he does not believe lightly. He has not, however, sufficient reason for scientific knowledge, hence he does not lose the merit.[49]

In his *Commentary on the Epistle to the Hebrews* Aquinas offers a universal theological anthropology rooted in salvation history together with a speculative treatment of the relationship between faith and reason. Pondering the affirmation of Hebrews 11:6, which teaches that without faith it is impossible to please God, and that the person of faith must believe that God is and that God rewards, Aquinas wonders whether holding that faith or assent to God's existence and remuneration are sufficient to merit salvation. He explains, first, that "after the sin of the first parent, no one could be saved … except through faith in the mediator." The nature of this faith, though, "was diversified regarding the mode of believing according to the diversity of time and states."[50] Those privileged to believe in Christ "are held the more to believe than those who were before the coming of Christ." Likewise, "[T]hose also, who lived under the Law, were held to believe more explicitly than those before the law."[51] Aquinas applies the same reasoning, though more remotely, to some pre-Christian gentiles: "They believed that God was a remunerator, which remuneration happened not except through Christ. Hence, implicitly they believed in a mediator."[52]

49. *ST* II-II, q. 2, a. 9, ad 3. "ille qui credit habet sufficiens inductivum ad credendum, inducitur enim auctoritate divinae doctrinae miraculis confirmatae, et, quod plus est, interiori instinctu Dei invitantis. Unde non leviter credit. Tamen non habet sufficiens inductivum ad sciendum. Et ideo non tollitur ratio meriti."

50. *Commentary on the Epistle to the Hebrews*, trans. Chrysostom Baer, O. Praem. (South Bend, Ind.: St. Augustine's Press, 2006), 237 [§576]. "post peccatum primi parentis, nemo potuit salvari a reatu culpae originalis, nisi per fidem mediatoris; sed ista fides diversificata est quantum ad modum credendi secundum diversitatem temporum et statuum."

51. Ibid. "Nos autem quibus est tantum beneficium exhibitum, magis tenemur credere, quam illi qui fuerunt ante adventum Christi: tunc etiam aliqui magis explicite."

52. Ibid. "sed gentiles, qui fuerunt salvati, sufficiebat eis, quod crederent Deum esse remuneratorem, quae remuneratio non fit nisi per Christum. Unde implicite credebant in mediatorem."

This explanation leaves Aquinas with the task of explaining how the diversity of modes of knowing that God is and that God rewards can be viewed as faith that is pleasing to God, when the existence of God can be known—seen—by demonstration apart from faith. To this question Aquinas responds: "Knowledge about God can be had in many ways. First, through Christ.... And this is only believed.... In the second way, that God alone is adored—this was also believed by the Jews. In the third way, that God is one—this was known also to those philosophers and does not fall under faith."[53]

Drawing on these insights from Hebrews 11, in the *secunda secundae*, when discussing the object of faith, Aquinas asks whether articles of faith have multiplied over time. He uses this question as a means of inserting his thoughts on Hebrews 11 into the discussion about faith in the *Summa*. "All the articles are contained implicitly in certain primary matters of faith [in aliquibus primis credibilibus]," among which Aquinas includes "God's existence, and His providence over the salvation of man, according to Hebrews 11: 'He that cometh to God, must believe that He is, and is a rewarder to them that seek Him.'"[54] His reason for maintaining this position is as follows: "For the existence of God includes all that we believe to exist in God eternally, and in these our happiness consists; while belief in His providence includes all those things which God dispenses in time, for man's salvation, and which are the way to that happiness."[55]

We can now see emerging in Aquinas's understanding of faith and reason the touchstone between those truths about God knowable by reason and what is assented to in faith. Charles Journet explains this aspect of Aquinas's thought accordingly, "The two statements, God is, God is providence, represent statements which are completely basic. They contain in themselves, implicitly, all that will finally be revealed."[56] According to Aquinas's own words, the truths of faith advance organically from these foundational credibilia: "We shall be advanced to this knowledge," he admits, "not by anything due to our nature but only by divine grace. So, even for this

53. Ibid., 237 [§577]. "quod de Deo potest multipliciter haberi notitia. Uno modo per Christum.... Et hoc tantum est creditum.... Secundo modo, quod solus Deus colendus est, et sic etiam erat creditum a Iudaeis. Tertio modo, quod est unus Deus, et hoc notum est etiam ipsis philosophis, et non cadit sub fide."

54. *ST* II-II, q. 1, a. 7. "omnes articuli implicite continentur in aliquibus primis credibilibus, scilicet ut credatur Deus esse et providentiam habere circa hominum salutem, secundum illud ad Heb. XI, *accedentem ad Deum oportet credere quia est, et quod inquirentibus se remunerator sit.*"

55. Ibid. "In esse enim divino includuntur omnia quae credimus in Deo aeternaliter existere, in quibus nostra beatitudo consistit, in fide autem providentiae includuntur omnia quae temporaliter a Deo dispensantur ad hominum salutem, quae sunt via in beatitudinem."

56. Charles Journet, *What Is Dogma?* trans. Mark Pontifex (San Francisco: Ignatius Press, 2011), 36.

perfect knowledge certain presuppositions must be offered at the beginning for our belief, and from these we are led to the full knowledge of the thing we believe from the beginning."[57]

Aquinas holds to a clear and organic continuity between the most speculative article of faith and the most basic preamble. The articles of faith develop, unfold, and perfect the basic content of the preambles. Though faith goes beyond reason and remains unseen, it does not propose articles to the mind for assent that are not integrally related to what the mind can know naturally, even if it be factually the case that someone may assent to God in faith who does not know the demonstrative arguments supporting the preambles.

What role then does reason have in the life of faith, if it be true that faith is necessary for salvation and about things that are unseen? Speaking again of the object of faith, Aquinas argues that philosophy ought to be used by the believer "in order to demonstrate the preambles of faith, which we must necessarily know in [the act of] faith. Such are the truths about God that are proved by natural reason, for example, that God exists, that he is one, and other truths of this sort about God or creatures proved in philosophy and presupposed by faith."[58]

Those truths which can be known by reason and presupposed by faith are, according to Aquinas, "reckoned among the articles of faith, not because they are believed simply by all, but because they are a necessary presupposition to matters of faith, so that those who do not know them by demonstration must know them first of all by faith."[59] Commenting specifically on this point, that of the role of philosophy in the life of faith, Lawrence Dewan notes the following: "The willingness to believe on divine authority alone all that is contained in revelation dominates what must remain secondary, the mere possession of the demonstrative argument. The attitude of faith must pervade the whole of our mental life vis-à-vis what God has revealed."[60]

---

57. *In Boeth. De Trin.*, q. 3, a. 1, c. See *Faith, Reason and Theology*, 67. "Et ad hanc cognitionem homo perducetur non ex debito suae naturae, sed ex sola divina gratia. Unde oportet quod huius etiam perfectae scientiae quaedam suppositiones primo ei credendae proponantur, ex quibus dirigatur in plenam cognitionem eorum quae a principio credit."

58. Ibid., q. 2, a. 3, c. See *Faith, Reason and Theology*, 49. "Primo ad demonstrandum ea quae sunt praeambula fidei, quae necesse est in fide scire, ut ea quae naturalibus rationibus de Deo probantur, ut Deum esse, Deum esse unum et alia huiusmodi vel de Deo vel de creaturis in philosophia probata, quae fides supponit."

59. *ST* II-II, q. 1, a. 5, ad 3. "ea quae demonstrative probari possunt inter credenda numerantur, non quia de ipsis sit simpliciter fides apud omnes, sed quia praeexiguntur ad ea quae sunt fidei, et oportet ea saltem per fidem praesupponi ab his qui horum demonstrationem non habent."

60. Lawrence Dewan, OP, "Communion with the Tradition: For the Believer Who Is a Philosopher," *Science et Esprit* XL (1988): 315–25, 317. See also McInerny, *Praeambula Fidei*, 30, where McInerny explains: "What, then, of a believer who is a philosopher and who fashions

Nature and Grace, Similitude and Connaturality

Whether known in rational demonstration or accepted by faith, the preambles are held by all who believe, just as the gift of grace presupposes nature. "So it is impossible that the contents of philosophy should be contrary to the contents of faith," Aquinas specifies, "but they fall short of them. The former, however, bear certain likenesses to the latter and also contain certain preambles to them, just as nature itself is a preamble to grace."[61]

Aquinas's description of the similitude or "likeness" between the preambles and the articles of faith makes clear the continuity between the two orders of knowing. The assent of faith is indeed supernaturally motivated, but it is nevertheless not *unnatural* to believe. Moreover, given the "likeness" that exists between the preambles and the articles of faith, the supernatural character of the articles of faith does not render them wholly alien or contrary to what the mind can naturally attain. Likeness is not equality, but it is a foundation for continuity.

The role of the preambles in relation to the articles of faith enables Aquinas to explain the way that reason works within and aids the life of faith and sacred doctrine. It is not, as Russell accuses, that the Church, fearing that faith's defects will be exposed by the so-called freethinkers, invents counterarguments and a dogma to plug the levy. On the contrary, "Since therefore grace does not destroy nature, but perfects it," Aquinas explains in the first question of the *prima pars*, "natural reason should minister to faith as the natural bent of the will ministers to charity."[62] Just as charity properly orders the will to love God above all things, philosophical arguments are not the authoritative sources of faith but they do help the intellect to see or know by nature foundational truths that all of the articles of faith presuppose. "What St. Thomas has in mind as a program for the believer," Lawrence Dewan explains, "seems to require that one retain a believing attitude toward all of revelation, yet all the while striving to provide rational argument for its truths wherever such argument is feasible."[63]

---

a cogent proof of God's existence? Does he stop believing that God exists? This follows on the truth that it is impossible to know and believe the same truth at the same time … doesn't the proof establish that God is one? It does, but to believe that God is one *and* a trinity of persons can only be believed."

61. *In Boeth. De Trin.*, q. 2, a. 3, c. See *Faith, Reason and Theology*, 48. "unde impossibile est quod ea, quae sunt philosophiae, sint contraria his quae sunt fidei, sed deficiunt ab eis. Continent tamen aliquas eorum similitudines et quaedam ad ea praeambula, sicut natura praeambula est ad gratiam."

62. *ST* I, q. 1, a. 8, ad 2. "Cum enim gratia non tollat naturam, sed perficiat, oportet quod naturalis ratio subserviat fidei; sicut et naturalis inclinatio voluntatis obsequitur caritati."

63. Dewan, "Communion with the Tradition: For the Believer Who Is a Philosopher," 317.

From a methodological standpoint Aquinas even maintains that sacred doctrine "can in a sense depend upon the philosophical sciences, not as though it stood in need of them, but only in order to make its teaching clearer. For it accepts its principles not from other sciences, but immediately from God, by revelation."[64] Sacred doctrine then, as the science of faith, does not lack truth that it needs to import from outside of Revelation, but the human mind needs assistance in seeing certain matters presupposed by faith. So Aquinas declares the following about the use of philosophical arguments in sacred doctrine: "That it thus uses them is not due to its own defect or insufficiency, but to the defect of our intelligence, which is more easily led by what is known through natural reason (from which proceed the other sciences) to that which is above reason, such as are the teachings of this science."[65] Describing the teaching of Aquinas and his commentators on this point, Dulles distinguishes between the "motive of faith," which is always God and God alone, and "motives of credibility," which do not per se prove the truthfulness of faith but do provide rational reasons in its favor.[66]

The gracious and supernatural character of faith as a theological virtue necessitates that two further elements need to be added to this consideration. The first pertains to the inner workings of grace that correspond to the external motives of credibility and the rational arguments in support of the preambles. For Aquinas, unlike for Kant in particular, speculative reason is not simply a cold, calculating faculty. In Aquinas's epistemology the object of knowledge (and of love) can become connatural with the knowing subject. Hence, even though the articles of faith remain unseen, there

64. *ST* I, q. 1, a. 5, ad 2. "haec scientia accipere potest aliquid a philosophicis disciplinis, non quod ex necessitate eis indigeat, sed ad maiorem manifestationem eorum quae in hac scientia traduntur. Non enim accipit sua principia ab aliis scientiis, sed immediate a Deo per revelationem."

65. Ibid. "Et hoc ipsum quod sic utitur eis, non est propter defectum vel insufficientiam eius, sed propter defectum intellectus nostri; qui ex his quae per naturalem rationem (ex qua procedunt aliae scientiae) cognoscuntur, facilius manuducitur in ea quae sunt supra rationem, quae in hac scientia traduntur."

See also Bruce D. Marshall, "Faith and Reason Reconsidered: Aquinas and Luther on Deciding What Is True," *The Thomist* 63 (1999): 1–48. In this very helpful article on the commonalities between Aquinas and Luther on the relationship between faith and reason, Marshall contends that the general presupposition that the Aquinas and Luther are worlds apart on the question of faith and reason is misguided. Marshall argues: "Aquinas and Luther hold basically the same view of faith and reason: the view that the most central Christian beliefs, those generated by communal interpretation of Scripture according to creedal rules, enjoy unrestricted primacy" (2). Although Marshall readily admits that Aquinas and Luther do genuinely disagree on "Aristotle and Philosophy" (47), it seems that the main thrust of his argument stands correct only relative to faith as such.

66. Dulles, *The Assurance of Things Hoped For*, 214. See also J. Jenkins, *Knowledge and Faith in Thomas Aquinas*, 161ff.

can be a quasi-experiential knowledge of them. This nuance in Aquinas's thought can be clearly discerned in the following text, where he explains the impact that faith has on the believer: "There arises here and now in us a certain sharing in, and a likeness to, the divine knowledge, to the extent that through the faith implanted in us we firmly grasp the primary truth itself for its own sake."[67]

In Aquinas's system the judgment of reason is, unlike in the case of Locke, not placed above faith such that it passes final verdict on it. Faith is "a faint stamp of the First Truth in our mind."[68] The mind is thus not cast against faith as a foreigner to it, but molded and inclined to it from within. Explaining Aquinas's position on this point, Bruce Marshall notes that "the believer's assent to the articles of faith springs not from a mere wish for what one would like there to be, but from a prior intimacy with the God who makes himself available to us in the articles as our last end. This grace-wrought intimacy with God—or 'connaturality,' as Aquinas sometimes puts it—spontaneously recognizes in the creedal articles the God of whose goodness and love it already enjoys a taste."[69]

Additionally, Aquinas teaches that two of the gifts of the Holy Spirit, understanding (*intellectus*) and knowledge (*scientia*), are also given to aid the infused virtue of faith in reaching its perfection. Because the natural powers of the human mind are finite whereas the object of faith is infinite, Aquinas argues: "Consequently man needs a supernatural light in order to penetrate further still so as to know what it cannot know by its natural light: and this supernatural light which is bestowed on man is called the gift of understanding."[70] Aquinas holds that this deeper penetration gives man a firm hold upon, or understanding of, the articles proposed for belief, which would not be possessed without the help of the gift of understanding. The gift of knowledge or science augments the grasp that the mind has of the articles of faith through understanding by enabling the believer to "have a sure and right judgment . . . so as to discern what is to be believed from what is not to be believed." Aquinas concludes that "for this the gift of knowledge is required."[71]

67. *In Boeth. De Trin.*, q. 2, a. 2, c. See *Faith, Reason and Theology*, 42. "sed fit nobis in statu viae quaedam illius cognitionis participatio et assimilatio ad cognitionem divinam, in quantum per fidem nobis infusam inhaeremus ipsi primae veritati propter se ipsam."

68. *In Boeth. De Trin.*, q. 3, a. 1, ad 4. See *Faith, Reason and Theology*, 69. "Lumen autem fidei, quod est quasi quaedam sigillatio primae veritatis in mente."

69. Marshall, "*Quod Scit Uetula*," 14.

70. *ST* II-II, q. 8, a. 1, c. "Indiget igitur homo supernaturali lumine ut ulterius penetret ad cognoscendum quaedam quae per lumen naturale cognoscere non valet. Et illud lumen supernaturale homini datum vocatur donum intellectus."

71. *ST* II-II, q. 9, a. 1, c. "ut habeat certum et rectum iudicium de eis, discernendo scilicet credenda non credendis. Et ad hoc necessarium est donum scientiae."

Conclusion

At the beginning of this chapter a few passages were put forth from Immanuel Kant, John Locke, and Bertrand Russell that broadly represent the assessment of not a few contemporary thinkers on faith's relationship to reason, but certainly not two of Aquinas's recent disciples, De Koninck and McInerny. What I have hoped to demonstrate here is not the obvious fact that Russell's and other like positions are at odds with a Christian outlook; little effort is needed to establish this. I have instead hoped to sketch how St. Thomas Aquinas understands the place of reason within the life of faith. This is all adroitly encapsulated by a line from Aquinas's *Expositio* on Boethius's *De Trinitate*: "The teaching of the philosophers," Aquinas explains, "is not to be used as though it held first place, in such a way that the truth of faith should be believed because of it."[72] In other words, Christians do not assent to God in faith because of human demonstration, but on account of God himself—hence, *Aristotelian-Thomists are not rationalists.*

72. *In Boeth. De Trin.*, q. 2, a. 3, ad 1. See *Faith, Reason and Theology*, 49. "doctrina philosophorum non sit utendum quasi principali, ut scilicet propter eam veritas fidei credatur."

CHAPTER EIGHT

Philosophical Starting Points

Reason and Order in Aquinas's Introductions to the *Posterior Analytics, De Caelo,* and *Nicomachean Ethics*

KEVIN WHITE

To go by the first article of Aquinas's *Summa theologiae*, as well as by the traditional order of seminary courses, the place of philosophy in theological education would seem to be before, or at least at, the beginning. To go by the *Summa* as a whole, and by the way in which theology is customarily taught, philosophy permeates theological education from beginning to end, although it is changed in doing so. Philosophy in theological education is a *principium* in two senses: it is both a point of departure and a continuing resource.

Philosophy is inquiry into the principles of things, all things. In philosophy, human reason discovers itself as a principle of awareness in the presence of its objects. Because of its interest in principles, philosophy cannot but be interested in the fact that it itself becomes a principle, that is, both a starting point and a pervasive influence, in theological education. Philosophy is reminded by this fact of its own beginnings and educational concerns. Philosophy is said to begin in wonder. How does one first address human reason, in the hope of provoking and encouraging its wonder? How does one perform the introduction of human reason to its objects and itself? How does one begin to teach philosophy?

If we turn to the works of Aquinas with these questions in mind, we are naturally drawn to the introductions of his twelve Aristotelian commentaries.[1] These introductions make up a set of philosophical starting points that are especially attractive to anyone looking for that apparently elusive thing in Aquinas's work, *philosophia pura*. In the bodies of the commentaries, Aquinas's self-effacement as expositor leaves him open to the suspicion that he is less than fully philosophically engaged in what he is expounding. His theological writings raise the contrary suspicion, that he is always philosophical in these writings, but always also more than philosophical; as he himself says, those who use philosophical teachings in sacred doctrine are not watering wine down, so to speak, but rather changing water into wine—in other words, turning philosophical teachings into theological ones.[2] But in the introductions to the Aristotelian commentaries, he seems, however briefly, to get the philosophical tone just right. From the opening words *Sicut dicit* with which he introduces an epigrammatic remark of Aristotle's from a work other than the one he is going to comment on, Aquinas speaks in these introductions with remarkable philosophical freedom.[3]

At first glance, the *Sicut dicit* opening of scholastic books might seem to be a formula of abject submission to authority. In fact, it is quite the opposite, namely, a way of using an authority to make it say what one wants to have said at the outset of one's remarks. If I simply tell you what someone has said, I make a neutral report; but if I introduce my quotation by saying "*As* he says," I imply my agreement with something said well, something I have appropriated that I expect you to find congenial also. The "as" makes all the difference. ("*So* he says," by contrast, conveys either neutrality or doubt.)[4] The *Sicut dicit* opening is a remote ancestor of the modern epigraph, likewise chosen by an author as a means of getting things going by having someone else say something, something on which author and reader

1. See *Thomas von Aquin Prologe zu den Aristoteles-Kommentaren*, ed. Francis Cheneval and Ruedi Imbach (Frankfurt am Main: Klostermann, 1993); and Jean-Baptiste Échivard, *Une Introduction à la philosophie: Les proèmes des lectures de saint Thomas d'Aquin aux principales oeuvres d'Aristote. 1. L'esprit des disciplines philosophiques fondamentales; 2. Science rationelle et philosophie de la nature; 3. Philosophie morale et politique; 4. Métaphysique* (Paris: François-Xavier de Guibert, 2004–6).

2. *Super Boetium De Trinitate*, q. 2, a. 3, obj. 5 and ad 5 (Leonine ed., 50:97.36–41, 100.213–16).

3. Aquinas's introductions to the *Physics* and the *Meteorologica* are unusual in not having the *Sicut dicit* opening.

4. "And a wide range of possibilities exists between belief and neutrality, between neutrality and disbelief: I can quote doubtfully, assuredly, with probability or with certainty, suspiciously or mockingly. Such doxic variations are made possible by the distinction between my own statement and what I quote." Robert Sokolowski, *Pictures, Quotations, and Distinctions: Fourteen Essays in Phenomenology* (Notre Dame, Ind.: University of Notre Dame Press, 1992), 33.

can implicitly agree, or at least something they can agree to think about, at the start of their relationship.[5] But whereas the modern author leaves it to the reader to find the connection between the epigraph and the work over which it stands, the art of the introduction as practiced by Aquinas consists in making the connection explicit, by generating from the epigraph other remarks that, in some at first unforeseeable but in retrospect inevitable way, will lead to the subject of the book at hand, and so to the book itself, allowing the exposition to begin. As he enlarges on his epigraph, speaking, as it were, in his own name and in his own voice, it is interesting to see, in each case, what Aquinas makes of the opportunity. In some of the introductions he moves quickly from epigraph to exposition; in others, he is more leisurely, starting from a remote vantage point that allows him to develop a sort of brief philosophical essay of his own, before getting down to the business of commenting.

The introductions typically refer to other books of the Aristotelian corpus as background and context of the book to be discussed.[6] The implication is that the Aristotelian corpus is an ordered whole that is, in a way, the whole of philosophy, and within which the book has an exact and explicable location. Aquinas presents the order of Aristotle's works as he does the order of topics in each book, that is, as an order of "consideration" that follows an order present in what is being considered. The introductions show how far he is from Descartes's procedure of supposing an order in things that are not themselves ordered; they also nicely illustrate the fact that *consideratio* and *considerare* are among his favorite words.[7] In this perspective, the order of the Aristotelian corpus is not some literary accident, but a reflection of the order of things, to the extent that this order has been uncovered and articulated by human reason.

Usually, then, Aquinas's introductions to Aristotle are concerned to clarify the rationale of the order of Aristotle's works. Three of them, however—the introductions to the *Posterior Analytics*, the *De caelo*, and the *Nicomachean Ethics*—begin, not with the commentator's "practical" task of placing the work to be discussed in the corpus, but with theoretical reflection on reason and order themselves, and on relations between them. I propose to

5. See the chapter on epigraphs in Kevin Jackson, *Invisible Forms: A Guide to Literary Curiosities* (London: Macmillan, 1999), 80–103.

6. Among the introductions to Aquinas's twelve Aristotelian commentaries, only the introductions to the commentaries on the *Politics* and the *Metaphysics* do not refer by name to books of the Aristotelian corpus other than the one being commented on.

7. "Consideration," for Aquinas, signifies the act of an intellect looking at the truth of a thing (*consideratio importat actum intellectus veritatem rei intuentis*). *Summa theologiae* II-II, q. 53, a. 4 (Leonine ed., 8:392a).

review these three introductions, tracing this double theme of reason and order that runs through them, and keeping in mind the question of how to begin the teaching of philosophy.[8]

The Art of Arts: Introduction to the *Posterior Analytics*

The introduction to the *Posterior Analytics* is an introduction to logic that begins with a quotation from Aristotle's *Metaphysics* on human life: humankind lives by art and reasons (*arte et rationibus*) (980b27–28).[9] In this remark, Aquinas says, the Philosopher seems to touch on a certain property (*proprium*) of man, by which he differs from other animals. Other animals are driven to their acts—*ad suos actus aguntur*, are passively "activated" in their acts—but man is directed in his acts by judgment of reason. Aquinas's comment shifts the focus from the human way of life of which Aristotle speaks to human acts. It also introduces and illustrates the logical notion of property.

The direction of human acts by reason explains why there are various arts that serve the carrying out of human actions in an easy and orderly way (*faciliter et ordinate*): for an art seems to be nothing but a definite ordering of reason (*certa ordinatio rationis*) as to how human acts may reach their due end through predetermined means. This is broader than the definition of art as right reason in making that Aquinas gives elsewhere.[10] The notion of human acts in the present discussion is correspondingly broad. Acts of making, as well as moral acts, are implicitly included, but neither making nor morality is emphasized at this point, although the art of building will be mentioned shortly. Art, broadly understood, then, involves a relation between reason and order from two points of view: it is itself an *ordinatio*, an ordering, established by reason, of means to ends; and its purpose is to ensure the successful execution of human acts in an easy and orderly way. Aquinas says that reason not only is able to direct the acts of "the lower parts," but also is directive of its own acts. Clearly it is the "parts" of human nature that he means, reason being highest among them. Reason is directive

8. On the notion of *ratio* in Aquinas's work as a whole, see: J. Peghaire, *Intellectus et Ratio selon S. Thomas d'Aquin* (Ottawa: J. Vrin-Institut d'études médiévales, 1936); and Georges M.-M. Cottier, "*Intellectus et ratio*," *Revue Thomiste* 88 (1988): 215–28. On the notion of *ordo* in his work, see Edward A. Pace, "The Concept of Order in the Philosophy of St. Thomas," *The New Scholasticism* 2 (1928): 51–72; and Brian Coffey, "The Notion of Order According to St. Thomas Aquinas," *The Modern Schoolman* 27 (1949): 1–18.

9. *Expositio libri Posteriorum* 1.1 (Leonine ed., 1*.2:1.1–7.127).

10. *ST* I-II, q. 57, a. 3 (Leonine ed., 6:366a–367b); *Sententia libri Ethicorum* 6.3 (Leonine ed., 47.2:339–43).

of its own acts because of a *proprium* of the intellective part, namely, that it bends back on itself (*in se ipsam reflectatur*). Intellect has intellection of it-self, and reason (a kind of intellect) can reason about its own act. This is the second property mentioned: just as it is a *proprium* of man among animals to be directed in his acts by judgment of reason, so it is a *proprium* of reason among the parts of man to be able to consider itself, and so to direct its own acts. Reason's ability to direct its own acts opens up the possibility of the art of logic.

It is because reason reasons about the action of the hand that arts of con-struction and carpentry were discovered, by which man can perform acts of building in an easy and orderly way. By the same reason (*eadem ratione*), an art is needed to direct acts of reason itself, an art by means of which man may proceed in acts of reason in a way that is easy, orderly, and free of error. (In other human acts, art aims at ease and order; in acts of reason, art aims at ease and order, but also at freedom from error. This is the introduction's first, albeit indirect, reference to truth.) The art by which reason directs its own acts is the art of logic or rational science. It is rational not only because it follows reason, as do all arts, but also because it has acts of reason as its subject matter. "Rational science" is reason's knowledge of its acts and of how its acts might be best conducted. Aquinas says that it seems to be the art of arts, because it directs us in acts of reason, and it is from reason that all arts proceed. His introduction of the art of logic by a comparison with arts of construction suggests that making is, in a sense, a paradigmatic hu-man act, and that art in the narrower sense of right reason in making is paradigmatic for understanding art in the broader sense of any humanly predetermined ordering of means to end in human action.

Aquinas spends the remaining three-quarters of his introduction sub-dividing logic, as he looks for the subject matter and the "place" of the *Pos-terior Analytics*. Once again, the notion of property is crucial to moving the discussion forward. Division of the parts of logic follows a distinction among three acts of reason. The first two acts belong to reason as a kind of intellect. One act is intellection of what is indivisible or incomplex, the action by which intellect conceives what a thing is; this is the subject of the *Categories*. The other is composition or division of intellected indivisibles into affirmations or denials, at which point there is true and false; this is the subject of *On Interpretation*. Reason, as a kind of intellect, performs both these acts that belong to any intellect; but it also has a third act that belongs to it because of a *proprium* it has among intellects, namely, an ability to "run" (*discurrere*) from one thing to another, so that through what is known it may arrive at knowledge of what is unknown. This third act of reason—

this *discursus*, also called a *processus* or "forward movement" of reason—is the subject of the remaining books of logic.

Aquinas says that acts of reason are something like acts of nature, which is why reason imitates nature as much as it can. In some of its acts, nature succeeds always and necessarily; in others, such as generation of a well-formed offspring, nature succeeds usually, but not always. Three kinds of acts of nature may be distinguished, then: those that succeed always; those, such as birth of a healthy animal, that are what happens usually and successfully; and those, such as births of deformed animals, that fail, because of corruption of a natural principle such as semen.[11] Analogously, reason's discourse or forward movement is of three kinds. One kind proceeds with necessity, producing the certainty of science; this is the subject of the "judicative" part of logic (*iudicativa*), treated in the *Prior* and *Posterior Analytics*. Another kind proceeds without necessity or certitude, but usually with some success; this is the subject of the "inventive" or "discovering" part of logic (*inuentiua*), treated in the *Topics*, the *Rhetoric*, and the *Poetics*. The third kind fails, due to failure to observe some principle of reasoning that ought to have been observed; this is the subject of the "sophistic" part of logic (*sophistica*), treated in the *Sophistical Refutations*. Note the implied comparison between corruption of a principle of natural operation, such as semen, and failure to observe a principle of reasoning: two very different, but analogous, disturbances at the point of departure of a process, with ruinous results in both cases.

The three books that come under the "inventive" part of logic correspond to three ways in which reason's movement, while failing to achieve the certitude of science, is nevertheless usually able to arrive at some truth. Aquinas presents these in order of the decreasing certitude they produce. (1) Sometimes, because the premises from which it proceeds are merely probable, reason's movement produces, not science, but settled opinion (*fides uel opinio*), because reason comes down wholly on one side of a contradiction, although with some apprehension that the other side *might* be right. This is the subject of topics or dialectics; the dialectical syllogism, which proceeds from probable premises, is treated in the *Topics*. (2) Sometimes, what is produced is not settled opinion, but an inclination to think something is true (*suspicio*), because, while reason does not come down wholly on one side of a contradiction, it does lean more to one side than to the other. This is the subject of rhetoric and of the *Rhetoric*. (3) Sometimes, there is only an evaluation (*estimatio*) that comes down on one side of a contradiction because of a representation of

11. Cf. Aristotle, *Physics* 2.8 (199b1–14).

something as repulsive or attractive. This is the subject of poetics and of the *Poetics*, for it belongs to a poet to draw on to what is virtuous by means of a decorous representation (*poete est inducere ad aliquid uirtuosum per aliquam decentem representationem*). Dialectic, rhetoric, and poetics all pertain to rational philosophy because all of them concern what belongs to reason: to lead on from one thing to another (*inducere enim ex uno in aliud rationis est*).

To the modern reader of Aristotle, used to finding the *Rhetoric* and the *Poetics* toward the end of the corpus, after the works on ethics and politics, it is surprising to find Aquinas placing them near the beginning, as it were, among the books on logic.[12] His placing of rhetoric and poetics, together with dialectic, in the intermediate, "inventive" part of logic—we might also call it the "probing" or "tentative" part—indicates a more expansive understanding of logic, of reasoning, and of reason than that of classical modern logic, which tends to dwell exclusively on the extremes in processes of reasoning, those that succeed necessarily and those that fail. Dialectic, rhetoric, and poetics—a threesome reminiscent of the trivium of speech arts in the liberal arts, namely, grammar, rhetoric, and dialectic—are closer to ordinary life and to the spoken word than are either the "judicative" part, which deals with the certainty of science, or the "sophistic" part, which deals with corruption of reasoning.[13] Dialectic is associated with conversation, both by the etymology of the word *dialectic* and by Aristotle's remark that the study of dialectic is useful for conversations (*Topics* 1.2 [101a27–30]). Poems, public speeches, and thoughtful conversations provide ready examples of reason's artfulness with respect to its own activity, its arrangement of means to ends, in ways that make its movements easy, orderly, and directed toward truth. In such examples, a beginner in philosophy can catch a first glimpse of a close connection between reason and order.

12. On the ancient Greek and Arabic sources of Aquinas's understanding of the *Rhetoric* and the *Poetics* as works of "logic," see the *apparatus fontium* in the Leonine edition of Aquinas's introduction to the *Posterior Analytics* (n. 9 above); and Deborah L. Black, *Logic and Aristotle's Rhetoric and Poetics in Medieval Arabic Philosophy* (New York: Brill, 1990).

13. As we will see, Hugh of St. Victor, in the twelfth century, had made grammar, rhetoric, and dialectic the divisions of logic. Aquinas makes poetics, rhetoric, and dialectic the divisions of the inventive part of logic; his apparent substitution of poetics for grammar is in keeping with the traditional understanding of grammar as the study, not just of elements of speech and rules of syntax, but also of the exemplification of these by poets. See Henri Marrou, *St. Augustin et la fin de la culture antique* (Paris: Boccard, 1983), 17–26; and Robert A. Kaster, *Guardians of Language: The Grammarian and Society in Late Antiquity* (Berkeley: University of California Press, 1988), 12.

The Works of Reason: Introduction to the *De caelo*

The introduction to the *Posterior Analytics* links reason and order through the notion of art; the introduction to the *De caelo* links them through the notion of works of reason.[14] The epigraph of the introduction to the *De caelo* is from the *Physics*: we think we know something when we know its first causes and principles, and down to its elements (*et usque ad elementa*) (184a13–15). By this, Aquinas says, Aristotle clearly indicates that there is in the sciences a "forward movement" or sequence that is ordered (*processus ordinatus*), inasmuch as one proceeds in the sciences from first causes and principles, down to proximate causes that are elements constituting the essence of a thing. This is reasonable, for the sequence of the sciences is a work of reason, a property of which is to set in order or arrange things (*opus rationis, cuius proprium est ordinare*). There is, in every work of reason, an order according to which one proceeds from one thing to another. This is evident both in practical reason, which considers what we make or do (*ea quae facimus*), and in speculative reason, which considers what is made or done by something other than ourselves (*ea quae sunt aliunde facta*). Aquinas describes four ways in which practical reason proceeds in an order—from something prior to something posterior—in the case of house building, then four analogous ways in which speculative reason proceeds in an order.

Reason proceeds from prior to posterior in house building: (1) according to an order of *apprehension*, inasmuch as a builder first apprehends the form of a house by itself (*absolute*), then introduces it into matter; (2) according to an order of *intention*, inasmuch as the builder intends to complete the whole house, and because of this does whatever work he does on the parts of the house; (3) according to an order of *composition*, inasmuch as he first cuts stones, then assembles them into a wall; and (4) according to an order of *structural support* (*sustentatio artificii*), inasmuch as he first lays a foundation, on which the other parts of the house are supported. Each of these four is a movement from prior to posterior, from a first to a second.[15]

There are four corresponding orders in the consideration of speculative reason. (1) The first is according as one proceeds from what is common to what is less common. This corresponds to the order of apprehension, for

14. *In libros Aristotelis De caelo et mundo expositio* 1.1 (Leonine ed., 3:1–3).

15. In an analysis of the notion of order, Aquinas enumerates three elements: correlation of prior and posterior, distinction of things ordered, and the notion of kinds of order (*Scriptum super librum I Sententiarum*, d. 20, q. 1, a. 3, qla. 2 [ed. Mandonnet, 1: 509]). As Aristotle says (*Metaphysics* 5.4 [1018b9]), *prior and posterior* are said in relation to a *principium*, a first, to which Aquinas adds that, wherever there is a *principium*, there is an order (*ST* II-II, q. 26, a. 1 [Leonine ed., 8:209a]). See Coffey, "The Notion of Order According to St. Thomas Aquinas," 3–7.

universals are considered with respect to form by itself (*secundum formam absolutam*), particulars with respect to application of form to matter. As Aristotle says, one who says *caelum* ("universe") names a form, but one who says *hoc caelum* ("this universe") names a form in matter (277b30–278a10). (2) The second order is from whole to parts, inasmuch as a whole is prior in consideration to the material parts of an individual.[16] This order corresponds to the order of intention. (3) The third order is from simples to composites, inasmuch as composites are known through simples as through their principles. This corresponds to the order of composition. (4) The fourth order is that according to which it is necessary to consider principal parts first, for example, heart and liver before arteries and blood. This corresponds to the order in practical reason that starts from the laying of a foundation. The implicit comparison between the house built on its foundation and the animal body "built on" its heart and liver is interesting. House and animal body are emblematic wholes, anticipating the great whole of the universe that is discussed next.[17]

Aquinas shows how these four orders in the works of speculative reason can be seen in the sequence of natural sciences. (1) First there is determined what is common in nature; this is done in the *Physics*, in which the moveable as moveable is treated. What remains to be done in the other books of natural science is to apply the common to the proper, that is, apply the common features of the moveable as such to particular subjects of motion. A subject of motion is both a magnitude and a body, and in bodies there are three other orders to consider: (2) according as the whole bodily universe is prior in consideration to its parts; (3) according as simple bodies are considered before mixed bodies; and (4) according as, among simple bodies, it is necessary to consider first what is prior, namely the heavenly body, on which all others are "supported" (*de caelesti corpore, per quod omnia alia firmantur*; cf. "firmament"). These three orders are treated in the *De caelo*, which teaches (2) some things pertaining to the whole universe (Book I); (4) some things pertaining to the heavenly body (Book II); and (3) some things pertaining to other simple bodies, that is, the four elements (Books III and IV). (Note that the sequence of the third and fourth kinds of order

16. Aquinas gives as examples *semicircle*, in the definition of which circle is included ("half a circle"), and *acute angle*, in the definition of which right angle is included ("angle less than a right angle"). Individual circles and right angles *happen* to be able to be divided in these ways. "Specific parts," by contrast, are prior in consideration to, and included in the definition of, their wholes; for example, flesh and bones are included in the definition of man.

17. For a somewhat different comparison between parts of a house and parts of the universe, see Aquinas, *In librum beati Dionysii De divinibus nominibus expositio* 4.6 (ed. Pera [1950], n. 364).

presented above is here inverted.) The *De caelo*, then, is reasonably placed (*rationabiliter … ordinatur*) immediately after the *Physics*; and it begins at once with a treatment of *body*, to which everything said about movement in the *Physics* must be applied.

Because several things are treated in the *De caelo*, Aquinas says, there was dispute among the ancient expositors of Aristotle as to its subject. (His information on this point comes from the introduction of Simplicius's commentary on the *De caelo*.) There were three opinions. (1) Alexander was of the opinion that the subject is the *caelum* in the sense of *the universe or world*, and that the work determines certain things pertaining to the whole universe, such as that it is finite and that it is only one. (2) Others thought that the subject of the work is the *caelum* in the sense of *the whole of the body that circles the earth*, and that other bodies are discussed either *ex consequenti*, inasmuch as they are contained and influenced by the heavenly body (the view of Iamblichus), or *per accidens*, inasmuch as knowledge of other bodies is used to clarify what is said about the heavenly body (the view of Syrianus). But this opinion is unlikely, for, after the discussion of the *caelum* in Book II, other simple bodies are the main consideration in Books III and IV, and Aristotle does not usually make what is taken up *per accidens* in a science into a main consideration.[18] (3) Therefore, it seemed to others, including Simplicius, that Aristotle's intention in the *De caelo* is to discuss simple bodies inasmuch as they all come under the general notion of *simple body*; and that, because the most important simple body is the *caelum*, on which the others depend, the whole book was named after the *caelum*. To this, Simplicius says, it is no objection that the *De caelo* discusses certain things pertaining to the whole universe, because these are conditions, such as being finite and eternal, that pertain to the whole universe inasmuch as they pertain to the body of the *caelum*; on the other hand, if his intention in the *De caelo* had been to discuss the universe or world, Aristotle would have extended his consideration to all parts of the world, including plants and animals, as Plato did in the *Timaeus*.

Aquinas turns this last way of arguing back on Simplicius: if Aristotle had principally intended to treat of simple bodies in the *De caelo*, he would have taught in it everything pertaining to simple bodies; as it is, he teaches only what pertains to their lightness and heaviness, leaving the rest to *On Generation and Corruption*. Aquinas finds more reasonable the opinion of Alexander, according to which the subject of the *De caelo* is the universe,

18. Aquinas reports that, in addition to meaning *the whole universe* and *the whole of the body that circles the earth*, caelum could also mean *the outermost of the heavenly spheres*; but none of the ancients, apparently, took the title of Aristotle's work to refer to this.

and simple bodies are treated in the work as parts of the universe. The corporeal universe, Aristotle holds, is constituted from its parts according to an order of position (*secundum ordinem situs*). Therefore, the *De caelo* discusses only parts of the universe that have position in the universe primarily and of themselves (*primo et per se*), namely, simple bodies; and it discusses the four elements not inasmuch as they are hot or cold and so on, but only with respect to their heaviness and lightness, by means of which a position in the universe is determined for them. Other parts of the universe, such as rocks, plants, and animals, have determinate position not of themselves, but because of the simple bodies of which they are composed, which is why they are not treated in the *De caelo*. Apparently thinking of Albert the Great, Aquinas concludes that this agrees with what is customarily said by "the Latins": that the *De caelo* treats of body as moveable to a position, or with respect to place (*de corpore mobile ad situm, sive secundum locum*), local motion being common to all parts of the universe.[19]

This account of the order of the universe and the order of natural science is, of course, quite alien to the modern reader, for whom modern natural science has put paid to Aquinas's Aristotelian beliefs that celestial spheres circle the earth, that there is a radical difference between the constitution of earthly and of heavenly bodies, and that the cosmic order is an eternal order of position of elements.[20] One might argue, on the other hand, that modern natural science does, in its way, acknowledge the four orders Aquinas finds in works of speculative reason; and, more generally, that it agrees with Aquinas's naïve and spontaneous philosophical view that reason is a faculty of order—a faculty of setting in order its own works, but also a faculty of seeking order in the things that it studies in natural science, from the immense totality of the visible universe that is the great stage setting for everything in human existence, to the vanishingly tiny particles and forces that underlie it all.[21] In this orientation of natural science to cosmic order, the beginner in philosophy can find another connection between reason and order.

19. See James A. Weisheipl, "The Commentary of St. Thomas on the *De caelo* of Aristotle," in *Nature and Motion in the Middle Ages* (Washington, D.C.: The Catholic University of America Press, 1985), 177–201. On Albert, see p. 188.

20. See Thomas Litt, *Les corps célestes dans l'univers de saint Thomas d'Aquin* (Paris: Publications Universitaires-Béatrice Nauwelaerts, 1963); and Oliva Blanchette, *The Perfection of the Universe According to Aquinas: A Teleological Cosmology* (University Park, Penn.: The Pennsylvania State University Press, 1992), 203–35.

21. "The driving force behind all empirical reasoning is the search for order." Thomas Nagel, *The Last Word* (New York: Oxford University Press, 1997), 82.

Considerations of Order: Introduction to
the *Nicomachean Ethics*

Aquinas's introductions to the *Posterior Analytics* and the *De caelo* begin
with reflections on reason and order that lead to discussion of the areas of
philosophy to which these works belong, rational science and natural science respectively. His introduction to the *Nicomachean Ethics* likewise begins with a reflection on reason and order, but one that leads to a survey of
the whole of knowledge.[22] The epigraph here, attributed to the *Metaphysics*,
is that it belongs to the wise man to set things in order: *sapientis est ordinare*. R.-A. Gauthier has pointed out that this is in fact a scholastic adage,
based on Aristotle's statement in the *Metaphysics* that "the wise man must
not be ordered but rather order" (928a28). The Greek verb Aristotle uses
(ἐπιτάττειν), like the English verb *to order*, can mean to give orders, but
also to set in order (and giving orders is obviously a way of setting things in
order or arranging things); Aristotle is playing on the ambiguity. Aquinas,
however, as his discussion of the adage *sapientis est ordinare* at the beginning of the *Summa contra gentiles* makes clear, takes it to refer exclusively
to the setting of things in order.[23] The point, for him, is simply that it is the
wise man who should arrange things.

The adage uses the so-called genitive of characteristic (*sapientis est*) to
express what is more formally conveyed by the nominalized adjective and
technical term *proprium* (cf. *poete est* and *rationis est* in the introduction to
the *Posterior Analytics*). The genitive of characteristic is customarily translated into English in terms of ownership ("It *belongs* to the wise man to set
things in order"), maintaining an original link between the genitive case
and the notion of possession. There is convergence between the ordinary
understanding of *property* as meaning *a possession, what is one's own*, and
the logical understanding of it as meaning a *distinguishing feature* predicated of a thing, a feature that "flows from," but is not part of, the thing's
essence; for the latter is also a possession, but a possession of a most formal
and metaphysical kind. Properties, in the logical sense, are the equipage of
essences. They are neither what things *are* (essences) nor what merely *be-
falls* things (accidents), but rather, coming between these, what things, in
their being, inalienably *have*, as a result of their essences.[24] Predications of
property are therefore quite naturally translated into the language of owner-

---

22. *Sententia libri Ethicorum* 1.1 (Leonine ed., 47.1:3.1–4.54).

23. René-Antoine Gauthier, Introduction to *Somme contre les gentils* (Paris: Editions Universitaires, 1993), 97–98.

24. See *ST* I, q. 77, a. 1, ad 5 (Leonine ed., 5:237b).

ship: it *belongs* to man to be directed in his acts by judgment of reason, as it belongs to the intellective part to reflect on itself, and it belongs to reason to advance from one thing to another, and to set things in order.

That it is a property of reason to set things in order is what Aquinas says in his introduction to the *De caelo*. In his introduction to the *Ethics*, he says rather that it belongs to the wise man to set things in order. This, he says, is because wisdom is the greatest perfection of reason, a property of which is to know order (*potissima perfectio rationis, cuius proprium est cognoscere ordinem*). Sense powers know certain things, but only one by one, in isolation (*absolute*); it belongs to reason alone to know the order of one thing to another. The property of reason is not, in the first place, the setting of things in order, which is the specialty, so to speak, of the wise man, the one whose reason has been perfected. The property that reason, perfected or not, has by nature, is ability to know order, to cognize or recognize it. This ability is what is most fundamental in the relation between reason and order: any setting of things in order (and any giving of orders) presupposes recognition of order.

Aquinas goes on to make two distinctions concerning order. His distinctions are starting to accumulate, and we must be careful to keep them distinct from one another. As we have seen, in the introduction to the *De caelo*, (1) he distinguishes (a) four kinds of order in works of practical reason and (b) four analogous kinds of order in works of speculative reason. Here, in the introduction to the *Ethics*, after establishing that it is a property of reason to know order, (2) he distinguishes two kinds of order in things, and then (3) he distinguishes four ways in which order is related to reason.

He takes the distinction between two kinds of order in things from Book 12 of Aristotle's *Metaphysics* (1075a13–15).[25] One is the order of coordination, the order of parts of a whole or a multitude to one another, as the parts of a house are ordered to one another. The other is the teleological order of subordination, the order of things to an end, and this order is prior to the former; as Aristotle says, the order of the parts of an army to one another is for the sake of the order of the whole army to its general. Aquinas introduces this distinction because he is going to use it to clarify what is proper to the consideration of moral philosophy. But first he makes a place for moral philosophy, by explaining the principal divisions of philosophy on the basis of four ways in which order is related to reason.

Order is the object of two actions of reason: *considerare* and *facere*. In a

---

25. Cf. Aquinas, *In duodecim libros Metaphysicorum Aristotelis expositio* 12.12 (ed. Cathala-Spiazzi [1950], nn. 2630–31).

prolongation of reason's original recognition of order, reason can consider
or ponder order; and reason can sometimes also make or produce order.
Accordingly, four kinds of order in relation to reason can be distinguished:
(1) order that reason does not produce, but only considers, such as the order
of natural things; (2) order that reason, in considering, produces in its own
act, when it orders to one another its conceptions, or the vocalizations that
signify its conceptions, that is, its words; (3) order that reason, in considering, produces in operations of will; and (4) order that reason, in considering, produces in exterior things of which it is a cause, such as a box or a
house.

A consideration of reason, Aquinas says, is perfected by "a habit of science" (*habitus scientiae*), that is, an acquired, settled, skillful way of knowing. "Sciences," therefore, are distinguished according to these different orders that it is proper to reason to consider (*quos proprie ratio considerat*). (1)
It pertains to *natural philosophy* to consider the order of things that human
reason considers but does not make—taking *natural philosophy* in a large,
non-Aristotelian sense that includes mathematics and metaphysics. (2) The
order that reason, in considering, produces in its own act pertains to *rational philosophy*, to which it belongs (*cuius est*) to consider the order of parts
of a sentence to one another and the order of principles to conclusions. (3)
The order of voluntary actions pertains to the consideration of *moral philosophy*. (4) The order that reason, in considering, produces in external things
constituted by human reason pertains to *artes mechanicae*. The products of
the mechanic arts are enmattered, manmade things, external to man in a
way that his reasoning and willing are not. These arts are not called *philosophy*, but they are included among the *habitus scientiae*, the ways of knowing
that perfect the ways in which reason considers order.

In this introduction to the *Ethics*, Aquinas is, of course, especially interested in moral philosophy. Applying his distinction between the order of
things to one another and the order of things to an end, he says that it is a
proprium of moral philosophy to consider human operations as ordered to
one another and to an end. Operations are "human" that proceed from the
will of man according to an order of reason; operations in man that do not
come under will and reason are not, properly speaking (*proprie*), human,
but "natural." As the subject of natural philosophy may be said to be either
motion or the mobile thing, so the subject of moral philosophy may be said
to be human action ordered to an end, or even man, as acting voluntarily
for the sake of an end.

As the introduction to the *Posterior Analytics* concludes by subdividing
logic into its parts, the introduction to the *Ethics* concludes by subdividing

moral philosophy into its parts. Man is naturally a social animal. Needing many things that he cannot provide for himself, he is naturally part of a group (*multitudo*) by which he is given help in living well. In fact, as he needs help in getting two sorts of things, he naturally belongs to two groups. (1) With respect to necessities of life, he is helped by a domestic group of which he is a part, receiving generation, nourishment, and instruction from his parents, and other help from other family members. (2) With respect to complete sufficiency of life, that is, everything that will allow him not just to live, but to live well, he is helped, physically and morally, by a political group of which he is a part. A family or a political group has unity only of order; it is not simply speaking one thing. A part or member of a family or political group therefore has an operation that does not belong to the whole; and the whole has an operation proper to itself. In the case of a whole that is, simply speaking, one thing in some sense, the parts have no operation that does not also belong to the whole; and it pertains to the same science to consider both the whole and the part. But it does not pertain to the same science to consider a whole that has unity only of order and the parts of this kind of whole. Therefore, as a human being is a whole, but also a part of two other wholes, wholes that have unity only of order, moral philosophy is divided into three sciences: *monostics*, which considers operations of one man as ordered to an end; *economics*, which considers operations of families; and *politics*, which considers operations of political groups. The *Nicomachean Ethics* teaches *monostics*.[26]

In light of this analysis, particular actions of individuals, of families, and of cities or countries can show the beginner in philosophy yet another distinctive way in which reason and order are connected.

The Mechanic Arts: Before Technology

Aquinas's four-part division of human knowledge in the introduction to the *Ethics* resumes the Stoic division of philosophical discourse into physics, logic, and ethics, as modified by Hugh of St. Victor's twelfth-century addition of the mechanic arts.[27] The four-part division is a piece of Aquinas's mental furniture that he tends to keep in reserve, usually giving preference

---

26. Cf. n. 32 below.

27. *Hugonis de sancto Victore Didascalicon de studio legendi: A Critical Text*, II.I, ed. Charles Henry Buttimer (Washington, D.C.: The Catholic University of America Press, 1939), 24. See Katerina Ierodiakonou, "The Stoic Division of Philosophy," *Phronesis* 38 (1993): 57–74; James A. Weisheipl, "Classification of the Sciences in Medieval Thought," *Mediaeval Studies* 27 (1965): 54–90, at 65–66.

to the divisions of philosophy by Aristotle and Boethius; the introduction to the *Ethics* seems to be the only occasion on which he mentions it. It is a noteworthy exception, however, in which he shows the basis of the four-part division in the different relations of reason and order.

The most obvious difference between the Stoic and Aristotelian divisions of philosophy concerns the meaning of *physics*, the study of nature. Aristotle divided philosophy into theoretical and practical philosophy, and theoretical philosophy into physics, mathematics, and theology; he seems to have regarded reason's study of its own operation, or logic, as an organon or instrument of philosophy proper. The Stoics were materialists interested in the operation of reason, as well as in human action in general, as is reflected in their division of philosophy into physics, logic, and ethics. Hugh of St. Victor's adaptation of the Stoic division makes the *physics* of this division coincide with Aristotelian *theoretical philosophy*, which Hugh further divides into physics properly so-called, mathematics, and metaphysics.[28]

The Latin Middle Ages knew of the Stoic division of philosophy from Augustine, who attributes it to Plato and who sees in it a reflection of the Trinity (*City of God* 8.4–8, 11.25). Although the division is formalized only in Stoicism, it does seem to derive from some of the oldest and deepest differences in philosophical thinking, differences between the natural philosophy of the Ionians, the dialectic of the Eleatics, and the moral and political thinking of Socrates. On the other hand, as Aquinas's analysis suggests, the threesome of physics (broadly understood), logic, and ethics transcends historical circumstances, representing as it does three permanent possibilities in the relations of reason and order.

Hugh of St. Victor makes his addition in a division of philosophy into theoretical, practical, mechanic, and logical philosophy. His *theoretical philosophy* corresponds to Stoic *physics*, his *practical philosophy* to Stoic *ethics*. His subdivision of theoretical philosophy follows the Aristotelian-Boethian division of it into theology, mathematics, and (in the Aristotelian sense) physics. Hugh incorporates the seven liberal arts into this scheme, making the arts of the quadrivium (arithmetic, music, geometry, astronomy) subdivisions of mathematics, and the arts of the trivium (grammar, rhetoric, dialectic) subdivisions of logical philosophy.[29] He introduces seven mechanic arts—woolworking, arms-production, navigation, agriculture, hunting, medicine, and theater—as complementary to the seven liberal arts; but more significant is his raising of the general category of mechanic arts to the level of the ma-

---

28. See Weisheipl, "Classification of the Sciences in Medieval Thought," 63.
29. *Didascalion*, II.III–XV (pp. 25–34), II.XXVIII–XXX (pp. 44–47).

jor divisions of philosophy, as a fourth member on a par with the three Stoic divisions.[30] This move was rejected by his follower Godfrey of St. Victor, to whom the mechanic arts seemed "unclean" in comparison with other kinds of knowledge that are less involved with matter and the body.[31]

In the thirteenth century, Hugh's recognition of the mechanic arts as an important kind of knowledge was received more sympathetically, not only by Aquinas, but also by Bonaventure, who, in his *De reductione artium ad theologiam*, written just a few years before Aquinas's commentary on the *Ethics*, incorporates the elements of Hugh's division of philosophy into his own very different four-part division of knowledge into four "lights" that come down from "the Father of Lights" (Jas 1:17): the *exterior* light of the mechanic arts (Bonaventure discusses the same seven mechanic arts as does Hugh); the *inferior* light of sense cognition; the *interior* light of philosophical cognition (which Bonaventure divides, in Stoic fashion, into *physica*, *logica*, and *practica*); and the *superior* light of grace and Sacred Scripture.[32] Aquinas's simpler division of knowledge in his introduction to the *Ethics* follows Hugh's four-part division more faithfully, while explaining it more philosophically, in terms of the underlying four kinds of order that reason considers: the order that it simply considers; the order that it introduces into its thoughts and words; the order that it introduces into human acts; and the order that it introduces into "external things of which it is a cause." Aquinas shows no interest in the particular mechanic arts that Hugh and Bonaventure discuss; he is rather interested in the distinctive relation of order to reason that the mechanic arts in general manifest. In making a place for this relation among the relations of order to reason, his account recalls Socrates's respect for the knowledge of craftsmen as a real, if limited, kind of human knowledge (*Apology* 22c–d). At the same time, it provides a setting for philosophical consideration of what is now casually referred to as *tech-*

30. Ibid., II.XX–XXVII (pp. 38–44).

31. See Edward A. Synan, "Verses and Wisdom in the Twelfth Century," in *"Truth" Is a Divine Name: Hitherto Unpublished Papers of Edward A. Synan, 1918–1997*, ed. Janice L. Schultz-Aldrich (New York: Rodopi, 2010), 95–108.

32. *St. Bonaventure's On the Reduction of the Arts to Theology: Translation with Introduction and Commentary*, ed. Zachary Hayes (St. Bonaventure, N.Y.: Franciscan Institute, St. Bonaventure University, 1996), 36, 40. Bonaventure's further subdivisions of the main divisions of philosophical cognition will be familiar: he subdivides *physica* into *physica* properly so-called (i.e., in the Aristotelian sense), *mathematica*, and *metaphysica*; he subdivides *logica* into *grammatica*, *logica*, and *rhetorica*; and he subdivides moral philosophy into *monastica*, *oeconomica*, and *politica* (p. 42).

For new light on the genre and the circumstances of Bonaventure's work, see Joshua C. Benson, "Bonaventure's *De reductione artium ad theologiam* and Its Early Reception as an Inaugural Sermon," *American Catholic Philosophical Quarterly* 85 (2011) (Special issue: Bonaventure, ed. Timothy B. Noone): 7–24.

nology—a "hazardous" term that seems to have come into its current use as a result of efforts to find a successor to the medieval term *mechanic arts* that would be adequate to the new kinds of "external things of which reason is a cause" that began to be produced in the modern age.[33] At first, *technology*, like *mechanic art*, referred to a kind of knowledge; now, of course, it usually means the artifacts—the devices, equipment, instruments—produced by the new kind of knowledge. The felt need for a new term to replace the old one suggests that these modern external things of which reason is a cause are radically different from the things of which it was a cause before. To complicate matters, the word *technology* is now sometimes projected backward onto products of the most primitive handicrafts. But perhaps the quaint term *mechanic art* is a more modest and transparent name for reason's introduction of a distinctive kind of order into matter, whether in simple shoemaking or in production of the most complex computers; the Greek root μηχανή points to the *devising* activity that distinguishes the special relation of reason to order common to these extremes. In considering such different instances of reason's devising, the beginner in philosophy can see yet one more way in which reason and order are connected.

Concluding Suggestions

On the basis of the foregoing, a few generalizations may be ventured in response to the question of how to introduce philosophy to beginners. Take an epigrammatic remark from Aristotle (or some other gnomic author) as your point of departure. Explain what a property is, and proceed by distinguishing things on the basis of their properties. Mention human reason and its connection with order early on. Note how reason (more or less clearly) sees order in things, and how it (for better or worse) introduces order into its own movements, human acts, and the work of human hands. With reference to these different relations between reason and order, point out some basic divisions of knowledge. Show the intelligible potency of such commonplace notions as *consideration* and *the setting of things in order*.

Confirmation of the philosophical importance of the theme of reason and order may be found in a recent work of philosophy in a style very different from that of Aquinas, Robert Sokolowski's *Phenomenology of the Human Person*.[34] This work is primarily an examination of the role of syntax in language and thinking, but it also discusses the syntax of pictures, the syntax

---

33. Leo Marx, "Technology: The Emergence of a Hazardous Concept," *Technology and Culture: The International Quarterly of the Society for the History of Technology* 51 (2010): 561–77.

34. New York: Cambridge University Press, 2008.

of action, and even the syntax of friendship. Such varied uses of the term *syntax* raise the question of its etymological sense, which is, of course, *co-ordination*, the setting of things in order in relation to one another. In suggesting that all thinking and all thoughtful activity are syntactic, Sokolowski comes close to saying that it is proper to reason to know and express order.

Theology is reason's consideration of an order that it could not have discovered by itself. On the extension of the theme of reason and order into theology, two very different recent works may be recommended. One is A.-I. Bouton-Touboulic's *L'ordre caché: La notion d'ordre chez saint Augustin*, which scrutinizes the vast work of Augustine to make the case that *ordo*—a Latin term that, in Augustine's usage, captures the semantic force of two Greek words, τάξις and κόσμος—is a master idea running through his thought, guiding his reflections on creation, sin, and redemption.[35] The other is James V. Schall's *The Order of Things*.[36] Schall begins with five epigraphs, among them Aquinas's account of the fourfold relation of order to reason, on the basis of which he develops a philosophical and theological meditation on "mind and order in the various levels of being, including the order within our own souls and our own politics."[37] As both works, in their different ways, show, philosophy can richly benefit from, as well as contribute to, theological exploration of the theme of reason and order.

It seems appropriate to close with some well-known lines on order by Wallace Stevens:

> O blessed rage for order ...
> The maker's rage to order words of the sea ...
> And of ourselves, and of our origins,
> In ghostlier demarcations, keener sounds.[38]

Stevens's poem describes a woman who sings by the sea, and who evidently stands for the figure of the poet ("the maker"), the practitioner of that subdivision of the "inventive" part of logic, as Aquinas might say, in which our reason is drawn on by means of decorous representation. "Blessed rage for order" might characterize the gift of reason itself, the happy privilege of the rational animal, who has an instinct for order, and who lives and moves in the medium of syntax. Philosophy and theology share poetry's ambition to make more refined distinctions ("ghostlier demarcations"), and deeper, more telling claims ("keener sounds"), than are usually made, when people speak about the world, ourselves, and, in particular, the origins and principles of our being.

---

35. Paris: Institut d'Études Augustiniennes, 2004.
36. San Francisco: Ignatius Press, 2007.   37. Ibid., 33.
38. "The Idea of Order at Key West."

CHAPTER NINE

Tunc scimus cum causas cognoscimus

Some Medieval Endeavors to Know Scripture in Its Causes

TIMOTHY BELLAMAH, OP

At the outset of the *Metaphysics*, Aristotle says that "all men suppose what is called wisdom (*sophia*) to deal with the first causes (*aitia*) and the principles (*archai*) of things," and that it is these causes and principles that he proposes to study in this work.[1] During the thirteenth century the recent recovery of Aristotle's works of natural philosophy (*Physics, Metaphysics, De anima, Meteora*), resulted in an evolution of the understanding of causality, which in turn resulted in remarkable developments in biblical interpretation.[2] Especially at the universities of Paris and Oxford commentators re-evaluated conventional anthropological presuppositions and reassessed the

---

1. *Metaphysics*, A.1 (981b28). Books I–IV of this work were translated from Greek into Latin by James of Venice during the first half of the twelfth century. The first complete Latin translation was produced by William of Moerbeke, c. 1265. A similar remark appears in *Posterior Analytics*, I, 2 (71b): "We possess scientific knowledge of a thing only when we know its cause." English translation, G. R. G. Mure, *The Basic Works of Aristotle*, ed. R. McKeon (New York: Random House, 1941), 110–86 (112). The Greek-Latin translation of the *Posterior Analytics* produced by James of Venice during the first half of the twelfth century was revised by William of Moerbeke during the 1260s.

2. Study of the *Libri naturales* (*Physics, Metaphysics, De anima, Meteora*), public or private, was prohibited in Paris in 1210 (*Chartularium Universitatis Parisensis [CUP]*, ed. Denifle [Paris, 1889] I, n. 11), and again in 1215 (I, n. 20). These measures failed to have lasting effect, and by 1255 the Arts Faculty at the University of Paris mandated lecturing upon them (I, n. 247).

human capacities for perception.[3] They also typically accounted for the biblical text's divine and human origins by appealing to a distinction between its primary and secondary efficient causes, namely, God and the human author. But the main influence for their account of primary and secondary causality was not Aristotle. For that we must turn to the *Elements of Theology* (*Elementationes theologiae*), a work of the fifth-century Athenian Neoplatonist Proclus, and then to the *Liber de causis*, whose composition recent scholarship situates in ninth-century Baghdad, in the circle of al-Kindi.[4] The latter work incorporated much of Proclus's thought, modified it, and transmitted it to the medieval Latin West. In this paper I propose to show that these developments allowed commentators, particularly St. Thomas Aquinas, to understand and explain with unprecedented clarity Scripture's literal sense as resulting from the twofold intention of its divine and human authors.

Proclus's Doctrine of Hierarchical Causality

To begin with the *Elements of Theology*, we find, in Propositions 56, 57, 70, and others like them, the source of the account of primary and secondary causality adopted by the *Liber de causis* and later by thinkers of the Latin West.[5] Here Proclus asserts the intrinsic causal presence of the transcendent

3. On these developments, see A. J. Minnis and A. Scott, *Medieval Literary Theory and Criticism* (Oxford: Oxford University Press, 1988), 197.

4. On this work's origins, see G. Endress, *Proclus Arabus; zwanzig Abschnitte aus der Institutio theologica in arabischer Übersetzung* (Wiesbaden, Beirut: Franz Steiner Verlag GMBH, 1973), 186–87; "The Circle of al-Kindi: Early Arabic Translations from the Greek and the Rise of Islamic Philosophy," in *The Ancient Tradition in Christian and Islamic Hellenism. Studies on the Transmission of Greek Philosophy and Sciences Dedicated to H. J. Drossaart Lulofs on His Ninetieth Birthday,* ed. G. Endress and R. Kruk (Leiden: Research School CNWS, 1997), 43–76; R. Taylor, "Remarks on the Latin Text and the Translator of the Kalam fi mahd al-khair/Liber de causis," *Bulletin de Philosophie Médiévale* 31 (1989): 75–102; C. D'Ancona Costa (to whom I owe the first reference), *Recherches sur le Liber de Causis* (Paris: Vrin, 1995), 36–45, 155–94; C. D'Ancona and R. Taylor, "*Le Liber de causis,*" in *Dictionnaire de Philosophes Antiques, Supplément,* ed. R. Goulet et alii (Paris: CNRS Éditions, 2003), 599–647.

5. Proclus, *Elements of Theology*, Proposition 56 (ed. and English trans. E. Dodds [Oxford: Oxford University Press, 1963], 55): "*All that is produced by secondary beings is in a greater measure produced from those prior and more determinative principles from which the secondary were themselves derived.* For if the secondary has its whole existence from its prior, thence also it receives its power of further production, since productive powers reside in producers in virtue of their existence and form part of their being. But if it owes to the superior cause its power of production, to that superior it owes its character as a cause in so far as it is a cause, a character meted out to it from thence in proportion to its constitutive capacity. If so, the things which proceed from it are caused in virtue of its prior; for the same principle which makes the one a cause makes the other an effect." Proposition 57 (ibid., 56–57): "But again, the powers which are present in the consequent are present in a greater measure in the cause. For all that is produced

One or Good in effects, that is, secondary beings. In classical Neoplation-ism it might seem that the transcendence of the One and the multiplicity of intermediate beings would attenuate the engagement of the One at the lower levels of being proceeding from it. In other words, the transcendent One might seem to be remote from the world of concrete particulars. And yet Proclus asserts, to the contrary, that because any secondary cause owes its existence to its prior cause, so too it owes all that it causes to its prior cause. This, certainly, is because the productive capacity of the secondary cause arises from its being, which derives from the primary cause. To be sure, Pro-clus has made use of Aristotle's understanding of instrumental causes, but he has adapted it to his own Neoplatonic perspective—the Stagarite does not explain instrumental causes as owing their existence to primary causes.[6]

What Proclus has in mind here is not a series of accidentally related causes after the fashion of natural generation or motion. It is rather a meta-physical hierarchy of causes wherein the causal activity of every subordinate cause depends on the causal agency of the first cause. Proclus was intent on describing the One's causal presence in everything posterior to it, that is, derivative from it. In Proclus's view, the multiplicity of secondary causes is produced only by the mediation of anterior secondary causes, and not im-mediately by the One.

Divine and Human Agency in the *Liber de Causis*

The *Liber de Causis* entered medieval Europe by way of the twelfth-century Arabic-Latin translation produced by Gerard of Cremona (d. 1187) at Toledo. Generally attributed to Aristotle during the thirteenth century, its inauthenticity was eventually documented by Aquinas late in his career (1270), subsequent to William of Moerbeke's translation of Proclus's *Ele-ments of Theology*.[7] Aquinas recognized the *Liber's* dependence on Proclus

---

by secondary beings is produced in a greater measure by prior and more determinative prin-ciples. The cause, then, is co-operative in the production of all that the consequent is capable of producing. And if it first produces the consequent itself, it is of course plain that it is operative before the latter in the activity which produces it. Thus every cause acts prior to its consequent and in conjunction with it, and likewise gives rise to further effects posterior to it." For these references and my remarks on the relationship between the *Elements of Theology* and the *Liber de Causis*, I am indebted to Richard Taylor. Responsibility for any errors in the application of his findings is entirely mine.

6. On Proclus's creative borrowing from Aristotle on this matter, see C. D'Ancona Costa, *Recherches sur le Liber de Causis* (Paris: Vrin, 2002), 224–27.

7. Albert the Great suspected the *Liber's* author to be Ibn Daoud, a Jewish Spanish contem-porary of Gerard of Cremona, but he never documented any connection with Proclus. It is not unreasonable to suppose that the first Christian scholar to recognize this dependence was

in its opening statement, "Every primary cause infuses its effect more abundantly than does a universal secondary cause."[8] Here, primary causality appears as the activity of a First Principle or First Cause conferring upon a secondary cause a formality by which it acts. Later, in proposition 18, we find that the First Principle is the sole originator and giver of being, while all other causes, that is, secondary causes, cause only by way of form. The salient formality here is being, which is the basis for the additional formalities of life and intellection. Taken together these constitute human being. Here, too, Aquinas recognizes the *Liber's* dependence on Proclus.[9] The First Cause is said to be primary inasmuch as it gives to secondary causes both their being and their power for acting from their own power. The *Liber* thus asserts the priority of the First Cause and its agency with respect to the being and agency of secondary causes. So understood, the First Cause is the First Agent of any action.

Richard Taylor has recently argued that this work was composed as a response to the occasionalist and theologically voluntarist views widely held at the time the circle of al-Kindi was active in Baghdad.[10] On this view, the *Liber* was meant to provide an account of the world's existence that allowed for the understanding of God as the sole creator and primary cause, on the one hand, as well as for the understanding of causality of secondary agents, particularly human ones, on the other. Thus, the purpose of the work was partly political—to show the compatibility of Greek philosophy with Revelation. But it also served a more properly theological end—to re-

---

Moerbeke, and that he translated the *Elements of Theology* to show it. According to manuscript indications, he completed the work at Viterbo by May 18, 1268. For an account of the *Liber's* attribution to Aristotle, see C. D'Ancona Costa, *Recherches sur le Liber de Causis*, 215–24.

8. *Commentary on the Book of Causes,* English trans. V. Guagliardo, OP, C. Hess, OP, and R. Taylor (Washington, D.C.: The Catholic University of America Press, 1996), 5. Thomas is unambiguous on the *Liber's* dependence on Proclus: "Proclus makes these three points in two propositions. The first is in Proposition 56 of his book," ibid., 7; *Sancti Thomae de Aquino Super Librum de causis expositio,* 1, ed. H.-D. Saffrey (Fribourg: Société philosophique, 1954), 5: "Omnis causa primaria plus est influens super suum causatum quam causa secunda universalis.... Quae quidem tria Proclus proponit in duabus propositionibus, primum in LVI propositione sui libri."

9. Ibid., 18 (Saffrey, 101): "*Res omnes habent essentiam per ens primum, et res vivae omnes sunt motae per essentiam suam propter vitam primam, et res intelligibiles omnes habent scientiam propter intelligentiam primam.* Et hoc idem dicitur in libro Procli CII propositione, sub his verbis: *Omnia quidem qualitercumque entia ex fine sunt et infinito, propter prime ens. Omnia autem viventia suiipsorum motiva sunt propter vitam primam. Omnia autem cognitiva cognitione participant propter intellectum primum.* Dicit autem quod *omnia sunt ex fine et infinito propter prime ens quia,* ut supra habitum est in 4 propositione, *ens creatum compositum est ex finito et infinito.* Ad huius autem propositionis intellectum primo quidem considerandum est quod omnes rerum gradus ad tria videtur reducere quae sunt esse, vivere et intelligere."

10. See references to R. Taylor's works cited in note 4 above.

fute a form of theologically voluntarist occasionalism that excludes any real moral responsibility from human agents. In other words, its main purpose for arguing for secondary causality was to settle a quarrel between rationalist philosophers, who tended to exclude divine agency from human affairs, and theological absolutists, who attributed all causality to God. Islamic theologians of ninth-century Baghdad tended to hold that God assigns actions, good or bad, to people with the result that they are subject to praise or blame without having any real choice in their actions. On Taylor's view, the *Liber* attempts to account for human agency and philosophic rationalism without doing violence to the legitimate claims of the theologians.

Assuming that Taylor's analysis is correct, it is not without interest to the history of the *Liber* in the medieval Latin West. The contexts within which thirteenth-century thinkers discussed primary and secondary causality were many—divine providence, the moral life, soteriology, Christology, the sacraments—to name a few of the more conspicuous examples. The present concern is biblical authorship.

Medieval Studies of Divine and Human Authorship

During the second half of the thirteenth century, biblical commentators showed unprecedented interest in the relation between divine and human authorial roles. This development is easily observable in the prologues to their commentaries, where we find their most explicit and elaborate methodological considerations, as well as the introduction of the various analytical techniques to be applied in their expositions.[11] Originating in the study of profane literature, these introductions to the author and his work, or *accessus*, became a standard feature of biblical commentaries in the latter part of the eleventh century. Eventually they were simplified according to an established pattern including an examination of the author's intention and mode of exposition, as well as the biblical book's title (*intentio, modus agendi*, and *titulus*). Subsequently, twelfth-century masters, notably Peter the Chanter and Stephen Langton, structured the *accessus* around an introductory biblical verse, generally taken from some book other than the one at hand.

With the development of university exegesis during the first half of the

---

11. See my *The Biblical Interpretation of William of Alton* (New York: Oxford University Press, 2011), 26–40; G. Dahan, "Les Prologues des Commentaires Bibliques," in *Les prologues médiévaux*, ed. J. Hamesse (Turnhout: Brepols, 2000), 427–28; A. Sulavik, "*Principia* and *Introitus* in Thirteenth Century Biblical Exegesis with Related Texts," in *La Bibbia del XIII Secolo. Storia del testo, storia dell'esegesi*, ed. G. Cremascoli and F. Santi, Millennio Medievale 49 (Florence: SISMEL—Edizioni del Galluzzo, 2004), 269–87.

thirteenth century, commentators had adopted another framework for the prologue, explaining a given book in terms of Aristotle's four causes. The author's intention, or the book's purpose, was discussed under the heading of final causality, its mode of exposition was considered as its formal cause, and its title as its material cause. It was not unusual for commentators to describe any one of these causes in a threefold manner, according to a book's literal, allegorical and tropological senses. An example appears in the prologue to a commentary on Lamentations by Aquinas's Dominican contemporary William of Alton, who indicates that the book's subject matter, or material cause, is Jeremiah's lament. Literally, his lament is for the destruction of Jerusalem at the hands of the Babylonians in his own time and at the hands of the Romans six centuries later. Allegorically, it is for the Church's falling away from the fervor of charity, the light of truth, and the constancy of solidity. Tropologically, it is the soul's falling away from justice into sin.[12] The book's formal cause, or mode of exposition, is lamentation.[13] Though this is not surprising, it is worth noting that William's idenification of lament as a distinct literary form is consistent with contemporary scholarship devoted to the form of the *planctus* or lament in the Old Testament as well as in Christian literature.[14] The final cause, or end, of Jeremiah's lament is a threefold call to mourning for sin according to the three senses William finds in the text. Literally, it is to bring the synagogue to mourn her sins; allegorically, to bring the Church to mourn hers; and tropologically, to bring the faithful soul to mourn hers.[15] Worth noting in this mode of analy-

12. William of Alton, *Super Threnos,* in *The Biblical Interpretation of William of Alton,* prologue, 218–19: "Causa materialis insinuatur per hoc quod dicitur, *aquam, fontem lacrimarum ut plorem interfectos.* Vehemens enim planctus quo Ieremias deplorat terre sue desolacionem siue deuastacionem, ciuitatis et templi destruccionem, populi sui et maxime regis Iosie afflicionem, et interfeccionem templi factam per Caldeos uel tunc faciendam per Titum et Vespasianum, per Romanos secundum sensum historicum, est materia huius libri. Item, notandum quod secundum sensum allegoricum materia huius libri est planctus pro recessu ecclesie a statu triplici, scilicet a feruore caritatis, a luce ueritatis, a constantia soliditatis. Feruor caritatis recessit a quibuscumque malis. Lux ueritatis a Iudeis, paganis et hereticis. Constancia firmitatis ab ypocritis. Secundum sensum moralem materia huius libri est planctus pro ruina siue lapsu anime fidelis a statu iusticie per peccatum cogitacionis, locucionis, et operi."

13. Ibid. (219): "Ex iam dictis patet modus agendi siue causa formalis in parte. Modus enim est triplici uersu in quadruplici alphabeto distincto dictos tres status deplangere."

14. See P. Dronke, "The Lament of Jephtha's Daughter: Themes, Traditions, Originality," *Studi medievali* 12.2 (1971): 819–63; G. Dahan, "Le sacrifice de Jephté (Juges 11, 29-40) dans l'exégèse chrétienne, du XIIe au XIVe siècle," in *Tous le temps du veneour est sanz oyseuseté: Mélanges offerts à Yves Christe pour son 65ème anniversaire, par ses amis, ses collègues, ses élèves,* ed. C. Hediger, Culture et société médiévales 8 (Turnhout: Brepols, 2005), 185–204.

15. William of Alton, *Super Threnos,* prol. (ed. cit., 219): "Causa autem finalis insinuatur in hoc quod dicitur: *filie populi mei,* ut li *filie* sit datiui casus. Planxit *filie,* id est ad utilitatem filie, id est sinagoge, ecclesie, et fidelis anime."

sis is the recognition of complexity in a given biblical book's subject matter, mode of exposition, purpose, and as we shall see, authorship.

Toward the beginning of the prologue to his commentary on Lamentations, William indicates that the book's principal efficient cause is the Holy Spirit and that the secondary and less principal one is Jeremiah. This is typical of commentaries of the period. As a consequence of evolving understandings of causality, university exegetes typically accounted for the biblical text's divine and human origins by appealing to a distinction between its primary and secondary efficient causes, namely, God and the human author. Put simply, they found in the *Liber de causis* a framework for accounting for the divine authority and authorship of Scripture on the one hand without prejudice to the integrity of the human author on the other.[16] On their view, both the divine and human authors understood and intended the literal sense, and sometimes multiple literal senses. Precisely because divine authorship was clearly established as the primary cause, it could be taken for granted, and human authorship could be subjected to unfettered analysis. This allowed commentators to take stock of differences between the perspectives of Scripture's various human authors without prejudice to the unity of revealed truth. So, for example, in his remarks on the title of the book of Lamentations, William illustrates the distinctiveness of Jeremiah's point of view with respect to those of several other prophets:

The title: the Book of Lamentations of Jeremiah, and just as the Canticle of Solomon is called the Canticle of Canticles, so this is called the Lamentation of Lamentations because it excels all others. The others are particular: Jacob's sons wept for their father, Samuel for Saul, David for Saul and Jonathan and Absalom, Hezekiah for his own imminent death predicted to him. But this one is made for every temporal and spiritual loss. Indeed, it exceeds the others in quantity, as is evident, and indeed in the mode of weeping.[17]

The same mode of analysis appears in William's commentary on the Book of Wisdom. In the prologue he introduces his discussion of the book's causes by invoking Aristotle's dictum that knowledge of any reality presupposes an examination of its causes: "In order to discern this book it is neces-

16. On divine and human authors as primary and secondary efficient causes, see A. J. Minnis, *Medieval Theory of Authorship* (Philadelphia: University of Pennsylvania Press, 1984), 73–117.

17. William of Alton, *Super Threnos*, prol. (ed. cit., 219–20): "Titulus: *Liber Trenorum Ieremie*, et sicut Canticum Salamonis dicitur *Canticum Canticorum*, sic ista lamentacio *Lamentacio Lamentacionum*, quia omnes excellit. Cetere enim particulares: fleuerunt enim filii Iacob patrem suum, Samuel Saulem, Dauid Saul et Ionathan et Absalonem, Ezechias mortem suam imminentem sibi predictam. Set hec fit pro omni dampno temporali et spirituali, excedit eciam alias in quantitate, ut patet, et etiam in modo plangendi."

sary to consider its causes. For we think we know a thing, says the Philosopher, when we know its causes. By this saying we may identify four causes of this book, namely, the efficient, formal, material, and final."[18] Though he credits Lamentations to the Holy Spirit,[19] William's ascription of Wisdom to the Word of God *per modum inspirationis* is hardly surprising in view of the Latin West's classical attribution of wisdom to the second person of the Trinity. And yet, he draws a further distinction within the secondary efficient cause, specifically, between remote and proximate human authors, the former being Solomon *per modum inuentionis*, and the latter Philo *per modum compilationis*.[20] Whereas the Church's liturgy testified to Solomon's authorship (readings from Wisdom were introduced by attributions to him), a somewhat vague ascription to Philo had been initiated by no less an authority than Jerome and had been perpetuated by Rabanus Maurus.[21] Faced with conflicting authorities, William differentiates between the role of an author and that of a compiler, the first belonging to Solomon, the second to Philo. After discussing both figures at some length, William mentions in passing that this conception of multiple human authorship applies as well to the book of Proverbs, the author and compiler of which, as he would have it, are respectively Solomon and unnamed subordinates of Hezekiah.[22] Concluding his discussion of the efficient cause, he cites the *Liber de causis*'s opening line to redirect his students' attention to the book's divine author: "Because 'every primary cause infuses its effect more abundantly than does a secondary cause,' by the custom of sacred Scripture this work is attributed

18. William of Alton, *Super Sapientiam*, prol. (*The Biblical Interpretation of William of Alton*, 214): "Cuius libri ut habeatur notitia oportet causas considerare. Scire namque, ait Philosophus, arbitramur unumquodque cum causas cognoscimus."

19. *Super Threnos*, prol. (ed. cit., 218): "Principalis enim efficiens Spiritus est.... Causa efficiens secundaria et minus principalis Ieremias est."

20. William of Alton, *Super Sapientiam*, prol. (ed. cit., 214): "Efficiens quidem huius libri causa triplex est. Prima per modum inspirationis, scilicet Verbum Dei.... Verbum Dei est efficiens causa prima. Secunda causa efficiens, scilicet per modum inuentionis, est Salomon.... Proxima causa efficiens per modum compilationis fuit Phylo sapientissimus Iudeorum." An equivalent text appears in another prologue associated with this commentary, which was wrongly ascribed to Bonaventure. See *Commentarius in librum Sapientiam*, (incipit: *Diligite lumen sapientiae*), *S. Bonaventurae Opera omnia* (Quaracchi: Fathers of the Collegium S. Bonaventure, Ad Claras Aquas, t. VI, 1893), 108a–b.

21. Jerome, *Praefatio in libros Salomonis* (PL 28, 1242): "Etenim multo est Philo iste, cui liber Sapientiae tamquam auctori, vel saltem interpreti tribuebatur." Rabanus Maurus, *Comm. in Sapientiam* (PL 109, 671): "quem tamen beatus Hieronymus asserit non a Salomone, ut usus habet, sed a Philone doctissimo Judaeo fuisse conscriptum."

22. William of Alton, *Super Sapientiam*, prol. (ed. cit., 214): "Vnde liber ipse *Sapientia Salomonis* inscribitur, et more ecclesiastico lectionibus de libro hoc sumptis premittitur: 'Dixit Salomon filiis Israel,' quia scilicet de eius sententiis liber iste, quamuis ab alio compilatus sit, sicut et liber *Prouerbiorum* pro magna parte a uiris Ezechie."

to the first cause, namely, the Word of God."[23] A similar analysis of causality appears in William's prologues to his other biblical commentaries.[24]

Aquinas's language is not so clearly fixed. In his biblical prologues he seldom mentions Aristotle's efficient, material, formal, and final causes, and he generally analyzes a given book of the Bible according to the earlier terminology of author, title, mode of exposition, and usefulness. In his very first work, his commentary on Isaiah, Aquinas names the Holy Spirit as the author and describes the prophet Isaiah as his minister.[25] In his commentary on Jeremiah from the same period, he names the efficient cause as the unity of the inspiring Spirit and the one prophesying by that Spirit,

23. Ibid.: "Quia 'omnis causa primaria plus est influens in suum causatum quam causam secundaria', ideo efficiens causa huius libri, more scripture sacre, cause prime, scilicet Verbo Dei, omissis ceteris attribuitur."

24. For the Latin texts of William of Alton's prologues to Ecclesiastes, Wisdom, Jeremiah, Lamentations, Ezekiel, and John, see my *The Biblical Interpretation of William of Alton*, 209–23. For the near contemporary William of Luxi's prologues to Jeremiah, Lamentations, Baruch, and the Minor Prophets, see A. Sulavik, *Guillelmi de Luxi: Postilla super Baruch, Postilla super Ionam* (Turnhout: Brepols, 2006), CCCM 219, 131–42. What follows are examples from a few anonymous commentaries from the second half of the thirteenth century: *Super Iosue*, incipit: *Fortis in bello* (MS Paris, BnF lat. 526 f. 210ra): "Fuit enim Iosue auctor secundarius inmediatus, Deus principalis et precipuus."; *Super librum Iudicum*, incipit: *Iudicabit Dominus populum suum* (MS Paris, BnF lat. 526 f. 224rb): "Auctor in hoc quod dicitur: *Dominus*, qui est auctor primus totius sacre scripture. Auctor secundarius qui compilauit et coniunxit facta istius libri, secundum Ysidorum, *Ethimologiarum*, libro sexto, capitulo II, Samuel; secundum alios, Esdras; secundum Magistrum in *Historia*, Ezechias qui parabolis Salamonis et librum Regum in unum collegit; de hoc Ysidore, libro sexto, capitulo secundo. Et licet aliquis istorum librum hunc in unum collegerit, dicunt tamen quidam quod singuli Iudices facta sui temporis in scripto redegerunt."; *Super Ruth*, incipit: *Breuis in uolatilibus est apis* (MS Paris, BnF lat. 526 f. 239rb): "<Causa> efficiens: *apis* … Per apim Filius Dei uel Spiritus sanctus intelligitur, qui est auctor principalis totius sacre scripture. Item, propter aliquas istarum, per apim potest designari Samuel, quem dicunt Hebrei et Ysidorus, Ethimol., libro VI, capitulo XII, auctorem secundarium istius libri, uel Ezechias rex, uel Esdras"; *Super I–IV Regum*, incipit: *Ad uos ergo o reges* (MS Paris, BnF lat. 526 f. 178ra): "Causa efficiens insinuatur ex persona loquentis in hoc quod dicitur: *mei*, Deus enim, qui per Salomonem hic loquentem, uel Spiritus Sanctus intelligitur est auctor principalis huius libri, secundariique non unus, set multi."; *Super Iob*, incipit: *Surgite postquam sederitis* (MS Basel, Univ. Bibl. B III 25, f. 2ra): "Causa autem efficiens principalis Deus est…. Causa autem secundaria in hoc libro fuit ipse Iob, licet enim, 'Alii Moysen,' ut dicit Ysid., *Ethimol.*, libro VI, 'alii unum uel aliquos de prophetis, hunc librum scripsisse autument'" (Isid. Hisp., *Etym.*, VI, 1, ed. Lindsay [Oxford, 1911], n. 13).

25. Thomas Aquinas, *Super Isaiam*, prol. (ed. Leonina, t. XXIII, 3a): "Ex verbis istis tria possunt accipi circa librum Ysaie prophete quem pre manibus habemus, scilicet actor, modus et materia. Circa primum tria ponuntur, scilicet actor, actoris minister et ministri officium siue donum. Actor ostenditur in dicentis imperio, unde premittitur: *Respondit michi Dominus et dixit: Scribe uisum*," etc. Actor enim Scripture sacre Spiritus sanctus est, infra xlviii: "Nunc misit me Dominus" etc., 2 Petri 1: "Non enim uoluntate humana," etc.; Spiritus enim "loquitur misteria," sicut dicitur I Cor. XIV. Minister ostenditur in scribentis actu; dicit enim *Scribe*: "fuit autem lingua prophete organum Spiritus Sancti."

namely Jeremiah.[26] In his literal commentary on Job, which dates to his stay in Orvieto (1261–65), the only author Aquinas mentions in the prologue is Job. Mentioning the view of some (*aliqui*) who say Job was a fictional figure rather than an historical one, Aquinas observes that this seems to run up against the authority of Scripture, as Job is mentioned in Ezekiel 14:14. But then he remarks that it is no part of his present intention to discuss questions concerning the time of the narrative, Job's ethnic origins, or even who the book's author may have been; that is, whether Job co-wrote it (*conscripserit*) about himself as if he were writing about someone else, or whether someone else wrote it about him.[27] In the prologue to his *Commentary on Matthew*, now generally dated to 1269–70, early on in his second Paris regency, the only author Aquinas mentions is Matthew (twice).[28] Similarly, in the prologue to his *Commentary on John*, dated with some probability to the years 1270–72 of his second Paris regency, he twice refers to the Evangelist as an author, without so mentioning anyone else.[29] In his prologue to the Pauline epistles, composed perhaps as early as 1265 (Rome), and perhaps as late as the end of his second Paris regency (1271–72) or even later, in 1272–73 (Naples), the only one he calls an author is Paul.[30] In sum, in Aquinas's

26. Aquinas, *In Jeremiam*, prol. (*Opera omnia*, ed. Parma, t. XIV, 1863, 577a): "Verba ista sunt Oniae summi sacerdotis ad Iudam Machabaeum, in visione Jeremiam commendantis. Ex quibus quatuor possunt accipi circa praesens opus quod prae manibus habetur; scilicet auctor, materia, modus, et utilitas. Circa auctorem tria designat praesens auctoritas; scilicet officium, affectum et actum. In officio ostenditur prophetalis dignitas: unde dicit: *Jeremias propheta Domini*." In prologum B. Hieronymi (ibid., 578a): "Et causam ostendit, unitatem Spiritus inspirantis, ibi, *Quippe qui eodem Spiritu prophetaverit*."

27. Aquinas, *Super Iob*, prol. (ed. Leonina, t. 26, 4b): "Quo autem tempore fuerit vel ex quibus parentibus originem duxerit, quis etiam huius libri fuerit auctor, utrum scilicet ipse Iob hunc librum conscripserit de se quasi de alio loquens, an alius de eo ista retulerit, non est praesentis intentionis discutere."

28. Aquinas, *Super Matt.*, in prologum B. Hieronymi (*Opera Omnia*, ed. Parma, t. X, 1a): "*Matthaeus ex Iudaea* etc. Evangelio Matthaei Hieronymus praemittit prologum, in quo tria facit: primo enim ipsum auctorem describit; secundo evangelii mysteria aperit, ibi, *Duorum in generatione Christi principia praesumens*; tertio suam intentionem ostendit, ibi, *Nobis autem in hoc studio argumenti fuit*. Auctorem vero ipsum describit ex quatuor. Primo ex nomine, cum dicit, *Matthaeus*; secundo ex origine, cum dicit, *ex Judaea*; tertio ex scribendi ordine, ibi, *Sicut in ordine primus ponitur*; quarto ex vocatione, ibi, *Cujus vocatio ad Dominum*, idest ad Christum."

29. Aquinas, *Super Iohannem*, prol. (*Opera Omnia*, ed. Parma, t. X, 281a): "Sequitur conditio Auctoris, qui quidem describitur in praemissis quantum ad quatuor: quantum ad nomen, quantum ad virtutem, quantum ad figuram, et quantum ad privilegium. Quantum ad nomen, quia Joannes, qui hujus Evangelii auctor fuit; Joannes autem interpretatur, in quo est gratia: quia secreta divinitatis videre non possunt nisi qui gratiam Dei in se habent."

30. Aquinas, *In Epist. Paul.*, prol. (*Opera Omnia*, ed. Parma, t. XIII, 1a, 2b): "*Vas electionis est mihi iste*, et cetera. Act. IX. Homines in sacra Scriptura inveniuntur vasis comparati propter quatuor; scilicet propter constitutionem, repletionem, usum et fructum.... Sic igitur ex verbis

early commentaries, the term *auctor* usually designates the divine author, while in his later ones it designates the human one, though always as subordinate, that is, as receiving and transmitting divine Revelation. Thus, it is not surprising that the human authors figure largely in his prologues. Their importance for him lies not in their intrinsic historical significance, but in their mediation of Revelation. While Aquinas's terminology is marked by a certain fluidity, he clearly subscribes to the twofold understanding of biblical authorship manifest in the work of his contemporaries.

All of this is in keeping with one of Aquinas's key contributions to the analysis of secondary causality, specifically, his frequently stated principle that God employs instruments according to the natures in which he created them (sometimes producing effects transcending their natural capacities), and that the defining feature of human nature is reason.[31] In Aquinas's view, if God makes use of biblical authors as instruments, he does so precisely by virtue of that which distinguishes them as human—their rationality, their capacity for understanding and intending, in this case understanding and intending what they write. There should be no need to say that Aquinas appreciates God's capacity for employing human agents as instruments without the slightest detriment to their freedom.

Authorial Intention and the Senses of Scripture

The framework of the *Liber*'s primary and secondary causes, in tandem with Aristotle's four causes, allowed university commentators to respond to two sets of questions with far greater precision than had previous generations. One concerns authorial intention, and the other the distinction between the various senses, literal and spiritual. Regarding the former, thirteenth-century biblical interpretation was characterized by a progressive tendency to identify the literal sense with the author's intention. In their methodological reflections as well as in their interpretations, Aquinas's contemporaries unambiguously designated the literal sense as the human author's intention, which they in turn identified with the divine author's intention. Aquinas held this view, refined it, and gave it a clearer theoretical basis.

As for the latter, the problem of differentiating between the literal and spiritual senses had attracted considerable attention during the century

---

praemissis possumus accipere quatuor causas huius operis, scilicet epistolarum Pauli, quas prae manibus habemus. Primo quidem auctorem in vase."

31. Throughout Aquinas's writings this principle appears in a broad range of contexts, e.g., creation, divine providence, the moral life, soteriology, and Christology. For a few examples drawn from only one work, see *Summa contra gentiles* II, 21; III, 78, 87, 103, 112, 147, 148; IV, 41.

preceding Aquinas's work. Largely due to the influence of Peter Abelard (d. 1142)[32] and Hugh of Saint Victor (d. 1141), interpreters had tended to expand the scope of literal exegesis to embrace figurative meanings. The literal sense had come to be more closely identified with the full scope of the human author's intended meaning rather than with a superficial reading of the biblical letter.[33] Yet it was not until the mid-thirteenth century that this tendency came to completion with the works of Dominican and Franciscan friars such as Guerric of Saint-Quentin, Bonaventure, Albert the Great, William of Alton, William of Luxi, and Aquinas.[34] As a result, thirteenth-century commentators took a keen interest in the human author's way of speaking. Involving consideration of the author's literary genre and historical background, such analysis had as its object the *intentio auctoris* from which the author's literal sense was to be had.[35] It is worth noting here that Aquinas often resolved problems of interpretation by appealing to a given biblical author's *modus loquendi*.[36]

32. In *Sic et Non* (PL 178, 1339–1610), Abelard addressed the problems of reconciling discordant texts and showed the importance of the philosophy of language in the interpretation of authoritative writings.

33. Hugh puts it as follows: "Expositio tria continet, litteram, sensum, sententiam. Littera est congrua ordinatio dictionum, quod etiam constructionem uocamus. Sensus est facilis quedam et aperta significatio, quam littera prima fronte prefert. Sententia est profundior intelligentia, que nisi expositione uel interpretatione non inuenitur. In his ordo est, ut primum littera, deinde sensus, deinde sententia inquiratur, quo facto, perfecta est expositio." *Didascalion* 3 (ed. Buttimer, 58). On the development of the literal sense, see G. Dahan, *L'exégèse chrètienne de la Bible en Occident Medieval, XIIe–XIVe siècle* (Paris, 1999), 240–41; B. Smalley, *The Study of the Bible in the Middle Ages*, 3rd ed. (Oxford, 1983), 93–95.

34. Note the qualification that, as they understood it, the literal sense is complex. As B. Smalley put it, "With St. Albert the 'literal truth' takes on a new meaning. It is not an easy preliminary but a difficult goal." *The Study of the Bible*, 299.

35. This process had been important for making sense of the Platonic styles of patristic authors, such as Augustine and Dionysius, which differed sharply from the dialectical language of the schools and universities. See M.-D. Chenu, *Introduction à l'étude de Saint Thomas d'Aquin* (Paris, 1950), 117–31.

36. In the first chapter of his commentary *Super Iohannem*, Aquinas adverts to the Evangelist's *modus loquendi* on eight separate occasions. What follows are two examples. In his exposition of Jn. 1:3 (*and without him was made nothing*), he mentions three heresies that have arisen from a misreading of John's manner of speaking in his usage of *nihil*, as if he meant that it were something created. Thomas replies by pointing out that John has used the term in a purely negative sense, *Super Io. 1, 3* (ed. Parma, t. X, 291b–292a): "Deinde dicit: *Et sine ipso factum est nihil.* . . . Nam, ex hoc modo loquendi quo Joannes hic utitur, ponens hoc quod dicitur *nihil*, in fine orationis, crediderunt, ipsum nihil teneri affirmative, quasi *nihil* sit aliquid, quod sine Verbo factum sit. . . . Sed omnes isti tres errores ex uno fonte procedentes, scilicet ex hoc quod ipsum *nihil* volunt affirmative accipi, excluduntur per hoc quod *nihil* non ponitur hic affirmative, sed negative tantum. Ut sit sensus: ita facta sunt omnia per Verbum, quod nihil est participans esse, quod non sit factum per ipsum." Commenting on 1:6 (*There was a man was sent by God, whose name was John*), Aquinas draws attention to the Evangelist's change of

Facilitating such analysis was the evolution of psychological presuppositions brought about by the study of Aristotle's anthropology. It will be recalled that in the Neoplatonic perspective, the soul exists as an integral reality dwelling within the body, and intellectual knowledge comes by way of enlightenment, not sense perception.[37] Such was the operative paradigm typical of much pre-thirteenth-century exegesis. Largely for this reason, medieval commentators of earlier generations, influenced as they were by patristic writers such as Origen, Augustine, and Gregory the Great, had viewed the spiritual senses as the primary medium of Revelation and had regarded the literal or historical sense as secondary.[38] Thirteenth-century interpreters, by contrast, influenced as they were by the recently diffused *libri naturales* of Aristotle, especially the *De anima*, called into question traditional anthropological assumptions and, making use of Aristotle's theory of knowledge, reconsidered the human endowments for perception. Particularly important for biblical interpretation was Aristotle's theory of the human intellect's dependence on the imagination. For Aristotle and his thirteenth-century followers, the soul was the form of the body and could not gain knowledge apart from the mediation of the senses and the imagination.

The importance of this doctrine with respect to Revelation was not lost on biblical commentators, upon whom its effect was twofold. First, they recognized in it the centrality of the literal sense with respect to the spiritual senses. As a result, allegory ceded pride of place to the literal sense. Though literal interpretation had figured in the expositions of even the most notorius allegorizers, such as Origen, Augustine, Gregory, and later, Rupert of Deutz and Bernard, it was seldom prominent. Now, it was considered essential. Second, thirteenth-century expositors realized the importance of the human author's imagination with respect to the literal sense. As a result,

----

manner of speaking as his subject changes from what is eternal, the Word, to what is temporal, John the Baptist (ibid., 296a): "Considerandum autem est circa primum, quod statim cum Evangelista incipit de aliquo temporali, mutat modum loquendi. Cum enim supra loqueretur de aeternis, utebatur hoc verbo erat, quod est praeteriti imperfecti, ostendens per hoc, aeterna interminata esse; nunc vero, cum loquitur de temporalibus, utitur hoc verbo, fuit, ad ostendendum quod temporalia sic praeterierunt quod tamen terminantur."

37. Augustine's account of human sensation is telling: "Nec sane putandum est facere aliquid corpus in spiritu, tamquam spiritus corpori facienti materiae vice subdatur. Omni enim modo praestantior est qui facit ea re, de qua aliquid facit. Neque ullo modo spiritu praestantius est corpus, immo perspicuo modo spiritus corpore."; and later: "Neque enim corpus sentit, sed anima per corpus, quo velut nuntio utitur ad formandum in seipsa quod extrinsecus nuntiatur." *De Genesi ad litteram libri*, XII, ed. J. Zycha (Vienna: 1894), CSEL 28.1, 402; 416.

38. In this connection Smalley remarks, "The allegorical method captivated the Latin world." *The Study of the Bible*, 20.

prophecies and rhetorical figures such as metaphor and irony were recognized as falling within the scope of the human author's intended meaning. As Aquinas puts it in the first chapter of his commentary on Job, "The literal sense is that which is first intended by the words, whether properly said or figuratively."[39]

University exegetes understood that coming to terms with a human author's *intentio*, that is, the literal sense of the inspired text, presupposes coming to terms with his perspective and interests, as well as the place his writings hold within the divine plan of redemption. Their concern for doing so is particularly conspicuous in their Old Testament commentaries, where we find them expatiating on prophecy as well as rhetorical figures, or tropes, as part of the literal sense. Returning to William of Alton's commentary on Lamentations, we find him taking Jeremiah's description of Israel's persecutors as referring literally not only to the Chaldeans of his own time, but also to the Romans who sacked Jerusalem and destroyed its temple some six centuries later.[40]

For his part, Aquinas does not doubt that human biblical authors could intend to signify many realities at once, as he occasionally finds a prophetic literal sense in his Old Testament commentaries. While he usually presents a plurality of literal senses as alternatives,[41] at times he puts all of them forward as intended by the human author.[42] With respect to his interpretation of the Psalms, something must be said of his understanding of the case of Theodore of Mopsuestia (c. 350–428).[43] In opposition to the allegorizing interpretations of Alexandrian commentators, Theodore had asserted that no

39. *In Iob* I (ed. Leonina, t. 26, 7b): "sensus litteralis est qui primo per verba intenditur, sive proprie dicta sive figurate."

40. The expositions of Lam 1:3 and 1:4 are typical: "*Omnes persecvtores eivs*, scilicet Caldei et Romani persequentes Iudeos fugitiuos," and "*Omnes portes eivs*, id est ciuitatis et templi, *destrvcte*, per Caldeos et Romanos." (Bellamah, "William of Alton's Commentary on the Book of Lamentations," *AHDLMA* 73 [2006]: 238–39). In William's perspective, Jeremiah's gift of prophecy allowed him to envision simultaneously two separate series of events and to describe them in one text. Enlightened by the Holy Spirit, the prophet saw and intended the ultimate signification of the words he wrote, viewing the present realities as *figurae* or *typoi*, and the future ones as their fulfillment. For a discussion of this mode of exegesis as it was practiced in William's time, see Minnis, *Medieval Theory of Authorship*, 88.

41. G. Dahan has identified the multiplication of alternative interpretations, at both the literal and spiritual levels, as a common feature of medieval exegesis, "Les Pères dans l'exégèse médiévale," *RSPT* 91 (2007): 109–26 (120).

42. What follow are two examples from Aquinas's literal commentary on Isaiah: "*Dominorum*: Assyriorum, Caldeorum, Romanorum" (*Super Isaiam* 19, 4, ed. Leonina, t. XXVIII, 105a); "ponit promissionem: *Cum transieris per aquas*, Egiptios, *flumina*, Chaldei, *igne*, Greci, *flamma*, Romani" (*Super Isaiam* 43, 2, ibid., 181a–b).

43. The present remarks are indebted to the discussion of Minnis in *Medieval Theory of Authorship*, 87–88.

more than five of the Psalms refer directly to Christ, though he allowed that others could be applied to him by adaptation. For this he was posthumously accused of denying that anything in the Old Testament referred literally to Christ. This mode of Old Testament interpretation was condemned at the Second Council of Constantinople in 553, with the result that Aquinas considered the prophetic literal sense a matter of doctrine and the denial of it a matter of heresy.[44] To avoid Theodore's pitfall he availed himself of a theory of prefiguration borrowed from Jerome. On this view, when the sages of the Old Testament described realities present to them, they recognized them as figures (*figurae*) or types (*typoi*) of future ones; while aiming to provide an account of things or events at hand, they primarily intended to describe what remained to be fulfilled.[45] Several examples of this mode of interpretation appear in his commentary on John's Gospel, once with reference to Theodore.[46]

It is doubtful that there is to be found anywhere in medieval literature a more rigorous theoretical account for this paradigm than in the writings of Aquinas. In what is probably the most often cited text in this connec-

44. *Super Ps.*, prol. (*Opera omnia*, ed. Parma, t. XIV, 149b) "Circa modum exponendi sciendum est, quod tam in Psalterio quam in aliis prophetiis exponendis evitare debemus unum errorem damnatum in quinta synodo. Theodorus enim Mopsuestenus dixit, quod in sacra Scriptura et prophetiis nihil expresse dicitur de Christo, sed de quibusdam aliis rebus, sed adaptaverunt Christo: sicut illud Psalm. 21: *Diviserunt sibi vestimenta mea* etc., non de christo, sed ad literam dicitur de David. Hic autem modus damnatus est in illo concilio: et qui asserit sic exponendas Scripturas, haereticus est." Later in the same work Aquinas returns to the matter, *Super Ps.* 21, 7 (ibid., 217b): "Et in synodo Toletana quidam Theodorus Mopsuestenus, qui hunc ad litteram de David exponebat, fuit damnatus, et propter hoc et propter alia multa; et ideo de Christo exponendus est." Several scholars have argued that Theodore's views were unfairly represented at the Second Council of Constantinople. See J. M. Lera, "Theodore de Mopsueste," *Dict. Sp.* 15 (1991): 385–400; E. Amann, "Théodore de Mopsueste," *DTC* 15.1 (1946): 235–79. For a less favorable appraisal of Theodore, as well as an overview of scholarly perspectives, see B. de Margerie, *Introduction à l'histoire de l'exégèse*, vol. 1 (Paris: 1979), 181–84.

45. *Super Ps.*, prol. (ed. Parma, t. XIV, 149b): "Beatus ergo Hieronymus super Ezech. tradidit nobis unam regulam quam servabimus in Psalmis: scilicet quod sic sunt exponendi de rebus gestis, ut figurantibus aliquid de Christo vel ecclesia." Though invoked by Aquinas against Theodore, Jerome's understanding of prefiguration is not far removed from the Antiochene perspective. De Margerie has even referred to it as "son intelligence «antiochienne» de la théôria," *Introduction à l'histoire de l'exégèse*, vol. 2, 175.

46. *Super Io.* 12, 41 (ed. Parma, t. X, 521b): "Videns ergo Isaias gloriam Filii, vidit et gloriam Patris; immo totius Trinitatis, quae est unus Deus sedens super solium excelsum.… Non autem ita quod Isaias essentiam Trinitatis viderit, sed imaginaria visione, cum intelligentia, quaedam signa majestatis expressit.… Per illud vero quod secundo dicitur, *Et locutus est de eo*, excluditur error Manichaeorum, qui dixerunt nullas prophetias in veteri testamento praecessisse de Christo, ut Augustinus narrat in Lib. Contra faustum, et Theodorum Mopsuestenum, qui dixit omnes Prophetias veteris testamenti esse de aliquo negotio dictas, per quamdam tamen appropriationem esse adductas ab Apostolis et Evangelistis ad ministerium Christi: sicut ea quae dicunt in uno facto, possunt adaptari ad aliud factum."

tion—*ST* I, q. 1, a. 10—he entertains the question of whether Scripture can have several senses under one letter (i.e., the literal, allegorical, tropological, and anagogical). At the outset of the reply, Aquinas says plainly that the author of sacred Scripture is God. Then he puts forward the classic solution, formulated by Augustine, according to which the literal sense is conveyed by biblical words signifying specific realities (*res*), while the spiritual senses are conveyed by realities (*res*) signifying other realities (*res*), as Moses's raising of a serpent on a staff (Num 21:9) signified Jesus's elevation on the cross (Jn 3:14).[47] On this account, the literal level of signification is intended by both the divine and human *auctores*, while the spiritual one is intended only by the divine one, in whose providence alone lies the capacity to employ contingent things and events to signify other realities. As a consequence, no sense of any spiritually signified reality can be had before the first (i.e., literal) signification is had. Aquinas concludes his reply by stating that the literal sense is the one intended by the author, and by reiterating that the author of Scripture is God.[48] In sum, for Aquinas, any text of Scripture may convey several senses, because such signification lies within the capacities of its divine author, namely, God.[49] Here Aquinas says nothing about multiple human intentionality. And yet, in another relevant text, *De quolibet* VII, q. 6, a. 1, ad 5, he unambiguously describes the human author as an instrumental efficient cause capable of intending to signify future events in their descriptions of present ones. As he puts it:

It is to be said that the principal author of sacred Scripture is the Holy Spirit, who understood much more in any single saying of sacred Scripture than is expounded or discerned by expositors. And yet, it is not unfitting that the man who was the in-

47. The capital text is Augustine's *De doctrina christiana*, I, 2: "Omnis doctrina uel rerum est uel signorum, sed res per signa discuntur. Proprie autem nunc res appellaui, quae non ad significandum aliquid adhibentur, sicuti est lignum lapis pecus atque huiusmodi cetera, sed non illud lignum, quod in aquas amaras Moysen misisse legimus, ut amaritudine carerent, neque ille lapis, quem Iacob sibi ad caput posuerat, neque illud pecus, quod pro filio immolauit Abraham. Hae namque ita res sunt, ut aliarum etiam signa sint rerum. Sunt autem alia signa, quorum omnis usus in significando est, sicuti sunt uerba" (CCSL 32, 7). For a discussion of this text and the legacy to medieval exegesis of Augustine's theory of signification, see Dahan, *L'exégèse chrétienne*, 299–307.

48. *ST* I, q. 1, a. 10, c. (ed. Leonina, t. IV, 25a–b): "Respondeo dicendum quod auctor sacrae Scripturae est Deus, in cuius potestate est ut non solum voces ad significandum accommodet (quod etiam homo facere potest), sed etiam res ipsas.... Quia vero sensus litteralis est, quem auctor intendit, auctor autem sacrae Scripturae Deus est, qui omnia simul suo intellectu comprehendit: non est inconveniens, ut dicit Augustinus XII *Confessionum*, si etiam secundum litteralem sensum in una littera Scripturae plures sint sensus."

49. On Aquinas's understanding of the possibility of plural literal senses, see M. Johnson, "Another Look at the Plurality of the Literal Sense," *Medieval Theology and Philosophy* 2 (1992): 117–41.

strumental author of sacred Scripture should understand many things in one statement, because the prophets, as Jerome says in his commentary on Hosea, spoke of
present events such that they even intended to signify future ones, hence it is not
impossible (for him) to understand many (things) insofar as one is the figure of another.[50]

The preceding affords us some background for examining another important text, *De potentia*, q. 4, a. 1, c., where Aquinas takes up the question
of whether the creation of things was preceded temporally by the creation
of unformed matter. At the outset of his reply, Aquinas differentiates between two aspects of the question, one having to do with the truth of things
(*una de ipsa rerum veritate*), the other having to do with the literal sense
(*alia de sensu litterae*). Regarding the latter, he indicates two pitfalls to be
avoided in the discernment of the literal sense. One is to assert what is pa-
tently false, because divine Scripture, as handed on (*traditae*) by the Holy
Spirit, is devoid of falsehood, as is the faith; the other is to impose an interpretation on Scripture in such a way as to preclude other senses which contain or can contain truth, and which are not at odds with their immediate
context (*circumstantia litterae*). At the outset he describes the literal sense
as that by which the divinely inspired Moses explains to us the world's beginning (*qua Moyses divinitus inspiratus principium mundi nobis exponit*).
Later in his reply, and in many other places in his works, he says that God
is the principal author of Scripture. By implication, Moses is a secondary,
instrumental author. It is Moses who does the explaining (*exponit*). It is his
meaning that must be understood:

Hence it is not inconceivable that Moses and the other authors of the Holy Books
were given to know the various truths that men would discover in the text, and that
they expressed them under one literary style, so that each truth is the sense intended
by the author. And then even if commentators adapt certain truths to the sacred text
that were not understood by the author, without doubt the Holy Spirit understood
them, since he is the principal author of Holy Scripture. Consequently every truth
that can be adapted to divine Scripture without prejudice to the circumstance of the
letter (*salva litterae circumstantia*) is its sense.[51]

---

50. *De quolibet* VII, q. 6, a. 1, ad 5 (ed. Leonina, t. XXV, 1, 29a–b): "Ad quintum dicendum,
quod auctor principalis sacrae Scripturae est Spiritus sanctus, qui in uno verbo sacrae Scripturae intellexit multo plura quam per expositores sacrae Scripturae exponantur, vel discernantur.
Non est etiam inconueniens quod homo qui fuit auctor instrumentalis sacrae scripturae in uno
uerbo plura intelligeret, quia prophete, ut Ieronimus dicit super Osee, ita loquebantur de factis
presentibus, quod etiam intenderunt futura significare, unde non est impossibile plura intelligere in quantum unum est figura alterius."

51. Aquinas, *De potentia*, q. 4, a. 1, c. (ed. Marietti, *Quaestiones Disputatae*, t. II, 33a): "Unde
non est incredibile, Moysi et aliis sacrae Scripturae auctoribus hoc divinitus esse concessum,

In evidence here is the aforementioned paradigm of primary and secondary efficient causality, whereby the primary author and efficient cause is God, and the secondary author and efficient cause is the biblical sage. With respect to the literal sense, wherein things or events (*res*) are signified by words (*verba*), the intentions of the two authors are identical, sometimes even for more than one meaning—for example, in prophecy. Put simply, the human author is capable of expressing multiple meanings in a single passage. And what about these truths that commentators adapt to the sacred text that were not understood by the human author? In speaking of "other senses" (*alios sensus*), of course, Aquinas is speaking of the spiritual senses, wherein things or events (*res*) are signified by other things or events (*res*). Lying only within the providential scope of the divine author, such signification by way of contingent events belongs to allegory, tropology, and anagogy. By noting the importance of the coherence of such senses with their literal context, Aquinas restates his view that the spiritual senses are based on the literal one.[52] By excluding such signification from the human author's ken and intentionality, Aquinas says much about divine providence and Revelation; he says nothing about the human author's involvement in the literal sense, and nothing about the exegete's task in grasping it.

Conclusion

Patristic and early medieval commentators, preoccupied as they were with expounding the allegorical senses, tended to accentuate similarities and obscure differences between biblical authors. During the thirteenth century, the four causes of Aristotle and the primary and secondary efficient causes of the *Liber de causis* provided scope for attributing to human biblical *auctores* an unprecedented degree of self-determination, as moved by divine inspiration, in regard to their writing; this constituted the matrix within which biblical texts were studied.[53] As a result, commentators were able at once to secure the divine authority of Scripture, on the one hand, and the integrity of the human author as a secondary efficient cause, on the other. This allowed them to account for genuine differences between the perspectives of human

---

ut diversa vera, quae homines possent intelligere, ipsi cognoscerent, et ea sub una serie litterae designarent, ut sic quilibet eorum sit sensus auctoris. Unde si etiam aliqua vera ab expositoribus sacrae Scripturae litterae aptentur, quae auctor non intelligit, non est dubium quin Spiritus sanctus intellexerit, qui est principalis auctor divinae Scripturae. Unde omnis veritas quae, salva litterae circumstantia, potest divinae Scripturae aptari, est eius sensus."

52. Cf. *De quolibet* VII, q. 6, a. 1, ad 4; *ST* I, q. 1, a. 10, ad 1.

53. Minnis, *Medieval Theory of Authorship*, 82.

biblical authors without fragmenting Revelation.[54] They were well aware of the arduousness of coming to terms with the human author's intended meaning, but confident in their ability to do so. Thomas was particularly explicit in designating this as his exegetical task.[55] As had Jerome, Augustine, and more recently, Hugh of St. Victor, he believed that the biblical sages were worth comprehending, despite their elusiveness. Not coincidentally, this was because he appreciated their capacities for seeing the Lord's glory and speaking of him.

54. So it is that we find William poignantly contrasting Jeremiah's point of view with that of several other prophets in the prologue to *Super Threnos* (see above, n. 15)

55. For a very small sampling of texts where Thomas looks for the meanings of biblical authors, *SCG*, Bk. IV, 2 (ed. Leonina, t. XV, 8a–b): "Ioannes etiam evangelista hoc frequenter ostendit.... Paulus etiam Apostolus haec verba frequenter interserit.... Et Paulus dicit ... Distinguit enim Apostolus Christum a Moyse sicut filium a servo"; *SCG*, Bk. IV, 4 (ibid., 10b–11a): "Apostolus autem e converso ostendit." Throughout his systematic and exegetical works Aquinas resolves problems by appealing explicitly to the biblical text's human author. What follows are a few examples from his exposition of Jn 1:3, where he appeals repeatedly to John's meaning, and Paul's (ed. Parma, t. X, 291a): "Cum ergo dicit Evangelista, *Omnia per ipsum facta sunt*, non est intelligendum simpliciter facta omnia, sed in genere creaturarum, et rerum factarum"; ibid., 291b, "Si autem recte considerentur verba praedicta, *Omnia per ipsum facta sunt*, evidenter apparet Evangelistam propriissime fuisse locutum"; ibid., 291b, "omnia quae Moyses per multa enumerat in productione rerum a Deo, dicens: 'Dixit Dominus, Fiat lux, Fiat firmamentum etc., haec omnia Evangelista excedens, uno verbo comprehendit, dicens: *Omnia per ipsum facta sunt*'"; ibid., 292a, "Sed instabit forsitan aliquis, dicens, hanc clausulam superflue fuisse appositam, si intelligatur negative, eo quod Evangelista dicens, *Omnia per ipsum facta sunt*, sufficienter videtur dixisse non esse aliquid quod non sit factum per Verbum"; ibid., 292b, "Ideo Evangelista, dum dixisset omnia per ipsum facta sunt, quae scilicet enumerat Moyses, ideo consequenter adiunxit sine ipso factum est nihil; quasi dicat: nihil eorum quae sunt, sive visibile sive invisibile, est factum sine verbo. Et hoc modo loquitur Apost. Col. I, dicens, omnia condita esse in Christo, sive visibilia, sive invisibilia. Ubi Apostolus specialiter mentionem facit de invisibilibus, quia de eis Moyses aperte mentionem non fecerat, propter ruditatem illius populi, qui supra sensibilia elevari non poterat."

PART FOUR

PHILOSOPHY IN SYSTEMATIC THEOLOGY

CHAPTER TEN

Ad aliquid

Relation in the Thought of St. Thomas Aquinas

GILLES EMERY, OP

Relation occupies a position of paramount importance in the thought of St. Thomas Aquinas. Several central themes of his theology are based on his use of the category of relation, such as his theology of the Trinity (the divine person as subsistent relation), creation (the relation of God to the world), and the Incarnation (the relation of the divine and the human natures in Christ). Relation receives attention of a philosophical and a theological order.[1] The philosophical approach is well attested in Aquinas's commentaries on the *Physics* and the *Metaphysics* of Aristotle. The theological interest explains why the most developed explications of relation are found in the treatises dedi-

A previous (much shorter) version of this essay appeared in *Saint Thomas d'Aquin*, ed. Thierry-Dominique Humbrecht (Paris: Cerf, 2010), 113–35, entitled, "*Ad aliquid*: la relation chez Thomas d'Aquin." English translation is by Jennifer Ramage, with modifications and additions by the author.

1. For further references, see A. Krempel, *La doctrine de la relation chez Saint Thomas: Exposé historique et systématique* (Paris: Vrin, 1952). Despite certain debatable interpretations and the dominance of the problem of transcendental relations in the argument, this study remains quite useful, and we have borrowed certain elements from it. See also Mark G. Henninger, *Relations: Medieval Theories 1250–1325* (Oxford: Clarendon Press, 1989), 13–39; Rolf Schönberger, *Relation als Vergleich* (Leiden: Brill, 1994), 63–76; Jeffrey Brower, "Medieval Theories of Relations," in *Stanford Encyclopedia of Philosophy* (Spring 2014 ed.), ed. Edward N. Zalta, at http://plato.stanford.edu/archives/spr2014/entries/relations-medieval/.

cated to the study of God and of Christ. A special difficulty comes from the fact that these explications are truly dispersed throughout his oeuvre. In this respect, the case of relation is comparable to that of the doctrine of analogy: Aquinas did not write a synthesis on relation. Rather, he develops his views when, in the course of treating certain subjects, he appeals to relation.

Aquinas's analysis of relation principally considers four elements:

1. the *subject* of the relation, that is, the *thing* which is ordered and the *name* which formally signifies this ordered thing (the "relative": *relativum*; *ea quae sunt ad aliquid*);
2. the *foundation* (*fundamentum*) or the cause of the relation, that which brings about the relation in the subject;
3. the correlative *term*, that toward which the relation tends;
4. the *order or relationship to the term* (*respectus, habitudo, ordo, comparatio*, etc.), which constitutes the formal reason (*ratio*) of the relation, and by virtue of which a thing is (and is called) relative.

We will see that the articulation of these different elements takes on different forms. The sources are numerous and complex: Aristotle, of course, but also Avicenna, Averroes, Augustine (and the patristic heritage that Augustine collected), Boethius, Anselm of Canterbury, Gilbert of Poitiers, Albert the Great, and so forth.[2] Aristotle's main focus was not on relations, but rather on *relatives* or *relative predicates* (at least in his *Categories*).[3] Aquinas, by contrast, pays a much greater attention to the *relation* itself; this is largely because Aristotle's *Categories* was received through the Neoplatonic tradition (which includes the Neoplatonic criticism of the Stoic theory of relation).[4] Further, the discussion of relation by the masters of the twelfth

2. For references, see Gilles Emery, *The Trinitarian Theology of Saint Thomas Aquinas*, trans. Francesca A. Murphy (Oxford: Oxford University Press, 2010), 78–102.

3. The distinction between *relations* (or relational properties) and *relatives* is sketched, however, in other places, notably in *Metaphysics* V, 15 (1021b6–7): "Further, there are the properties in virtue of which the things that have them are called relative." *Aristotle's Categories and De Interpretatione*, trans. with notes by J. L. Ackrill (Oxford: Oxford University Press, 1963), 98. We should also note that Aristotle consistently speaks of "πρός τι," and not of "σχέσις" (relation). The word σχέσις appears quite rarely in Aristotle, and in other contexts; cf. Hermann Bonitz, *Index Aristotelicus*, 2d ed. (Graz: Akademische Druck- und Verlagsanstalt, 1955), 739. The absence of "σχέσις" in *Categories* 7 might well be deliberate (given the difficulty of finding the unity of the different kinds of relatives); see Françoise Caujolle-Zaslawsky, "Les relatifs dans les *Catégories*," in *Concepts et Catégories dans la pensée antique*, ed. Pierre Aubenque (Paris: Vrin, 1980), 167–95, here at 174 and 181.

4. See, for instance, Plotinus, *Ennead* VI.I.6–9. Plotinus deals not only with the "πρός τι" (the relative), but also formally with "σχέσις" (relation, relationship); *Plotini Opera*, Tomus 3: *Enneas VI*, ed. Paul Henry and Hans-Rudolf Schwyzer (Oxford: Oxford University Press, 1982), 8–14. The understanding of the relative (πρός τι) in terms of relation (σχέσις) is even clearer

and thirteenth centuries is often in the background of Aquinas's arguments, even when he does not mention them explicitly. In what follows, we will pay special attention to Aquinas's reading of Aristotle.

Our argument comprises four sections. The first presents the category of relation and its constitutive elements, as part of the doctrine of predicaments; the second examines the distinction between real relations and relations "of reason"; the third deals with the most significant properties of relations, and considers some particular difficulties; finally, the last section shows briefly Aquinas's usage of the category of relation in his account of the relationship of God and the world.[5]

Ad aliquid

Relation has its place among the ten predicaments or ten "genera of being" (*genera entis*) into which Aquinas divides extramental being (*ens quod est extra animam*).[6] This analogical division of being takes place according to the "mode of being" (*modus essendi*). Aquinas explains the name "predicament" (*praedicamentum*) by the correspondence or proportion between the modes of being and the modes of predication: "A different mode of predication flows from (*consequitur*) a different mode of being."[7] The mode of *predication* depends on the thing's mode of *being*, with reference to our mode of *understanding*.[8] When one *predicates* one thing of another, one af-

---

in Porphyrius, who underlines the formality of the relation (σχέσις) as such. See, for instance, Porphyrius, *Commentary on Aristotle's Categories* 124.21–125.5; 125.16–17; critical Greek text in Porphyre, *Commentaire aux Catégories d'Aristote*, Edition critique, traduction, introduction et notes par Richard Bodéüs (Paris: Vrin, 2008), 404, 406, and 408; English translation: Porphyry, *On Aristotle's Categories*, trans. Steven K. Strange (London: Duckworth Publishers, 1992), 133–34. For Porphyrius, "relatives consist in the relation (*skhesis*) of subjects to one another" (133). On this, see Matthieu Raffray, "Les origines antiques de la relation," *Revue Thomiste* 112 (2012): 419–65. See also below, n. 52.

5. Citations of the works of St. Thomas Aquinas refer to Latin editions whose bibliographic details can be found in Jean-Pierre Torrell, *Saint Thomas Aquinas*, vol. 1, *The Person and His Work*, revised edition, trans. Robert Royal (Washington, D.C.: The Catholic University of America Press, 2005), 330–59 and 424–38. The translations are at times made with the help of available English translations (cited in Jean-Pierre Torrell's work, or found at http://dhspriory.org/thomas). Translations of Aristotle are drawn from: *The Works of Aristotle*, 2 vols., ed. W. D. Ross, Great Books of the Western World, vols. 8–9 (Chicago: Encyclopædia Britannica, 1952). In what follows, I refer to Aquinas's commentary on Aristotle's *Metaphysics* as a *Sententia*, whereas his commentary on the *Physics* is cited as an *Expositio* (my thanks to Fr. Adriano Oliva, OP, for this clarification).

6. *Sententia libri Metaphysicae*, lib. V, lect. 9 (Marietti edition, n. 889).

7. Ibid. (Marietti edition, n. 890): "Oportet, quod ens contrahatur ad diversa genera secundum diversum modum praedicandi, qui consequitur diversum modum essendi."

8. *Summa theologiae* I, q. 13, a. 9, ad 2: "For names do not follow upon the mode of being

firms that "this is that" (*hoc esse illud*); this is why the ten "genera of being" are called "predicaments."[9]

In his commentaries on Aristotle's *Physics* and *Metaphysics*, which give a classification of the predicaments, Aquinas explains that a predicate can relate to a subject in three ways.[10] (1) In the first case, the predicate signifies the subject itself (*id quod est subiectum*) or what concerns the essence of the subject. This is the predicament of substance. (2) In the second case, the predicate is said of something which "inheres" *in* the subject (*secundum quod inest subiecto*). This inherence can be of two modes. First, when that which is predicated inheres "per se and absolutely" in the subject, we are dealing with the predicament "quantity" which flows from the matter, or with the predicament "quality" which flows from a form. Secondly, when that which is predicated relates to something which inheres in the subject "not absolutely but in connection to something else" ("*non absolute, sed in respectu ad aliud,*" "*per respectum ad alterum*"), we are in the presence of the predicament "*ad aliquid*" which Aquinas also calls "predicament of relation" (*praedicamentum relationis*). (3) In the third case, that which is predicated is said of something exterior to the subject itself (*aliquid extrinsecum*): it can be something which is totally exterior to the subject, and thus we find the predicaments "equipped with" (*habitus*), "time when" (*quando*), "place where" (*ubi*), and "position" (*situs*); it can also concern something which is located in a certain way in the subject, as we see in the predicament "action" (because the principle of the action resides inside the subject) and in the predicament "passion," inasmuch as the effect of an action is found in the receiving subject.

These first explanations already show the special place that Aquinas assigns to relation. On the one hand, relation is not related to a subject as identical to this subject (substance), nor as flowing from a reality external to the subject (accidents taken from something exterior). Aquinas places rela-

---

that is found in things, but upon the mode of being as it is in our understanding" (*nomina enim non sequuntur modum essendi qui est in rebus, sed modum essendi secundum quod in cognitione nostra est*). Cf. *De potentia*, q. 7, a. 2, ad 7 (about our knowledge of God): "Modus significandi in dictionibus quae a nobis rebus imponuntur sequitur modum intelligendi; dictiones enim significant intellectuum conceptiones, ut dicitur in principio *Periher*. Intellectus autem noster hoc modo intelligit esse quo modo invenitur in rebus inferioribus a quibus scientiam capit."

9. *Expositio libri Physicorum*, lib. III, lect. 5, §15 (Marietti edition, n. 322): "Praedicando enim aliquid de aliquo altero, dicimus hoc esse illud: unde et decem genera entis dicuntur decem praedicamenta."

10. *Sententia libri Metaphysicae*, lib. V, lect. 9 (Marietti edition, nn. 890–92); *Expositio libri Physicorum*, lib. III, lect. 5, §15 (Marietti edition, n. 322). On these two passages, see John F. Wippel, *The Metaphysical Thought of Thomas Aquinas: From Finite Being to Uncreated Being* (Washington, D.C.: The Catholic University of America Press, 2000), 212–24.

tion among the accidents which affect the subject "intrinsically," as it were. On the other hand, although relation is predicated according to "what inheres in the subject," it differs from the absolute accidents, which are taken with regard to the subject itself: relation concerns the *connection or order to something else*. The formal "proper reason" of the relation (*propria ratio*: that by which a relation is a relation) presents a quite singular character.

In each of the nine genera of accidents, as Aquinas explains, one must consider two elements or two aspects.[11] (1) The first element is the mode of being (*esse*) which belongs to each accident as accident, that is to say, the "existing in" (*inesse*) which characterizes the accident as such. Whereas substance is "that to which it belongs to have existence not in a subject," the accident is characterized as "that to which it belongs to have existence in a subject."[12] Aquinas notes here the accidental mode of being of relation in and by the substance in which this relation inheres. (2) The second element is the "*ratio propria*" of each genus of being, that is to say, the proper nature, the formal reason of each accident. It is this generic *ratio* which is expressed by the quasi-definition of relation and which the name "relation" formally signifies.[13] Here is the quasi-definition: "The relation (*relatio*), according to its generic reason as such (*secundum rationem sui generis*), … consists in the connection to something (*quod sit ad aliquid*)"; "Relatives (*ea quae ad aliquid dicuntur*), according to their own proper *ratio*, signify only a relationship to another (*solum respectum ad aliud*)"; "The being [the essence] of a relative is to be referred to another (*relativi esse est ad aliud se habere*)"; "The specific reason of a relative consists in being referred to another (*ratio specifica relativi consistat in hoc quod ad aliud se habet*)"; "Relation … consists only in the fact of being referred to something else (*relatio … consistit tantum in hoc quod est ad aliud se habere*)."[14] We see here the second definition of the "πρός τι" given by Aristotle in his *Categories*: "*Sunt ad aliquid quibus hoc ipsum esse est ad aliquid quodam modo habere*" (Boethius's Latin

---

11. *ST* I, q. 28, a. 2, c.; cf. *Scriptum super primum librum Sententiarum* (henceforth I *Sent.*), dist. 8, q. 4, a. 3, c.; I *Sent.*, dist. 31, q. 1, a. 1, c.; etc.

12. *ST* III, q. 77, a. 1, ad 2: "Quidditati seu essentiae substantiae competit habere esse non in subiecto; quidditati autem sive essentiae accidentis competit habere esse in subiecto." On these formulations (required by the theological account of the Eucharist), see Ruedi Imbach, "Le traité de l'Eucharistie de Thomas d'Aquin et les Averroïstes," *Revue des Sciences Philosophiques et Théologiques* 77 (1993): 173–228.

13. "Quasi-definition" because, properly speaking, there is no definition of the ten genera of being, since real definition, bearing on a species, is a composite of genus and difference. See I *Sent.*, dist. 2, q. 1, a. 3, c.; *Sententia libri Metaphysicae*, lib. V, lect. 4 (Marietti edition, n. 805).

14. Respectively: *De potentia*, q. 2, a. 5, c.; *ST* I, q. 28, a. 1, c.; *ST* I, q. 28, a. 2, obj. 3; *ST* I, q. 40, a. 2, ad 4; *ST* I, q. 32, a. 2, c.; *Expositio libri Physicorum*, lib. III, lect. 1, §6 (Marietti edition, n. 280).

translation).[15] Examining this Aristotelian definition of the "πρός τι," Aquinas adds this clarification:

When one says that "the relatives are that whose being consists in being referred to something else" (*ad aliquid sunt, quorum esse est ad aliud se habere*), one must understand that this concerns the being (*esse*) which is the quiddity of the thing, signified by the definition; because the very nature of the relation (*ipsa natura relationis*), by which it is constituted in its genus, is to be referred to something else (*ad aliud referri*); but it does not concern the being (*esse*) which is the act of the essence (*actus essentiae*): because the relation holds this latter being from what causes it in the subject, that is to say, insofar as this being [of the relation] does not refer to something else but to the subject (*subiectum*), like all accidents.[16]

Later, we will return to the existence of the relation in the subject. For the moment, we must observe that the "*ratio generis*" of the relation possesses a feature which is unique among the accidents: this *ratio* is not taken in reference to the subject itself, nor in reference to the cause which brings about its existence in the subject, but with reference to the correlative term ("something else").[17] Indeed, while the generic *ratio* of the other accidents is taken with regard to the subject ("quantity is a measure of substance, quality is a disposition of substance, and similarly in the other genera"),[18] "the proper reason of relation is not taken from its respect to that in which it is, but from its respect to something outside."[19] According to its formal reason, the relation "does not posit anything in the subject."[20] "From the proper rea-

---

15. Aristotle, *Categories* 7 (8a31–32); Latin translation from: Aristotle, *Categoriae vel Praedicamenta*, "Aristoteles Latinus I, 1–5," ed. Lorenzo Minio-Paluello (Paris: Desclée de Brouwer, 1961), 22. Cf. 8a39–b1: "Relativis autem hoc est esse, ad aliquid quodammodo habere" (ibid.). The translation by William of Moerbeke (c. 1266) stresses even more the formal reason of the relatives: "Sunt ipsa ad aliquid quibus esse idem est cum hoc quod est ad aliquid aliquo modo se habere" (101). As for the first definition given by Aristotle (6a36–37), its translation by Boethius reads as follows: "Ad aliquid vero talia dicuntur quaecumque hoc ipsum quod sunt aliorum dicuntur, vel quomodolibet aliter ad aliud ... dicitur" (18). On this double definition of the relatives in the *Categories*, see F. Caujolle-Zaslawsky, "Les relatifs dans les Catégories," 185–91. By contrast with the first definition, which applies to all relatives, the second definition refers more specifically to what is "essentially relative" (Aristotle, *Categories* 7 [8a33–35]).

16. I *Sent.*, dist. 33, q. 1, a. 1, ad 1. Cf. *De potentia*, q. 8, a. 2, ad 12: "Cum relatio sit accidens in creaturis, esse suum est inesse; unde esse suum non est ad aliud se habere, sed esse huius; sed ad aliquid est ad aliud se habere."

17. *ST* I, q. 28, a. 2, c.; *ST* III, q. 2, a. 7, ad 2; *ST* III, q. 2, a. 8, obj. 1.

18. I *Sent.*, dist. 8, q. 4, a. 3, c.; see also *ST* I, q. 28, a. 2, c. and ad 1.

19. *ST* I, q. 28, a. 2, c.: "Sed ratio propria relationis non accipitur secundum comparationem ad illud in quo est, sed secundum comparationem ad aliquid extra."

20. I *Sent.*, dist. 26, q. 2, a. 1, c.: "Ex hac ratione non habet quod ponat aliquid in eo de quo dicitur." Cf. I *Sent.*, dist. 30, q. 1, a. 1, c.: "Sed relatio secundum rationem suam non habet quod ponat aliquid in eo de quo dicitur; sed ponit tantum habitudinem ad aliud."

son of its genus, relation does not posit *aliquid*, but *ad aliquid*."[21] One can thus consider relation under two aspects: (1) inasmuch as it is an accident, it inheres in a subject (accidental *esse* of the relation); (2) but "as relation," that is to say, in its proper formal *ratio*, the relation does not regard the subject which bears the relation, but it concerns only the connection (*respectus*) to something else. This is the reason why the Porretan school, considering only this formal reason, spoke of the relations as "assistant" (*assistentes*) or "fixed from outside" (*extrinsecus affixae*).[22]

The "ecstatic" purity of the relation's formal reason (second aspect) has several consequences. One of these is that certain relations, having no foundation *in re*, do not have real existence in a subject: in this case, we observe only a pure connection to something else, with no addition to the subject itself.[23] By virtue of the generic *ratio* of the relation, "there are certain relations which posit nothing within that of which they are said."[24] This consideration shows the difficulty of our knowledge of relation. There are relations "of reason," but there is neither "quantity of reason" nor "quality of reason." We will return below to these relations "of reason." Following Averroes's interpretation of Aristotle,[25] Aquinas notes several times that, because of its formal reason, relation possesses "the weakest being" ("*debilioris esse*," "*debilissimum esse*," "*minimum habet de ente*," "*minimum habet de natura entis*"), since it consists solely in *the connection to something else*,[26] which

21. *Quodlibet* IX, q. 2, a. 3, c. (Leonine edition, vol. 25/1, p. 96): "*Ad aliquid* ex propria sui generis ratione non habet quod ponat aliquid, sed ad aliquid." Cf. *De potentia*, q. 2, a. 5, c.: "Nam ipsa relatio secundum rationem sui generis, in quantum est relatio, non habet quod sit aliquid, sed solum quod sit ad aliquid."

22. See, for instance, *ST* I, q. 28, a. 2, c.; I *Sent.*, dist. 33, q. 1, a. 1, c.; *De potentia*, q. 8, a. 2, c. (with reference to the relation's "mode of signifying").

23. See, for example, I *Sent.*, dist. 33, q. 1, a. 1, c.

24. Ibid., dist. 26, q. 2, a. 1, c.: "Et ideo inveniuntur quaedam relationes nihil ponentes in eo de quo dicuntur." See also *Quodlibet* IX, q. 2, a. 3, c. (Leonine edition, vol. 25/1, p. 96).

25. Averroes, *Commentarium in Aristotelis Metaph.*, lib. XII (text. 19), in *Aristotelis opera cum Averrois commentariis*, vol. 8 (Venetiis: Apud Iunctas, 1562; Reprint: Frankfurt am Main: Minerva, 1962), 306 B: "Et dicit proprie relationem: quia est debilioris esse aliis praedicamentis: ita quod quidam reputaverunt ipsam esse ex secundis intellectis." For explicit references to Averroes on this issue, see Aquinas, I *Sent.*, dist. 26, q. 2, a. 2, sc: "Sed inter omnia alia relatio est debilioris esse, ut dicit Commentator, adeo quod quidam reputaverunt eam esse de intentionibus secundis." III *Sent.*, dist. 2, q. 2, a. 2, quaestiuncula 2, c.: "Minimum habet de natura entis, ut Commentator, XII Metaph., dicit." For a modern translation of Averroes, see *Ibn Rushd's Metaphysics: A Translation with Introduction of Ibn Rushd's Commentary on Aristotle's Metaphysics, Book Lam*, ed. and trans. Charles Genequand (Leiden: Brill, 1986), 113: "Relation is singled out because it is less being than the other categories." For Aristotle himself, see: Aristotle, *Metaphysics* XIV, 1 (1088a22–24 and 29–30), in *The Works of Aristotle*, vol. 1, trans. W. D. Ross (Chicago: Encyclopædia Britannica, 1952), 620: "What is relative is least of all things a kind of entity or substance … the relative is least of all a substance and a real thing."

26. Among many passages, see *Expositio libri Physicorum*, lib. III, lect. 1, §6 (Marietti

explains moreover why certain thinkers reduced relation to a pure concept ("second intention").[27] Following these explanations, the created real relation has being which is "last in order and quite imperfect" (*et postremum et imperfectissimum esse habet*): last in order, since the relation's being requires not only the being of the substance in which it inheres, but also the being of the accidents that cause it, as we shall see below; and quite imperfect, because the relation depends on the being of the correlative term.[28] Aquinas maintains firmly the existence of real, extramental relations, but he has no difficulty in recognizing this "weakness" of relation. Moreover, it is common among the theologians of the thirteenth century to take advantage of this characteristic of relation to explain its role in the distinction of the divine persons: having the weakest being among all the genera, relation neither modifies nor divides the divine essence; it is therefore fitting to introduce the "smallest distinction" ("small" in the sense of the "quantity" of this distinction), that is to say, the real distinction of the consubstantial divine persons.[29]

The formal reason of relation explains its great value for discourse about God. This is one of the reasons Aquinas is particularly interested in it. Indeed, all other accidents are excluded from proper speech about God not only insofar as they are accidents (dependence and composition) but also under the aspect of their generic *ratio*, because the *ratio* of their genus is taken with regard to the subject which these accidents modify or determine.[30] As for relation, since it consists solely in the connection to another

---

edition, n. 280); *Summa contra gentiles*, Bk. IV, ch. 14 (Marietti edition, n. 3508); III *Sent.*, dist. 2, q. 2, a. 2, quaestiuncula 2, c.; *De potentia*, q. 7, a. 9, c.; q. 8, a. 1, obj. 4 and ad 4; q. 9, a. 5, ad 2; q. 9, a. 5, ad 14.

27. See above, n. 26. Cf. also I *Sent.*, dist. 26, q. 2, a. 1, c.; *De potentia*, q. 7, a. 9, c.; *De potentia*, q. 8, a. 2, c. (with reference to the relation's "mode of signifying"). These thinkers who denied the relation's real existence are found among the Stoics, although Aquinas does not name them explicitly; see below, n. 52.

28. *SCG*, Bk. IV, ch. 14 (n. 3508). See below, n. 41.

29. See I *Sent.*, dist. 26, q. 2, a. 2, ad 2: "minima distinctio realis quae possit esse"; *SCG*, Bk. IV, ch. 14 (Marietti edition, n. 3508); *De potentia*, q. 9, a. 5, ad 2; q. 9, a. 5, ad 14; *ST* I, q. 40, a. 2, ad 3.

30. I *Sent.*, dist. 8, q. 4, a. 3, c.: "Sed in unoquoque novem praedicamentorum duo invenio; scilicet *rationem accidentis* et *rationem propriam illius generis*, sicut quantitatis vel qualitatis. Ratio autem accidentis imperfectionem continet: quia esse accidentis est inesse et dependere, et compositionem facere cum subjecto per consequens. Unde *secundum rationem accidentis nihil potest de Deo praedicari*. Si autem consideremus *propriam rationem cujuslibet generis, quodlibet aliorum generum, praeter ad aliquid, importat imperfectionem*; quantitas enim habet propriam rationem in comparatione ad subjectum; est enim quantitas mensura substantiae, qualitas dispositio substantiae, et sic patet in omnibus aliis. *Unde eadem ratione removentur a divina praedicatione secundum rationem generis, sicut removebantur per rationem accidentis*" (emphasis mine). Certain perfections found in these accidents will be properly attributed to God (science, for example): these perfections nevertheless do not concern the *generic ratio* of these accidents, but only some of their *species* (science is a species in the genus of quality).

thing, its generic *ratio* introduces no positive determination in the subject. So, unlike all other accidents, relation can be *properly* attributed to God according to its generic reason. Under the aspect of its *ratio*, relation has no need to be refashioned in order to be applied to God: in itself it befits the divine simplicity and perfection. When Christian doctrine affirms real relations in God, these relations retain their formality as relations. "Its formal content being free of the bondage and limitation of the material subject, this notion can be immediately transposed into the spiritual world," because "what it says about its subject is this order, this pure looking outwards toward the [correlative] term, leaving the positive richness of the subject untouched."[31] This is why, following St. Augustine and Boethius (in the wake of St. Basil of Caesarea), Aquinas retains only two modes of proper predication concerning God: that of substance and that of relation.[32]

The uniqueness of relation, by virtue of its *ratio*, is also seen in its "mode of signifying" (*modus significandi*). Some accidental predicaments "signify" by the mode of an accident which inheres in the subject. This is the case with quantity and quality: one speaks of the size of a house, of the whiteness of a mouse, and the size and the whiteness are *signified* as "inhering in" the house and the mouse. But relation does not "signify" by the mode of accidental inherence: the relative predicate ("greater," "master," "son," etc.) "does not signify as something of the subject in which it is found (*ut aliquid eius in quo est*), but as toward something exterior (*ut ad id quod extra est*)"[33] or "as passing toward something else (*ut in transitu quodam ad aliud*)."[34] We find here again the difficulty that, in Aquinas's view, leads astray those who reduce all relations to a pure concept in refusing them the consistence of an accident existing in things, or who consider in the relation only the connection to another thing. This difficulty stems from the relation's mode of signifying (*modus significandi*), which leads us back to the distinction be-

---

31. Hyacinthe Dondaine, in Saint Thomas d'Aquin, *Somme théologique, La Trinité, 1a, Questions 27–32* (Paris: Desclée, 1950), 234–35: "Libre, en son contenu formel, des servitudes et limites du sujet matériel, cette notion se transpose d'emblée dans le monde spirituel"; "ce qu'elle exprime à propos du sujet, c'est cet ordre, ce pur regard vers le terme, qui laisse inviolée la richesse positive du sujet."

32. I *Sent.*, dist. 8, q. 4, a. 3, c.; *De potentia*, q. 8, a. 4, sc; *ST* I, q. 28, a. 2, ad 1.

33. *De potentia*, q. 8, a. 2, c.: "*Ad aliquid* vero non significatur secundum rationem accidentis: non enim significatur ut aliquid eius in quo est, sed ut ad id quod extra est. Et proper hoc etiam dicit Philosophus, V Metaph., quod scientia, inquantum est relatio, non est scientis, sed scibilis."

34. Ibid., q. 7, a. 8, c. (with reference to Boethius). The same applies to the personal relations in the Trinity: "Relationes autem divinae, licet significent id quod est divina essentia, non tamen per modum essentiae, quia non per modum inexistentis, sed per modum se habentis ad aliud" (ibid., q. 8, a. 2, ad 4).

tween the formal reason and the accidental being of the relation.[35] Aquinas
does not weary of emphasizing that, even when the relation really *exists* in
a subject by mode of inherence (*est res aliqua*), this relation is *not signified*
in the manner of a property that inheres *in* the subject; rather, it is signified
as referring to something else. "Nothing prevents something to be inhering,
which nevertheless is not signified as inhering."[36]

"Real" Relations and Relations "of Reason"

The examination of the formal *ratio* of relation has already given rise to
clarifications concerning the existence (*esse*) of relation; let us look at them
more closely. First, certain relations really exist in things: Aquinas speaks
here of "real relation" (*relatio realis*), "real relationship" or "real respect"
(*respectus realis*), relation or connection which exists "really" (*realiter*), "according to reality" (*secundum rem*), "in the nature of things" (*in ipsa natura
rerum*), in things outside the soul (*in rebus extra animam*), and so forth.
Secondly, there are other relations which lack such a consistence of being in
extramental reality: he thus speaks of a "relation of reason" (*relatio rationis*)
or "according to reason alone" (*secundum rationem tantum*), "according to
the mode of knowing" (*secundum modum intelligendi*), and so forth; such
a relation is a "thing of reason" (*res rationis tantum*) which exists only "in
the intellect" (*in intellectu tantum*) or "in the apprehension of reason" (*in
ipsa apprehensione rationis*).[37] Here we must also note that Aquinas refers to
Aristotle himself in order to distinguish between real relations and relations
of reason. This is especially clear in his discussion of the difference between
the relation of the science to the thing known (real relation), and of the
thing known to the science (relation of reason).[38] The difference between
these two sorts of relations does not concern the generic *ratio* of the relation, which is found in both cases, but it touches on the existence (*esse*) of
the relation. Let us begin with real relations.

35. Ibid., q. 7, a. 9, ad 7: "Ipsa relatio quae nihil est aliud quam ordo unius creaturae ad
aliam, aliud habet in quantum est accidens et aliud in quantum est relatio vel ordo. In quantum
enim accidens est, habet quod sit in subiecto, non autem in quantum est relatio vel ordo; sed
solum quod ad aliud sit quasi in aliud transiens, et quodammodo rei relatae assistens. Et ita
relatio est aliquid inhaerens, licet non ex hoc ipso quod est relatio."

36. Ibid., q. 8, a. 2, c.: "Nihil prohibet aliquid esse inhaerens, quod tamen non significatur
ut inhaerens." See also *ST* I, q. 40, a. 1, c.: "non significant ut in aliquo, sed magis ut ad aliquid."

37. For this vocabulary, see Krempel, *La doctrine de la relation*, 487–89.

38. See, for instance, *De potentia*, q. 7, a. 1, ad 9 ("ut patet per Philosophum"); q. 7, a. 10, sc 2;
q. 7, a. 11, ad 1 (with reference to *Metaphysics* V, 15 [1021a29–30]). See below n. 49.

Real Relations

Several conditions are required for two things to have a real relation. It is necessary, first, that the two terms in relation be real (*quod utrumque sit ens*); second, that the two terms be really distinct; third, that they belong to a "same order"; fourth, that the relation results from a foundation which causes it to be in the subject.[39] The relation depends on the correlative term to be constituted as "*ad*," but its reality in the subject ("*in*") depends on the substance *and* on the foundation (*fundamentum*), that is to say, on that which *causes* this relation in the subject.[40] Referring to Aristotle (*Metaphysics* V [Δ], 15 [1020b26–1021a26]), Aquinas holds that *only two foundations* can cause a real relation: (1) quantity, and (2) action/passion, which are accidents (and which differ from the subject itself). Here we return again to an aspect associated with the "imperfection" of the being of the relation: the existence (*esse*) of the real relation is grounded in an *accident* which is presupposed (as a prerequisite) to this relation, and which causes this relation in the subject.[41] "According to the Philosopher in *Metaphysics* V, every relation is based (*fundatur*) either on quantity, e.g., double and half; or on action and passion, e.g., maker and made, father and son, master and servant, and the like."[42]

In the case of relations founded on quantity and action/passion, things are relative because each is referred to something else, and not because something else is referred to it.[43] This analysis of the relation explains, for example, the structure of the first three questions of the *Summa*'s treatise on "the distinction of the divine persons": since the divine person will be understood as a subsisting relation (*ST* I, q. 29), the study of the person requires a teaching on real relations (q. 28), which in turn *presupposes* a study of the processions (q. 27), since we grasp the Trinitarian relations as founded on actions ("notional acts": to beget, to spirate) and on the processions

---

39. *ST* I, q. 13, a. 7, c.; I *Sent.*, dist. 33, q. 1, a. 1, c.; *De potentia*, q. 7, a. 11, c.

40. *SCG*, Bk. IV, ch. 14 (Marietti edition, n. 3508): "Relatio realiter substantiae adveniens … non solum praeexigit esse substantiae, sed etiam esse aliorum accidentium, ex quibus causatur relatio … propria relationis ratio consistit in eo quod est ad alterum, unde esse proprium, quod substantiae superaddit, non solum dependet ab esse substantiae, sed etiam ab esse alicuius exterioris." I *Sent.*, dist. 2, *expositio textus*: "Relationes fundantur super aliquid quod est causa ipsarum in subjecto, sicut aequalitas supra quantitatem, et dominium supra potestatem." I *Sent.*, dist. 33, q. 1, a. 1, ad 1; etc.

41. See, for example, *SCG*, Bk. IV, ch. 14 (Marietti edition, nn. 3507–8).

42. *ST* I, q. 28, a. 4, c. See *Sentientia libri Metaphysicae*, lib. V, lect. 17 (Marietti edition, nn. 1001–2); *Expositio libri Physicorum*, lib. III, lect. 1, §6 (Marietti edition, n. 280). See also *De potentia*, q. 7, a. 9, c.; q. 8, a. 1, c.; q. 8, a. 3, obj. 7; q. 10, a. 3, obj. 2; etc.

43. *Sentientia libri Metaphysicae*, lib. V, lect. 17 (Marietti edition, n. 1026).

which correspond to these actions (to be begotten, to proceed): therefore, the order of teaching is: processions, relations, and persons.

Considering the other predicaments, Aquinas specifies that substance and quality are not the foundation of real relations except "*per accidens*," that is to say, insofar as substance and quality present an aspect considered under the formal *ratio* of quantity or of action/passion; for example: the unity (quantity) of quality entails the relation of similitude. As for the other genera (when, where, position, and habitus), "they do not cause a relation but they rather follow upon a relation."[44] In his explanations concerning the second foundation, that is, "action and passion," Aquinas specifies that it is a matter either of the act itself or of "the active and passive power" (*virtus activa seu passiva, or: potentia activa, potentia passiva*),[45] or "in general every active and passive."[46] In some cases, only the "active and passive power" is mentioned. For the same second foundation, Aquinas also speaks of movement (*motus*), to the extent to which action and passion are movements.[47] In *Metaphysics* V, 15 (1020b30–32), Aristotle adds a third kind of relatives (besides those taken according to quantity and action/passion), namely, the relatives "as the measurable to the measure, and the knowable to knowledge, and the perceptible to perception." In this third case, by contrast with the relatives taken according to quantity or action/passion, "that which is measurable or knowable or thinkable is called relative because something else involves a reference to it."[48] We will return below to this third *modus*, in our discussion of "relations of reason" and of "pairs of relations." In sum: "One thing (*res*) is ordered (*ordinatur*) to another either as to quantity or as to active or passive power: for

44. *Sententia libri Metaphysicae*, lib. V, lect. 17 (Marietti edition, n. 1005): "Alia vero genera magis consequuntur relationem, quam possint relationem causare."

45. Ibid.; *Expositio libri Physicorum*, lib. III, lect. 1, §6 (Marietti edition, n. 280); *De potentia*, q. 7, a. 9, c.; *De potentia*, q. 7, a. 10, c.; etc. Cf. Aristotle, *Metaphysics* V, 15 (1021a15–16): "κατὰ δύναμιν ποιητικὴν καὶ παθητικήν."

46. *Sententia libri Metaphysicae*, lib. V, lect. 17 (Marietti edition, n. 1002): "et universaliter omne activum et passivum." Cf. Aristotle, *Metaphysics* V, 15 (1020b30).

47. I *Sent.*, dist. 26, q. 2, a. 1, c.: "motum quemdam supra quem fundatur"; IV *Sent.*, dist. 41, q. 1, a. 1, quaestiuncula 2, c.: "actionem vel passionem, aut motum." *Expositio libri Physicorum*, lib. V, lect. 3, §2 (Marietti edition, n. 661): "Secundum autem quod motus consideratur ut est in hoc ab alio, vel ab hoc in aliud, sic pertinet ad praedicamentum actionis et passionis."

48. Aristotle, *Metaphysics* V, 15 (1021a29–30). Cf. Aquinas, *Sententia libri Metaphysicae*, lib. V, lect. 17 (Marietti edition, n. 1026): "[Aristotle] says that this third mode (*modus*) differs from the foregoing in this way, that each of the foregoing things is said to be relative because each is referred to something else (*dicitur relative ex hoc, quod ipsum ad aliud refertur*), not because something else is referred to it. For double is related to half, and conversely; and in a similar way a father is related to his son, and conversely. But, according to this third mode, something is said to be relative only because something [else] is referred to it (*hoc tertio modo aliquid dicitur relative ex eo solum, quod aliquid refertur ad ipsum*)."

on these two counts alone can we find in a thing something in connection to an exterior thing."[49] By means of the foundation which causes the relation in the subject, the being (*esse*) of this relation depends on the substance which bears it, and it differs from the being of this substance.[50]

In numerous texts, Aquinas strives to demonstrate the existence of real relations (this was already a concern of Plotinus and of other Neoplatonic philosophers in opposition to the Stoics—although Aquinas's demonstration differs from the thought of Neoplatonic philosophers).[51] Aristotle is frequently invoked by Aquinas in support of the existence of real relations. Aquinas notes that the Stagirite placed relation (*ad aliquid*) among the predicaments, and he specifies that these predicaments concern extramental realities (*res extra animam existens*): Aristotle spoke of the "being of reason" precisely in distinguishing it from the being which admits of the ten predicaments.[52] More profoundly, Aquinas points to *the order of the universe* (*ordo universi*).[53] The goodness of things consists not only in the absolute perfections which they possess in themselves, but also in the order which these things have to other things. The good of the universe is the good of order (*bonum ordinis*), rooted in the singular goods. The good of the universe consists precisely in the mutual ordering of its parts, and in its ordering toward God, the first order existing because of—and in view of—the second.[54] Recognizing an ordered universe, following the double order (*du-*

49. *De potentia*, q. 7, a. 9, c.: "Ordinatur autem una res ad aliam vel secundum quantitatem, vel secundum virtutem activam seu passivam. Ex his enim solum duobus attenditur aliquid in uno, respectu extrinseci."

50. I *Sent.*, dist. 33, q. 1, a. 1, c.: "In … realibus relationibus in creaturis existentibus est aliud esse relationis, et substantiae quae refertur; et ideo dicuntur inesse; et secundum quod insunt, compositionem faciunt accidentis ad subjectum." See also *SCG*, Bk. IV, ch. 14 (Marietti edition, n. 3508): "Oportet quod eorum esse sit superadditum supra esse substantiae, et ab ipso dependens." *De potentia*, q. 8, a. 1, ad 5: "de relatione reali, quae habet aliud esse ab esse substantiae cui inest."

51. Some Stoics understood the relation as a judgment of our intellect comparing things: this led Plotinus to argue in favor of the relation's real existence; see Concetta Luna, "La relation chez Simplicius," in *Simplicius: Sa vie, son oeuvre, sa survie*, ed. Pierre Hadot (New York: Walter de Gruyter, 1987), 113–47, here at 115–16. For references to Plotinus, see above n. 5. In Plotinus, the relation is not only a matter of language or logics, but rather of metaphysics: the relation is a Form which is participated by the relative (p. 115). Simplicius also maintained the real existence of the relation, and he understood the relatives as "those things which have a relation (*schesis*)" (pp. 130–31).

52. *De potentia*, q. 7, a. 9, c.: "In nullo enim praedicamento ponitur aliquid nisi res extra animam existens. Nam ens rationis dividitur contra ens divisum per decem praedicamenta ut patet V *Metaph*. Si autem relatio non esset in rebus extra animam non poneretur ad aliquid unum genus praedicamenti." Cf. Aristotle, *Metaphysics* V, 15.

53. We find a good example of this in *De potentia*, q. 7, a. 9, c.

54. See, for example, *SCG*, Bk. I, ch. 78 (Marietti edition, n. 663); *ST* I, q. 103, a. 2, ad 3: "Finis quidem universi est aliquod bonum in ipso existens, scilicet ordo ipsius universi: hoc

plex ordo) which constitutes its good, leads to recognizing the existence of real relations which are found *in* things: "Consequently there must be order in things themselves (*in ipsis rebus*), and this order is a kind of relation (*hic autem ordo relatio quaedam est*). Wherefore there must be relations in things themselves (*oportet ergo in rebus ipsis relationes quasdam esse*), whereby one is ordered to another."[55]

This doctrine is distinct from the subsequent nominalism, which tends to reduce relations to comparisons made by the mind and thus to situate these relations "between" things rather than "in" things. For William of Ockham in the fourteenth century, the predicament of relation will be composed exclusively of names, that is to say, of relative *words*, and not of things existing outside the mind (all that exists is the singular thing in its irreducibility).[56] Ockham will expel the existence of relations from the reality of things; he will maintain the existence of real extramental relations only "where faith obliges" (the doctrine of the Trinity), thereby creating a rupture between the philosophical approach and the theological approach. To fully grasp the thought of Aquinas, it is thus necessary to note his insistence on the concrete existence of certain relations in the very reality of things, outside of our minds. Before Aquinas, this was already the position of St. Albert the Great, although with other nuances.[57]

Relations "of Reason"

According to Aquinas, there is relation "of reason alone" when one of the conditions mentioned above does not obtain, that is to say, if the correlative terms or extremes are not really distinct (for example, in the case of the relation of identity of a thing with itself), if they lack objective reality (relation to a non-existent), if they do not belong to the same order, if the foundation (that is, quantity and action/passion) is lacking, or if we are dealing with relations of relations.[58] The relation "of reason" does not exist concretely in the very reality of things, it does not inhere in the things in the manner of

---

autem bonum non est ultimus finis, sed ordinatur ad bonum extrinsecum ut ad ultimum finem." Cf. Aristotle, *Metaphysics* XII, 10 (1075a11–25).

55. *De potentia*, q. 7, a. 9, c. The text continues by indicating the two foundations that can cause the existence of real relations (quantity and action/passion), and it concludes by affirming the double *ordo*: "ordo qui est partium universi ad invicem, est per ordinem qui est totius universi ad Deum."

56. See Béatrice Beretta, *Ad aliquid: La relation chez Guillaume d'Occam* (Fribourg: Editions Universitaires, 1999).

57. See Gilles Emery, "La relation dans la théologie de saint Albert le Grand," in *Albertus Magnus: Zum Gedenken nach 800 Jahren*, ed. Walter Senner (Berlin: Akademie Verlag, 2001), 455–65.

58. I *Sent.*, dist. 26, q. 2, a. 1, c.; *De veritate*, q. 1, a. 5, ad 15; *De potentia*, q. 7, a. 11, c.

an ontological determination, but its consistence is that of a concept.[59] The real relation enters into composition with its subject (by virtue of its accidental being),[60] but the relation of reason differs only conceptually from the subject to which it is attributed.

Observing that "the relation of reason consists in the order of concepts (*in ordine intellectuum*)," Aquinas specifies two modalities.[61] This teaching, which is too often neglected, will be important for grasping correctly the relation of God to the world. (1) According to the first modality, the order of concepts is posed or "invented" (*adinventus*) by our intellect, which attributes it to the things *insofar as these things are known* (*rebus intellectis, prout sunt intellectae*). Such is the case, for example, of the relation of genus and species. "Our reason discovers these relations by considering the order of that which is in the intellect to things that are outside the intellect, or again the order of concepts to one another."[62] (2) The second modality is found when the relation "of reason" flows from our mode of knowing (*modus intelligendi*).[63] In this case, grasping A in relation to B inasmuch as A is the term of the real relation of B to A, although the relation is not real in A, our intellect attributes the relation *to the thing (A) itself.*[64] Aquinas invokes this second modality of relations "of reason" to account for mixed pairs of relations: when, by virtue of the real relation that one thing maintains with another (for example, the relationship of the science to the thing known), our intellect grasps in the corresponding term a relation that does not fulfill the conditions required for a real relation (the relation of the thing known with the science), our intellect necessarily attributes to this corresponding term a relation "of reason." Let us look at this more closely.

Pairs of Relations

In his teaching about real relations and relations of reason, Aquinas recognizes three sorts of *pairs of relations*. (1) The first class is constituted by

59. *Compendium theologiae* I, ch. 53: "Illae enim relationes sunt rationis tantum quae non consequuntur ad aliquid quod est in rerum natura, sed ad aliquid quod est in apprehensione tantum."

60. See, for example, I *Sent.*, dist. 8, q. 4, a. 3, c. See above, n. 51.

61. *De potentia*, q. 7, a. 11, c.

62. Ibid.: "Has enim relationes ratio adinvenit considerando ordinem eius quod est in intellectu ad res quae sunt extra, vel etiam ordinem intellectuum ad invicem." These are, properly speaking, "logical relations."

63. Ibid.: "Alio modo secundum quod huiusmodi relationes consequuntur modum intelligendi, videlicet quod intellectus intelligit aliquid in ordine ad aliud; licet illum ordinem intellectus non adinveniat, sed magis ex quadam necessitate consequatur modum intelligendi."

64. Ibid.: "Et huiusmodi relationes intellectus non attribuit ei quod est in intellectu, sed ei quod est in re." See below, n. 96.

relations which are real in each of the two correlative terms. Recall that this necessitates that the two correlative terms be endowed with real existence (*res naturae*), that they belong to the "same order," and that the two relations be based on one of the two foundations capable of causing a real relation in the subject. This is the case of all relations founded on quantity (e.g., double-half); it is also the case of certain relations founded on action and passion (e.g., father-son) when the conditions for a real relation are verified in the two correlatives. (2) The second class includes the pairs of relations which are bilaterally "of reason." It includes, for example, relations of the same to the same (that is, of a thing to itself), relations with a non-existing thing (*non ens*), relations of genus and species, relations of relations, and so forth. (3) The third class of pairs of relations is constituted by a relation which is "real" in one term, with a relation "of reason alone" in the correlative term. Aquinas constantly uses the example of the relations of the science and the thing known, or of the sensation and the sensible (cf. Aristotle, *Metaphysics* V, 15 [1020b31–32]): the relation is real in the science and in the sense, but the thing known (as such) has only a relation of reason to the science or the sense. This lack of reality is explained by the absence of *fundamentum* in the thing known itself, and more profoundly by the fact that the science and the thing known "are not of the same order," inasmuch as the thing known, which exists in the order of natural being (*esse naturale*), is found outside the order of sensible being and of intelligible being as such (*extra ordinem esse sensibilis et intelligibilis*).[65] Thus, the "knowable" or the "known" implies a relation of reason: following the *modus intelligendi* (second modality of "relations of reason" explained above), our intellect attributes to the thing known a relation of reason which necessarily corresponds to the real relation that the science maintains with this thing known. This third class (mixed pairs, when the relation is real in one of the correlative terms but is only "of reason" in the other) concerns relations founded on action and passion since, as we have already noted, the relations founded on quantity are bilaterally real: thus, for example, equality ("one in quantity") is a real relation in its two correlative terms (its two "extremes"), because it is founded on the quantity which exists in both terms.[66]

To account for the Trinitarian faith, Aquinas examines the first class of pairs of relations (bilaterally real relations) with the greatest care. He pays equally special attention to the third class of pairs of relations, because it is

---

65. *ST* I, q. 13, a. 7, c.; cf. q. 42, a. 1, ad 4; I *Sent.*, dist. 30, q. 1, a. 3, ad 3; *De potentia*, q. 11, a. 7, c.

66. See *ST* I, q. 13, a. 7, c.; *De potentia*, q. 7, a. 10, c.; I *Sent.*, dist. 31, q. 1, a. 1, c.; *Expositio libri Physicorum*, lib. V, lect. 3, §8 (Marietti edition, n. 667).

this which allows an account of the relationship of God and his creatures, as well as of the hypostatic union (the union of God and man in Jesus Christ is a relation). We will return briefly to this point below.

Complementary Clarifications

Aquinas's study of relations offers several precisions which cannot be examined in the limited scope of the present study. We will nonetheless point to some of the most significant ones.

Firstly, following Aristotle's *Physics* V, 2 (225b11–13), "There is no motion (κίνησις) in respect of the relative (πρός τι): for it may happen that when one correlative changes, the other ... does not itself change, ... so that in these cases the motion is accidental."[67] This means that there is no movement (*motus*) *per se* in the predicament *ad aliquid*, but only *per accidens*.[68] On the one hand, this allows Aquinas to account for the immutability of the divine relations: the Trinitarian relations do not introduce any change in God.[69] On the other hand, Aquinas reckons that certain created relations, including real relations, can come upon a subject without any change in this subject. When speaking of a relation "of reason," this hardly poses any difficulty. But the problem is more serious when discussing a real relation: this is a point that Aquinas judges to be "difficult."[70] For example, a person changes: by this change, he becomes equal to me, and correlatively I become equal to him. I have thus acquired a new real relation (namely, equality) without any change (*mutatio*) occurring in myself: the change occurred in the other person. This case appears only in the genus of relation.[71] Aquinas maintains the reality of such a relation as he explains: "That equality was in me in advance, in a certain way, as in its root (*radix*), from which that equality has real existence: for since I have such and such a quantity, it belongs to me to be equal to all who have the same quantity as me. Hence, when someone newly acquires that quantity, that common root of equality reaches this person: that is why nothing new happens to me when I begin to

---

67. A similar statement is found in *Metaphysics* XI, 12 (1068a11–13) and XIV, 1 (1088a29–35); this last reference (*Metaphysics* XIV, 1) is quite famous: "A sign that the relative is least of all a substance and a real thing is the fact that it alone has no proper generation or destruction or movement."

68. *Expositio libri Physicorum*, lib. V, lect. 3, §7 (Marietti edition, n. 666).

69. See, for instance, Aquinas, I *Sent.*, dist. 9, *expositio textus*: "Secundum Philosophum, V *Physic.*, in 'ad aliquid' non est motus: et ita adventu relationis non potest concludi aliqua mutabilitas." The context is the patristic debate with the "Arians."

70. *Expositio libri Physicorum*, lib. V, lect. 3, §8 (Marietti edition, n. 667).

71. Ibid., lib. VII, lect. 6, §5 (Marietti edition, n. 923).

be equal to someone by virtue of a change in this other person."[72] Similarly, a real relation can be destroyed by the destruction of the foundation (the "root"), or by the cessation of the relationship to the correlative term when this correlative term disappears.[73] The explanation, one sees, insists upon the "root" or cause (*fundamentum*) of the relation in the subject, as well as on the "*ratio*" of the relation which consists precisely in the connection to the *correlative term*. The foundation in a subject remaining unchanged, the relation appears or disappears with its correlative term.

Secondly, the *unity or plurality* of the real relation is taken from the subject and from the foundation rather than from the correlative term itself (that toward which the relation tends). Thus, on the *ontological* level, it is by one and the same relation of filiation that a human being is referred as "son" or "daughter" to his or her father and mother: there is *in me* only one real filiation by which I am the son of my father and of my mother (I am one son, one subject), because I was engendered by a unique generation (foundation), although the relationships (*respectus*), which concern the pure formality of the relation, are diverse (here again we find the singular characteristic of the *ratio* of the relation). This applies also to the relation of the teacher toward his students, inasmuch as the teacher (subject) instructs his disciples by one and the same teaching (foundation); it is the same for the real relation of equality that I have with numerous equals, and so forth. And even when the causes (foundations) are multiple, if these causes are of the same species they do not create multiple relations *in* one and the same subject (on the ontological level). It is by one and the same paternity that, *onto-*

72. Ibid., lib. V, lect. 3, §8 (Marietti edition, n. 667): "Si aliquis per suam mutationem efficiatur mihi aequalis, me non mutato, ista aequalitas primo erat in me quodammodo, sicut in sua radice, ex qua habet esse reale: ex hoc enim quod habeo talem quantitatem, competit mihi quod sim aequalis omnibus illis, qui eandem quantitatem habent. Cum ergo aliquis de novo accipit illam quantitatem, ista communis radix aequalitatis determinatur ad istum: et ideo nihil advenit mihi de novo per hoc quod incipio esse alteri aequalis per eius mutationem." Cf. §7 (Marietti edition, n. 666): "Contingit de novo verum esse aliquid relative dici ad alterum altero mutato, ipso tamen non mutato." In IV *Sent.*, dist. 41, q. 1, a. 1, quaestiuncula 1, ad 3, showing that such a relation of equality is *really founded* in the two extremes, Aquinas specifies: it is by an anterior movement that I reached the quantity that I have now: "Sicut aequalitas fit inter duos homines per augmentum unius sine hoc quod alius tunc augeatur vel minuatur; sed tamen prius ad hanc quantitatem quam habet, per aliquem motum vel mutationem, pervenit; et ideo in utroque extremorum talis relatio realiter fundatur."

73. I *Sent.*, dist. 26, q. 2, a. 1, ad 3; *De potentia*, q. 7, a. 9, ad 7. See also *De potentia*, q. 7, a. 8, c.: "Et propter hoc etiam probat Philosophus V *Phys.*, quod in *ad aliquid* non potest esse motus: quia, sine aliqua mutatione eius quod ad aliud refertur, potest relatio desinere ex sola mutatione alterius." *De potentia*, q. 7, a. 8, ad 5: "Et tamen non oportet, ad hoc quod de aliquo relatio aliqua de novo dicatur, quod aliqua mutatio in ipso fiat, sed sufficit quod fiat mutatio in aliquo extremorum."

logically, a father of several children is father; there are not multiple paternities in him but one alone: he is *one father*. The guiding principle to these explications is the following: multiple forms of the same species cannot exist simultaneously in the same subject. Nevertheless, when their causes are of different species, nothing prevents real relations from multiplying in the same subject: the master who teaches grammar to certain pupils and logic to others possesses different relations toward the two groups of pupils.[74]

Thirdly, we must also clarify the distinction between relatives "*secundum esse*" and relatives "*secundum dici*." This vocabulary, which comes from the reception of the two Aristotelian definitions of the "πρός τι" (in the *Categories*) through Boethius, often brings about confusion. For Albert the Great, for example, the relatives "*secundum esse et dici*" concern real relations flowing from a change in the two correlatives, while the relative "*secundum dici tantum*" concerns a relation of reason, devoid of real existence in the subject, which is attributed to a term because of a change which occurs in the correlative term.[75] Aquinas objects to such an interpretation: "This distinction between relatives *secundum esse* and relatives *secundum dici* has nothing to do with the reality of the relation."[76] For Aquinas, the relatives *secundum esse* signify the relations themselves (*ispas habitudines, ipsas relationes*) or principally these relations (for example: master, servant, father, son, lord, etc.); for their part, the relatives *secundum dici* signify that upon which the relation is founded, or a reality which implies a relation, that is to say an absolute which is accompanied by a relation (science, motion, Creator, Savior, etc.).[77] Some relatives *secundum esse* (the *thing* and the *name* which formally signify it) concern a relation of reason, while certain relatives *secundum dici* concern a real relation.[78]

Fourthly, among the properties of the "πρός τι" enumerated in Aristotle's *Categories* 7, Aquinas pays special attention to the following three: (1) all the relatives have their correlatives, (2) they are simultaneous, and (3) one

74. *Quodlibet* IX, q. 2, a. 3 (Leonine edition, vol. 25/1, pp. 96–97); *ST* III, q. 35, a. 5. Here Aquinas shows that Christ Jesus does possess only one real relation of filiation (filiation has the person for subject): his filiation toward his divine Father.

75. Albertus Magnus, *Summa theologiae* I, tract. 13, q. 52, c. and ad quaest. 2, ad 2; Albertus Magnus, *Opera omnia*, ed. Auguste Borgnet, vol. 31 (Paris: Vivès, 1895), 536 and 538. For more details, see Emery, "La relation dans la théologie de saint Albert le Grand," 456–57.

76. *De potentia*, q. 7, a. 10, ad 11: "Distinctio ista relativorum secundum esse et secundum dici, nihil facit ad hoc quod sit relatio realis."

77. *ST* I, q. 13, a. 7, ad 1; cf. I *Sent.*, dist. 30, q. 1, a. 2, c.

78. *De potentia*, q. 7, a. 10, ad 11: "Quaedam enim sunt relativa secundum esse quae non sunt realia, sicut dextrum et sinistrum in columna; et quaedam sunt relativa secundum dici, quae tamen important relationes reales, sicut patet de scientia et sensu."

knows the one when knowing the other. There is no difficulty with the first property because it flows from the very definition of the relative: "It is inconceivable that one thing be said in relation to (*relative ad*) another unless, conversely, the latter be said in relation to it."[79] If we consider the *ratio* of the relation, the third property is equally clear: "In one relative is found the notion (*intellectus*) of the other relative";[80] consequently: "Whoever knows one of the relatives also knows the other."[81] The simultaneity of the relatives is given a more detailed explanation. Sometimes Aquinas affirms, without further qualifications, that the relatives exist simultaneously according to nature, according to time (since the relatives appear and disappear together) and according to our understanding (since a relative is defined as such by the relation to its correlative).[82] Nevertheless, certain relatives have no natural simultaneity as absolute entities: this is the case, for instance, of the knowable that preexists the science. Aquinas thus specifies that the simultaneity of nature (*simul natura*) is found in the relatives which have the same reason for their mutual relationship (e.g., father and son, master and servant, double and half), or which are in act *as relatives* (e.g., the known and the science). In sum, the *subjects*, considered in themselves, are not necessarily simultaneous by nature (a father, *as a human being*, exists before his son), but the *relations* themselves are by nature simultaneous.[83]

These observations lead us to a final consideration: relative opposition. Every formal distinction has some opposition as its principle,[84] so that among immaterial things there can be no distinction except by some opposition.[85] Commenting on Aristotle, Aquinas notes four modes by which we speak of

79. *SCG*, Bk. II, ch. 11 (Marietti edition, n. 906).

80. *De potentia*, q. 7, a. 10, ad 4: "In uno enim relativo est intellectus alterius relativi." Cf. I *Sent.*, dist. 19, q. 3, a. 2, c.; *ST* I, q. 42, a. 5, c.: "Unum oppositorum relative est in altero secundum intellectum" (in the context of the mutual "esse in" of each divine person in the other two divine persons). See also *ST* I, q. 13, a. 7, ad 6. This applies to relatives *as such* and calls for an examination of the "mode of signifying" of the relative words.

81. II *Sent.*, dist. 38, q. 1, a. 4, c.: "Qui novit unum relativorum, novit et reliquum." See also *De veritate*, q. 2, a. 3, sc 2; etc.

82. I *Sent.*, dist. 9, q. 2, a. 1, c.: "natura ... tempore ... et etiam intellectu." See also *ST* I, q. 40, a. 2, ad 4 ("simul natura").

83. *De potentia*, q. 7, a. 8, ad 1; *ST* I, q. 13, a. 7, ad 6; q. 42, a. 3, ad 2.

84. I *Sent.*, dist. 26, q. 2, a. 2, c.: "Omnis autem distinctionis formalis principium est aliqua oppositio." *De potentia*, q. 10, a. 2, obj. 2 (with reference to *Metaphysics* X): "Omnis autem formalis distinctio est per aliquam oppositionem, et maxime eorum quae sunt unius generis." Cf. Aristotle, *Metaphysics* X, 8 (1058a9–10); Aquinas, *Sententia libri Metaphysicae*, lib. X, lect. 10 (Marietti edition, nn. 2120–21).

85. *SCG*, Bk. IV, ch. 24 (Marietti edition, n. 3612): "In rebus enim, remota materiali distinctione, ... non inveniuntur aliqua distingui nisi per aliquam oppositionem." *Compendium theologiae* I, ch. 60: "Formalis distinctio non est nisi per oppositionem."

"opposites" (*opposita*): contradictories, contraries, according to privation and possession, and relatives (*ad aliquid*).[86] He therefore holds: (1) the opposition of affirmation and negation, (2) the opposition of contrariety (*contrarietas*, which implies a diversity of form), (3) the opposition of possession and privation, and (4) the opposition of relation (*oppositio relationis*).[87] In Aquinas's interpretation, the opposition of relation is the only one that does not suppress one of the terms and which, in itself, does not imply any imperfection in one term by comparison with the other term.[88] This characteristic holds special interest for Trinitarian theology: it allows us to show that the consubstantial divine persons are distinguished and constituted by "opposed relations of origin." We grasp these relations as founded on "notional acts" (to beget, to spirate) and on "processions" (to be begotten, to proceed). Notional acts are indeed identical to relations, although our mode of signifying (which follows upon our mode of understanding) is different.[89] The same goes for the processions: "In God, processions and relations are not really distinct, but only according to the mode of understanding."[90] We should also note that "to proceed" (the Son is *begotten* by the Father, the Holy Spirit *proceeds* from the Father and the Son) is an *act*. "The only 'passive' that we posit among the divine persons is grammatical, according to our mode of signifying; i.e., we speak of the Father begetting and of the Son *being begotten*."[91] In this way, processions come back to relations: "Generation *signifies relation by way of an operation.*… And although 'to beget' does not belong to the Son, this does not

86. *Sententia libri Metaphysicae*, lib. V, lect. 12 (Marietti edition, n. 922): "Contradictoria, contraria, privatio et habitus, et ad aliquid." Cf. Aristotle, *Categories* 10 (11b15–13b35; on "things opposed as relatives," see 11b24–33); *Metaphysics* V, 10 (1018a20–21); *Metaphysics* X, 4 (1055a38–1055b1).

87. *SCG*, Bk. IV, ch. 24 (Marietti edition, n. 3612).

88. Ibid. See also *De potentia*, q. 7, a. 8, ad 4: "Oppositio relationis in duobus differt ab aliis oppositionibus: quorum primum est quod in aliis oppositis unum dicitur alteri opponi, in quantum ipsum removet.… Non autem est hoc in relativis.… Et ex hoc causatur secunda differentia, quia in aliis oppositis semper alterum est imperfectum.… Hoc autem in relativis non oportet, immo utrumque considerari potest ut perfectum, sicut patet maxime in relativis aequiparantiae, et in relativis originis, ut aequale, simile, pater et filius." See also I *Sent.*, dist. 26, q. 2, a. 2, c.: "In omnibus autem oppositionibus alterum est ut perfectum, alterum ut imperfectum, praeter relationem." *De potentia*, q. 8, a. 1, ad 13.

89. *ST* I, q. 41, a. 1, ad 2: "Actus notionales secundum modum significandi tantum differunt a relationibus personarum; se re sunt omnino idem.… Cum in divinis non sit motus, actio personalis producentis personam, nihil aliud est quam habitudo principii ad personam quae est a principio. Quae quidem habitudines sunt ipsae relationes vel notiones." *ST* I, q. 40, a. 4, c.: "Relatio, inquantum huiusmodi, fundatur super actum." For further clarifications, see Emery, *The Trinitarian Theology of Saint Thomas Aquinas*, 51–55, 74–77, and 96–102.

90. *De potentia*, q. 10, a. 3, c.: "Processiones autem et relationes non distinguuntur in divinis secundum rem, sed solum secundum modum intelligendi."

91. *ST* I, q. 41, a. 1, ad 3.

mean that there would be some operation belonging to the Father and not to the Son. Rather, it is by one and the same operation that the Father begets and the Son is begotten, but this operation is in the Father and in the Son according to two distinct relations (*sed haec operatio est in Patre et Filio secundum aliam et aliam relationem*)."[92] The same applies to the procession of the Holy Spirit.

The Relation of Creatures to God the Creator

Without entering further into the use of the philosophical elaboration of relation in Trinitarian theology, we must note its importance for understanding the relationship of God and the world. Aquinas considers the relations of God and the creature as a pair of relations wherein one is real (in the creature) and the other of reason (in God).[93]

Taken in the active sense, *creation* signifies an act of God: it is "a divine action which is God's essence with a relation 'of reason' toward creatures."[94] On the one hand, observing the real relation of creatures toward God, our mind necessarily attributes the corresponding relation to God. On the other hand, since God is not of the same order as creatures ("God is totally outside the order of creatures"), this relation can only be "of reason" in God; this flows from the conditions required for the existence of a real relation: there are no bilaterally real relations when the relatives are not of the same order. God's relation to creatures pertains to the second modality of relations "of reason" noted above: such a relation does not concern the order of concepts "invented" by our intellect, but it flows from the "mode of knowing" and is attributed to God himself.[95]

---

92. I *Sent.*, dist. 20, q. 1, a. 1, ad 1.

93. *ST* I, q. 13, a. 7, c. For a more extensive treatment of this topic (in Aquinas, Bonaventure, Henry of Ghent, and Duns Scotus), see Gilles Emery, "La relation de création," *Nova et Vetera* [French ed.] 88 (2013): 9–43.

94. Ibid., q. 45, a. 3, ad 1: "Creatio active significata significat actionem divinam, quae est eius essentia cum relatione ad creaturam. Sed relatio in Deo ad creaturam non est realis, sed secundum rationem tantum. Relatio vero creaturae ad Deum est relatio realis, ut supra dictum est, cum de divinis nominibus ageretur." See also II *Sent.*, dist. 1, q. 1, a. 2, ad 4; *De potentia*, q. 3, a. 3, c.; *De potentia*, q. 3, a. 3, ad 2: "Creatio active accepta significat divinam actionem cum quadam relatione cointellecta, et sic est increatum."

95. *De potentia*, q. 7, a. 11, c.: "Quandoque vero [intellectus] accipit aliquid cum ordine ad aliud, in quantum est terminus ordinis alterius ad ipsum, licet ipsum non ordinetur ad aliud: sicut accipiendo scibile ut terminum ordinis scientiae ad ipsum; et sic cum quodam ordine ad scientiam, nomen scibilis relative significat; et est relatio rationis tantum. Et similiter aliqua nomina relativa Deo attribuit intellectus noster, in quantum accipit Deum ut terminum relationum creaturarum ad ipsum; unde huiusmodi relationes sunt rationis tantum." See above, nn. 64 and 65.

Taken in the passive sense, *creation* signifies a relation of the creature toward God as the principle of the creature's existence (*esse*). More precisely, "If creation is taken in the passive sense, it is a certain accident in the creature, and so it signifies a certain reality which is not in the predicament of passion, properly speaking, but in the genus of relation (*in genere relationis*): it is a certain relationship of the thing having being from another, resulting from divine operation."[96] Inasmuch as creation is a real relation in the creature itself, it has the creature as its subject; the correlative term of this relation is God from whom the creature has its being; and the foundation of this relation is the reception of being by virtue of the divine operation (action/passion, under the pure aspect of relation, since creation is not a movement).[97]

Here we should note that the Incarnation, that is to say, the personal union of the Son of God with the assumed human nature, is explained in a similar way: "Every relation which we consider between God and the creature is really in the creature, by whose change the relation is brought into being; whereas it is not really in God, but only in our way of thinking, since it does not arise from any change in God. And hence we must say that the union of which we are speaking is not really in God, except only in our way of thinking; but it is really in the human nature, which is a creature."[98] In the assumption of the human nature by the Son, the subject of the real relation is the assumed humanity; the correlative term of the assumption is the divine person of the Son;[99] and the foundation of the "relation of Incarna-

96. II *Sent.*, dist. 1, q. 1, a. 2, ad 4: "Creatio potest sumi active et passive.... Si autem sumatur passive, sic est quoddam accidens in creatura, et sic significat quamdam rem, non quae sit in praedicamento passionis, proprie loquendo, sed quae est in genere relationis, et est quaedam habitudo habentis esse ab alio consequens operationem divinam." Cf. *ST* I, q. 45, a. 3, c., ad 1 and ad 2.

97. *De potentia*, q. 3, a. 3, c.: "Creatio potest sumi active et passive.... Si autem passive accipiatur, cum creatio, sicut iam supra dictum est, proprie loquendo non sit mutatio, non potest dici quod sit aliquid in genere passionis, sed est in genere relationis." *ST* I, q. 45, a. 3, c.: "Unde Deus, creando, producit res sine motu. Subtracto autem motu ab actione et passione, nihil remanet nisi relatio, ut dictum est. Unde relinquitur quod creatio in creatura non sit nisi relatio quaedam ad creatorem, ut ad principium sui esse."

98. *ST* III, q. 2, a. 7, c.: "Omnis relatio quae consideratur inter Deum et creaturam, realiter quidem est in creatura, per cuius mutationem talis relatio innascitur; non autem est realiter in Deo, sed secundum rationem tantum, quia non nascitur secundum mutationem Dei. Sic igitur dicendum est quod haec unio de qua loquimur, non est in Deo realiter, sed secundum rationem tantum: in humana autem natura, quae creatura quaedam est, est realiter." See also III *Sent.*, dist. 5, q. 1, a. 1, quaestiuncula 1.

99. III *Sent.*, dist. 2, q. 2, a. 2, quaestiuncula 3, ad 2: "Unio relatio quaedam temporalis est: quae quidem realiter est in ipsa natura assumpta, sed in persona assumente secundum rationem tantum; sicut et de aliis relationibus ex tempore de Deo dictis." The divine essence is really identical with the divine person (*ST* I, q. 39, a. 6). However, the case of the Incarnation is more

tion" lies in the fact that this humanity is assumed by the Son, by virtue of an action common to the whole Trinity (passion/action).[100]

Let us return to creation. The thesis that posits the relation of creation as an *accident* in the creature is far from being insignificant. In fact, a large current of Christian thinkers hesitates to recognize the accidentality of this relation and tends to consider it as a reality that belongs to the essence of creatures, or as identified with creatures' very substance. As St. Bonaventure explains: "The creature, as to its first being, depends essentially [on God]: and such a relation, which expresses this dependence [upon God], is not accidental to the creature but is rather essential to it,"[101] so that "creation is not really something else than the creature."[102] Later, Duns Scotus holds that the relation of the creature to God is really identical to created being: in this case, the "foundation" (here, the created being) is "an absolute that contains a relation by identity."[103] In this context, Duns Scotus appeals to

complex than that of creation, since in the Incarnation we must distinguish between the divine nature (or the whole Trinity) as the *cause* of the hypostatic union, and the distinct person of the Son as the *term* of this union; see next note.

100. The "assumption" is "terminated" in the person of the Son, but the act of uniting is common to the three divine persons: "Prima et principalis differentia inter unionem et assumptionem est quod unio importat ipsam relationem, assumptio autem actionem secundum quam dicitur aliquis assumens, vel passionem secundum quam dicitur aliquid assumptum.... Uniens et assumens non omnino sunt idem. Nam omnis persona assumens est uniens: non autem e converso. Nam persona Patris univit naturam humanam Filio, non autem sibi: et ideo dicitur uniens, non assumens" (*ST* III, q. 2, a. 8, c. and ad 2). Accordingly, Aquinas explains that "Assumption (*assumptio*) implies two things, namely, the act of the one who assumes (*actus assumentis*) and the term of assumption (*terminus assumptionis*). Now the act of the one who assumes proceeds from the divine power, which is common to the three persons, but the term of the assumption is a person, as stated above. Hence that which pertains to action in the assumption is common to the three persons (*quod est actionis in assumptione, commune est tribus personis*); but what pertains to the term belongs to one person in such a manner as not to belong to another; for the three persons caused the human nature to be united to the one person of the Son (*tres enim personae fecerunt ut humana natura uniretur uni personae Filii*)" (*ST* III, q. 3, a. 4, c.).

101. St. Bonaventure, I *Sent.*, dist. 30, dubium 4: "Dicendum, quod creatura quantum ad esse primum essentialiter dependet; et talis relatio, quae exprimit illam dependentiam, non est creaturae accidentalis, sed magis essentialis." S. Bonaventura, *Opera omnia*, edita studio et cura PP. Collegii a S. Bonaventura, vol. 1 (Quaracchi: Ex typographia Collegii S. Bonaventurae, 1882), 528.

102. Bonaventure, II *Sent.*, dist. 1, pars 1, a. 3, q. 2, resp.: "Et ideo concedendum, quod creatio non est aliud secundum rem a creatura." S. Bonaventura, *Opera omnia*, edita studio et cura PP. Collegii a S. Bonaventura, vol. 2 (Quaracchi: Ex typographia Collegii S. Bonaventurae, 1885), 35.

103. Duns Scotus, *Ordinatio* II, dist. 1, qq. 4–5, n. 275: "Ita dico in proposito quod fundamentum non est tantum relatio (quam continet per identitatem), sed est ita absolutum ... quia illam relationem continet per identitatem, ita quod ipsa continentia praevenit accidentalitatem realtionis ne ipsa possit esse accidens, quia perfecte continetur in substantia." Ioannes Duns

the notion of "transcendental relation."[104] He specifies: "I concede that 'relations in creatures are accidents' in the case of relations of creatures toward that upon which they do not depend essentially; but toward all that upon which a thing depends essentially, this essential dependence toward that [upon which this thing depends essentially] is not an accident; that is to say, it is not really something else."[105] The following example makes it very clear: "I say that the relation to God, common to all creatures, is really identical with its foundation.... Because what is properly said to inhere in something, and without which this thing cannot exist without contradiction, is really identical with this thing. Now, the relation to God properly inheres in the stone, in such a way that without this relation the stone cannot be without contradiction. Hence, this relation is really identical with the stone."[106] In this teaching, the relation of dependence on God (without which the creature cannot exist) *is identified with the creature itself.*

The thought of Aquinas, about which some theologians have reproached him for a certain "naturalism," differs from these views. He firmly holds that, in the creature, the relation of creation (relation of causality) is an accident. His teaching on this subject involves three main aspects. Firstly, Aquinas maintains the accidental nature of the relation of creatures to their Creator, in specifying: "The relation to the cause does not enter into the definition of a being that is caused, but nonetheless it follows from those things that do belong to its *ratio*; for from the fact that something is a being through participation it follows that it is caused by another."[107] We can

---

Scotus, *Opera omnia*, Studio et cura Commissionis Scotisticae edita, vol. 7 (Vatican City: Typis Polyglottis Vaticanis, 1973), 136.

104. Duns Scotus, *Ordinatio* II, dist. 1, qq. 4–5, n. 277: "Potest tamen dici—consequenter ad dicta alias—quod huiusmodi relatio est transcendens, quia quod convenit enti antequam descendat in genera, est transcendens; sed quod convenit omni enti, convenit sibi antequam descendat in genera; ergo quod est tale, est transcendens et non alicuius generis. Et ideo istae relationes quae consequuntur ens antequam descendat in entia cuiuscumque generis, cum sint transcendentes, non erunt alicuius generis determinati" (ed. cit., pp. 137–38).

105. Duns Scotus, *Ordinatio* II, dist. 1, qq. 4–5, n. 278: "Concedo, quod 'relationes in creaturis sunt accidentia', de relationibus creaturarum ad illa ad quae non dependent essentialiter; ad quaecumque autem essentialiter dependet aliquid, ipsa dependentia essentialis eius ad illa non est sibi accidens, hoc est, non est aliud realiter" (ed. cit., pp. 138–39).

106. Duns Scotus, *Ordinatio* II, dist. 1, qq. 4–5, n. 260-61: "Dico quod relatio ad Deum, communis omni creaturae, est idem realiter fundamento.... Quia illud quod proprie dicitur inesse alicui, sine quo illud non potest esse sine contradictione, est idem sibi realiter; relatio autem ad Deum proprie inest lapidi, et sine ea non potest lapis esse sine contradictione; ergo illa relatio est realiter idem lapidi" (ed. cit., pp. 128–29).

107. *ST* I, q. 44, a. 1, ad 1: "Licet habitudo ad causam non intret definitionem entis quod est causatum, tamen sequitur ad ea qua sunt de eius ratione: quia ex hoc quod aliquid per participationem est ens, sequitur quod sit causatum ab alio." Aquinas insists that "being caused" does not belong to "being" (*ens*) per se: "Sed quia esse causatum non est de ratione entis simpliciter,

therefore "scientifically" define a being (its essence, which the definition signifies) without bringing in its relation to God. Secondly, although the relation to God is not an essential property of creatures, it is not a mere accident. Rather, it is a *proper* accident (*proprium accidens*) of creatures, that is, an accident that necessarily belongs to created beings—a determination that is not part of the essence of a being but that necessarily "follows from those things that do belong to the *ratio*" of a created being. Aquinas gives the following example: "A being by participation cannot exist without being caused, just as man cannot exist without being capable of laughing."[108] In this way, a creature cannot exist without the "relation of creation": this relation is an accident that necessarily follows from the created substance, by the very fact that this substance is created.[109] Thirdly, Aquinas specifies that *esse* is the "proper *ratio*" of the object of creation,[110] "the most common first effect and more intimate than all other effects."[111] In line with this, he explains: "Although the first cause that is God does not enter into the essence of creatures, yet *esse* which is in creatures cannot be understood except as derived from the divine *esse*: even as a proper effect cannot be understood save as derived from its proper cause."[112] This explanation has recourse to the real difference between essence and existence: while the *essence* of

propter hoc invenitur aliquod ens non causatum" (ibid.). See also *De potentia*, q. 7, a. 9: although the creature's substance can be considered as the "cause of the relation" to God (*sicut secundum causam relationis*), the creature is *formally* (ontologically) referred to God by a relation (ad 4) which is an accident that inheres in the subject (ad 7).

108. *ST* I, q. 44, a. 1, ad 1. On "proper accidents" (*accidentia propria*), see *ST* I, q. 3, a. 4, c.; I-II, q. 2, a. 6, c.; *De veritate*, q. 3, a. 7, c. ("accidentia propria … secundum esse nunquam a suis subiectis separantur"); *Quaestiones disputatae De anima*, q. 9, c. (Leonine edition, vol. 24/1, p. 81): "accidentia propria que necesse est ei inesse." In his *Sententia libri de sensu et sensato* (tractatus I, ch. 9, dubitatio 1; Leonine edition, vol. 45/2, p. 54), Aquinas gives the example of heat with relation to fire: "Heat is present per se in fire (*calor per se inest igni*) not as its substantial form, but as its proper accident (*proprium accidens eius*)."

109. *Quodlibet* VII, q. 4, a. 3, ad 4 (Leonine edition, vol. 25/1, pp. 23–24): "Ex hoc ipso quod substancia creata comparatur ad Deum, consequitur ipsam aliquod accidens, sicut ipsa relatio creationis, aut servitutis, aut alia similis relatio; unde, sicut Deus non potest facere quod creatura non dependeat ab ipso, ita non posset facere quod esset absque huiusmodi accidentibus; posset autem facere quod esset absque aliis accidentibus."

110. *ST* I, q. 45, a. 4, ad 1: "Cum dicitur, prima rerum creatarum est esse, ly esse non importat subiectum creatum; sed importat propriam rationem obiecti creationis."

111. *De potentia*, q. 3, a. 7, c.: "Ipsum enim esse est communissimus effectus primus et intimior omnibus aliis effectibus."

112. *De potentia*, q. 3, a. 5, ad 1: "Licet causa prima, quae Deus est, non intret essentiam rerum creatarum; tamen esse, quod rebus creatis inest, non potest intelligi nisi ut deductum ab esse divino; sicut nec proprius effectus potest intelligi nisi ut deductus a causa propria." Cf. *SCG*, Bk. II, ch. 18 (Marietti edition, n. 952): in the creature, creation is "the very dependence of created existence with respect to the principle by which it is established (*ipsa dependentia esse creati ad principium a quo statuitur*); it therefore belongs to the genus of relation."

things can be grasped without reference to creation, the *existence* of things can be grasped only as coming from God. The whole argument is clarified through the doctrine of participation. In this way, Aquinas's understanding of the "relation of creation" accounts for both the "religious status" (or "religious condition") of the world *and* the proper consistency of created beings.

In conclusion, among the traits characteristic of Aquinas's understanding of relation, we can list the following aspects: an approach to relation as an accident among the ten predicaments; the strict connection of metaphysics and language in interpreting Aristotle; the tight analysis of the formal reason (*ad aliud*) and of the being (*esse*) of the relation—together with the "mode of signifying" proper to the relation; the recognition of real relations and the attention given to the foundation of such relations; the place of "relations of reason" (and the distinction between two kinds of "relations of reason"), as well as the study of pairs of relations (which receive the most attention in the exposition of theological doctrines). Relation is at the heart of the metaphysical understanding of unity and plurality in the created world ("ordered" universe) and in God himself (the Trinity). Far from being marginal, the *philosophical analysis* of relation, clearly guided by the Aristotelian tradition, assumes a decisive importance for the elaboration of fundamental theological teachings, especially the Trinity, creation, and the Incarnation.

CHAPTER ELEVEN

Aquinas on the Procession of the Holy Spirit

JOHN BOYLE

In his memoir, *I Alone Have Escaped to Tell You*, Ralph McInerny spoke to the current state of philosophy, especially in Catholic institutions:

This habit of prescribing more of what has caused the problem is a mark of our age. Philosophers, aware that something has gone wrong in their discipline, do not see the need for a 180-degree turn. What are considered radical solutions, merely plunge us deeper into nihilism and relativism. In short, the culture and its philosophy have grown worse since 1879, and the remedy Leo XIII proposed remains the only cure. The human mind must again be measured by reality rather than make futile attempts at the reverse. How ironic that Catholic philosophy since the Council has taken on the coloration of modernity and all but abandoned its traditional roots. Our departments of philosophy now have a majority of members for whom what I have been saying would be as unintelligible as doubtless it would be at Meatball Tech. It is a melancholy thought that now, when the salutary impact of traditional philosophy is most urgently needed, we who are its presumed representatives have abandoned ship and are crowding the rails of the Titanic.[1]

If such is the state of philosophy, one might well shudder at the prospects for theology, which is in its speculative work so dependent upon philoso-

---

1. Ralph McInerny, *I Alone Have Escaped to Tell You: My Life and Pastimes* (Notre Dame, Ind.: University of Notre Dame Press, 2006), 105.

phy. As McInerny so keenly appreciated, St. Thomas Aquinas has much to teach us. In considering "Aquinas on the Procession of the Holy Spirit," I would like to consider one specific text of Aquinas that sheds light on the topic of procession, and in so doing speaks to Aquinas's understanding of the place of philosophy in theological education.

In the middle of his career, Aquinas was instructed to return from Paris to the Roman Province of the Order of Preachers, where he was to teach beginning theology to his confreres. As Tolomeo of Lucca tells us, Aquinas taught, for one year, 1265–66, book I of Peter Lombard's *Sentences* to his young students. The surviving student reportatio of that year of teaching is illuminating for our topic.[2] Throughout the articles of this *Lectura romana*, Aquinas is careful to build on the philosophical training of his students as he leads them into theology. We find attention to the signification and analysis of words and of propositions; to the definition of words, and to the imprecisions of words; to the careful analysis of the analogies that undergird the theologian's work.[3] Of course, all of this is also found in Aquinas's other works; but in the *Lectura romana*, such considerations seem rather more pronounced. There is, we might say, a greater density of such basic and essential philosophical considerations. The point, obviously, is not to teach his students philosophy, but rather to show how the philosophy they have learned is to be in the service of theology.

Much of the *Lectura romana* is concerned with the doctrine of the Trinity. This essay concerns one article, in which Aquinas asks whether the Holy Spirit can be said to be begotten.[4] The answer is theologically obvious: the Holy Spirit is not begotten; the Son is the only begotten Son of the Father. In his other systematic works, this question does not get the extended, separate treatment it does in the *Lectura romana*. Generally Aquinas raises the question in the context of a procession of love in the will as the analog to understand why the Holy Spirit is spirated and not begotten, as in *Summa theologiae* I, 27, 4; and *Summa contra gentiles* IV, 19, 9.

Our question—whether the Holy Spirit can be said to be begotten—is situated at the end of Aquinas's consideration of the procession of the Holy Spirit. In fact, Aquinas has already laid out, within the confining strictures of Lombard's order, the essential contours of his teaching on the procession of

2. Thomas Aquinas, *Lectura romana in primum Sententiarum Petri Lombardi*, ed. L. E. Boyle and John F. Boyle (Toronto: Pontifical Institute of Mediaeval Studies, 2006). Hereafter cited as *LR*.

3. For a consideration of the character of the work, especially as a product of Aquinas's classroom, see John F. Boyle, "Thomas Aquinas and his *Lectura romana in primum Sententiarum Petri Lombardi*," in *Mediaeval Commentaries on the Sentences of Peter Lombard*, vol. 2 (Leiden: Brill, 2010), 149–73.

4. *LR* 13.3, pp. 173–74.

the Holy Spirit. So why raise this question at all? It is an opportunity to consider more precisely the place of philosophical analysis in the heart of theology. Aquinas begins his response by stating that this question is raised by the heretic Macedonius, who held that the Holy Spirit is not God but a creature. Macedonius's argument, as Aquinas formulates it, goes like this: The Holy Spirit either receives the nature of the Father or not. If it receives the nature of the Father, then it is begotten. But the Holy Spirit cannot be called begotten. Therefore it does not receive the nature of the Father and is thus a creature.[5] We have here an argument, an exercise of reason, that would seem to use Catholic doctrine (the Holy Spirit is not begotten) against Catholic doctrine (the Holy Spirit is God). In answering this argument, Aquinas introduces no new theological material into his classroom; rather, he guides his students in understanding what has gone wrong philosophically in the Macedonian argument.

Aquinas tips his hand as he begins his response to this argument by saying that this question is rather more about the signification of words than about the reality of the Holy Spirit.[6] It is a question of how to use and understand words: why is it that we can say the Son is begotten but not the Holy Spirit?

To get this signification of the words right, Aquinas speaks to what causes diversity among words. He says that in the words we use, we follow our concepts; a difference in the *ratio* of our concepts is the cause of the diversity of words.[7] The problem with an argument such as that of Macedonius is that it fails see the proper *ratio* of things.

With this principle articulated, Aquinas now turns his attention to the question at hand. He says, "Now the Holy Spirit proceeds as love, but the Son as word."[8] He thereby signals the two key concepts: love and word. The question is, what are the *rationes* according to which these two concepts are different such that there is a proper diversity of words according to which these two instances of procession are to be properly distinguished.

Aquinas first articulates the defining *ratio* of word, and he does so in this

---

5. *LR* 13.3.resp., p. 174: "Responsio. Dicendum quod hanc quaestionem movet Macedonius qui ponebat Spiritum Sanctum esse creaturam. Cuius ratio ad hoc erat quia Spiritus Sanctus aut recipit naturam Patris aut non. Si recipit, ergo est genitus; sed non potest dici genitus, ergo non recipit; et sic est creatura."

6. Ibid.: "Sed haec quaestio magis est de significatione nominis quam de re, ut scilicet sit quaestio quare Spiritus Sanctus non dicatur genitus sicut Filius."

7. Ibid.: "Ad quod dicendum est quod in nominibus imponendis sequimur conceptiones nostras, et differentia quae sit secundum rationem ipsarum conceptionum est causa diversitatis nominum."

8. Ibid.: "Spiritus autem Sanctus procedit ut amor, Filius vero ut verbum."

way: "The Word, inasmuch as it is word, has the likeness of that from which it proceeds."[9] Note the language: the Word, inasmuch as it is word. The *ratio* here of word is that it has the likeness of that from which it proceeds.[10] For this reason, Aquinas continues, the procession of the divine Word has a likeness to that procession which is according to nature.[11] A procession according to nature is a procession in the created order in which something proceeds from another and is of the same nature. It is for this reason, Aquinas concludes, that in speaking of the procession of the Word, we use words which properly pertain to that procession which is according to nature. In other words, there is an analog in the natural order for the procession of the Word. At this point, Aquinas introduces a middle position in the line of analogies; he says, "Hence in the procession of word we use words which properly pertain to the procession which is according to nature, as we are said to conceive what we understand."[12] In the case of human intellection, there is a likeness between what we understand and the thing understood such that we say we conceive it. We use the language of natural generation, of procession according to nature. Thus there is a threefold progression in the analogy: natural procession, human intellection, and divine intellection. In each case, what proceeds is in the likeness of that from which it proceeds. Thus it is that the very *ratio* of "word" as likeness holds for both human and divine intellection and, precisely because of this *ratio* of likeness, this procession of word, both human and divine, is analogous to natural procession.

At this point, Aquinas makes a critical move in this long sentence I have been quoting: "Hence in the procession of word, we use words which properly pertain to the procession which is according to nature, as we are said to conceive what we understand, for which reason that which proceeds as word is said to proceed as begotten and as son, because it has the species of that from which it proceeds, as a son has the species of his father."[13] Here Aquinas's astute students would appreciate the analogical distinctions. Consider the procession of a son from a father—begetting—in the natural or-

9. Ibid.: "Spiritus autem Sanctus procedit ut amor, Filius vero ut verbum. Verbum autem in quantum verbum habet similitudinem eius a quo procedit et etiam immediate procedit."

10. St. Thomas adds "et etiam immediate procedit" which also distinguishes word from love, but he does not return to this in the article.

11. Ibid.: "Et ideo processio verbi habet similitudinem illius processionis quae est secundum naturam."

12. Ibid.: "Vnde in processione verbi utimur nominibus quae proprie competunt processioni quae est secundum naturam, sicut quod intelligimus dicimur concipere."

13. Ibid.: "Vnde in processione verbi utimur nominibus quae proprie competunt processioni quae est secundum naturam, sicut quod intelligimus dicimur concipere, propter quod illud quod procedit ut verbum dicitur procedere ut genitus et ut filius, quia habet speciem eius a quo procedit, sicut filius habet speciem patris."

der. The son is begotten—meaning, precisely, he has the same nature as the father. In the case of human intellection, there is likewise a likeness which proceeds from the action of the thing known upon the intellect, such that we can say we conceive an idea, as we are passively acted upon by the thing known. The concept is of the same species, but not strictly of the same nature. And then there is the case of God. In the case of God, what is known is himself, and thus he himself begets the Word. And because of the perfection of divine knowing, that Word is indeed of the same divine nature as the Father who has begotten him. Thus the divine procession of the Word is analogous to both human intellection and to natural procession by way of generation, taking something from each: Word and Son. But in both instances of the analogical ascent, Aquinas has maintained the defining *ratio* of having the likeness of that from which it proceeds. Each of the two created analogs of procession clarifies a central aspect of the divine procession of the Word. Aquinas says nothing here that he has not already said in the *Lectura romana* with regard to trinitarian doctrine; he is, rather, spelling out the precise *ratio* under which the terms are working in the analogy of the Word.

At last, Aquinas can now turn to the procession of the Holy Spirit. He says, "But in the procession of love, this is not the case, because love does not proceed as a likeness of that from which it proceeds, but rather more as a kind of impression of the lover on the beloved."[14] As Aquinas frequently says about love, it is an impetus, a movement of the lover toward the beloved. There is a procession here in that there is a movement, a movement toward the beloved, but it is a movement toward the beloved without the communication of likeness. Such communication of likeness is simply not the *ratio* of love.

This brings Aquinas to his conclusion: "And thus, although the Holy Spirit does receive nature as does the Son, nevertheless, the *ratio* of the procession does not entail that he be called Son or begotten."[15] The point is exquisitely articulated. Yes, the Holy Spirit does, of course, receive the nature of the Father and the Son; however, that communication of nature is not in the *ratio* of love, as it is in the *ratio* of word. Even though the Holy Spirit receives the nature of the Father and the Son, we still do not call him "begotten" because such is not entailed in love.

From this Aquinas comes to his final conclusion: "And thus we do not at-

14. Ibid.: "In processione vero amoris non est hoc, quia amor non procedit ut similitudo illius a quo procedit, sed potius ut impressio quaedam amantis in amatum."

15. Ibid.: "Et ideo licet accipiat naturam sicut Filius, tamen ratio processionis non importat ut dicitur filius sive genitus."

tribute to the Holy Spirit words of natural procession, such that he could be called begotten, but he is said to proceed as love and as gift."[16]

Part of the difficulty in all of this is the lack of proper terms for the procession of the Holy Spirit. The reply to the third objection turns on this. Aquinas again addresses the foundation of the analogies in the created order. In created things, a person proceeds only by way of nature, that is, begetting, and for this reason, all the words of procession are applied according to natural procession. Since in the procession of the Holy Spirit there is entailed no likeness of that from which it proceeds, it can take no name from natural procession. Because there is no word proper to the created order, the procession of the Holy Spirit lacks a proper name, and thus is expressed in the common name of "procession." There is no proper term for the procession of the Holy Spirit for the simple reason that there is no strict natural analog.[17]

In this article, Aquinas rehearses elements of his teaching on procession that he has already articulated here in the *Lectura romana*. What is the point? In part it is to answer an heretical argument. But something more is at work here. Macedonius makes an argument, and Aquinas's response is to show that the argument fails because it fails to get the philosophy right. It does not get the philosophy right because it does not get the interplay between reality, human concepts, and analogy right. Thus the concern with the signification of words, which is really a matter of understanding the *rationes* of things. In the end, the problem is an analogical failure. Macedonius's argument had failed to recognize the analogical shifts in the term "procession" from word to love. The tipoff was not simply that one ended up in an heretical position, although that is a pretty good tipoff. The tipoff was that the natural condition of things was not attended to with proper precision. The argument failed to see that our relation to an object known is different from our relation to an object loved. It moved too quickly to impose a univocal meaning of procession from nature. In fact, we are stuck with the generic term "procession" in the case of the Holy Spirit because we do not have sufficient terms to capture the analogical disjuncts in the case of the Holy Spirit. In the case of the Son, the complementarity of Son and Word is most fitting. But in the case of the Holy Spirit, we have a procession of love.

16. Ibid.: "Et ideo non attribuimus ei nomina naturalis processionis, ut scilicet possit dici genitus, sed dicitur procedere ut amor et ut donum."

17. *LR* 13.3.ad 3m, p. 174: "Ad tertium dicendum quod in rebus creatis nulla persona procedit nisi per modum naturae. Ideo omnia nomina processionis imponuntur secundum processionem naturalem. Vnde cum in processione Spiritus Sancti non importetur similitudo illius a quo procedit, non sortitur nomen processionis naturalis ut dicatur nativitas, quanquam proprio nomine careat, sed tamen communi nomine processionis exprimitur."

And thus there is the twofold problem. We have no proper term for the personal termination of the procession of love that is comparable to "Word" for the procession of intellection. And second, in the created order there is no procession of persons that is not a procession of nature. The more natural term—"begotten"—is precisely disanalogous in the case of the Holy Spirit.

I think this little article with its analogical clarification is intended by Aquinas as an example for his students of philosophical precision in theological reflection. Theological errors all too easily have their origins in philosophical errors. In this case, Aquinas shows his students that they must give serious attention to the natural analogs that they will be applying to the divine life. They must understand those analogs well, and in that understanding they will be able more faithfully to apply those analogs insightfully to the mysteries of God. It is a salutary thought for our own time. If we crowd the railings of the Titanic, we render our theological reflections at best opaque, at worst erroneous. Here too, as Professor McInerny would remind us, St. Thomas is a good teacher.

CHAPTER TWELVE

Christology of Disclosure in Robert Sokolowski

GUY MANSINI, OSB

This chapter seeks to honor the esteemed Ralph McInerny by exploring what Robert Sokolowski has to say about the role of philosophy in theology and theological education. He has addressed this issue many times, in many ways. I begin with some evidently sensible advice that he has given to seminary educators about philosophy. There follows a description of what he calls the "theology of disclosure." Third, I gather up some of the "disclosures" he has made in Christology. Last, I try to press things just a little further in one or two matters Christological.

A First Step

I will begin with an essay of 1987 titled "Acquiring the Philosophical Habit," in which Sokolowski delimits two reasons for including philosophy in a theological education.[1] One reason is that philosophy can provide an antidote to the skepticism of contemporary culture about such things as friendship and political life, human freedom and virtue, moral and religious truth.[2] We doubt the reality of such things, and are tempted to consign them

---

1. Robert Sokolowski, "Acquiring the Philosophical Habit," *Theology Today* 44 (1987): 319–28.
2. Ibid., 323.

to the realm of ideological fictions. Philosophy can help to restore such human things to us, human things that Christianity presupposes as grace does nature. This is, so to speak, a propaedeutic service of philosophy to theology. There is another and more properly theological reason for turning to philosophy within theology, however. This reason is that we come to appreciate supernatural things by contrast with philosophically appreciated natural things. For instance, we appreciate Christian faith for what it is more fully, more exactly, in contrast to human belief and trust. Or again, he says, we appreciate the sacraments more fully if we see them in contrast to human signs, memorials, and performatives. "The reason why philosophy is important in a theological education is that it articulates the human and worldly things that serve as the basis and the contrast for theological definition."[3] This reason, evidently, is related to the use of analogical language for things theological, and it hints at the manner in which theological things become manifest to us in the first place.

It only hints, however. In other words, with this second reason for including philosophy in a theological education, we approach but do not quite arrive at what Sokolowski elsewhere calls "the theology of disclosure." However, if we step from the things compared to the very comparing of the things, we do arrive. The contrast that it is possible to draw between natural and supernatural things presupposes that the supernatural things have already in some measure come to light. The theology of disclosure examines just this coming to light. So to speak, we can examine supernatural things within the light of their manifestation, part of which is given in the contrast with natural things, but this is not to turn our attention to this light just in itself. That is what the theology of disclosure does. "The theology of disclosure examines how the things of the faith must be presented; it attempts to state essential distinctions that must occur in the emergence of what Christians believe."[4] To return to the topic of analogy: when we see that analogy cannot be taken as a moment subsequent to Revelation, concerned merely with how we shall talk about what has already been seen and known as revealed, but as structural to Revelation, then we have entered the theology of disclosure.[5]

3. Ibid., 320. These two reasons for theology students and seminarians to study philosophy are revisited in Sokolowski's "Philosophy in the Seminary Curriculum," in *Christian Faith and Human Understanding: Studies on the Eucharist, Trinity, and the Human Person* (Washington, D.C.: The Catholic University of America Press, 2006), 299–310. For an extended treatment of the first reason, see his "Intellectual Formation in Catholic Seminaries," *Seminarium* 46 (2006): 827–46.

4. Sokolowski, *The God of Faith and Reason: Foundations of Christian Theology* (Washington, D.C.: The Catholic University of America Press, 1982), 97.

5. See Sokolowski's essay, "Christian Religious Discourse," in *Christian Faith and Human Understanding*, 51–65.

It is worth noting that the 1987 essay introduces a puzzle that it does not wholly resolve, at least explicitly. In his introduction, Sokolowski notes that theology and philosophy are alike in that both aspire to deal with the whole of things, and our place within that whole. There cannot, however, be "two comprehensive doctrines" of the one whole, the one reality. How does Sokolowski answer the implied question of the relation of philosophy to theology? In its aspiration to offer a comprehensive doctrine, furthermore, does not philosophy threaten theology? The last question is answered by adverting to the doctrines of creation and incarnation. It cannot be that the deployment of human reason in its maximum length and breadth—philosophy—should threaten the revelation of the God who created it, nor rightly be at odds with the Son of God who assumed it as the instrument of his saving work in assuming our nature. "When human nature is elevated into grace, therefore, reason does not need to be replaced or denied."[6] The special status of the doctrine of Creation, moreover, suggests at least a partial solution to the first question about wholes. Although Sokolowski observes that reason did not on its own discover the relation of the world to God as created to Creator, it proved able to grasp it once revelation taught us this relation.[7] In this way, philosophy has been enabled to tell some of the same story theology tells. The first article of the Creed, so to speak, provides common ground. And although it remains that the subsequent two articles are beyond the reach of reason, as is the Trinity of Persons itself as a whole and to which the three articles of the Creed correspond, this still goes some way toward ensuring the possibility not only of peaceful coexistence, but of mutual enrichment. This seems to mean, however, that philosophy tells a less comprehensive tale than theology, especially with regard to the destiny of man, and, even considering Creation, with regard to the ultimate relation of identity and distinction in the First Cause.

In this article, Sokolowski is content to let these fields remain fallow—the field of wholes and parts, the field of the kinds of distinction needed to handle Christian realities. They are rather cultivated in the theology of disclosure.

6. Sokolowski, "Philosophical Habit," 327.

7. Ibid., 328. Note that Sokolowski is arguing that it is revealed that God freely creates the universe. This can be affirmed, even if, with Dr. Long (see his essay above), one argues against claiming that the Unmoved Mover was immanent within the universe. As "Actus Purus" Aristotle's God could be transcendent, but would never be without the universe since God causes the universe eternally—the "sempiternitas mundi." Aquinas shows how the contingency of God's creating is known by revelation.

The Theology of Disclosure

The "theology of disclosure" names a determinate way in which philosophy can come to the handmaidenly service of theology. It enlists philosophy in its expressly Husserlian, phenomenological form.[8] Sokolowski has offered us two rather more extended presentations of the theology of disclosure, the first in *The God of Faith and Reason: The Foundations of Christian Theology* (1982) and the second in *Eucharistic Presence: A Study in the Theology of Disclosure* (1994).[9]

In *The God of Faith and Reason*, the theology of disclosure emerges as the needed reflection through which may be solved certain puzzles that arise in thinking of Christian things in contrast to natural things. The question of the relation of the philosophical whole to the theological whole is one such puzzle. *The God of Faith and Reason* gives a lengthy discussion of another such puzzle. When we realize that the theological virtues are absolutely necessary for us to attain the *de facto* end to which God has called us, the natural virtues as known by Plato and Aristotle can seem unreal, even "false" virtues. Is this seeming disparagement right and just?[10] These problems are resolved or rather dissolved according as we understand how it is that Christian things come to light in the first place, and to do so is to engage in the "theology of disclosure."

Sokolowski locates this theology in relation both to simple faith and to

8. Is phenomenology only one form or style of philosophy, or is it philosophy as such? It is philosophy, simply speaking. See Sokolowski, *Husserlian Meditations: How Words Present Things* (Evanston, Ill.: Northwestern University Press, 1974), 189–204, where the enquiry concerns "philosophy"; similarly, Sokolowski's *Presence and Absence: A Philosophical Investigation of Language and Being* (Bloomington, Ind.: Indiana University Press, 1978), chaps. 13 and 14. There is discussion in Sokolowski, *Introduction to Phenomenology* (Cambridge: Cambridge University Press, 2000), chap. 13. See also "The Science of Being as Being in Aristotle, Aquinas, and Wippel," in *The Science of Being as Being: Metaphysical Investigations*, ed. Gregory T. Doolan. Studies in Philosophy and the History of Philosophy 55 (Washington, D.C.: The Catholic University of America Press, 2012), which says of metaphysics: "First philosophy clarifies what we are as agents of truth. We are a special kind of entity because being is an issue for us, and because we are an issue for ourselves. The science of being as being is called in Latin the science of *ens qua ens*, but it is also the science of *mens qua mens* .... I would suggest that Aristotle's manoeuvre into first philosophy is similar to the transcendental reduction of Husserl" (15). There is also Sokolowski's "Husserl on First Philosophy," Husserl Memorial Lecture of 2009, in *Philosophy, Phenomenology, Sciences: Essays in Commemoration of Edmund Husserl*, ed. Carlo Ierna, Hanne Jacobs, and Flip Mattens. Phaenomenologica 200 (Dordrecht: Springer, 2009), where he develops the equivalence of the science of being as being with the science of mind as mind.

9. Sokolowski, *Eucharistic Presence: A Study in the Theology of Disclosure* (Washington, D.C.: The Catholic University of America Press, 1994).

10. Sokolowski, *God of Faith and Reason*, 78–84.

a more standard style of theology which he calls "the theology of Christian things."[11] Simple faith possesses things natural and supernatural in an uncomplicated unity in which both are lived but not thought about in relation to one another. With regard to the virtues, for instance, we are happily motivated to be just and temperate both "because that's what a good man does" and "because our Lord wants you to." Or with regard to the whole within which we believe and hope and love, we do not ask what we could know without faith, or what we could do without grace.

In the theology of Christian things, however, we are concerned precisely with what supernatural faith is in itself; we are concerned precisely with what infused temperance gives us that acquired temperance does not; and we explicitly raise questions about what revelation tells us that we could not otherwise know. These concerns in turn lead us to say such things as that natural virtue is not really and truly virtue or that philosophy must always lead us astray because it will ineluctably mistake partial things for integral things, provisional things for final things.

Enter the theology of disclosure. If we pay attention to how Christian things first appear to us, how they come to light, such puzzles disappear. Supernatural virtue does not appear except with the appearance of a supernatural end. If we distinguish ends, natural and supernatural, natural virtue is restored to its dignity, which, however, is not the same dignity as supernatural virtue. Or again, if we pay attention to the very way in which the God who is beyond the world manifests himself to us, and the very way in which that manifestation adjusts our discourse about the whole of things, and if further we notice the openness and tentativeness of pre-Christian philosophy before questions answered definitively by Revelation, we will not antecedently condemn philosophy to blindness and error.[12]

In *Eucharistic Presence*, the theology of disclosure is located by contrast not only to the theology of Christian things, the sort of theology we are to see in scholasticism, but by contrast to positive theology, where the task is to see what Scripture and Tradition teach us about Christ, the Trinity, the sacraments, and so on. In saying that the theology of disclosure attends to

---

11. Ibid., 88–93.

12. It will be recalled that St. Bonaventure seems perilously close to doing this in the *Collationes in Hexaemeron*. Sokolowski's concern is not idle. According to Mark Jordan, philosophy began to oppose theology when it pretended to the clarity and certainty with which revelation answers ultimate questions, a clarity and certainty the ancients did not claim. That is, the opposition was a temptation of philosophy only after it had been exposed to the fullness of the Christian revelation. See his "The Terms of Debate over 'Christian Philosophy,'" *Communio* 12 (1985): 293–311.

how Christian things come to light, we might suppose that it is something like the history of doctrine. This is not the case, however.

While historical theology examines facts, the theology of disclosure examines structures of disclosure; it describes the forms of manifestation proper to Christian things. It tries to describe how Christian things must display themselves, in keeping with what they are, and how they must distinguish themselves from things that resemble them and with which they may be confused.[13]

Positive theology is concerned with how in fact certain things appeared to certain people and how in fact they expressed them. The theology of disclosure is concerned with how Christian things must appear if they are to show up to anyone at anytime, and how they must be expressed if they are anywhere to be communicated. In comparison with *The God of Faith and Reason*, therefore, *Eucharistic Presence* supplies a more satisfying, because more comprehensive, differentiation of the theology of disclosure from other theological tasks. "Thus, the theology of disclosure differs from speculative theology because it examines the manifestation of Christian things and not, primarily, their nature, definition, and causes, and it differs from positive theology because it is concerned with essential structures of disclosure, which would hold in all times and places, and not with matters of historical fact."[14] We might say that while metaphysics is the instrument of speculative theology and history of positive theology, phenomenology is the instrument of the theology of disclosure.[15]

Sokolowski conceives the theology of disclosure as a bridge between positive theology and speculative theology. Rather than attending to the necessities of the nature of Christian things immediately after the positive theological task is complete, we first attend to the necessities of their coming to light at all, the necessities of their revelatory form. The *de facto* deliverances of positive theology are as it were informed with how anyone must come to see the thing in question, and the foundation and footings of speculative theology are thus strengthened. Some aspect of necessity is embedded in the concrete of history, in the sense that if something happens, it necessarily happens.

Like *The God of Faith and Reason*, *Eucharistic Presence* claims that the theology of disclosure addresses the peculiar problem modern philosophy

13. Sokolowski, *Eucharistic Presence*, 8.

14. Ibid. While the congenital temptation of speculative theology is rationalism and of positive or historical theology historicism, the congenital temptation of the theology of disclosure is psychologism; ibid., 7–8.

15. However, see above, n. 8, on the identity of philosophy, especially metaphysics, and phenomenology. Also, regarding the significance of Karol Wojtyła's metaphysically informed phenomenology see Introduction to this volume.

bequeaths us, that of the relation of *what* appears to the human mind to its *appearances*. What the modern mind has difficulty negotiating, the theology of disclosure easily negotiates, and a good thing, too, especially in those places where the Christian thing in question is evidently bound up with the working and reality of appearances and representations, as in the theology of the sacraments or the theology of icons. But *Eucharistic Presence* details more of the features and consequences of modernity, according to which the individual human being is isolated from the world, enclosed in the "cabinet" (Locke) of his self-consciousness, forgetful or unable to see any longer the forms of things, and so also tone deaf to the music of the ends of things and the excellences of things as determined by their forms.[16] Here, we rejoin "Acquiring the Philosophical Habit," and see that the theology of disclosure comprises both reasons there adduced for installing philosophy in a theological education: the theology of disclosure both addresses the reality of the human things of which modernity is suspicious, and the objectivity of human mind, and works to enable philosophically appreciated natural things to become the foil of Christian things.[17] We must reckon once again with the possibility in the modern world that properly philosophical work may be accomplished most easily under the shelter provided by faith and theology.[18]

Evidently, if Sokolowski is right, then together with metaphysics—without which we cannot be responsible receivers of the theological tradition and we would be unable really to understand and appreciate, much less develop, what is bequeathed to us—there should also be considerable attention paid to the kind of philosophical formation that informs the theology of disclosure. Furthermore, Sokolowski points out that such attention will by no means be foreign to the Church's mission in the broader society and culture. Precisely the things the modern world is most confused about will find needed clarification.[19]

Eucharistic Presence lists the great themes of the theology of disclosure. They are (1) presence and absence, especially that absence which is the transcendence of God; (2) wholes and parts, especially and architectonically the whole of the world as distinguished from the God who could be all there is in undiminished greatness and glory; (3) the role of distinctions in thinking, and especially and again, the Christian distinction of God and the world;

16. Sokolowski, *Eucharistic Presence*, 180.
. 17. In addition to the studies listed above in n. 3, see also Sokolowski's "Formal and Material Causality in Science," *American Catholic Philosophical Quarterly* 69 (1995): 57–67, which pays particular attention to the loss of form in modernity, as does his *Phenomenology of the Human Person* (Cambridge: Cambridge University Press, 2008), 112–16.
18. This is a theme of St. John Paul II's encyclical letter of 1998, *Fides et Ratio*.
19. Sokolowski, *Eucharistic Presence*, 186–90; and "Intellectual Formation," 836–43.

and (4) the reality and functioning of symbols. As the first three of these themes show us, it is the "Christian distinction" between God and the world that presides over the theology of disclosure. In *The God of Faith and Reason*, Sokolowski begins the Christian distinction as from a first principle. In *Eucharistic Presence*, he ascends to it from the *priora quoad nos* of the Eucharist. Whatever order is followed, it remains the strategic distinction, on the boundary between philosophy and theology, reason and Revelation.[20]

The Christology of Disclosure

I now want to gather up some of the things Sokolowski has provided for thinking about Christ and the manifestation of Christ.

Part of the theological importance of the Christian distinction is that it provides the framework within which the Christian mysteries can be asserted without incoherence. In *The God of Faith and Reason*, Sokolowski shows this in the first place in respect to the incarnation. Attention to the Christian distinction between God and the world helps us with the very conceivability of the incarnation. The Church teaches that God, the Son of God, became man. This is possible only if God is "not himself a competing part of the world," Sokolowski says.[21] What is he getting at? God is not a part of the world at all, and since even if the world did not exist he could be without any loss of greatness or glory, he is not even defined by not being the world. He does not need not to be the world in order to be himself. Parts of the world, by contrast, do need not to be one another in order to be themselves. In order to be what they are, pigs cannot have wings, but neither can pigeons have a low and powerful frame for routing the forest floor and still fly. Pigs and pigeons are "competing parts," which is to say, the weaving together of the same and the other constitutes their natures. A pig could not become a pigeon without ceasing to be a pig, and vice versa.

God, however, precisely because he is not defined by what he is not, can really and truly become man without ceasing to be himself, and without humanity suffering some alteration or truncation. "The reason the pagans could not conceive of anything like the incarnation is that their gods are part of the world, and the union of two natures in the world is bound to be, in some way, unnatural, because of the otherness that lets one thing be itself only by not being the other."[22]

---

20. The Christian distinction is cognitively prior to the knowledge of the Trinity.

21. Sokolowski, *God of Faith and Reason*, 36.

22. Ibid., 36. See also Sokolowski, *Eucharistic Presence*, 52–53. There are expressions of this insight already in patristic times. See Tertullian, *On the Flesh of Christ*, chap. 3, (6): "God is able

In this way, the Christian distinction allows us to think the incarnation; on the other hand, the incarnation requires us to think the distinction more deeply.

The Incarnation perfects the understanding of divine transcendence that was revealed in the Old Testament. In the Old Testament it would not have seemed possible for God to become incarnate in his own creation.... The New Testament not only adds belief in the Holy Trinity to the faith of the Old Testament; it also deepens the understanding of God's nature and transcendence, precisely by revealing that his becoming part of creation does not lessen the difference between him and the world. God is revealed to be so transcendent that he can enter into his creation without suffering limitation in his divinity.[23]

The Incarnation does not cancel our sense of the transcendence of God but rather highlights it by a sort of unsurpassable contrast between the God who is with us and the God who is our creator.

In order to clarify how the celebration of the Holy Eucharist makes present the action of Christ on Calvary, *Eucharistic Presence* first undertakes to study that action itself as accomplishing our salvation. Sokolowski explores how this action is at once both the action of Christ, the incarnate Son, and the action of the Blessed Trinity.[24] In doing so, he shows that only as incarnate can one Person obey another. Only with the incarnation does the Second Person have a will distinct from the one will of God by which he can align himself to the Father.[25] This last point is important to note, lest things true only in the economy of salvation, in virtue of the temporal missions of the Person, be imputed to the Persons themselves, in virtue of the eternal processions.[26]

Sokolowski has also taken up the issue of the manifestation of the Trinity, which is to say, the revelation of just who it is who takes flesh in Jesus

---

both to change into everything and yet to continue such as he is.... Otherwise, God will be on a level with things which, when they have changed, lose what they have been" (Norris translation, *The Christological Controversy* [Philadelphia: Fortress Press, 1980], 66), and St. Gregory of Nyssa, *An Address on Religious Instruction* ("The Great Catechism"), n. 24: "It does not startle us to hear it said that the whole creation, including the invisible world, exists by God's power, and is the realization of his will. But descent to man's lowly position is a supreme example of power—of a power which is not bounded by circumstances contrary to its nature" (trans. C. C. Richardson, in E. R. Hardy, *Christology of the Later Fathers* [Philadelphia: Westminster Press, 1954], 300–301). See also clarification in note 7 above.

23. Sokolowski, *Eucharistic Presence*, 53–54. See also *God of Faith and Reason*, 123 (Christ implies the Christian distinction), 127 (the incarnation modifies our sense of the divine transcendence).

24. Sokolowski, *Eucharistic Presence*, chap. 6; see especially 64–70 and 70–76.

25. Ibid., 75–76.

26. An introduction to this question can be found with Bruce Marshall, "The Unity of the Triune God," *The Thomist* 74 (2010): 1–32.

the Christ. "The Revelation of the Holy Trinity" brings forward the use of the first personal pronoun in order for a speaker to express himself as a rational agent, and indeed "as actually exercising his rationality at the moment he uses the word."[27] Sokolowski shows us that in order to reveal himself as who he is in distinction from his Father, Christ must deploy this distinctive use of I, differentiating himself from the Father in his very act of speaking, in order for the Persons of the Trinity to be revealed.[28] In order for the divine Persons to be talked about, one of them must first come to manifestation in his immediate personal authority and agency, but as distinct from the others.

By way of complement to "The Revelation of the Trinity," "God the Father: The Human Expression of the Holy Trinity," shows the necessity for the revelation of the Trinity to be accomplished not only in word but also in deed.

Christ revealed the Holy Trinity by more than just the words he used.... His Resurrection from the dead is not an outcome of the latent energy of the world. It manifests a source and resource beyond that, and it reveals this source more fully than creation does.... It brings being and life, not just out of nothing, but out of the deeper nihilism of sin and death, and thus saves us from both desperation and ironic Cynicism.[29]

The Resurrection thus "provides a glimpse of the Holy Trinity," beyond what any word of any prophet could do, and beyond what any action of any created being could show.[30]

The Word Who Becomes Flesh

In what follows I want to extend the theology of disclosure a little further into Christology, exploring the significance of the fact that it was the Second Person of the Trinity, the Word, who became flesh, and not the Father and not the Spirit. Second, I want to pick up on something Richard Bauckham has attended to recently, the necessity of eyewitness testimony to Christ.

Sokolowski has said a lot over the course of his career about words, what they do, how they do it in contrast to other signs and representations, and—most difficult to say—what they are, or maybe even better (as to difficulty) where they are. This invites us to think about the Word of St. John's Gospel, the Word who is made flesh.

27. Sokolowski, "The Revelation of the Holy Trinity," in *Christian Faith and Human Understanding*, 136.

28. Ibid., 134–35.

29. Sokolowski, "God the Father: The Human Expression of the Holy Trinity," *The Thomist* 74 (2010): 33–56, at 47.

30. Ibid., 47–48.

1. Human words make the absent things spoken of present to us. Of course, we can speak of things that are before us. But words always negotiate absence. If I speak of the side I can see of the object between us, I am speaking of what is missing from your visual field. In their phonemic constitution, words depend on opposed pairs of phonemes that cannot be both operative at the same point.[31] Further, words are realized only across some time, according as one word of a sentence is finished as heard (or seen) and another anticipated, and even according as one syllable is over and another expected. Furthermore, words can come to be detached from their original speaker. They can be quoted later by another, recorded and replayed elsewhere, written and re-read after the speaker is dead. Words are always in some way and often in many ways at the same time involved in the play of presence and absence.

The Word of God is not like that. The Word does not express something absent, but the infinite intelligibility of the Godhead that the Word is. It is not different from what it expresses. And it is not temporally realized, nor is it constituted across binary phonemic possibilities. It is indeed different from the speaker, the Father. But it is not detachable from its speaker the way human words are. Wherever the Word is present, in the way it is present, so is the Father (cf. Jn. 14:9). The unity of the divine essence forestalls such an absence of the Father, since Father and Son not only possess specifically the same nature, but are the same numerically one nature. The circumincession of the Persons of the Trinity also forestalls the absence of Spoken from Speaker in the Trinity, or perhaps, is just a way of indicating it.

Compared with human words, the divine Word is not involved in absence, and, within the Trinity, cannot be.[32] To know this is to know that presentability and re-presentation are good in themselves and not just as overcoming absence. It is only as incarnate that the Word of God becomes involved with absence.

2. Human words make the intelligibility of what they name present. They do more than signal, bringing something to mind, as does a call or a whistle. When we name things, we bring them forward as subjects of predication, as the to-be-articulated by accidental and if necessary essential predicates. This is to bring forward their intelligibility, for things are understood according as they are subject to syntax.[33] But knowing the name of God,

---

31. Sokolowski, *Presence and Absence*, chap. 7.

32. In a way transcendent to the world, the same and the other are verified in the mystery of the Triune God. But presence and absence are not verified there, nor are motion and rest, which last seems to require potency.

33. See especially Sokolowski, *Phenomenology of the Human Person*, 166–67, on naming as making the intelligibility of a thing present.

or the names of the divine persons, does not make the divine intelligibility present. We have a name, indeed, a God-given name for God in Exodus (3:14). Should we say that God exists in us cognitively, and that we understand what he is, Sokolowski asks? By no means. And Sokolowski continues: "The name of God is not like other names. It is not the word for one kind of being among others. It is the name for the source of things."[34] It is the name for the we-know-not-what whence comes the world whose parts we can name so as to present their intelligibility. Of course, this is not to say we cannot speak of God and say many meaningful things about him, not only reporting what he does, but truly characterizing him. The "accidents" of God's free actions in history enable us to fix such "properties" of God as loving-kindness, faithfulness, truthfulness, patience, and "jealousy."[35]

Do things change with the incarnation? Does the assumed humanity of Christ tell us more about the nature of God than the Old Testament does? According to what was said above, it rather deepens our sense of the transcendence of God. In that way, paradoxically, the unsurpassable nearness of the Son of God in our flesh accentuates the absence of God.

What is rendered by the incarnation is not the intelligibility of the nature, but only the identity of the person.[36] The distinction of persons, distinct according to opposed relations of origin, is made present by the names "Father" and "Son." And the incarnation itself, of course, is the incarnation of the Person of the Word, not the divine nature. We say that the union is hypostatic—in and according to the hypostasis. That is, the Word is incarnate only in his distinction from Father and Spirit—for that is what constitutes him—not in and according to the one divine nature. We might almost say that the incarnation is the incarnation of a distinction, except that that would seem to imply that both Father and Son are incarnate. What is certain, however, is that it is the incarnation of an already constituted personal identity, and presupposes a distinction already made. Created human persons distinguish themselves according to their moral action. That is to say, by their decisions and action, they constitute the personal identity that is the answer to the question, "Who are you?"[37] But Christ reveals an eternal

---

34. Sokolowski, "God's Word and Human Speech," *Nova et Vetera* 11 (2013): 189–212, adds that of God's name it can be said that it is "the most proper of all names" (203).

35. On the manifestation of properties via accidents, see Sokolowski, *Phenomenology of the Human Person*, 117–20.

36. The glorified humanity of Christ doubtless renders something more of the divine nature to those who beheld it.

37. Sokolowski addresses the constitution and manifestation of personal identity in many places. See *God of Faith and Reason*, 66–67, and his *Moral Action: A Phenomenological Study* (Bloomington, Ind.: Indiana University Press, 1985), 156–62.

distinction, an eternal personal identity: he is, as Sokolowski points out, not chosen but rather sent.[38]

3. A Christology of disclosure can also shed light on the question of the *convenientia* of the incarnation of the Word, and not the Father or the Holy Spirit. Saint Thomas Aquinas identifies three reasons for the suitability of the incarnation of the Son, the first of which is evocative of the theme of manifestation.[39] The Word is the eternal exemplar of all creatures, and it is fitting that like be joined to like. Moreover, there is a particular likeness between the Wisdom of God and the wisdom by which human nature is perfected.[40] There are further suitabilities in the order of disclosure, however, for the incarnation of the Son. In the first place, we should recall Sokolowski's demonstration that God could not reveal the Trinity of Persons to us, as long as we are in this life, without the medium of human words. There must be an incarnate Person who says "I" both to us and to another divine Person. But also, there must be many human words preparing for the incarnation, establishing the "grammar" of the articulation and identification of a divine Person in human form, and there must be words, human words, reporting the incarnation and repeating the words of the incarnate one. That is, there must be the words of the Old Testament, and the subsequent words of the New Testament.[41] It is therefore fitting, and just as a matter of disclosure, that it was the Word who took flesh of Mary the Virgin. The culmination of all the prior words, and the referent of all the subsequent ones, is the fulfillment achieved in the incarnation of the Word.

Moreover, the suitability of the Word as the one to be incarnate comes to light if we think of one of the other New Testament ways for identifying the Second Person of the Trinity, and that is the language of "image," according to which, as the Letter to the Colossians says, "he is the image of the invisible God" (1:15). And the Letter to the Hebrews has it that "he reflects the glory of God and bears the very stamp of his nature" (1:3). That the Second Person of the Trinity is also a reflection, as in a mirror, or bears an impression, as in a material, engages the eye just as "word" engages the ear. Both ways of characterizing the Second Person should be considered together, and allowed to illumine one another.

Sokolowski has in fact already done this is in the natural order. When he wishes to focus for us what words are and what they do, the required strat-

38. Sokolowski, *Eucharistic Presence*, 124–25.

39. Aquinas, *Summa theologiae* III, q. 3, a. 8.

40. The other two reasons are that, as we are predestined to be sons, it is fitting that the Son be incarnate, and that as we sinned in Adam by eating from the tree of knowledge, it was fitting that the "Word of true knowledge" come to our aid.

41. Sokolowski, *Eucharistic Presence*, 144–56.

egy is to play off words against pictures.[42] For one thing, when we consider pictures, he says, we are less likely to locate them in our mind. The picture of Eisenhower is on the wall. The picture that makes Eisenhower present is on the wall, over there, in front of and not behind my eyes. So also words are on the page, or in the auditory space. The distinction of pictures relative to the pictured, and the objectivity of pictures, their being over against me, help me to verify the same things as to words. Not all things are the same, of course. Pictures, Sokolowski says, are a sort of embodiment of the thing pictured. Eisenhower is presented in his various intelligibilities in the picture, but the picture is also a kind of instance of them.[43] Words, on the other hand, do not similarly embody what they speak of. They are leaner than pictures. Just so, we think they are too thin to be outside us, on the page, in the air, and this is a mistake. But also, in their leanness they do nothing but call to mind the sheer intelligibility of what they name.

If this is so, then in calling the Second Person "Word," there is indicated the sheer and perfect presencing of the intelligibility of God. And as "Image," there is indicated a sort of embodying, which is already to look toward a further embodying in the incarnation.[44] In any event, in being both Word and Image, the Second Person of the Trinity includes seemingly exclusive ways of representation, the ways of speaking and picturing that we are acquainted with. From our perspective, the Second Person becomes something like "Representability" as such. And as such, he is the most suitable Person to be presented in the flesh of Christ.

Witnesses of the Word Made Flesh

The manifestation of a personal identity must be by way of both word and action: word, for the person is an agent of truth; action, for the person is an agent of moral truth, the truth installed in action.[45] Moreover, the

42. Sokolowski, *Phenomenology of the Human Person*, 161–67; and "God's Word and Human Speech."

43. Ibid., 167.

44. Speaking of things in the natural order, Sokolowski says, that these ways of presencing work together: "we cannot speak philosophically about words and what they do except in conjunction with picturing, imagining, and perceiving, because words work only in conjunction with these other ways of intending" (ibid).

45. Is it not possible that we may have only someone's words, someone's mind declaring only what he thinks is so, with no record of his own moral action? Still, as soon as we have read what he thinks is so about the human good, and about what is to be done, then we have the form of prudence, proximate to moral action itself. And the other way round, it is possible that we be the witnesses of the moral action of a silent agent. Even so, the action itself, if taken in a large enough context, will make plain its prudential soul, how the agent sizes up—and would declare—the world in which he acts.

words must be part of a conversation, and the actions must have other persons as their target.[46] Thus, in the Old Testament, the Trinitarian persons as such and in their distinction from one another cannot come to manifestation.[47] There must be an incarnation where the Son can say "I" to his Father and to us, and where, in distinction from Father and Spirit, he can act morally and be seen to act on and receive the action of other persons.

Now actions, according to the perfection of the agent, find reverberations in the moral universe, in the thought and actions of other moral agents. Large actions have large consequences and more and louder echoes in the other agents affected by them and witnessing them, and in that way, the actions, for all that they are over and done, do not really pass away.[48] On the other hand, if there are no reverberations of an action, then there has been no action; nothing has been done. The culminating action of Christ on Calvary remains in an especially vibrant and full way in the sacraments and especially in the Eucharist. The sacraments are as it were the expanding circle of the effects of the stone once dropped into the pond. But the Eucharist is the very action of Christ's sacrifice made present and so as to include us in this action. Sokolowski addresses this in *Eucharistic Presence*.

There is an analogous consideration to be made regarding words. According as they are real and concern more of reality, they cast a shadow. They are quoted, answered, recapitulated, commented on. And unless this happens, nothing has been said. So, just as the Eucharist is necessary for the completion of the action of Christ in its universality and in the completeness with which it refashions our relation to God and to men, so the New Testament is necessary for the continuing presencing of the mind of Christ. Just as the Eucharist is necessary for the completion of the action of Christ, so also the Scriptures are necessary for the continuing presence of Christ. As already noted, the words of the Old Testament, the law and the prophets and the wisdom books, are necessary for him to have the categories by which to express his identity and action; we must hear his appropriation of these categories; we must hear his appropriation recapitulated in the apostolic books. The necessity of a written record just as such for the preservation of the gospel is addressed in *Eucharistic Presence*.[49]

In considering the necessity with which his words are to be quoted and recapitulated and his action reported in speech and in writing, however, we

---

46. Sokolowski, *God of Faith and Reason*, 120, for the necessity of seeing how people react to Christ's speech and deeds in order for us to understand them.

47. This is an implication of Sokolowski, "The Revelation of the Holy Trinity."

48. Sokolowski, *Moral Action*, 162.

49. Sokolowski, *Eucharistic Presence*, chap. 11, "Disclosure in the Scriptures." See also his "God the Father: The Human Expression of the Holy Trinity," 51.

discern a special necessity for eyewitness testimony, as it were, at the origin of tradition, and giving itself to us just as such.

Here, I turn to the work of Richard Bauckham. In his *Jesus and the Eyewitnesses*, he proposes by way of both historical and theological argument that the gospels mediate testimony to Jesus from those who were "participant eyewitnesses" to the events.[50] They saw and heard Jesus; also, they were involved, morally and religiously, with him. Whether this is so or not is a matter of historical fact. Additionally, however, Bauckham argues that if we Christians, many a year after the events, are to believe the message of the gospels, that Jesus is the Son of God, the Word made flesh, who died and rose for our salvation, then that message, the gospel news, must be credibly the report of participant eyewitnesses.[51] The credibility of the gospel message is bound up with this logically prior credibility.

This is so because the story of Jesus is "uniquely unique," as Bauckham explains it, borrowing this category from Paul Ricoeur. There are some historical narratives for the reception of whose truth we do not require either that the reporters be eyewitnesses or, if they were, that they be participant eyewitnesses to the events. For reports of what happened in the past, our background knowledge of what usually happens functions in such a way that we do not have to be assured either of the reporter's first-hand credentials as to place and time (we might simply trust his inferences) or his personal involvement in the events (rather, sometimes we prefer "neutrality"). For the uniquely unique, however, we do. The destruction of the Jews of Germany and Eastern Europe counts as an example of the uniquely unique. We cannot credit such barbarity, of such enormous scale, without the testimony of those who were subject to it.

The story of Jesus is likewise uniquely unique in that it cannot be told "without reference to God."[52] For this story, to credit that a human being made such claims as Jesus, did such things as he is said to have done, suffered such things as he is described as suffering, and was raised from the dead, we require participant eyewitness testimony. This is to say that we require Persons who use the declaratory "I," as Sokolowski understands that. As has been noted, Christ, in order to reveal himself as Son, has to say "I" in this required sense. Furthermore, those in whose presence he addresses the Father, and those to whom he speaks, saying "But I say," those whom he heals, and those to whom he shows himself after his resurrection must

---

50. Richard Bauckham, *Jesus and the Eyewitnesses: The Gospels as Eyewitness Testimony* (Grand Rapids, Mich.: Wm. B. Eerdmanns, 2006).

51. Ibid., 491–92, 499–502.

52. Ibid., 507.

also say in their own persons "I attest," "I saw," "I heard," "I touched." The completion of revelation calls for a most vivid realization of the "I" in its declarative function on the part of the original hearers of revelation. Revelation requires them to become more personal, more actualized agents of truth. For the truth in question is a more than worldly truth. It is also a divine truth. Only on the basis of participant testimony can we who hear the witnesses say, as we ought, "I believe," in our own Christian and more than natural actualization of the declarative I.

I say that our own "I believe" is a more than natural actualization of the declarative I. The act of faith, which responds purely to the authority of the revealing God, cannot respond unless it is elevated by faith. The "I" of the one who asserts the creed is a more empowered "I," since it shares in the very knowledge of things that God has, which surpass reason, and do so on the sole ground that God reveals them.[53] The mediation of this revelation, I am saying, and what Bauckham shows, must be by human agents whose "I" of attestation is similarly potentiated.

Since the story of Jesus cannot be told without reference to God, God as present and acting, those who attest to it must have faith in it. They must be involved in the events, involved in Jesus of Nazareth, in just this way. Now, this is a requirement of revelation itself, since part of the event of revelation is its acceptance, as Bauckham notes.[54]

Thus, the gospels are credible only if they are reports of eyewitness, as indeed the third and fourth gospels expressly claim, and only if they are written from faith, for faith. Only if they come to us in this way can we have any hope to know the story of Jesus.

Christ as a Presentational Form

So far, we have been engaged with issues in coming to identify Christ, issues in how he discloses himself to us, in the representational forms involved in this disclosure. Thus, the Christian distinction, the declaratory "I" of the incarnate Christ, the written word of Scripture, are all involved in our coming to identify Jesus of Nazareth as the incarnate Word of God. But also, Christ in turn functions as a representational form himself. That is, it is the task of a Christology of disclosure not only to identify the presentational forms needed to identify him, but also to recognize him as himself establishing a presentational form. Analogously, the Christian distinction

---

53. Sokolowski compares natural and supernatural faith in "Philosophy and the Christian Act of Faith," in *Christian Faith and Human Understanding*, 25–37.

54. Bauckham, *Jesus and the Eyewitnesses*, 508, who is relying on Francis Watson.

not only lets Christians behold the divine in a new way, absolutely incommensurable with pagan divinity but also introduces a new presentational dimension for other things, all other things, as well. "The being of the Christian God brings with it a new presentational mode. The world and everything in it are now understood as capable of being seen from a new point of view, that of the transcendent Creator.... The world and the things in it are now seen as being known and chosen to be by the Creator."[55]

Once we have beheld the action of the incarnate Son as giving himself over to suffering and death for our redemption, a new dimension of human beings is similarly disclosed. I must understand every human being I see not only as chosen by the eternal and infinite God, and so existing with more reality than can be appreciated in any accidental universe, but I must understand every human being I see as one for whom God, the Son of God, died. In this way a Christology of disclosure verifies the dictum of *Gaudium et Spes,* according to which it is only in the light of Christ that man is fully revealed to himself (n. 22). It is the vision of Christ himself, who tells us in Matthew 25, where he limns the last judgment over which he will preside, that he is to be recognized in every man, and the least most of all. It is the point taken also by St. Paul, who says that since "one has died for all, therefore all have died," and so "we regard no one from a human point of view" (2 Cor. 5:14, 16).

A Christology of disclosure is especially suited to capture the revelational excellence of Christ. He is the summit of Revelation, not only in the sense that he reprises and fulfills the Old Testament, and not only in the sense that he reveals the Trinity, and not only in the sense that the incarnation deepens the sense of the divine transcendence, but also in the very important sense, especially important today, that he lights human beings in the rays of an unsurpassable dignity.

---

55. Sokolowski, *Eucharistic Presence,* 204.

CHAPTER THIRTEEN

Ego sapientia

The Mariology of Laval Thomism

ROMANUS CESSARIO, OP

Introduction

This chapter aims to illuminate the intercession of the Blessed Virgin Mary. It views what the Church holds about her maternal mediation as an application of Aristotelian efficient instrumental causality within the order of grace. Specifically, the chapter evokes the notion of "physical causality" that the grand Thomist tradition employs when speaking about the sacraments. While the crisis over instrumental causality reaches beyond the theology of the sacraments, one nonetheless recognizes it rather acutely there. This crisis stems from several sources, such as developments in both natural philosophy and theological method. It is wondrous to observe that several approaches to Thomism have maintained the place that philosophical physics holds in Aquinas's account of metaphysics and theology. Even during the peak of the crisis, that is, during the mid-twentieth century, outstanding Thomists who developed these approaches were able not only to recognize the nature of the problem but also to begin to formulate a properly theological response. They enacted what the Church has long counseled her savants: To philosophize in Mary.

Reverends Ryan Connors, Christopher Seiler, Reginald Lynch, OP, and Cajetan Cuddy, OP, kindly assisted me with this chapter.

To break open the discussion, the chapter starts with a citation from a theological text from the Christian tradition:

The efficacy of the sacraments is due solely to the blessing of Christ and the working of his Spirit. The Spirit, it is to be ever remembered, is a personal agent who works when and how He will. God has promised that his Spirit shall attend his Word; and He thus renders it an effectual means for the sanctification of his people. So He has promised, through the attending operation of his Spirit, to render the sacraments effectual to the same end.[1]

To knowledgeable Catholics of our period, these words may sound like an excerpt from a late-nineteenth-century manual of Romantic dogmatic theology.[2] For those less well-instructed Catholics—say, from our universities and schools—the language may strike their ears as foreign, effectual means. "What's that about?" Again, not a few average Catholics might just nod their heads in agreement: "Sounds right to me! Christ and the Holy Spirit." The above text, I regret to inform you however, comes from the pen of Charles Hodge (1797–1878), a longtime Calvinist professor of theology and Bible at Princeton, who wrote explicitly against Catholic teaching on the sacraments. How, one may puzzle, do we find ourselves in such a situation?

The chapter proceeds in three movements: first, it observes the affinities between River Forest Thomism and a certain champion of Leonine Revival Thomism who directed the graduate studies of the young Ralph McInerny, Charles De Koninck (1906–65) of Laval. If some students merit being called pious, McInerny surely ranks among them.[3] At the end of his illustrious career, he returned to his beginnings, and so gave proof to the poet's insight that "In my beginning is my end."[4] The last works published by Professor McInerny include two volumes of *The Writings of Charles De Koninck*.[5] McInerny translated these writings from the French originals.[6] In the second

1. Charles Hodge, *Systematic Theology*, vol. 3 (Grand Rapids, Mich.: Wm. B. Eerdmans, 1940), 500.

2. Perhaps significantly, a two-volume abridgement of Matthias Joseph Scheeben's "Dogmatik" refers readers to other authors for the celebrated question of whether the sacraments operate with a moral or physical causality. See *A Manual of Catholic Theology*, vol. 1, ed. Joseph Wilhelm and Thomas B. Scannell (London: Kegan Paul, Trench, Trübner & Co., 1909), 363–64. At the same time, in the author's *Mysterien des Christentums* (Freiburg, 1865–97) one finds a discussion of these two views of sacramental causality. See his *The Mysteries of Christianity*, trans. Cyril Vollert, SJ (St. Louis, Mo.: B. Herder Book, 1946), 569–72. For his part, however, Scheeben would prefer the expression "hyperphysical" instead of physical causality (*loc. cit.*, 571).

3. For example, see his "Charles De Koninck: A Philosopher of Order," *The New Scholasticism* 39 (1965): 491–516.

4. T. S. Eliot, "East Coker," no. 2 of "Four Quartets," I.

5. *The Writings of Charles De Koninck*, ed. and trans. Ralph McInerny, 2 vols. (Notre Dame, Ind.: University of Notre Dame Press, 2008, 2009).

6. In the preface to his translation, McInerny explains his project: "It would be disingenu-

of these volumes we find an early piece that expresses the Flemish philosopher's contemplative Mariology, *Ego Sapientia*.

Second, the chapter considers Mary and the natural sciences. That Charles De Koninck would have composed a volume of Marian theology (with two others to follow) may come as a surprise to some persons. De Koninck is best known as a philosopher, one who took seriously the place of natural philosophy in both his exposition of Saint Thomas Aquinas and the philosophical dialogues that he undertook with those scholars of his day who engaged in empirical science.[7] Why then did De Koninck, who spent his professorial life at Laval University in Quebec, compose a meditation based on classical allegorical interpretations of the sapiential books of the Old Testament? What hath Mary to do with cosmology? A clever response would suggest that De Koninck, by composing *Ego Sapientia*, wanted to show how the Blessed Virgin Mary steadies the cosmos of Sir Arthur Stanley Eddington (1882–1944). He of course was the English author and scientist of the early twentieth century, who—to borrow an expression from Fr. Matthew Lamb—"popularized" the findings of Einstein.[8] However, more can—and in this moment, ought to—be said about the relationship between Mary and both the natural sciences and the philosophy of nature.

Lastly, after our philosophical and devotional excursuses, we move to a properly theological question crucial for Catholic theology today: the practically total eclipse of the notion of sacramental efficacy, especially as theologians up to the 1960s explained this Catholic teaching by reference to the classical philosophical categories of principal and instrumental causality.[9] I

---

ous of me to suggest that the writings of Charles De Koninck are for me simply an important trove of materials in the Thomistic Revival. A year or two ago, for quite accidental reasons, I began to reread Charles De Koninck. I was overwhelmed. One night, having finished an essay of his on the Eucharist, I sat back and said aloud, 'Thank God that I studied under this man.' Soon I began to see the desirability of bringing out the collected works of Charles De Koninck. Thomas De Koninck was enthusiastic, but pointed out that a French edition of his father's works was in the planning. No matter, I had in mind an English edition. And so it began" (*Writings*, vol. 1, p. viii).

7. For further information, see De Koninck's "Are the Experimental Sciences Distinct from the Philosophy of Nature?" (*Writings*, vol. 1, pp. 443–56); "Three Sources of Philosophy," his Medalist's Address in History and Philosophy of Science, in *Proceedings of the Thirty-Eighth Annual Meeting of the American Catholic Philosophical Association 1964* (Washington, D.C.: The Catholic University of America Press, 1964), 13–22; and his "The Unity and Diversity of Natural Science," in *The Philosophy of Physics*, ed. Vincent E. Smith, St. John's University Studies, Philosophical Series, 2 (New York: St. John's University Press, 1961), 5–24.

8. For more on De Koninck's views on Eddington, see the author's "The Philosophy of Sir Arthur Eddington" in *Writings*, vol. 1, 99–234.

9. There are several signs that this long eclipse is coming to an end. Philosophers have taken up the topic. For example, Steven A. Long, "The Efficacy of God's Sacramental Presence," *Nova et Vetera* (English ed.) 7 (2009): 869–76. Theologians too have; for example, Bernhard

refer especially to what came to be identified among the better Thomists of the modern period as "physical causality." That is, the sacraments act after the manner of physical causes.[10] My purpose, as they say, remains heuristic. It falls now to a new generation of Catholic theologians to put Humpty Dumpty together again. Humpty Dumpty stands for the classical teaching on sacramental causality, which must include the account of double agency that Aquinas borrowed from Aristotle. Double agency recognizes both principal and instrumental causes in the production of a given effect.

What follows then should be placed under the category of clues. And let me forewarn you, it is not elementary, Watson.[11] The big challenge for future Catholic scholars stems from problems that are long in the making. The theological and pastoral controversies that the Church faces and will face in the first decades of the twenty-first century arise as the result of theological currents whose proximate origins may be traced to certain movements, especially in Europe, and after the Second Vatican Council, also in the United States, that have been ongoing since roughly after World War I (1914–18).[12]

Laval Thomism and the River Forest School

In an informative essay published in the *festschrift* for his fellow Dominican and Thomist, James A. Weisheipl, Father Benedict M. Ashley, OP, provides a goldmine article that introduces his reader to the specific methodological outlooks of the River Forest School. Why River Forest Thomism? Starting in 1939, the philosophy *studium* of the Dominican Province headquartered in Chicago was located in a suburb of that city called River Forest. The leader of the *studium* school was a certain Dominican priest, William Humbert Kane (1901–70), known affectionately as "Humph Kane."[13] Of the eight theses Ashley stipulates as those that characterized the kind of

Blankenhorn, OP, "The Instrumental Causality of the Sacraments: Thomas Aquinas and Louis-Marie Chauvet," *Nova et Vetera* (English ed.) 4 (2006): 255–94, and my "The Sacraments of the Church," in *Vatican II: Renewal Within Tradition*, ed. Matthew L. Lamb and Matthew Levering (Oxford: Oxford University Press, 2008), 129–46.

10. For the best defense of Aquinas's views on the question of "physical causality," see Cardinal Cajetan's commentary on the *Summa theologiae*, III, q. 62.

11. From dialogue between Watson and Holmes in "The Crooked Man," in *The Complete Sherlock Holmes* (New York: Doubleday), 412.

12. On this theme, see the fascinating account of Roberto De Mattei, *Il Concilio Vaticano II. Una storia mai scritta* (Turin: Lindau, 2010).

13. For further information, see William H. Kane, OP, *Approach to Philosophy: Elements of Thomism* (Washington, D.C.: The Thomist Press, 1962). Although it is a compilation of several articles Fr. Kane wrote for *The Thomist*, it is some of the clearest exposition of the River Forest position. See also *The Dignity of Science: Studies in the Philosophy of Science Presented to William Humbert Kane, O.P.*, ed. J. A. Weisheipl (Washington D.C.: The Thomist Press, 1961).

work done at River Forest, the final one seems especially pertinent to our present considerations. Ashley formulates his thesis in this way: the "task of revising modern science on the basis of its original foundations cannot be evaded by a flight to metaphysics or theology."[14] Gifted young Dominicans, who approached the history of science without the usual prejudices, took up the task of showing demonstrably that this eighth thesis, unlikely though it may have sounded to many of their contemporaries, contained a salutary warning for those who wished to do philosophy with an eye toward working in Catholic theology.

The River Forest Thomism research on the proper way to read Aquinas on Aristotle went on especially at the Albertus Magnus Lyceum, a think tank whose scholars sought, in a word, to reverse the Enlightenment position that modern science should critique rather than illuminate Catholic theology. The Dominican *studium* in River Forest also attracted university students who were being inspired by the well-known renewal of Aristotelian (and Thomist) studies that got underway during the late 1930s at the University of Chicago. Robert Maynard Hutchins (1899–1977) and Mortimer Adler (1902–2001) led this *ressourcement*. Certain of these young intellectuals came into full communion with the Catholic Church, and, significantly, they later exhibited great devotion to the Blessed Virgin Mary.[15]

The Albertus Magnus Lyceum enjoys a special place in the history of Catholic theology. While the Church claims no philosophy as her own, such as that one could speak of *una filosofia* della *Chiesa*, there are philosophies that find themselves very much at home within the Church, *una filosofia* nella *Chiesa*. River Forest Thomism ranks among them. To appreciate the singularity of this enterprise, one should recall that during its somewhat tumultuous thirty-year lifespan, most Catholic thinkers who were neither Marxists nor materialist pragmatists remained content to work within the confines of a metaphysics separated from the natural sciences and, of course, of a theology that increasingly took its bearings from historical studies—the Fathers, and so forth—scriptural exegesis, liturgical studies, and even from the ecumenical movement. These Catholics theologians of the post-war period may have inquired rhetorically, "Why bother with the natural sciences when you have such rich theological resources at hand?"

14. Benedict M. Ashley, OP, "The River Forest School and the Philosophy of Nature Today," in *Philosophy and the God of Abraham. Essays in Memory of James A. Weisheipl, O.P.*, ed. James R. Long (Toronto: Pontifical Institute of Mediaeval Studies, 1991), 12.

15. Among these we find the Jewish psychoanalyst turned Trappist monk, the late Father M. Raphael Simon, OCSO (1909–2006), and the distinguished convert and medical doctor, Herbert Ratner (1907–97), an early supporter of the *La Leche League*, who gave a philosophical clarity to those who wished to stress the importance of breastfeeding for children.

The River Forest School enjoyed much in common with the thought of Charles De Koninck.[16] So much, in fact, that for a long time I thought of myself as a latter-day Laval Thomist, thanks to the instruction that I had received from my professor of cosmology and the philosophy of science, William A. Wallace, OP. This Lyceum ally published his voluminous research in the 1970s and the 1980s. The most celebrated of Wallace's work remains *Galileo and His Sources*.[17] While affinities exist between the approaches of De Koninck and the Chicago-based Lyceum, the immediate intellectual lineage of River Forest Thomism can be traced back to another source. William "Humph" Kane had studied in Rome, at the Angelicum, where he learned from Fr. Aniceto Fernández Alonso (1895–1981)—later Master of the Dominican Order (1962–74)—the central place that cosmology or natural philosophy holds in the exposition of Thomist thought.[18] Fernández Alonso had received his instruction in Spain, and so was a direct inheritor of the methods of the Spanish Thomists of the sixteenth and seventeenth centuries, especially Domingo de Soto (1494–1560).[19] They upheld and preserved an insight set down by St. Albert the Great in his *Sentence* commentary, namely, that those thinkers who neglect what is sensible and mobile in nature deceive themselves and others.[20]

Why Charles De Koninck Wrote *Ego Sapientia*

The Christian tradition has allegorized the sapiential books of the Old Testament; Marian allegories appear especially in commentaries on Proverbs, Ecclesiastes, the Song of Songs, Wisdom, and Sirach. When in 1943 De Koninck published his *Ego Sapientia: La Sagesse qui est Marie*, he inserted himself within this tradition.[21] In order to recognize that De Koninck's sources come almost exclusively from what we today would call the spiritu-

16. See Ashley, *The Way Toward Wisdom: An Interdisciplinary and Intercultural Introduction to Metaphysics* (Notre Dame, Ind.: University of Notre Dame Press, 2006), 469, n.103: "Charles De Koninck and his students at Laval University emphasized the dialectical character of modern science, but in conversations with me also accepted this [River Forest] position, as has Ralph McInerny of the University of Notre Dame." Also see Ashley, "River Forest," 2.

17. William A. Wallace, *Galileo and His Sources* (Princeton: Princeton University Press, 1984).

18. See his "Scientiae et Philosophia secundum S. Albertum Magnum," *Angelicum* 13 (1936): 24–59. For more on Fr. Fernandez, see *Padre Aniceto Fernandez (Recuerdos y testimonies)*, ed. Jaime R. Lebrato, OP (Rome, 1981).

19. See his "Scientia et Philosophia secundum S. Albertum Magnum," *Angelicum* 13 (1936): 24–29, as well as Bernard T. Vinanty, OP, "Les rapports entre la philosophie et les sciences: L'enseignement de la cosmologie a l'Angelicum,'" *Angelicum* 61 (1984): 19–62, esp. 32–37.

20. "Qui (enim) in natura rationes motus et sensus negligit, cum tota natura sit de sensibilibus et mobilibus, parat se ad decipiendum se et alios." *In Sent.* II, d. 1, a. 4; t. XXVII, p. 14.

21. Quebec: Laval-Fides, 1943.

al writings of the saints, one only need examine the footnotes. The question before us at this juncture of our heuristic inquiry is why would a philosopher, especially one whose "teaching centered chiefly around philosophy of nature, philosophy of science, and mathematics," take time from his research and writing to produce what many might take as a book of Marian piety?[22] The answer is simple: *Ego Sapientia* can be read as a philosophical text, one moreover that is dense and thus difficult to summarize briefly. If however I were obliged to characterize the essay, albeit with a certain obscurantism, I would say that De Koninck shows the authentic Thomist philosophical undergirding of Saint Louis-Marie Grignion de Montfort's *True Devotion*. In other words, De Koninck explains the speculative underpinnings of De Montfort's Marian and Christological blueprint for Christian living: *Ad Iesum per Mariam.*

Why do we speak of Mary as Wisdom? De Koninck answers the question at the start of the treatise. "'*Sapientis est ordinare*—It is for the wise man to order.' … Two things are included in the notion of order: distinction and principle. Principle is that from which something proceeds in any way whatsoever. Principle implies proceeding."[23] The thesis that interests us in *Ego Sapientia* proposes Mary as the human person who best embodies the principle of order in the economy of salvation, just as God remains the principle for the natural and philosophical sciences. No cause for alarm or confusion. Neither De Montfort nor De Koninck thought Mary held a place in the Trinity. They did not. They could not. They would not have found it decorous, to adapt John Duns Scotus's celebrated phrase. De Koninck however did recognize that God gave Mary a place within the order of grace and therefore related her to nature as perfective of it. This place that Mary occupies, De Koninck reveals in his judicious use of the traditional verses from the Latin Vulgate, for example, "Ego sapientia" (Prov 8:12), "Nigra sum sed formosa" (Sg 1:4). For De Koninck, Mary's place, her maternal mediation, is best described as ontological, not moral. For Mary's position stems from her divine maternity, which cannot be explained only in moral terms without reducing the Virgin Mother to a disciple of Christ who happens to provide a sterling example of Christian living. As the Church teaches, Mary embodies a principle of order in the economy of salvation: "Mary is not only the model and figure of the Church; she is much more.… It is a motherhood in the order of grace."[24] She not only illustrates grace, she communicates it. So St. John Paul

22. Thomas De Koninck, "Charles De Koninck: A Biographical Sketch," in De Koninck, *Writings*, vol. 1, p. 75.

23. De Koninck, *Ego*, no. 2, in *Writings*, vol. 2, p. 6.

24. St. John Paul II, encyclical letter, "Mother of the Redeemer" (*Redemptoris Mater*), §44.

II writes: "It can be said that motherhood 'in the order of grace' preserves the analogy with what 'in the order of nature' characterizes the union between mother and child."[25] And as De Koninck suggests, this feature of the Marian mystery, sages had foretold from the beginning.

Ego Sapientia takes us back to creation itself, to the beginning of what is sensible and mobile, and there we find the mysterious presence of the Blessed Virgin Mary. *Quasi rota in medio rotae.* The following passage provides an important key for De Koninck's perceptive placement of the Blessed Virgin Mary within the divine order of things.

> There is thus established a circular motion between her [Mary's] dignity as a separated principle and her dignity as the noblest part of pure creation, a circular motion which embraces the very order of the parts of the universe. The order and dignity inherent in the universe are thus all the more intimately linked to the separated principle insofar as this principle is at the same time the principal intrinsic part of the universe. This circular motion imitates in a way the circular motion between the incarnate Wisdom and the mother of this Wisdom, which in turn imitates more deeply still the circular motion between the Father and the perfect consubstantial image of the Father, *as it were a wheel within a wheel—quasi sit rota in medio rotae.*[26]

The phrase comes from Ezekiel 1:16. So Mary in some way occupies a place from the beginning of things. No wonder John Paul encouraged Catholics to emulate the counsel of the saints and *"philosophari in Maria."*[27]

De Koninck's use of the patristic and medieval authors, especially St. Bernard, shows the perennial relevance for contemporary theology of a very large body of literature (cited in the 212 footnotes from texts mostly overlooked today). As *Ego Sapientia* unfolds, however, De Koninck the philosopher reveals that the saints held Mary to be the sort of principle that is a cause, a principle, with dependence on being. The message is clear: Christians who appreciate the practice of Catholic life, including its sacramental action, find no difficulty describing Mary as a principle, and so identify her person with the Wisdom that "is mobile beyond all motion, and [which] penetrates and pervades all things by reason of her purity" (Wis. 7:21). Let one example from late Spanish Thomism, namely John of St. Thomas (1589–1644), suffice to illustrate this comparison. He writes: "Mary is the *Mater divinae gratiae,* and so is our mother with respect to the generation of redemptive grace."[28] The multitudinous footnotes in *Ego Sapientia* show that

25. Ibid., §45.

26. De Koninck, *Ego,* no. 13, in *Writings,* vol. 2, pp. 17, 18.

27. Encyclical Letter of John Paul, *Fides et Ratio,* §107. John Paul also cites Pseudo-Epiphanius, a monk of the East.

28. De Koninck, *Ego,* no. 30, in *Writings,* vol. 2, p. 38, citing *Cursus Theologieus,* t. 8, d. 10, a. 3.

our ancient teachers in the faith understood this Marian principle, namely, that Mary exercises a causality in our redemption.

Only with the advent of the Thomist tradition would the full dynamics of how Mary works in Catholic life be exposed with philosophical and theological clarity. This clarity originates in Aristotle's intuition about double agency or causality, a thesis first taught not in metaphysics but in natural philosophy. *Ego Sapientia* affords a good example of what I call, simply, Thomism, or the Thomist commentatorial tradition. Throughout the assemblage of patristic texts, De Koninck masterfully appeals to both Aquinas and, crucially, his commentators (as well as to the medieval Mariologist Albertus Magnus) in order to put, well, order into what otherwise can appear as the enthusiastic exclamations of holy men about the woman whom they revere devoutly as Queen and Mother.

Wisdom and the Sacraments

To complete this sketch of the significance of Laval Thomism and Mariology for our present ecclesial and theological circumstances, I wish to apply our findings to the question of the sacraments. In what follows, I provide the briefest of sketches for a response to a problem that continues to afflict the renewal of sacramental theology in the Church. Whatever one's views on Thomism may be, one must see that this problem adversely affects all Christians. To marginalize the sacraments or to reduce the sacraments to protestative signs opposes the authentic practice of the Catholic faith. Ignorance about the sapiential ordering that the sacraments introduce into Christian living also undermines the special vocations that exist within the Church. Each vocation embodies an order. Each vocation invokes Mary as its Queen. And through the deprediation of the sacramental economy, each vocation suffers: Marriage suffers inasmuch as the natural ordering of man to wife and of conjugal love to the rearing of children is undermined; Holy Orders suffers inasmuch as the priest is reduced to a designated or credentialed functionary instead of the gift and mystery that he is, that is, instead of being a Head, a Shepherd, and a Bridegroom. The place of consecrated life as an objectively superior state is no longer recognized within the hierarchy, that is, the *order*, of vocations. When these vocations within the Church fail, then there exists no alternative but to view the Church as the last outpost of communitarian humanism. The logical outcome of this kind of ecclesiology appears in the abandonment of worship and then, after a while, of the places of worship. We shutter up churches, and sell them.

The remote and general background for the eclipse of sacramental causality can be traced back to the well-known Enlightenment aversion to the "scandal of particularity." The egalitarian spirit takes umbrage at the thought that only one Savior exists, that only one Church offers the full means to attaining salvation, that only seven sacraments duly celebrated within this Church communicate divine grace. Today however, most Catholics encounter the "scandal of particularity" when they engage studies that include interreligious dialogue and religious multiculturalism. Few present-day authors have observed the deleterious wreckage that inclusivism (which is the Enlightenment remedy for avoiding the scandal of particularity) introduces into the context of sacramental theology. The Congregation for the Doctrine of the Faith issued during the Great Jubilee of the Year 2000 a declaration titled *Dominus Jesus*. The declaration, a prophetic text for the Church in the new millennium, of course deals explicitly with "particularity" in Christology, soteriology, and ecclesiology: "On the Unity and Salvific Universality of Jesus Christ and the Church." However, only in an oblique way does it treat sacramental theology, that is, when the text mentions the "fullness of the means of salvation" available within the Church gathered around Peter. The footnote refers to Pius XII's 1943 encyclical, *Mystici corporis*.[29]

To explain the full story of the eclipse of causality in modern sacramental theology would, as I have mentioned already, require a long study—but liturgy, ecumenical studies, and patristic thought would be discovered to have a lot to do with the historical explanation.[30] The focus on these studies—liturgical, ecumenical, historical—with the concomitant neglect of the classical dogmatic synthesis and its deployment of philosophical categories such as efficient causality has obscured and undermined the traditional notion of sacramental causality. Modern philosophy itself played a role, especially after the development of modern empirical science in the seventeenth century—the so-called scientific revolution. The rupture that occurred returns us to De Koninck and his efforts to restore friendly relations between science and philosophy. There are other factors to consider: the *de facto* eclipse of efficient causality as a category of explanation; the preference for formal and final causality in modern German philosophy; the wearisomeness that countries like Holland and Switzerland experienced after 400 years of being split almost evenly by religion; the two world wars of the twentieth century.

Many occurrences conspired to make what had become regarded as a juridico-sacramental system appear as obsolete and impersonal and obstructionist to religious experience. By contrast, the effervescent liturgical

29. Declaration *Dominus Jesus*, no.22, n.92.
30. I offer some justification for this broad claim in my article "Sacraments of the Church." See note 9 above.

movement encouraged an unstoppable production of all kinds of personal experiences, social, musical, choreographic, political. Unfortunately the juridical aspects of sacramental theology, which still cannot be ignored, were judged intricately linked to the use of cause in sacramental theology. Prior to the Second Vatican Council, canon lawyers often taught sacramental theology.[31] With the advent of transcendental philosophy, the category of sign soon dominated theological attempts to explain the sacraments, and this was understood by many as a way to escape falling back into the old particularity. Karl Rahner's *Real Symbol* ranks among the best examples. At the same time, other philosophical categories entered into the service of sacramental theology; these are largely drawn from the several varieties of twentieth-century personalism, such as encounter and presence. Edward Schillebeeckx's work is best known. However the only theologian that I know who remained faithful to sacramental causality and at the same time exposed the sacramental economy as profoundly personalist is my teacher, Colman O'Neill, whose books still serve Catholic education in the United States.[32]

What is important to reflect on is the following: how does the fear of violating the unspoken Enlightenment-mandated code to distance oneself from the scandal of particularity emerge as a driving force even in the areas of liturgical, ecumenical, and especially historical studies? Consider these clues:

1. the liturgical movement—one thinks especially of Dom Odo Casel— sought to broaden the categories of efficacy; Belgian Cardinal Godfried Danneels recognized in 2000 that no satisfactory replacement for the sacramental causality problem has been found.[33]
2. The ecumenical movement sought to overcome divisions—the figure of the Benedictine Lambert Beauduin (1873–1960), another Belgian priest, who combined his interest in the liturgical movement with ecumenical activism at Chevetogne, is worthy of study.[34]

31. For example, see Nicholas Halligan, OP, *The Administration of the Sacraments: Some Practical Guides for Priests and Seminarians* (Staten Island, N.Y.: Alba House, 1963).

32. It pleased me to hear Bishop Charles Morerod, a Swiss Dominican who studied under Father O'Neill, recall with appreciation the latter's contribution to sacramental theology.

33. See Cardinal Godfried Danneels, "Current Challenges for Sacramental Theology," *Antiphon* 5.2 (2000): 44–45.

34. For favorable accounts in English, see Sonya Quitslund, *Beauduin, a Prophet Vindicated* (New York: Newman Press, 1973). For a more recent and quite thorough study, see Raymond Loonbeek and Jacques Mortiau, *Un pionnier, dom Lambert Beauduin (1873–1960): Liturgie et Unité des chrétiens*, 2 vols., Université Catholique de Louvain: Recueil de Travaux d'Histoire et de Philologie, 7 Série, Fascicules 12–13 (Louvain-la-Neuve: Collège Erasme, 2001).

3. Historical studies and method, which finds endorsement in *Optatam Totius*, tend to locate an exposition of how Aquinas revolutionized Catholic theological method within a spectrum of historical development. For instance, recall the celebrated battle that began in 1944, "l'affaire de Fourvière."[35] It developed around the publication by Henri Bouillard (1908–81) of *Conversion et grâce chez saint Thomas d'Aquin.*[36] The author had written a thesis on a minor point of development in the thought of St. Thomas Aquinas concerning the role of human freedom in the preparation for the reception of divine grace. He went on to argue that all theological systems suffer from the constraints of their cultural setting, both religious and secular, and so these "systems" need to be understood within a relative context.

These clues suffice to intimate, at least, that the movements—liturgical, ecumenical, and historical—that achieved a certain recognition at the Second Vatican Council have caused a decided derailment of the category of sacramental causality. It is also true to observe that the biblical studies of the same period did not provide a lifeboat for this important element of Catholic thought that Aquinas had presented with exquisite philosophical adornments.

River Forest Thomism prided itself on studying the commentaries on Aristotle in order to learn about the philosophy of Aquinas, and not, as Gilson had done, to read Thomist philosophy out of the theological pages, mostly of the *Summa theologiae.*[37] Take away philosophy or reduce philosophy to a commentary on a theological truism and the category of efficient causality emerges as something of the proverbial bogeyman, something alien to inclusivist sensibilities and a mechanical reduction of what comes freely as a divine gift to man. The loss of a sapiential sacramental theology owes much to the liturgical renewal and its twin, the ecumenical movement.[38] But a lot else was going on during the 1930s, the decade when Europe had begun to get up on its feet after the First World War.

Consider the case of Humbert Boüessé (1901–75), a former student of

35. For further information, see Étienne Fouilloux, "Dialogue théologique? (1946–1948)" in *Saint Thomas au XXe siècle, Actes du colloque du Centenaire de la "Revue thomiste", 25–28 mars 1993*, ed. S.-T. Bonino (Paris, 1994), 153–95; and Aidan Nichols, "Thomism and the Nouvelle Théologie," *The Thomist* 64 (2000): 1–19.

36. See Étienne Fouilloux, "Henri Bouillard et Saint Thomas d'Aquin (1941–1951)," *Recherches de Science Religieuse* 97 (2009): 173–83.

37. Ashley, "River Forest," 3.

38. For more about the liturgical-ecumenical movement relationship, see Étienne Fouilloux, *Les catholiques et l'unité chrétienne du XIXe au XXe siècle. Itinéraires européens d'expression française* (Paris: Le Centurion, 1982).

the future cardinal Emmanuel Suhard (1874–1949) at the Grand Séminaire de Laval (France). Suhard later became known as one sympathetic to the ecumenical movement when, in the late 1940s, he helped Yves Congar arrange for Catholic attendees at the 1948 Amsterdam Conference of the World Council of Churches—an arrangement that failed to win approval at Rome. As for Boüessé himself, he became a Dominican in the province de Lyon.[39] His article in the *Revue thomiste*, "La Causalité efficiente instrumentale de l'humanité du Christ et des sacrements chrétiens," appeared in 1934, just as De Koninck took up his teaching post at Laval (Canada). The author describes the order of sacramental action by appeal to the general sacramentality of the Risen Christ, and then asks: "... physical causality. Should one acknowledge that one regrets the expression? We never find it flowing from the pen of Aquinas. Perhaps better to leave Aquinas with his own language."[40] One may wonder whether this kind of new theological argument, which we recognize appears as early as the 1930s, did not prompt Charles De Koninck deliberately to place Mary and natural philosophy side by side in his first spiritual writing.

39. His other works: *Un seul chef, Jésus-Christ* (Paris, 1950); *Le Sauveur du monde en deux tomes*: (1) La Place du Christ dans le plan de Dieu. Essai spéculatif, suivi d'une Étude critique sur la pensée scotiste et la pensée patristique en collaboration avec le R.P. F.M. Lemoine, Collège théologique dominicain, Chambery Leysse, (1951); (2) De la convenance de l'incarnation ou de la sagesse divine, le mystère de l'incarnation, en son essence et en ses modalités, de l'union en ses modalités, de la science du Christ, les infirmités coassumées, dans ses conséquences, les conséquences de l'union face à Dieu, le Père face au Christ, le moi du Christ, Collège théologique dominicain, Chambery Leysse, (1953); *Problèmes actuels de christologie* (avec J. J. Latour); *Le Sacerdoce chrétien* (Desclée De Brouwer 1957); Biographie du cardinal Suhard, ouvrage inédit du fait de la mort de l'auteur.

40. Humbert Boüessé, "La Causalité efficiente instrumentale de l'humanité du Christ et des sacrements chrétiens," *Revue thomiste* (1934): 383.

CHAPTER FOURTEEN

Reflections on Ralph McInerny's *Dante and the Blessed Virgin Mary*

KEVIN FLANNERY, SJ

In the second semester of the academic year 2005–6, Ralph McInerny was the Joseph Visiting Professor in the Faculty of Philosophy at the Gregorian University. The course was entitled *Praeambula fidei* and was basically an exposition of the book of the same title that came out later that year.[1] For at least a couple of years prior to that, Fr. Paul Mankowski and I had been meeting on Sunday evenings in order to translate *The Divine Comedy* to (or at!) each other, one canto per sitting; so, knowing of McInerny's interest in Dante, we invited him to join us, which he did willingly. The evenings were always very enjoyable as we hacked away at Dante's archaic Italian, rendered yet less tractable for being set in hendecasyllabic *terza rima*. If memory serves me, we added a bottle of wine to the regime in order to entice McInerny to come along. I am sure, of course, that he came for the poetry and not the wine!

I recall McInerny's saying on one of these occasions that he was working on a book about Dante and the Blessed Virgin. I am pretty sure that he also said then that he had been working on it for some time. I mention this because it says something about the special character of the book eventually

---

1. Ralph McInerny, *Praeambula Fidei: Thomism and the God of the Philosophers* (Washington, D.C.: The Catholic University of America Press, 2006).

published as *Dante and the Blessed Virgin*, about which I will be speaking.[2] *Dante and the Blessed Virgin*, which is just over 150 pages in length, was published in 2010 and was the last book that Ralph published. That means that he had worked on it for *at least* six years—and probably for more. Anyone who knows anything of McInerny's work ethic will know that this was unusual. When he got the idea of writing anything—whether a novel or a philosophical tome—he carried out the task expeditiously, including the project in his daily order, which was as strict as any monk's (and certainly as any Jesuit's) and which turned out its products as efficiently as any natural process. Like good drama for Aristotle, the process of writing a book had, for McInerny, a beginning, a middle, and a definite end. But *Dante and the Blessed Virgin* was a book he lingered over.

The result of this slow gestation is a book of several levels. At one level we find a large number of things said—sometimes directly, sometimes seemingly incidentally—about art. At a second level, we find philosophical and/or theological reflection on themes that occupied our friend over his lifetime. At a third level, and most prominently, we find a meditation on Our Lady. The larger edifice containing these various levels is, of course, a commentary on Dante: in particular, on the *Divine Comedy*.

So then, regarding the first level, in reading *Dante and the Blessed Virgin*, anyone must needs be struck by its constant—and yet non-obtrusive—citation of authors from a wide range of times, cultures, propensities, and languages (besides English and Italian, especially French). At one point he refers to Flannery O'Connor's self-description as a "hillbilly Thomist," at another to the paedophile André Gide's doubts about his own writings, at yet another to (the) *Treatise on True Devotion to the Blessed Virgin Mary* by St. Louis-Marie Grignion de Montfort. The epilogue consists largely of a long quotation (with commentary) from the seventeenth-century French mathematician Blaise Pascal. Inclusion among those cited does not depend on McInerny's agreeing with an author, as the example of Gide shows—not to mention the acknowledgment of a helpful point made by Fr. Andrew Greeley in a prickly review of McInerny's *The Noonday Devil*.[3] This itself says something about the informing virtue of this book and of McInerny's character in general: generosity (or, I suppose Aristotle would call it, "magnanimity"). In this, *Dante and the Blessed Virgin* is the polar opposite of Etienne Gilson's book *Dante the Philosopher*, which is an extended polemic *against* Pierre

2. McInerny, *Dante and the Blessed Virgin* (Notre Dame, Ind.: University of Notre Dame Press, 2010).

3. The review appeared in the *New York Times*, March 31, 1985.

Mandonnet, OP.[4] This is by no means to suggest that there is no place for polemics in the scholarly world: one need only think of McInerny's opposition to Cajetan's analysis of analogy in St. Thomas Aquinas—although, even in this regard, it is significant that, later in life, he became an ardent defender of Cajetan's reputation as commentator on the Angelic Doctor.[5]

Dante and the Blessed Virgin in a way discusses this, its own magnanimity, in its first lines: "One of the marvels of art is that our appreciation of it does not require that we share the outlook of the artist. There must, of course, be sympathy, and more than sympathy, with the protagonist and with his manner of viewing his plight. A reader in the third millennium can be drawn into a Greek tragedy and experience the anguish of a character whose culture is utterly alien to his own." McInerny acknowledges that the "bracketing of differences" is not always easy—and he mentions the "dilemma of Oedipus"; but he adds that "nonetheless, it may well be said that beneath the undeniable strangeness is the note of familiarity, a familiarity due to our common humanity." The differences to be bracketed might be religious or even ethical. He cites the case of Conrad's Kurtz in the *Heart of Darkness*. That we are mesmerized by his voice is an indication that we share with him, at the very least, a sense of "the horror, the horror, the horror."

And he mentions Matthew Arnold, who considered Christianity the "casualty of nineteenth-century philology and science"—a thesis which McInerny certainly rejects—and yet he acknowledges also a certain *frisson* when he reads of the "melancholy, long, withdrawing roar" of the once full Sea of Faith: "Retreating, to the breath / Of the night-wind, down the vast edges drear / And naked shingles of the world." McInerny experiences no such distance between himself and the Dante who wrote the *Divine Comedy,* and he acknowledges that there can be an advantage in this for one seeking to understand and expound the poem—"a possibility only," he says, and "nothing inevitable." But his primary motivation in *Dante and the Blessed Virgin* is clearly to invite the reader *in*—into a world (or world view) that can hardly fail to be attractive, no matter what one's own point of view, for its philosophical and theological consistency and its artistic perfection.

The common humanity between individuals who do not share the same beliefs is also a major theme in the *Divine Comedy*, where Dante is guided, until he reaches the Garden of Eden at the pinnacle of purgatory, by

---

4. Etienne Gilson, *Dante the Philosopher*, trans. David Moore (London: Sheed & Ward, 1948) (originally published as *Dante et la philosophie*, Études de philosophie médiévale, 28 [Paris: J. Vrin, 1939]). Gilson also published a collection of essays on Dante: *Dante et Béatrice: Études dantesques*, Etudes de philosophie médiévale, 61 (Paris: J. Vrin, 1974).

5. See McInerny, *Praeambula Fidei*, 39–90.

the pagan poet Virgil. "What an odd choice to guide Dante to heaven," remarks McInerny. "As a pagan, unredeemed by the grace of Christ, paradise is closed to him, and that means that human happiness in its fullness cannot be his." A pagan like Virgil cannot even have the explicit longing for the Messiah that gives the Jews access to paradise.[6] And yet Dante was well able to relate to Virgil's poetry: indeed, it was this pagan's poetry he emulated; it was this pagan's poetry that (at least for a time) most stirred his soul.

At one point in the poem (*Purgatorio* XXI), Dante and Virgil encounter Statius, a Roman poet who died in AD 96 and who, according to Dante's imaginings, converted to Christianity having read Virgil's Fourth *Eclogue*, which speaks of a child descending from on high and was therefore considered a prophecy of the birth of Christ: "Per te poeta fui, per te cristiano," he tells Virgil: "Because of you I was a poet, because of you a Christian" (*Purgatorio* XXII, 73).[7] Statius was certainly the lesser poet (in comparison with either Virgil or Dante) and yet both of them depend on him to guide them along the correct path forward (*Purgatorio* XII, 121–26). Although Virgil's verses brought others to the faith, they helped him not at all in that regard: they could not since, whereas Statius's conversion was caused by grace, Virgil's verses issued from human reason. And yet Dante was well able to relate to Virgil's poetry. As he did in art, here in purgatory, he hangs upon his arm as together they stumble toward the paradise only one of them may enter.

That brings us to the second level of *Dante and the Blessed Virgin*, that of philosophical and/or theological reflection. A few years ago, a waggish colleague (or two) made reference to the "McInerny Identity Thesis": the thesis, that is, that Aquinas *was* Aristotle.[8] And it is true: McInerny would often insist, especially against Gilson and company, that the relationship between Aquinas and "the Philosopher," upon ten of whose works he wrote commentaries, was not "the chasm" imagined by Gilson.[9] But what becomes very apparent in *Dante and the Blessed Virgin* is that McInerny agrees with the Florentine that there is a very clear line to be drawn between the realm where Aristotle dwelt (along with such figures as Plato, Homer, and Virgil) and the realm accessible to those who are saved in Christ. If, as the Gos-

---

6. See *Paradiso* XXXII.

7. The words in Virgil (*Ecl.* IV, 5–7) are as follows: "magnus ab integro saeclorum nascitur ordo. / iam redit et Virgo, redeunt Saturnia regna; / iam nova progenies caelo demittitur alto." One notes that a Virgin is mentioned here, although this does not find its way into Dante's paraphrase (at *Purgatorio* XXII, 70–72). There *Virgo* becomes simply *giustizia*. On this, see Charles Southward Singleton, *Dante Alighieri: The Divine Comedy*, Bollingen Series, 80 (Princeton, N.J.: Princeton University Press, 1970–75), 2.2.528.

8. See McInerny, *Praeambula Fidei*, 293.

9. I take the word from McInerny: ibid.

pel of Luke tells us, there is a chasm (*chasma mega*: Lk 16:26) between the pauper Lazarus and the sinfully rich Dives—such that even one wanting to cross over it could not do so—between Aristotle (who represents human reason) and Aquinas (who represents reason informed by Revelation), the gap *is* traversable. But only for Aquinas, not for Aristotle.

Dante puts Aristotle, "'l maestro di color che sanno" ("the master of those who know"), in the first circle of hell, to which he refers also as "limbo" (*Inferno* IV, 45), where he sits "among a philosophical family" that includes, close by, Socrates and Plato—and, less close by, such figures as Democritus ("who attributed the world to chance"), Empedocles, Euclid ("the geometer"), Ptolemy, Avicenna, and Averroes (*Inferno* IV, 130–47). The place where these learned men gather is described as a "meadow of fresh greenery" (*Inferno* IV, 111), and it is only *after* leaving this place that Dante comes to another "ove non è che luca" ("where there is nothing that shines") (*Inferno* IV, 151). The light that does shine in limbo is the light of the natural world, which itself reflects the light of God; but it also represents the light of reason that can take man a certain distance, but no farther. "Rest content, oh human race, with the *quia* / for were you able to see all, there had been no need for Mary to give birth."[10] The *quia* referred to here is (or are) such truths as *that* God exists, *that* he is one, and so on. Aristotle was able to arrive at knowledge of these truths about God but not at knowledge of the *proper quid*, that is, an understanding of his very essence: the pagan's knowledge stopped short of *seeing* God, which is possible only in and through Christ. In the final canto of the *Divine Comedy*, Dante himself is granted this vision. He writes: "Thus my mind, wholly suspended, admired fixed, immobile and attentive, and was ever alight to admire."[11] Having gazed on the essence of God, Dante cannot turn away, for every desire is there satisfied and calmed; outside, anything is defective.[12]

This no man's land—or, perhaps better, this few men's land—between reason and reason-informed-by-faith was a major concern of McInerny's, especially in the culmination of his career: both in his Gifford Lecture (*Charac-*

10. "State contenti, umana gente, al quia; / ché se potuto aveste veder tutto, / mestier non era parturir Maria" (*Purgatorio* III, 37–39). He goes on to say, "I speak of Aristotle and of Plato and of many others" (43–44).

11. "Così la mente mia, tutta sospesa, / mirava fissa, immobile e attenta, / e sempre di mirar faceasi accesa" (*Paradiso* XXXIII, 97–99). The next stanza runs: "A quella luce cotal si diventa, / che volgersi da lei per altro aspetto / è impossibil che mai si consenta" (100–102).

12. One wonders then how Dante could have returned to earth to write the *Divine Comedy*; but in the final lines of the poem he says that his desire and will were "*moved*, by the love that moves the sun and the other stars" ("ma già volgeva il mio disio e 'l velle, / sì come rota ch'igualmente è mossa / l'amor che move il sole e l'altre stelle"), that is by God (described in distinctively Aristotelian terms).

ters in Search of their Author: the "characters" being the whole pantheon of recent philosophy, which he describes as largely hostile to natural theology) and in *Praeambula Fidei*, which, as he says in its preface, is "about the negative attitude toward natural theology that is found among those one would have expected to be defenders of it."[13] Here in *Dante and the Blessed Virgin*, he discusses at some length Dante's credo, as he is examined by St. John on the (theological) virtue of charity:

> E io rispondo: Io credo in uno Dio
> solo ed etterno, che tutto 'l ciel move,
> non moto, con amore e con disio;
> e a tal creder non ho io pur prove
> fisice e metafisice, ma dalmi
> anche la verità che quinci piove
> per Moisè, per profeti e per salmi,
> per l'Evangelio e per voi che scriveste
> poi che l'ardente Spirto vi fé almi. [*Paradiso* XXIV, 130–38][14]

The initial lines here refer to Aquinas's five ways of proving that God exists, but these are based (some more, some less immediately) upon passages in Aristotle's *Physics* and *Metaphysics*. The truths so proved are, therefore, part of the *praeambula fidei*. But this presents a problem, notes McInerny, since to be a *praeambulum fidei* is to be connected to the faith; and, indeed,

---

13. McInerny, *Praeambula Fidei*, ix (where recent philosophy is described as hostile to natural theology). Although *Characters in Search of Their Author* (that is, *Characters in Search of their Author: The Gifford Lectures, Glasgow, 1999–2000* [Notre Dame: University of Notre Dame, 2001]) was published before *Praeambula Fidei*, it grew out of this latter, more thorough treatment of the same themes. *Characters in Search of Their Author* has to do especially with such figures as Descartes, Heidegger, and A. J. Ayer; *Praeambula Fidei* has chapters devoted to—and critical of—Gilson, de Lubac, and Chenu. In an early draft, the preface to *Praeambula Fidei* made critical mention also of the then Prefect of the Congregation for the Doctrine of the Faith, Joseph Cardinal Ratzinger. Before publishing the book, out of respect for the man and his new office as pope, McInerny pulled the remark, which had to do with following words: "I am of the opinion that Neo-Scholastic rationalism failed which, with reason totally independent from the faith, tried to reconstruct the *preambula fidei* with pure rational certainty. The attempts that presume to do the same will have the same result. Yes, Karl Barth was right to reject philosophy as the foundation of the faith independent from the faith. If it were such, our faith would be based from the beginning to the end on the changing philosophical theories" (*Relativism: The Central Problem for Faith Today*). This passage comes in an address given at a meeting in Guadalajara, Mexico, in May 1996; the full address can be found in various places on the Internet. One notes that the quoted remark begins with the words, "I am of the opinion …"

14. "And I respond: 'I believe in one God / unique and eternal, who moves the whole heavens, / unmoved, with love and desire; / and in believing thus I have not just proofs / physical and metaphysical, but given me / is also the truth that rains down / through Moses, through the prophets, and through the psalms, / through the Gospel and through you who wrote / after the fiery Spirit made you bountiful'" (*Paradiso* XXIV, 130–38).

most believers know certain of the *praeambula* (such as that God exists) before they are even capable of saying what a philosophical proof *is*.

In short, the truths about God that philosophers can prove and have proved are included among the truths about God that have been revealed. Before the believer knows (by way of a philosophical proof) that God exists, he or she believes it. By calling such truths preambles of faith, Aquinas is comparing them to faith, a comparison that only a theologian, not an ancient philosopher, would make. Does this render the relationship between the known and believed hopelessly ambiguous?[15]

McInerny's (and Dante's) answer is a firm no: there have been human beings, such as Aristotle, who, quite independently of any Judeo-Christian influence, knew what we call *praeambula fidei*. If grace comes through Jesus Christ, who spoke through the prophets—but not through Aristotle or Homer or the Orphic poets—about things not otherwise knowable by them, there are two distinct types of knowledge, one human, the other divine (but given by grace to men).

But, to press McInerny's point, what is the *use* of the *praeambula fidei* to believers? Well, for one thing, the fact that the Church (believers) can step back across the line—in Dantesque terms, from paradise to purgatory or even to hell, to argue (in the latter case) with individuals whose reasoning is demonically confused—allows her to keep a watchful eye upon her own teaching. For she knows that, if that teaching ever contradicts reason, it can no sooner be part of the faith than it can be part of the *praeambula fidei*: the articles of the faith are subject to the same logical principles as are the *praeambula fidei*. The occasional tussle in the realm of shadows or even in the heart of darkness is good training in the use of these logical principles. A skilled believer might even gain a soul for Christ in this way, by showing that supposed intellectual impediments to faith are no such things. But in order to have such success, the believer needs to appreciate his adversaries. He needs to be at ease with the likes of Virgil, Matthew Arnold, and Conrad's Kurtz.

Remaining in argumentative form is also a good thing for believers themselves. "The fact is," writes McInerny, "that holding truths on the basis of faith is not a natural mode of the human mind."[16] A purely charismatic faith, cut off from philosophical argumentation, is always in danger of declining into sentimentality, which itself leads to *lack* of faith, since it lacks traction in those parts of the human soul that breed conviction. Says McInerny: "If some of the truths that have been revealed—the preambles—can be *known* to be true, this suggests that the whole of revelation consists of

15. McInerny, *Dante and the Blessed Virgin*, 117–18.
16. Ibid., 118.

intelligible truths, truths that will be understood and grasped as true in the next world."[17] So appreciation of the fact that the *praeambula fidei* can be known and proved gives believers confidence in their own more supernatural beliefs. It also gives them courage as they step into the "public square" *as Christians* to make the Church's case about such matters as concern humanity itself. There is no need—or excuse—for cowering behind the thesis that religion is a matter of personal choice, "so do what you will and leave us to our eccentric ways."

This brings us finally to the third level of *Dante and the Blessed Virgin*: Dante's (and McInerny's) meditation upon Our Lady. The concerns of this level are not unconnected with those of the previous level. One of the presuppositions of Mc Inerny's book is that Beatrice—with whom Dante fell in love when he was nine, she eight years old—is a "screen lady," a "stand in," for Dante's true object of love, Mary the Mother of God.[18] And at one point, in clear contrast with Dante's own prizing of philosophical reasoning, Beatrice lambastes the debates of the schools on earth: "Down there, you do not follow a single path in your philosophizing, so much does love of appearance and your own thought transport you!" In McInerny's own translation of these lines, he speaks of "showing off," and he is obliged to acknowledge that "the theology of the philosophers is a difficult achievement; metaphysical proofs of God's existence, however cogent, are subject to endless discussion."[19] In a better world, suggests Beatrice, there would be—there *is*—"a single path" even of human reasoning. In effect, this is Mary saying to academics, "Listen to your mother." Having overheard the shouting and witnessed perhaps a punch or two in the nose, she steps in and says: "All right now, stop your wrangling: here is the one thing you are to believe."

This is Mary's role throughout the *Divine Comedy*, that is, to call sinners to the calm humility in which they can listen to one another—even to Matthew Arnold and Andrew Greeley—and in which they can listen, especially, for those elements of the truth in what others say as they too struggle up the way to true beatitude, where anxious striving ceases. A large portion of *Dante and the Blessed Virgin* is an explanation of how different remarks by or about Our Lady constitute the counterpoints to the capital sins expiated on the "Seven Story Mountain" of purgatory. (That is the expression that McInerny uses; he never mentions Thomas Merton by name, but the wholly

17. Ibid., 119, emphasis mine.

18. Ibid., 9–11.

19. Ibid., 117–19. The Italian of the translated passage is as follows: "Voi non andate giù per un sentiero / filosofando: tanto vi trasporta / l'amor de l'apparenza e 'l suo pensiero!" (*Paradiso* XXIX, 85–87).

non-ironical allusion is apparent.) On the first story—or terrace—those who were led astray in this life by the sin of pride hear the words: "Behold, I am the handmaid of the Lord; let it be to me according to your word" (Lk 1:38). On the second terrace, where sins of envy are expiated, are heard the words: "they have no wine" (Jn 2:3). Writes McInerny: "Imagine how differently those words might be spoken by another, you or I perhaps, with a little lilt in the voice, widened eyes, lifted brows, calling attention to the impending embarrassment of the hosts" (p. 65)—especially (I might add) if they happen to be our ideological antagonists.

On the third terrace, peopled by those carried away in this life by anger, Dante makes reference to the passage in which the youthful Jesus is found by Mary and Joseph in the Temple: "Son, why have you treated us so? Behold, your father and I have been looking for you anxiously" (Lk 2:48, RSV). It is strange that *these* words should be proposed as the *antidote* to anger, for Mary in them appears indeed angry. But McInerny provides an interpretation of the words with which Dante would certainly agree, for it is Thomistic. "Thomas," says McInerny, "recalls the ancient quarrel between Stoics and Aristotelians, the former treating all anger as a vice, whereas the latter held that sometimes anger is good."[20] Mary's anger was not the sinful anger atoned for on the third terrace of purgatory—for that always involves the irrational desire to harm its object—but the sort of clearheaded and proper anger that is informed by meekness. Indeed, it is meekness that is the opposite of sinful anger; and so, when we hear Mary's rebuke to the youthful Jesus, we should attend to how it is tempered by that virtue. Dante exploits in this regard the Vulgate translation of *odunōmenoi* as *dolentes*— "Ecce pater tuus et ego *dolentes* quaerebamus te"—in order to get this point across; he speaks too of Mary in this scene as *dolce* (sweet).[21] For the Stoics, *any* agitation of the soul was evil, but that is not the Christian way, since agitation of the soul *in itself* is natural and therefore part of God's creation. In the Temple, Mary's soul is clearly agitated—as it was at the Annunciation—but she remains open to (if not yet fully understanding of) the reasonable, if *also* a bit agitated, explanation of the Son of God: "Why were you seeking me? Did you not know that I must be about my Father's business?" (Lk 2:49). One of the purposes of poetry is to capture and convey such subtle moral distinctions.

In the subsequent terraces of purgatory, the pattern is the same: each sin

---

20. Ibid., 68; see also Aquinas, *Summa theologiae* II-II, q. 158, a. 1, ad 1.

21. "Ivi mi parve in una visione ... / e una donna, in su l'entrar, con atto / dolce di madre dicer: 'Figliuol mio / perché hai tu così verso noi fatto? / Ecco, dolenti, lo tuo padre e io ti cercavamo'" (*Purgatorio* XV, 85–92).

is purged by countervailing inspired words pertaining to the Virgin: sloth by "Mary arose and went with haste to the hill country" (Lk 1:39); avarice by "And she laid him in a manger, because there was no room for them in the inn" (Lk 2:7); gluttony by another allusion to the wedding feast at Cana (Jn 2:1–11), Dante noting that Mary thought more of her hosts "than of her own mouth";[22] and lust by the words: "How shall this be, since I know not man?" (Lk 1:34).

All these words point, of course, to Mary's humility, but in paradise the emphasis is on her majesty and glory. When she finally appears in person, she is in the company of her Son. And, although the angel of the Annunciation is present too, there is no talk of an *ancilla* (although it is not excluded either) but rather of Mary's making the highest sphere of heaven yet more divine by entering into it (*Paradiso* XXIII, 107–8). Shortly afterwards, the hosts of heaven burst out singing the *Regina coeli*, which McInerny quotes in full (106):

> Regina coeli, laetare, alleluia!
> Quia quem meruisti portare
> Resurrexit, sicut dixit, alleluia!

One could well emphasize the word "meruisti" here: "Because he whom you *merited* to bear, has risen, as he said."

This majesty of the Queen of Heaven is due to her continued union with her Son. She is, as McInerny says, "the mediatrix of grace" (135). Among graces that come through her is doubtless the grace of the human and divine truth taught by the Church.

To conclude, then, as one would expect of a work addressing the themes of a lifetime, the argument of this, Ralph McInerny's final book, is not simple. At its base is what we might call a sort of liberalism: an ear open to all and sundry, whether they share one's convictions or not. Together with this, however, we find a frank willingness to engage in controversy and to say forthrightly that another person has things wrong—by, for instance, failing to recognize the proper distinction between reason and reasoned informed by the light of faith. This tendency—even desire—to wade into the crowd in the public square and land a punch or two is tempered by the truth to which Beatrice points: that much philosophical controversy is just "showing off," which is not the way to paradise, not the way to truth itself. That way is the way of humble obedience to our Mother the Church. Such obedience is not, however, abject or blind obedience. It is not abject, since it remains confident and strong; it is not blind, since it is the epitome of reason itself.

---

22. "Più pensava Maria onde / fosser le nozze orrevoli e intere, / ch'a la sua bocca" (*Purgatorio* XXII, 142–44).

PART FIVE

PHILOSOPHY IN MORAL THEOLOGY

CHAPTER FIFTEEN

Moderating the Magnanimous Man

Aquinas on Greatness of Soul

MARC D. GUERRA

In a still-influential book published sixty-three years ago, Harry Jaffa argued that St. Thomas Aquinas "mistakes Aristotle's intention," and for that reason Thomas endeavors to "save" the character of the *Nicomachean Ethic's* magnanimous man "in accordance with what Thomas evidently considers a higher standard of perfection."[1] The higher standard of perfection Jaffa has in mind is "Christian ethics," as revealed in an epigram from Winston Churchill that Jaffa uses to open his book: "It is baffling to reflect that what men call honor does not correspond always to Christian ethics." Jaffa's argument is not simply that Aristotle's account of the magnanimous man differs from Aquinas's; it is that Aquinas failed to understand that his account of magnanimity was not identical to Aristotle's. Against this view, a growing number of Catholic scholars have argued that Aquinas did not get Aristotle's account of greatness of soul wrong. In fact, he adopted it while appending to it a distinctively Christian teaching on the demands of humility and charity. The argument advanced by these scholars "is not that Aristotle's magnanimous man is a Christian but that his virtue ... is compatible with Christianity."[2]

1. Harry V. Jaffa, *Thomism and Aristotelianism* (Westport, Conn.: Greenwood Press, 1972), 141.
2. Carson Holloway, "Christianity, Magnanimity, and Statesmanship," *The Review of Politics* 61, no. 4 (Fall, 1999): 595.

While these two camps claim to be in fundamental opposition to each other, they are in reality closer to each other than either one cares to recognize. Both claim that Aquinas understood his teaching on the virtue of magnanimity to be identical to Aristotle's. And both claim that Aquinas's account of magnanimity is, to greater and lesser degrees, necessarily wedded to and framed by his teachings on humility and the infused, theological virtue of charity. However, in my view both of these positions miss the mark, although in different ways. Careful attention to Aristotle's account of magnanimity in the *Nicomachean Ethics* and to Aquinas's presentations of greatness of soul in his commentary on the *Ethics* and in his *Summa theologiae* reveals that neither is the case. Aquinas's teaching on magnanimity knowingly parts company with Book IV of the *Ethics*'s account of the magnanimous man in important and in substantive ways. Aquinas implicitly critiques the *Ethics*'s surface presentation of the magnanimous man even as he incorporates much of this account's teachings into his own views.[3] Aquinas's view of magnanimity's role in political life is not predominantly shaped by his understanding of the roles that the virtues of Christian humility and the infused theological virtue of charity play in political life. Rather, it is most relevantly rooted in his recognition of the way in which justice, "the most excellent of all the moral virtues,"[4] informs, ennobles, and transcends the realm of human affairs.

Aristotle's presentation of magnanimity (*megalopsychia*) in Book IV of the *Ethics* diverges in subtle but perceptible ways from the manner in which he has previously spoken of particular virtues in this work. Aristotle here does not speak of magnanimity primarily as a mean between two extremes, as he had done in Book III when giving accounts of the ethical virtues of courage and moderation. Rather, Book IV's discussion of magnanimity

3. Mary Keys makes a similar argument in her impressive *Aquinas, Aristotle, and the Promise of the Common Good* (New York: Cambridge University Press, 2006). Keys sees "Aquinas as offering a subtle yet far-reaching critique of Aristotelian magnanimity, one with roots in Aquinas's theology yet also comprising a philosophic reappraisal of Aristotle's account of human excellence." She notes that her account concurs "with Vaclav Havel (1991), among others, that reflection on the totalitarian experiences of the twentieth century reveals the humanity and nobility of a magnanimity informed by humility." See Keys, *Aquinas, Aristotle, and the Promise of the Common Good*, 144. Although I am in broad agreement with Keys on this score, I think Aquinas's own teaching on the virtue of magnanimity is, as I will argue, more relevantly informed by his understanding of the created nature of nature and the natural demands of justice that are upheld by the created natural order than by his "theology" or by his teaching on "humility" or by his emphasis on "natural human sociability" (*Aquinas, Aristotle, and the Promise of the Common Good*, 154).

4. St. Thomas Aquinas, *Summa theologiae* I-II, q. 66, a. 4. All references to this work in this paper are to the following edition: Aquinas, *Summa theologica*, trans. The Fathers of the English Dominican Province (Westminster, Md.: Christian Classics, 1981).

brings to light the form that this comparatively rare virtue actually takes in the great-souled man. The magnanimous man subsequently is described as he comes to sight in his own eyes, in the eyes of serious men (*spoudaios*), in the eyes of decidedly lesser men—and, in between the lines, in the eyes of Aristotle himself. As Aristide Tessitore artfully puts it, in "the same way one views a statue by walking around it, Aristotle invites readers to ponder the magnanimous person from several different and even conflicting points of view."[5] Aristotle deliberately invites his reader to contemplate magnanimity not in the abstract but incarnate, that is, in the person of the great-souled man. Presenting his reader with a portrait of the great-souled man, Aristotle gives an account of the magnanimous man's great deeds and the great honors he rightly claims, and at the same time provides an insightful, if not unproblematic, glimpse into the inner psychic life that characterizes such a man. As we shall see, by choosing to proceed in this way Aristotle quietly draws attention to an irreducible tension that marks the life of the magnanimous man he describes. For on the one hand, the great-souled man "is incapable of living with a view to another—except a friend—since doing so is slavish";[6] on the other, he nevertheless seeks "great honor" from others and looks to perform the kind of "great deed" that necessarily requires others with whom one lives.[7]

From the time it is first mentioned in the *Ethics*'s opening catalogue of the virtues,[8] Aristotle carefully distinguishes magnanimity from the more ordinary love of honor. Unlike its unnamed counterpart, magnanimity concerns the love of honor on a grand scale. As his name indicates, the magnanimous man is not simply animated by a love of honor (*philotimia*). He esteems the kind of great honor that is associated with and accompanies the performance of "great deeds."[9] Illustrative of this fact, he is not a man of constant, active civil engagement. He is both seen and said to be slow to act. Although his actions are few, they are "great and notable ones."[10] What is more, he knows that he is in fact worthy of great honors. To underscore the connection between his deeds and his greatness, Aristotle draws a comparison between greatness of soul and greatness of body. As men who are worthy of little and know that they cannot be great-souled, so too can "those who are small ... be elegant and well-proportioned but not beautiful."[11]

---

5. Aristide Tessitore, *Reading Aristotle's* Ethics: *Virtue, Rhetoric, and Political Philosophy* (Albany, N.Y.: State University of New York Press, 1996), 28.

6. Aristotle, *Nicomachean Ethics*, trans. Robert C. Bartlett and Susan D. Collins (Chicago: The University of Chicago Press, 2011), 1124b31–1125a1.

7. Ibid., 1124b25.

8. Ibid., 1107b21–1108a1.

9. Ibid., 1124b25.

10. Ibid., 1124b26.

11. Ibid., 1123b6–7.

Aristotle's comparison of greatness of soul and greatness of body points to a connection between the magnitude of a man's deeds and the magnanimity he possesses. At the same time, it also hints at a factor that would seem to qualify the self-sufficiency of the great-souled man. For the comparison leads one to wonder whether magnanimity depends on chance in the way that beauty is said to depend on chance. The small, after all, do not choose to be small; their body size is given to them. Could the traits that enable greatness of soul be like this? Could they be traits that men might be able to hone, like the small are capable of honing their graceful features, but whose very possession initially and ultimately depends on a gift from chance or nature or the gods?

Other problems associated with greatness of soul are indicated by Aristotle's claim that "in truth" it is difficult to be magnanimous, since "it is not possible without gentlemanliness (*kalokagathia*)."[12] A true account of greatness of soul must show that this virtue effects the humanly desirable but rare union of the beautiful or the noble (*to kalon*) and the good (*to agathon*). As Aristotle makes clear in his *Ethics* and *Politics*, the beautiful and the good traditionally are said to be united in a particular type of man, the *kalokagathos* or the gentleman. Viewed in this light, the *kalokagathos* is said to be the political man in the most proper sense of the term. In contrast to merely good men, who act virtuously for the sake of attaining such naturally good things as wealth and honor, the gentleman acts virtuously "for the sake of the noble, for this is the end of virtue."[13] Truly political men, the men Aristotle calls gentlemen, are quite rare. Indeed, "the majority of those engaged in politics are not correctly called political men, for they are not truly political ... [but] embrace this sort of life for profit and gain."[14] Aristotle, in not-so-subtle terms, thus emphasizes the difference between the kind of men who are "in truth" honorable and the kind of men who are commonly honored in public life. Aristotle's great-souled man thus comes to the fore as the most excellent man among political men, the great political actor or statesman *par excellence*. As such, he deserves the highest honors of men.

The great-souled man's concern with honors is qualified, however, in some decisive respects. He is neither unduly preoccupied with, nor overly pleased by, the reception of honors. Quite the contrary, he takes moderate pleasure in honors and even then only when they come from "serious human beings," since he recognizes that "there could be no honor worthy of complete virtue."[15] As the last phrase indicates, greatness of soul "seems to

---

12. Ibid., 1124a3–4.

13. Ibid., 115b12–13.

14. Aristotle, *Eudemian Ethics*, 1216a23–27.

15. Aristotle, *Nicomachean Ethics*, 1124a8–9.

be like a kind of *cosmos* of the virtues."[16] The virtue of magnanimity seems to adorn the other virtues; it appears as the peak of moral virtue, a rare but recognizable form of excellence that the great-souled man wears on his head like a crown. Somewhat perplexingly, however, the reference to magnanimity being a *cosmos* also suggests that it is an ordered "whole" that comprehends all the virtues. Aristotle adds yet another piece to this puzzle by intimating that magnanimity by all accounts seems to include "what is great in each virtue."[17] The likening of greatness of soul to a *cosmos* thus calls attention to an ambiguity concerning that virtue's treatment in the *Ethics*. While the question of whether it crowns or comprehends all of the other virtues remains unclear, Aristotle nevertheless suggests that the virtue of magnanimity is a complete or comprehensive virtue.

Greatness of soul is the first of three moral virtues, the other two being justice and prudence, that Aristotle suggests are comprehensive in character. Juxtaposing Aristotle's accounts of the comprehensive virtues of magnanimity in Book IV and justice in Book V brings to light a tension that apparently plagues the life of the great-souled man. Like greatness of soul, justice also "is often held" to be "the greatest of the virtues."[18] Aristotle distinguishes between two senses of justice. In its comprehensive sense, the virtue of justice includes all of the moral virtues.[19] It represents "not a part of virtue but the whole of virtue."[20] Understood in this way, justice is associated with law-abidingness.[21] But in its more narrow sense, justice designates a particular virtue. Justice understood in this way denotes a concern with the equal (*to ison*). It reflects a specific form that justice can, and to some extent does, take in regimes.

The initial equation of complete or comprehensive justice with the virtue of law-abidingness, however, proves to be problematic upon closer scrutiny. For Aristotle further draws a distinction between what is "just unqualifiedly (*to haplos dikaion*)" and what is just in "the political sense."[22] Political life necessarily cobbles together the natural and the conventional: "of the just in the political sense, one part is natural, the other, conventional."[23] Governing free and equal men who share a common life together and who are capable of "ruling and being ruled" in turn, the type of justice one finds embodied in the laws of actual cities, ultimately falls short of the kind of justice that would inform "the best regime," the regime "in accord with na-

16. Ibid., 1124a1–2.   17. Ibid., 1123b30.
18. Ibid., 1129b29.   19. Ibid., 1129b25–30.
20. Ibid., 1130a8–10.   21. Ibid., 1129b19–25.
22. Ibid., 1134a24–26.   23. Ibid., 1134b18–19.

ture."[24] Political justice, in other words, cannot perfectly achieve the lofty goals demanded by a strict adherence to justice. And yet it does allow for a way of life—and hence a place in nature, namely, the city—where men can (most perfectly) cultivate the excellences of their given nature. Both "in living together and in sharing in speeches and actions,"[25] political life points to a natural end that transcends the real but humanly limited good of "mere life," that is, a life lived for self-preservation. Inasmuch as it provides the indispensable floorboards and some of the walling—but not the ceilings[26]—of citizens' and statesmen's aspirations to excellence, political justice helps secure the grounds of political life's humanizing pursuit of the just and the noble.[27]

Whereas the justice operative in actual regimes seeks to rule the mutual relations between free and equal citizens, magnanimity points not to an established equality among citizens but rather to a great and important difference between them. It is the virtue of the man whose special form of greatness recognizably elevates him above his fellow citizens. Juxtaposing the "two virtues," Ronna Burger perceptively observes, expresses "two independent principles—the just as a principle of equalization and the *kalon* as a principle of distinction—each of which, in its claim to represent the whole of ethical virtue, stands in potential conflict with the other."[28] This is reflected in the *Politics*'s discussion of the problem raised by the presence of a man of outstanding virtue, whose very presence in the city raises the question of whether he should be allowed to rule or should be ostracized. Viewed together, Aristotle's treatments of the comprehensive virtues of magnanimity and justice permit his reader to reflect upon the twin peaks of moral virtue from two related perspectives, namely, in terms of the most preeminent citizens within actual regimes and in terms of the way of life that binds all citizens and statesmen together in cities.

The complicated relation that the magnanimous man has with his fellow citizens is further analyzed in Aristotle's treatment of magnanimity in the *Posterior Analytics*. In that work, Aristotle brings up magnanimity amidst a discussion of the use of equivocal terms. This virtue is used there to illustrate such an equivocation. Aristotle juxtaposes, on the one hand, Alcibiades, Achilles, and Ajax—real and poetically portrayed political men who

24. Ibid., 1135a5.

25. Ibid., 1126b11–12.

26. See Leo Strauss, "On Natural Law," in *Studies in Platonic Political Philosophy*, ed. Thomas Pangle (Chicago: University of Chicago Press, 1983), 140.

27. Aristotle, *Nicomachean Ethics*, 1094b13.

28. Ronna Burger, *Aristotle's Dialogue with Socrates: On the* Nicomachean Ethics (Chicago: University of Chicago Press, 2008), 84.

performed great deeds on the battlefield and who were unwilling to succumb to political dishonor (to the point that their unwillingness to suffer dishonor finally pitted them against their fellow soldiers or citizens),[29] with Lysander and Socrates, on the other, two men who remained "unaffected by good and bad fortune."[30] Of the five men mentioned here, Socrates alone failed to distinguish himself in political life. If Socrates is a model of magnanimity, he is not a particularly political model, at least as that term is generally understood and used in the *Ethics*'s account of greatness of soul.

Aristotle's remarks in the *Posterior Analytics* raise the specter of a form of greatness of soul that is not explicitly political but instead unmistakably philosophic. Like its political counterpart, the possession of philosophic magnanimity would seem to engender an uneasy relationship between its possessor and his fellow citizens. Despite his claim to be a good—perhaps even the best of—citizens, Socrates's fate resoundingly testifies to the conflict the citizens of democratic Athens believed they had with the philosopher. Yet it also seems that, to the extent that Socrates understood philosophic greatness of soul and the good it pursues to be informed by an order that transcends the horizons of the moral and political life, it enabled him not to call direct attention to the distance that separated him from his fellow citizens. Socrates, we should recall, was famous for his use of irony. Although the depreciation of one's own abilities and worth can be a vice, the studied, ironic understatement of one's true greatness, a practice Aristotle explicitly identifies with Socrates, can be a "refined" and effective way of avoiding the ire of others who take exception to one who appears pretentious.[31]

Aristotle brings Book IV's treatment of magnanimity to a close by describing a series of traits that seem to characterize the magnanimous man as magnanimous man. What we could call "the surface presentation" of these traits casts many of them in a less than flattering light. Aristotle here does not go out of his way to soften this impression. Some of these traits appear to be amusing. The magnanimous man is said to speak in a deep, firm voice and possess a slow, deliberate gait. Other traits amplify the impression that the great-souled man consciously maintains a remarkably attenuated connection to those with whom he must live. He, for instance, remembers the favors he has done for others, but "not those that have been done" for him.[32] Still other traits call into question the limits of viewing human beings and

29. See Tessitore, *Reading Aristotle's* Ethics, 32–33.
30. Aristotle, *Posterior Analytics*, 97b25.
31. Aristotle, *Nicomachean Ethics*, 1127b25–26.
32. Ibid., 1124b14–15.

the life of virtue simply within the moral/political horizon. Aristotle states that the magnanimous man is not prone to feel admiration[33] and that in his view "nothing is great."[34] On this score, Book IV's magnanimous man proves to be further unlike the Socrates spoken of in the *Posterior Analytics* whose capacity for admiration is connected to his ability, as Aristophanes and Plato note, to wonder about the things "aloft." As if to further emphasize this fact, Aristotle remarks that the great-souled man chooses to possess "beautiful and useless things more than useful and beneficial ones, for this is more the mark of a self-sufficient person" (*autarchia*).[35]

The magnanimous man's belief in his own self-sufficiency, that is, his belief that he is a whole unto himself, moves him away from the demands of both justice and truth. While relating that the great-souled man fails to remember the good deeds that others have done for him, Aristotle invokes the Homeric images of Thetis and Zeus. Thetis did not remind Zeus, the king of the gods, of the favors she had done for him.[36] That would have displeased him, by bringing before him evidence of his need for others. The magnanimous man's belief in his Zeus-like self-sufficiency proves to be as untrue of him as it is of the Olympian god himself. It is tenable only as long as the great-souled man chooses to ignore the fact that he is dependent upon the city he inhabits and, by extension, upon his fellow citizens, for the very venue in which he can put his particular form of virtue on display. In this respect he *is* reminiscent of Aristophanes's Socrates, inasmuch as the magnanimous man too is depicted as being radically unappreciative of the social, moral, and political preconditions that allow for his particular way of life. Moreover, the magnanimous man's belief in his own self-sufficiency requires him to deny the role that chance seems to play in the exercise of magnanimity: for the exercise of greatness of soul necessarily requires one to live in a place and at a time when great deeds are both needed and can be performed. In short, as Robert Faulkner eloquently points out, Aristotle allows us to see how the "great-souled forget their dependence and, like Shakespeare's Caesar, incline to imagine themselves gods."[37]

The account of magnanimity given in the *Ethics* thus cuts both ways. Insofar as it invites us to reflect upon the magnanimous man as he actually comes to sight in political life, the reader is able to catch a glimpse of the full array of qualities and tensions that typify such a man. This is one of the great strengths of Aristotle's presentation of magnanimity in Book IV of the *Ethics*.

33. Ibid., 1125a2–3. 34. Ibid., 1125a4.

35. Ibid., 1125a11–12. 36. See Homer, *Iliad*, I, 503–4.

37. Robert Faulkner, *The Case for Greatness: Honorable Ambition and Its Critics* (New Haven, Conn.: Yale University Press, 2007), 42.

Aristotle's complex portrayal of the great-souled man simultaneously elicits our admiration for this rare man's qualities and deeds, even as it lays bare, and forces us to recoil from, those bumptious and problematic characteristics that mark the lives of the magnanimous men one encounters in political life.

In his commentary on Aristotle's *Nicomachean Ethics*, Aquinas does not pass over in silence the less attractive features of Aristotle's portrait of the magnanimous man.[38] For the most part, he carefully explicates the surface argument of Aristotle's text. He does, however, conspicuously smooth out some of this character's more noticeable rough edges. That Aquinas consistently does so indicates that he is well aware of what he is doing in the commentary. The tactic that he takes in this work is in keeping with his acknowledged effort in the *Summa theologiae* to reflect upon the virtue of magnanimity not principally as it comes to sight in the person of the *Ethic*'s great-souled man, but rather in a context that is not as studiously limited to the moral and intellectual confines that characterize the city and political life as such. His argument quietly but firmly has the overall effect of minimizing the opportunity for the political order to arrogate to itself the sole horizon or responsibility to determine the content of moral virtue. The thrust behind this approach is captured by Aquinas's remark in his commentary, which finds no exact parallel in the *Ethics*, that the magnanimous man's "whole attention is taken up with the goods of the community and God."[39]

Aquinas's effort to widen the sphere in which magnanimity (*magnanimitas*) is viewed vividly comes to sight in his comments on Aristotle's claim that the magnanimous man thinks nothing great and is not prone to admiration. Whereas Aristotle had left it at saying that "nothing is great" to the magnanimous man, Aquinas remarks that "there is nothing great for him among the things that can happen *externally*, because his whole life is busy with internal goods, which are truly great."[40] This statement is in keeping with his general tendency in this commentary to affirm and maintain the great-souled man's capacity to discriminate between "external" and "internal" goods. For example, when Aristotle asks, "why would someone to whom nothing is great do anything shameful,"[41] Aquinas remarks that the great-souled man "does not place so great a value on any external thing

---

38. Aquinas, *Commentary on Aristotle's* Nicomachean Ethics, trans. C. I. Litzinger (Notre Dame, Ind.: Dumb Ox Books, 1993), 171–82.

39. Ibid., 779.

40. Ibid., 777.

41. Aristotle, *Nicomachean Ethics*, 1123b32.

(*rem exteriorem*) that he would wish to do a shameful action for it."[42] Along similar lines, when Aristotle notes that the magnanimous man's deep and steady voice and deliberate and measured walk reflect the fact that one who thinks nothing great does not get excited, Aquinas states that the great-souled man "holds nothing external of value."[43] To be sure, the magnanimous man found in Book IV of the *Ethics* is genuinely concerned with what Aquinas here refers to as internal goods. The great-souled man is repeatedly said to be drawn to and actively to pursue virtue, the *kalon* and the good. But it cannot be overlooked that in the cases mentioned above, Aquinas consistently chooses to accentuate the great-souled man's active discrimination between external and internal goods in a way that Aristotle, for whatever reason, chooses not to accentuate in the corresponding passages in the *Ethics*.

Aristotle, as well as Plato's Socrates, affirms that philosophy begins in wonder.[44] Wonder is the spark that ignites a life that pursues an activity, the contemplation of *something greater than one's self*, namely, "the whole," that is ultimately done for its own sake. In contrast to his reference to Socrates in the *Posterior Analytics*, Aristotle in Book IV of the *Ethics* remains silent about the magnanimous man's interest in, or actual pursuit of, philosophic activities. His incapacity to wonder in fact would argue against it. In other words, the magnanimous man appears to be a model of a particular kind of human excellence, the kind of excellence that can and ought to be pursued in political life. He excels and shines in the realm of action, more specifically, in the realm of great action.

Aristotle's announcement at the opening of Book VII of the *Ethics* that he now makes a new beginning, however, signals that the question of virtue and human flourishing needs to be examined from a different perspective, other than that of the gentleman's, if it is to be treated adequately. In the sequel, the best judge of virtue and human flourishing turns out to be the "one who engages in philosophic inquiry about politics." Thus, somewhat unexpectedly, the political philosopher is announced as "the architect of the end with a view to which we speak of each thing as being bad or good in an unqualified sense."[45] It is the philosophic life—the life of Socrates, not the

---

42. Aquinas, *Commentary on Aristotle's* Nicomachean Ethics, 747.

43. Ibid., 782.

44. See Aristotle, *Metaphysics*, 982b12; and Plato, *Theaetetus*, 155d.

45. Aristotle, *Nicomachean Ethics*, 1152b1–3. For an account of one way in which this new beginning or "another beginning" at the opening of Book VII reverberates back on Aristotle's previous arguments in Books I–VI see my "Aristotle on Pleasure and Political Philosophy: A Study in Book VII of the *Nicomachean Ethics*," *Interpretation: A Journal of Political Philosophy* 24:2 (Winter, 1997): 171–82.

life of Alcibiades or Ajax or Achilles or Lysander—that is seen to possess the greatest kind of greatness of soul. The account of virtue given in the preceding six books of the *Ethics*, Aristotle intimates at this point, must be returned to and each of its claims about the nature of virtue and happiness must now be reexamined in light of Aristotle's announced second sailing.

It is then rather remarkable that in his commentary on Book IV Aquinas indicates that the magnanimous man is prone to speculative reflection. Aquinas, as Mary Keys pointedly notes, in this case "endeavors" to paint "magnanimity in the context of a more unified, harmonious existence, indicating that greatness of soul conduces to both moral and intellectual excellence."[46] Amid a discussion of pusillanimity, a vice opposed to magnanimity that inclines a man to resist engaging "in great things" rightly and "according to their dignity,"[47] Aquinas straightforwardly states that those who "are ignorant of their worth ... suffer ... damage to their goodness ... they abandon works of virtue and the pursuit of speculative truths, as if they were unfitted for and unequal to things of this kind."[48] Aquinas strongly implies that the great-souled man is not simply defined by the realm of political life, even the heights or peaks of that life's honorable pursuit of the just and the *kalon*. While undoubtedly presented only in passing, the image of greatness of soul hinted at here reflects a greater degree of wholeness or completion than the tension-ridden account of the magnanimous man that Aristotle gives in Book IV of the *Ethics*.

Aquinas's account of magnanimity in the *Summa theologiae* leaves little doubt that he sees something inadequate, and in important respects distorting, about viewing greatness of soul predominantly in terms of the political order.[49] It also leaves little doubt that he reads Aristotle's account of magnanimity in Book IV of the *Ethics* as doing just this. Addressing the disposition of humility (a virtue, it should be noted, not explicitly mentioned in the *Ethics*) to moderate exaggerated and misguided hopes, Aquinas states that the Philosopher "intended to treat of virtues as directed to civic life, where the subjection of one man to another is defined according to the ordinance of the law, and is consequently a matter of legal justice."[50] Aquinas's own account of magnanimity in the *Summa theologiae* refuses to treat magnanimity principally in terms defined by the political order. Instead, it insists upon situating this virtue in a natural order of justice that informs political life

---

46. Keys, *Aquinas, Aristotle, and the Promise of the Common Good*, 151.
47. Aquinas, *Commentary on* Nicomachean Ethics, 786.
48. Ibid., 787.
49. Aquinas, *ST* II-II, q. 129.
50. Ibid., q. 161, a. 1, ad 5.

even as it transcends the limits of political life. As Ernest Fortin notes, by so doing Aquinas settles the "issue between justice and magnanimity" unambiguously "in favor of justice" in a way that Aristotle in his *Ethics* does not.[51]

In the *Summa theologiae*, Aquinas presents magnanimity as a part of courage or fortitude. Courage, one of the four cardinal virtues, helps perfect the irascible appetite.[52] By putting reason into the irascible passions, it strengthens a man's resolve to persevere in the good in the face of hardship and the "dangers of death."[53] Building on this line of thought, Aquinas states that magnanimity moves a man to take up great deeds and great works in the presence of formidable obstacles and perils. Furthermore, employing the classic distinction between form and matter, Aquinas affirms that "the proper matter" of the virtue of magnanimity "is great honor, and that the magnanimous man tends to such things as are deserving of honor."[54] Here, Aquinas's enlargement of the realm in which the magnanimous man is seen and in which he is said to act starts to become clear. The magnanimous man is explicitly said to exist within, and to be properly related to, a created natural order that transcends the legitimate but limited order that nature upholds in the life of the city. Moreover, even this is connected with the divine. Aquinas notes that there "is in man something great which he possesses through the gift of God.... Accordingly magnanimity makes a man deem himself worthy of great things in consideration of the gifts he holds from God."[55] Viewed in this heightened light, the magnanimous man recognizes that his greatness is something given to him; it is something he possesses but for which he cannot take authorial credit.

Aquinas's magnanimous man thus understands his particular form of greatness to have its roots in a gift he has received from God. The magnanimous man recognizes this dependence as a matter of natural justice. This recognition is in keeping with the natural virtue of religion, "a moral virtue ... [that] is a part of justice."[56] For it belongs to the dictate of natural reason, he argues, that man recognizes that it is God "to Whom we ought to be bound as to our unfailing principle; to Whom also our choice should be resolutely directed as to our last end."[57] The virtue of religion, he insists, "is not a theological virtue whose object is the last end, but a moral virtue which is properly about things referred to the end."[58] In sharp contrast

---

51. Ernest L. Fortin, *Classical Christianity and the Political Order: Reflections on the Theologico-Political Problem*, ed. J. Brian Benestad (Lanham, Md.: Rowman & Littlefield, 1996), 169.

52. *ST* I-II, q. 61.

53. *ST* II-II, q. 129, a. 5.

54. Ibid., a. 2.

55. Ibid., a. 3, ad 4.

56. Ibid., q. 81, a. 5, ad 3.

57. Ibid., a. 1.

58. Ibid., a. 5.

to the great-souled man of Book IV of the *Ethics*, Aquinas's magnanimous man acknowledges not only a cosmos above himself, but a cosmos that is ordered by and to a Being infinitely greater than the magnanimous man himself. That acknowledgment walks hand in hand with Aquinas's claim that the Old Law's moral precept to observe the Sabbath is itself part of the natural law "in so far as it commands man to give some time to the things of God."[59] It also walks hand in hand with his claim that the offering of sacrifices to God is also "of the natural law" inasmuch as this act reflects "natural reason['s]" recognition that man "is subject to a higher being."[60]

Aquinas's magnanimous man, however, not only looks up in a way that the *Ethics*'s great-souled man has great difficulty doing, he also looks around him. He recognizes that he needs "human assistance ... to provide for his own life" in a way that the Aristotelian magnanimous man's exaggerated belief in his self-sufficiency prevents him from doing.[61] This recognition is also demanded by justice; it is a demand of the special virtue of piety.[62] The virtue of piety acknowledges that "man becomes a debtor to other men in various ways, according to their various excellences and the various benefits received by them."[63] After God, all men, including magnanimous men, are said to owe their greatest debts to their parents and their country—not simply for the contributions that one's parents and country make to the preservation of mere life, but more importantly for their contributions to the cultivation of the good life, since the city as city "seeks the highest among all human goods, for it aims at the common, which is better and more divine than the goods of one individual."[64]

A full account of the ways in which the various demands of justice that Aquinas explicitly mentions in the *Summa theologiae*'s thematic account of magnanimity frame his understanding of that virtue would obviously have to take into consideration the complex roles that natural law, human law, and prudence play in his rich reflections on the nature and scope of the realm of human affairs. Such a consideration goes well beyond the bounds of this chapter.[65] But on the basis of what has been said here it should be

---

59. *ST* I-II, q. 100, a. 3, ad 3.

60. *ST* II-II, q. 85, a. 1.

61. Ibid., q. 129, a. 6, ad. 1.

62. Ibid., q. 101, a. 3.

63. Ibid., a. 1.

64. Aquinas, *Commentary on Aristotle's Politics*, trans. Ernest L. Fortin and Peter D. O'Neill, quoted from *Medieval Political Philosophy: A Sourcebook*, ed. Joseph C. Macfarland and Joshua Parens (Ithaca, N.Y.: Cornell University Press, 1991), I, 1, 11.

65. For insightful discussions of the relation between natural law, human law, and prudence in Aquinas's thought see Fortin, *Classical Christianity and the Political Order*, 151–75; 209–15; and 265–86.

clear that Aquinas's treatment of magnanimity and the magnanimous man's relation to his fellow citizens remains in constant contact with his teaching on the natural law. By retaining this connection, Aquinas is able to find room in the city for the magnanimous. Put somewhat differently, Aquinas points to a way in which one can be a magnanimous man and still take part in the ennobling political good that all citizens, the ordinary and the great-souled, substantively share in common.

CHAPTER SIXTEEN

Charles De Koninck and Aquinas's Doctrine of the Common Good

SEBASTIAN WALSHE, O PRAEM

Introduction

Charles De Koninck taught Prof. McInerny at the University of Laval in Quebec in the mid-1950s, and (as those of us who knew him can attest) McInerny considered himself a disciple of De Koninck. In later years, McInerny would express ever-increasing gratitude to De Koninck for the formation he received in Thomistic thought, and was even responsible for editing and publishing the works of his former teacher as an expression of his gratitude.

While De Koninck taught and wrote on virtually every subject that occupied the mind of St. Thomas Aquinas: the philosophy of nature and of the soul, ethics and politics, metaphysics, theology, even mathematics; one of his most significant and lasting contributions to the *philosophia perennis* was his exposition of Aquinas's doctrine of the common good. This chapter aims to impart a clearer and more profound understanding of Aquinas's doctrine of the common good with De Koninck as our guide. To this end, I will first expose some pitfalls that can impede our understanding of Aquinas's doctrine; second, I will lay out some important distinctions which De Koninck proposed as keys to understanding Aquinas's doctrine; and third, I will briefly identify some important ways that this doctrine contributes to theology.

Some Difficulties

There are a number of difficulties that could impede a correct understanding of Aquinas's doctrine on the common good. I will consider three that are particularly important.

The first difficulty facing those who want to understand Aquinas's doctrine on the common good correctly is that Aquinas himself never wrote a treatise dedicated to the common good as such. His discussions of the common good are spread piecemeal throughout his works in widely diverse contexts. Given the difficulty of the subject and the various and contradictory understandings of it even among those who claim to be disciples of Aquinas, the modern student of Aquinas may be left saying to himself: "Alas! if only Aquinas had written a *Quaestio Disputata De Bono Communi.*"[1]

The second difficulty faced by those attempting to attain to a scientific understanding of the common good is the wide latitude of meanings to which the phrase is susceptible.[2] Taken separately, both terms "common" and "good" are used in widely diverse senses: we speak of common sense and of the common wealth; of good ice cream and good arguments. And so when these words are brought together the likelihood of confusion of meanings is not merely added, but multiplied. The highway system, children, world peace, and God are all called common goods. Therefore, a large part of explaining Aquinas's doctrine on the common good is making those distinctions necessary for an accurate understanding of the meaning or meanings Aquinas had in mind in the different contexts in which he wrote.

A third difficulty encountered in coming to a distinct understanding of the common good is arriving at a sapiential perspective on the common good: that is, not only understanding the distinct meanings of the expression "common good," but ordering those meanings in such a way as to see which meaning or meanings are primary and of most interest to the wise man. The meaning of the common good in which Aquinas was most interested, the sense which he identified as most profound and important in both philosophy and theology, is a meaning very far removed from our senses or imagination. It is therefore a meaning less known to us. And since the human mind habitually falls back upon better-known meanings of

1. It is of interest to note that one of St. Thomas Aquinas's contemporaries, Remigio de Girolomi, did indeed write a treatise on the common good which includes a number of objections and replies.

2. See G. Froelich, "The Equivocal Status of Bonum Commune," *The New Scholasticism* 63 (Winter, 1989): 38–57; and "On Common Goods," *The Aquinas Review* 15 (2008): 1–26.

words, we must constantly be on our guard not to confuse a better-known meaning with the one we are seeking to treat here. Our task therefore is to order those meanings in such a way as to lead the mind from those pedestrian meanings of the expression, which are better known *quoad nos*, to that most intelligible and proper concept of the common good most relevant to wisdom.

As we shall see, it is precisely because De Koninck was keenly aware of these three difficulties that he is such a valuable guide to understanding Aquinas's doctrine on the common good.

Approaching an Understanding of the Common Good

The first things to which we give the name "good" are sensible goods and the pleasures that accompany them. Ice cream and warm hugs are good in this sense. We find that we have a natural desire to possess them and rest in them. As we grow and become aware of things beyond the realm of sense experience, we start to recognize that we also have a desire for these non-sensible things as well: we desire our parent's love and approval; we desire justice (children, even at a very young age, will insist that they be treated fairly); we desire to know the truth. These things are not the same kind of things as sensible goods, but since they too are objects of our desires, we give them the same name "good," but with the vague realization that they are not good in the same sense of the word. After some time, as we reflect more upon our experience of the world, we recognize that in all things there seem to be natural inclinations to act and be acted upon. Rocks tend downward. Plants tend to grow and reproduce. New life, seeds and embryos, tend to develop from the imperfect toward the perfect. We see that they tend toward determinate ends, and because those ends are like the objects of our desires, we call them "goods" as well. And so a new meaning of the word "good" comes to be, different, but related, to our original meaning. We say that it is good for a tree to bear fruit and even for a rock to be down. This final application of the term good is universal, and one could even say "metaphysical," since it is applied to all beings: it belongs to being, as being.

Bound up in our experience of these different but related goods is the experience of cause and effect. We notice that these goods are somehow a cause of the actions (and sometimes even the very being) of the things for which they are good. The good ice cream is a cause of my opening the freezer and scooping a heaping bowlful for myself after dinner. This is not to deny that sometimes goods can also be effects. But observe that even when we notice that some good is an effect, it is also a cause in a different way: the good music is an effect of the skill of the musician who produces it; but it is also the reason why he acquires and employs his skill. Health is the effect of walking, but it can also be the cause for which someone walks. Natural things too appear to act for the sake of goods, as if the good is somehow a cause of the activities or being of natural things. Even if philosophers of nature and natural scientists disagree about whether the good really is a cause in nature, they all agree that it looks that way at face value; and naturalists from Empedocles to Darwin and beyond have devised intricate theories to explain why these appearances are merely that: apparent but not real. So the idea that the good is somehow a cause, even among non-rational beings, is where we start: it is something very familiar to us.

Let this suffice for a first approach to the idea of that which is good. The good is what is desirable, the object of an intrinsic inclination. And it is somehow also experienced or perceived as a cause.

Key Distinctions

When Aquinas spoke about a common good as contrasted with a private good, what precisely did he mean by the terms "good" and "common"? Here is where De Koninck serves as an invaluable guide. As I mentioned before, Aquinas never wrote a systematic treatise on the common good. His texts are found scattered though dozens of works in various contexts. In his work "On the Primacy of the Common Good: Against the Personalists,"[3] and in his more polemical "In Defense of Aquinas"[4] which followed, De Koninck brought together many of the most important texts of Aquinas on this question. In these works, De Koninck makes a number of key distinctions (themselves found in Aquinas) in order to lay out Aquinas's doctrine clearly and in order. Here I shall focus on three key distinctions.

Distinction 1: Integral Whole vs. Universal Whole vs. Potential Whole

Since that which is common is universal and a kind of whole, one key distinction that De Koninck uses to interpret Aquinas's doctrine on the common good is the distinction among the kinds of wholes. Aquinas distinguishes three chief kinds of wholes and corresponding parts: the integral whole, the universal whole, and the potential whole. Here is one text explaining the distinction:

3. *The Aquinas Review* 4:1 (1997): 1–70; hereafter PCG.
4. *The Aquinas Review* 4:1 (1997): 171–349; hereafter DST.

The division of the [angelic] hierarchies into orders is of a potestative whole into its potential parts, just as the soul is divided into its powers: and this whole is as if a medium between the universal whole and the integral whole. For the universal whole is in each of its parts according to essence and complete power, hence it is predicated equally of each of its parts. But the integral whole is not in each of its parts according either to essence or complete power, and therefore, it is in no way predicated of its parts. But the potential whole is present according to essence in each of its parts, but it is present according to complete power [only] in its highest part, since the superior power always has in itself more completely those things which are in the inferior powers.[5]

De Koninck is aware that of the three kinds of whole, the integral is best known, the universal second best known, and the potential whole is least known to us. A sign of this is that Aquinas explains the potential whole by means of the other two. As I mentioned before, we have a tendency to fall back upon meanings of terms that are better known to us. And thus we should expect that the less known senses of the term "whole" will sometimes be confused with the better known senses of the term "whole." An interesting example of this is found in the Platonic dialogue *Parmenides*. There the young Socrates attempts to defend his doctrine of universals against the objections of the older, wiser Parmenides. At one point in the dialogue, Parmenides tricks Socrates into confusing the universal whole with the integral whole: Socrates falls back upon a better-known sense of the word "whole," after which he finds himself in a maze of contradictions.

It is not surprising, therefore, that when there is talk of the common good, what comes first to mind is a kind of aggregate or sum of private goods. Indeed, this is one legitimate sense of the expression (for example, Aquinas speaks of this kind of common good in relation to distributive justice).[6] But it is not the most profound or metaphysically important sense of common good. The sense of common good that we are after is that which is most of all the perfection of beings, especially persons, and which is the foundation for societies of persons. Explaining why the common good is not an aggregate or sum total of singular goods, De Koninck says: "The common good is greater not because it includes the singular good of all the singulars. In that case, it would not have the unity of the common good which comes from a certain kind of universality in the latter, but would merely be a collection, and only materially better than the singular good."[7] The good which is the foundation of society, on the other hand, is common

5. *In II Sent.*, d. 9, q. 1, a. 3, ad 1.
6. See, for example, Aquinas, *Summa theologiae* II-II, q. 61, a. 1, ad 1.
7. PCG, 16.

as a perfective cause: one whose essence belongs to each member of the society.

The common good is not a good other than the good of the particulars, a good that is merely a good of the collectivity looked upon as a kind of singular. In that case, it would be common only accidentally; properly speaking it would be singular. But when we distinguish the common good from the particular good, we do not mean thereby that it is not the good of the particulars; if it were not, then it would not be truly common.[8]

Confusion of a good which is common as a collection and a good which is common as a cause perfecting the particulars to which it is communicated can result in serious errors. De Koninck identifies totalitarianism as one of these errors: "In totalitarian regimes, the common good is singularized, and it is opposed as a more powerful singular to the singulars which are purely and simply subjected. The common good loses its distinctive character; it becomes alien. It becomes subordinate to this monster of modern invention which is called the State."[9]

Also to be avoided is the confusion of the common good as a cause, which is a potential whole, with the good common only according to predication.[10] The name "good" can be said of many individuals, and this is to be common, or universal, in predication. On the other hand, the good can be a real, determinate being and a universal cause in things. The good which is universal in predication is less distinct and determinate than the specific goods receiving the universal name "good." In contrast, the good which is a cause and a potestative whole is the reason for the determination and specificity in the goods it causes. For example, the good of victory determines completely the order and movements of all the parts of the army. These orders and movements are themselves certain intermediate goods caused by the determinate victory toward which they are ordained: each one is chosen only to the extent that it seems to lead to the good of victory.

The common good which, according to De Koninck, is of most interest to the wise man, that good which is the foundation for the society of rational beings and the whole order of the universe, is a good common as a cause and potential whole,[11] taking potential here in the sense of an active power. As Aquinas teaches:

8. Ibid., 17.

9. Ibid., 66. One thinks immediately of the Leviathan of Hobbes, whom De Koninck most certainly had in mind as he wrote this passage.

10. On this distinction see R. MacArthur, "Universal *in Praedicando*, Universal *in Causando*," *Laval Théologique et Philosophique* 18.1 (1962): 59–95.

11. See, for example, DST, 233.

Something can be called common in two ways. In one way through predication. But in this way the common is not the same in number in the diverse instances.... The other way is something common according to participation of one and the same thing according to number. And this community is most of all able to be found in those things which pertain to the soul, since through it there is reached that which is the good common to all things, namely God.[12]

Distinction 2: The Good as Efficient Cause and the Good as Final Cause

Another key distinction is between the good understood as final cause and the good understood as efficient cause.[13] De Koninck begins "The Primacy of the Common Good" with these lines: "The good is what all things desire insofar as they desire their perfection. Therefore, the good has a notion of a final cause."[14] Later, in his work "In Defense of Aquinas," De Koninck adds further that "it should be clear that the most proper and profound meaning of the term 'good' is *perfectivum alterius per modum finis*."[15] The good is not any cause, but the final cause which is perfective of the thing for which it is good.

Let us look in greater detail at this distinction. De Koninck brings forth two texts of Aquinas that are especially important in understanding the distinction between the good as final cause and the good as efficient cause. The first is taken from the *Summa contra Gentiles*:

The communication of being (*esse*) and goodness proceeds from goodness. Which indeed is clear both from the nature itself of the good, and from its notion. For naturally the good of any one thing is its act and perfection. Moreover, anything acts from this: that it is in act. Furthermore, by acting it pours out being (*esse*) and goodness into other things. Hence, also it is a sign of perfection of something that it is able to produce its like: as is clear from the Philosopher in the fourth book of the Meteorology. But the notion of the good is from this: that it is desirable. This is the end, which also moves an agent to acting. Because of which the good is said to be diffusive of itself and of being (*esse*).[16]

In this text the good is considered under two aspects, its nature and its notion or definition (*ratio*). According to its nature a good thing is something in act, and it therefore has the capacity to move other things from potency

---

12. *In IV Sent.*, d. 49, q. 1, a.1a, obj. 3 and ad 3. Also see *Summa contra Gentiles*, Bk. III, c. 17.

13. Beginning in 1992, with an article published by W. N. Clarke ("Person, Being and St. Thomas," *Communio* 19: 601–18), a series of debates emerged on this issue, including contributions by D. L. Schindler, S. Long, G. A. Blair, and B. T. Blankenhorn. For a summary of the debate see B. T. Blankenhorn, "The Good as Self-Diffusive in Thomas Aquinas," *Angelicum* 79.4 (2002): 803–37.

14. PCG, 14.

15. DST, 253.

16. *SCG* I, 37.

to act as an efficient cause. According to its proper notion or definition, however, the good is something desirable. Under this latter formality, the good is a cause in another mode. Aquinas makes this clear in a second text from his *De veritate*:

> When it is said that the good is diffusive according to its notion, diffusion is not to be understood as it implies the operation of an efficient cause, but as it implies the relationship of a final cause. And such a diffusion is not by the mediation of some super-added power. Moreover, the good signifies the diffusion of a final cause, and not of an agent cause: first since an efficient [cause], insofar as it is such, is not the measure and perfection of a thing, but rather its beginning, and then since the effect participates in the efficient cause according to assimilation of form only, but a thing obtains the end according to its whole being (*esse*), and the notion of the good consists in this.[17]

Here Aquinas carefully distinguishes what is meant by the self-diffusion of the good as final cause from the self-diffusion of an efficient cause. While implying that the notion of self-diffusion is more apparent to us in the case of efficient cause, he nevertheless denies that all self-diffusion of causes is reduced to a kind of efficient causality. More than this, he even indicates that the more profound sense of self-diffusion is attributed to the good as final cause, for the good brings the *whole* being to its *whole* perfection.

In summary, it can be said that the good, as something in act (which every good thing is), diffuses itself by way of efficient and exemplar causality.[18] It can even be said that this is the sense of diffusion which is better known to us. This explains why we tend to fall back upon this sense in which the good is a cause.[19] De Koninck was aware of this and was careful to keep in mind that the good, considered precisely *as good*, diffuses itself not as an efficient cause, but by way of final causality.[20]

For De Koninck, the failure of many modern philosophers to account correctly for the relationship between the person and society results from a failure to approach the problem from the perspective of final causality:

17. Aquinas, *De veritate*, q. 21, a. 1, ad 4.

18. See *ST* I, q. 19, a. 2, c.

19. This seems to have been the cause of one of the more serious errors of Fr. Eschmann, to whom De Koninck was responding in this article.

20. Upon close examination it becomes apparent that these two modalities of self-diffusion of the good have a determinate order to each other. The final cause is the cause of the causality of the efficient cause. If the good were not diffusive, as good (i.e., by way of final causality), it would not be diffusive as something actual (i.e., by way of efficient causality), for the very inclination which is correlated to the good in the subject which desires the good is the principle of acting in that subject. Without this inclination, without some determinate end, the agent would have no reason to act one way rather than another, and so it would not act at all. Moreover, by being drawn closer to the end which is its good a being becomes more and more actual, and hence, more and more capable of acting upon others by way of efficient causality.

Instead of discussing the problem in terms of "person" and "society," I approach it in the fundamental terms of "proper good" and "common good." Ultimately, person and society are not to be judged by what they *are* absolutely, but by what is their perfection, *i.e.*, by what is their good; that is the only way in which Aristotle and Aquinas ever discussed this problem. To look upon the absolute comparison of the person and society as the most basic consideration is distinctly modern. It is also distinctly modern to accord absolute priority to the subject.[21]

Distinction 3: The Good Perfecting the Speculative Intellect vs. the Good Perfecting the Practical Intellect

The third distinction which De Koninck lays out is the distinction between the good as perfective of the rational creature in the speculative order and the good as perfecting the rational creature in the practical order. De Koninck understands Aquinas to teach that in the speculative order and the order of separated substances, the primacy of the common good has its truest application. Here is the text of Aquinas, with the objection first followed by his response.

It appears that beatitude consists more in an act of the practical intellect than of the speculative intellect. For to the degree that some good is more common, so much more is it divine, as is clear in the first book of the *Ethics*. But the good of the speculative intellect singularly belongs to him who beholds, while the good of the practical intellect is able to be common to many. Therefore, beatitude consists more in the practical intellect than in the speculative intellect.

And now for the response:

To the first objection it ought to be said that the good to which the speculative intellect is united through cognition is more common than the good to which the practical intellect is united, inasmuch as the speculative intellect is more separated from the particular than the practical intellect whose cognition is perfected in an operation which consists in singulars.[22]

---

21. DST, 319.

22. *In IV Sent.*, d. 49, q. 1, a. 1, obj. 1 & ad 1. Aquinas goes on in his response to make further precisions which do not, however, alter the first observation he made in the beginning of his response. He adds: "But this is true, that the attainment of the end to which the speculative intellect arrives, inasmuch as it is such, is proper to the one attaining; but the attainment of the end which the practical intellect intends is able to be proper and common, inasmuch as through the practical intellect someone directs both himself and others to the end, as is clear in the ruler of a multitude. But someone from the fact that he beholds, is himself singularly directed unto the end of speculation. However, the end itself of the speculative intellect surpasses the good of the practical intellect as much as its singular attainment exceeds the common attainment of the good of the practical intellect. And therefore, the most perfect beatitude consists in the speculative intellect." This part of the response overcomes the fallacy of transgressing genera or orders of good. For it is true that a private good of a higher order may be preferable to a common good of a lower order.

De Koninck comments:

Aquinas avoids distinguishing the major ("Quanto aliquod bonum est communius tanto est divinius") [To the degree that a good is more common, so much more is it divine]. On the contrary, he shows that the *dictum authenticum* applies more perfectly to the good of the speculative intellect than to that of the practical. And we must note carefully that Aquinas calls "communius," not the good which consists in the *act* of the speculative intellect, but the "bonum *cui* intellectus speculativus *conjungitur* per cognitionem," [the good to which the speculative intellect is united through cognition] and this is objective beatitude. The good of the speculative intellect as such is more common because it is formally more abstract, more separated from the singularity of the operable which involves potentiality, and hence, more communicable.[23]

If one considers the dictum "The more common a good is, the more divine it is" accepting "good" here to mean that which is perfective of another as an object and end, then the dictum holds more perfectly in the speculative order since the notion of diffusion and communicability can be more perfectly applied to that which is more separated from matter and particulars. So the common good in this most profound sense extends even beyond the moral sciences: it is a cause which extends to being as such. The words of Aristotle at the beginning of his *Metaphysics* are to the point: "The supreme science, and superior to any subordinate science, is the one which knows that for the sake of which each thing must be done. And this is the good in each case, and in general the highest good in the whole of nature … it is this science which must investigate the first principles and causes, and the good or final cause, is one of the causes."[24] I think this is a point on which the eminent Thomist Jacques Maritain was in error. According to Maritain, the good of the speculative order, as opposed to a good of the practical order, is not a common good in the strict sense.[25] Maritain seems to fall back upon a more known sense of the term "good," which prevents

23. DST, 312.

24. Aristotle, *Metaphysics*, Book A, chap. 2, 982b5–10. This text comes at the end of an argument in which Aristotle reasons from a nominal definition of wisdom (the best kind of knowledge) to an essential definition of wisdom (the knowledge of the first and most universal cause or causes). And since the final cause is the cause of the causality of the other genera of causes, Aristotle ultimately concludes in this text that wisdom is most of all a knowledge of that good which is the ultimate cause of being as such.

25. Maritain argues that not only is the principle "the common good is more divine than the private good" to be understood analogously but also that its primary analogate is found in its application to human society and human goods. Aquinas gives this *dictum authenticum* "its full value in strictly social matters" (PCG, 19–20). He applies the same principle later in the same work where he states: "The common good of the intellects can be understood in two ways: in the first way, it is truth and beauty themselves, through the enjoyment of which minds receive a certain natural irradiation or participation of the Uncreated Truth and Beauty or of the separated common good. This common good of the intellects is obviously superior to the

him from appreciating the full amplitude and import of the common good: a good which is not only the foundation for every society of rational beings, men and angels, but is absolutely first in the whole order of causes.[26]

Applications to the Science of Theology

It is not difficult to see the importance of this doctrine on the common good for the science of theology. The goodness of God is the ultimate explanatory principle of all his works, both of nature and grace. Moreover, the whole of moral theology in particular begins and ends with a consideration of God as our beatitude. De Koninck makes clear that, for Aquinas, the object of this beatitude is formally attained as a common good in the line of final causality.[27] This explains why the theological virtue of charity necessarily has a social dimension: we are to love God precisely as he is communicable to others.

This doctrine on the common good also is crucial for formulating a correct understanding of the Church in relation to its members. The Church has as its principle of unity that very same good which is the beatitude of

personal act by which each intellect conquers a fragment of it; but it is not a social good, a common good in the strict sense" (PCG, 73).

26. It seems to me that the explanation for Maritain's particular reading of Aquinas on this point stems from an approach to metaphysics that tends to ignore the role of essences and causality in favor of being. While, according to Aquinas, being *qua* being is the subject-genus of metaphysics and while the distinction between *esse* and essence is fundamental for Aquinas, there is much more to a science than its subject. Neither is being the most fundamental consideration for every metaphysical problem. Indeed, for Aquinas metaphysics is first of all wisdom, and wisdom has to do with the first causes, especially the final cause since it is the first among causes. A metaphysical approach which restricts itself to the consideration of being and the *actus essendi*, which pertains properly to the consideration of formal causality, is impoverished precisely because it cannot account for the whole of reality, from pure act to pure potency.

27. This is something that Fr. Eschmann failed to understand, and it resulted in serious errors. Fr. Eschmann, as De Koninck points out, has understood *bonum universale in causando* to refer only to causes in the line of efficient and exemplary causality, the causality by which God causes goodness in others. He failed to recognize or understand the many texts where Aquinas shows that, most properly, *bonum universale in causando* refers to a common good in the line of final cause. As a consequence, Fr. Eschmann concludes that our participation in the divine goodness is not by way of final causality. Moreover, God is not formally a common good for beatified souls, but a private, personal good. But if this is so, the goodness of the beatified soul will be formally the same as God's goodness, so that the divine goodness is wholly communicated to the beatified soul. That is to say, the beatified creature becomes as good as God himself! And hence, it would be false to say that God should be loved more than the saints, or that we ought to love ourselves or the saints for God's sake. It is not difficult to see the harm which comes from such an error. Germain Grisez carries the consequences of this error further, arguing at one point that "strictly speaking, God is not the ultimate end toward which we should direct our lives." From *The Restless-Heart Blunder*, 2005 Aquinas Lecture, Center for Thomistic Studies, University of St. Thomas, Houston, Texas.

all its members. Unlike temporal societies, the end to which membership in the Church is ordained is our ultimate end. For this reason, membership in the Church touches us even at the level of our conscience: the Church has from Christ an authority even in those areas most intimate to our persons. For this reason also, membership in the Church can never be coerced: all the children of the Church must be free.

The doctrine of the common good is so universal in its application that failure to understand the nature of the primacy of the common good in relation to private goods in the same order can result in the obfuscation of even the clearest doctrines of the Church. When the private good of individual souls is held up as the ultimate good and end for which God acts, traditional doctrines like the existence of hell, the necessity for baptism or membership in the Church for salvation, and the doctrine of predestination become all but impossible to understand. According to this mistaken view, there is nothing better than the salvation of an individual soul; therefore, a loving God could never have a reason for permitting a soul to be lost. Hence, salvation is automatically assured no matter whether one keeps the commandments or not, or is baptized or not, or is a member of the Church or not. But if there is a common good of the elect which is a greater good than any individual's private salvation, and if this surpassing good is what God primarily loves and acts to bring about, all of these traditional doctrines of the Church make sense.

Conclusion

This brief survey of Aquinas's teaching on the common good with the help of Charles De Koninck manifests that not only are there several analogous meanings of the expression common good, but also manifests that there is a primary meaning which, though least known to us, has the fullest notion of common good. It is most perfectly common because it is communicable in the highest degree: to being as such. It most fully has the notion of goodness because it is most of all perfective, bringing the whole being of each thing to its perfection in the mode of an end. It is this primary meaning of the common good that has significance far beyond the boundaries of ethics or political science. It is a metaphysical concept of the greatest importance that even touches upon and is of greatest service in theology. For the object sought by the wise man in first philosophy is the first and most universal cause of all beings. And this cause is some good. And this good, precisely as common, is the highest beatitude of all rational creatures, and is the ultimate reason for being of all things.

CHAPTER SEVENTEEN

Reading Aquinas's Commentary on Aristotle's *Nicomachean Ethics*

A Reply to Mark D. Jordan

CHRISTOPHER KACZOR

Numerous questions arise in connection with St. Thomas Aquinas's commentaries on Aristotle. Aquinas devoted a great deal of time to these commentaries through his professional responsibilities focused on commenting on Scripture. In terms of overall volume, they constitute about 13 percent of his entire corpus, roughly matching the 13.5 percent of the *opera omnia* devoted to commenting on the Bible. Should these works be construed as theology or philosophy? What were Aquinas's goals in writing them? Were they notes in preparation for writing the moral parts of the *Summa theologiae*? Were they expositions to provide his brother Dominicans a guide to Aristotle in preparation for their pastoral ministry?

I would like to consider a different question about these commentaries, but in particular the commentary on the *Nicomachean Ethics*. Should they be read as Aquinas's own work, or should they rather be understood simply as an interpretation of Aristotle but not Aquinas's own understanding of the matters in question? In this chapter, I would like to contribute to the ongoing conversation about the *Sententia libri ethicorum* by responding to the most recent contributions to the debate, a debate that the late Ralph

McInerny followed with great interest, given his interpretation of Aquinas as fundamentally an Aristotelian.

By way of context, a short summary of one discussion in the literature is necessary. I will first present the views of Mark D. Jordan, Andrew W. Mellon Professor of Christian Thought at Harvard, who has offered a strong answer to this question. Next, I will summarize briefly a critique of these views. Finally, I will present a summary and evaluation of Jordan's response to this critique.

Jordan's View of the *Sententia libri Ethicorum*

On Jordan's view, Aquinas notifies alert readers in various ways that they ought not to confuse Aquinas's own views—as expressed, say, in the *Summa contra Gentiles* or *Summa theologiae*—with the interpretations Aquinas gives of Aristotle in his *Sententia libri ethicorum*. Although his teacher Albert the Great offered explicit remarks that alerted readers that they should not mistake Albert's reading of Aristotle with Albert's own views, on Jordan's view Aquinas does provide at least implicit "disclaimers" that accomplish the same purpose as Albert's explicit disclaimers.

First, Aquinas sometimes explicitly disagrees with Aristotle, and at other times implicitly critiques the Stagirite, indicating that Aristotle's views are not his own. Jordan writes:

[Aquinas] notes, against the apparent sense of the Aristotelian text, that virginity cannot be seen as an extreme beyond the virtuous mean.[1] He records that the ancients allowed marriages to be dissolved because of sterility,[2] that they posited semi-divinities known as daemons,[3] that they deified heroes.[4] Throughout the text, Thomas remarks that Aristotle speaks "more gentium" in calling the separate substances or planetary bodies "gods."[5]

In such passages, and more could be added, Aquinas alerts readers that the *Sententia libri ethicorum* is merely a commentary and should not be mistaken for Aquinas's own understanding of the matters under discussion.

1. Thomas Aquinas, *Sententia libri Ethicorum*, 2.2: ed. R. M. Spiazzi (Turin: Marietti, 1949), #263; (Leonine edition 47:81.124–31).

2. Ibid., 8.12, Spiazzi #1724 (LE 47:488.285–88).

3. Ibid., 4.7, Spiazzi #719 (LE 47:222.23–26).

4. Ibid., 7.1, Spiazzi #1298 (LE 47:381.88–90). See also Mark D. Jordan, "Aquinas Reading Aristotle's *Ethics*," in *Ad Litteram: Authoritative Texts and Their Medieval Readers*, ed. Mark D. Jordan and Kent Emery Jr. (Notre Dame, Ind.: University of Notre Dame Press, 1992), 229–49, at 248.

5. *Sent. Eth.* 1.14.167 (LE 47:50.66–76), and elsewhere. See, too, Jordan, "Aquinas Reading Aristotle's *Ethics*," 236.

Secondly, Aquinas supplements Aristotle in various ways—to take just one example, by adding virtues unmentioned by Aristotle—faith, hope, and love—to the list of virtues. Jordan writes:"Thomas often enough notes a lacuna in Aristotle and then proceeds to fill it."[6] These additions include linguistic and doctrinal supplements to the text of Aristotle, again, on Jordan's view, indicating that the *Sententia* is not to be confused with Aquinas's views.

Thirdly, Aquinas remarks on the limited scope of the *Nicomachean Ethics*. In Jordan's words: "A third way in which Thomas marks his distance is the insistence upon the limited scope of an Aristotelian inquiry.... Thomas reiterates, for example, that the *Ethics* is concerned only with the happiness of the present life."[7]

Fourth, Aquinas indicates the limitations of Aristotle's views made necessary in light of the rhetoric that Aristotle uses. "A fourth way of marking distance," continues Jordan, "emphasizes the particular rhetorical limitations under which Aristotle labors. As Thomas sees plainly, Aristotle needed to teach a particular audience. The audience held certain beliefs that Aristotle appropriates for dialectical purposes, even if erroneous."[8]

Fifth, Jordan notes that there are contradictions in the ordering of the moral life between the commentary on the *Nicomachean Ethics* and the *Summa theologiae*:

First, Thomas separates the definitions of virtue and other principles or elements much more strictly from the treatment of particular virtues. Thomas insists ... on the sufficiency of the four cardinal virtues as a comprehensive organization of all moral virtue.... Third, Aristotle's separate treatment of the intellectual virtues is suppressed by Thomas.... Thomas regards his revision of the order of the *Ethics* as an improvement in clarity and comprehensiveness.[9]

A signature part of Aquinas's contribution to Christian wisdom is not just the views he expressed but the organization of various topics that he brought to the discussion. Aquinas organized the patristic patrimony so as to better bring out its clarity and truth. When looking at other authors, including biblical writers, Boethius, Pseudo-Dionysius, and Aristotle, Aquinas took their organizational strategies quite seriously, lending plausibility to the idea that we too should not ignore how Aquinas structured his account of the moral life. Aquinas's account of the moral life as expressed in the *Summa theolo-*

---

6. Jordan, "Thomas Aquinas' Disclaimers in the Aristotelian Commentaries," in *Philosophy and the God of Abraham: Essays in Memory of James A. Weisheipl, O.P.*, ed. R. James Long (Toronto: Pontifical Institute of Mediaeval Studies, 1991), 109.

7. Ibid., 109.

8. Ibid.

9. Jordan, "Aquinas on Aristotle's *Ethics*," 238–39.

A Reply to Mark D. Jordan   281

giae differs quite significantly from how the same topics are expressed in the *Sententia libri ethicorum*. This difference in organization makes clear that the *Commentary* cannot be regarded as Aquinas's own thought.

The final way Aquinas distances himself from Aristotle is that a commentator is not generally held to accept as true what he expresses in a commentary. "The genre of literal exposition just by itself constitutes a kind of disclaimer. It need not suggest that the commentator disavows what is taught in the underlying text, but it does suggest that additional warrant will be required for attributing what is taught to the commentator.... The expositor of a text cannot in general be taxed with the views being expounded."[10] We do not believe that when commenting on Plato, Stanley Rosen accepts and personally holds those assertions made by different participants in the conversation of the *Symposium*. It would be fallacious to assume that contemporary scholars of the Gospel of John personally accept as true all the assertions made in the Gospel. In other words Aquinas, by his choice of genre, indicates that only Aristotle's views, and not his own, will be discussed.

A Critique of Jordan's View

I have challenged these considerations of Jordan's in an article entitled "Is the *Sententia libri ethircorum* of Thomas Aquinas Only an Interpretation of Aristotle?"[11] I argue that these considerations offered by Jordan do not justify the conclusion that the views expressed in the commentary are not expressive of Aquinas's own views. Let me summarize these arguments.

It is true that Aquinas occasionally corrects the views expressed by Aristotle, and it is in these very corrections that it is becomes evident that Aquinas is communicating his own views. "Indeed, passages in which Aquinas corrects Aristotle are passages in which Thomas *undoubtedly* speaks in his own voice. Thus, the evidence supplied by Jordan of Thomas's disagreeing with Aristotle would seem to controvert his conclusion more than support it."[12]

It is also true that Aquinas supplements the text of Aristotle—answering questions left unanswered in the text, but similar supplements are also found in Aquinas's scriptural commentaries. "Thomas considers whether

10. Jordan, "Disclaimers," 104, 107. See also Jordan, *The Alleged Aristotelianism of Thomas Aquinas*, Etienne Gilson Series, vol. 15 (Toronto: Pontifical Institute of Mediaeval Studies, 1990), 11.

11. Christopher Kaczor, "Is the *Sententia libri ethicorum* of Thomas Aquinas only an Interpretation of Aristotle?" *American Catholic Philosophical Quarterly* 78 (Summer 2004): 353–78.

12. Ibid., 363.

the term *cognitio* applies to the Word of God, though the term appears no-where in this section of the Gospel and is Thomas's technical addition. He also speaks about the many senses of the word *principium*. Further on, he treats the different senses of *de, a,* and *ex* in Latin without reference to the Greek."[13] Everyone agrees that in the commentaries on Scripture—commentaries similar in form and genre to the *Sententiae* on Aristotle—Aquinas is both giving his reading of the text as well as communicating what he takes to be true about the matters under discussion.

In response to Jordan's third way in which Aquinas allegedly distances himself from Aristotle by noting the limited scope of the Aristotelian inquiry, I argue that subordinate sciences may nevertheless be true, useful.

We would not be justified, I believe, in saying that the Thomas of these philosophical works [*De unitate intellectus* and *De principiis naturae*] is not to be confused with the Thomas of his theological works on account of the limitations of the inquiry. We would be justified in saying that these works do not reflect *all* that he said about these matters (but the very same caution applies to the *Summa theologiae* itself), but not that what he said in a philosophical context he really did not hold on account of the limits of this type of inquiry. *Mutatis mutandis,* Thomas's remarks about the limits of Aristotle's inquiry do not *of themselves* indicate that the commentary is not representative of Thomas's thought.[14]

Fourth, rhetorical strategies are also found in Aquinas's commentaries on Scripture that are similar to the strategies used in the commentary on the *Ethics,* so these strategies alone cannot indicate that the commentary is merely an interpretation. "The fourth disclaimer, noting the rhetorical limitations of Aristotle, also seems to prove too much, since in the Gospels Christ himself, according to Thomas's reading, often speaks in a certain way for rhetorical purposes in addressing a particular audience."[15]

Fifth, while it is true that the ordering of material in works that are un-doubtedly Aquinas's own differs from the ordering of material in the commentary, we also find reordering among works that are undoubtedly Aquinas's own.

A reordering of the treatment of God's characteristics is evident in a comparison of the *Summa contra Gentiles* with the *Summa theologiae.* Although both begin with a demonstration of God's existence, the *Summa contra Gentiles* orders the discussion of God's characteristics by treating first God's eternity, and then God's simplicity, … perfection, goodness, and finally infinity. In contrast, the *Summa theologiae* takes up these matters in an entirely different order beginning with God's simplicity, and

---

13. Ibid., 370, notes omitted.
15. Ibid., 373–74.

14. Ibid., 373.

moving to God's goodness, perfection, infinity, ... and finally eternity. Factors other than "distancing" must account for the reordering of the treatment in these cases, which lends some plausibility to the idea that these other factors may also account for the differences in the order of presentation of virtues between the *Summa theologiae* and the *Sententia libri ethicorum*. Perhaps it is not a deep dissatisfaction with prior treatments that underlies these reorderings but rather considerations of various audiences, the nature and scope of the works involved, or a desire to cast light on a topic from various perspectives.[16]

Finally, Jordan's hermeneutical assumption that the commentator cannot be burdened with the views expressed in the commentary does not square well with several considerations. First, it is generally the case that medieval expositions reflected not just an interpretation of the text in question but also the views of the commentator. Several scholars, including Francesco del Punta, Joseph Owens, Marie-Dominque Chenu, B. C Bazán, and Jean-Pierre Torrell, support this contention.[17]

Second, in Aquinas's reading of other people's commentaries on Aristotle, Aquinas frequently writes as if the commentary represents not merely the commentator's view of Aristotle but also the commentator's own view of the matter under consideration. For example, Thomas writes as if Themistius's commentary on the *De anima* represents Themistius's own views:

16. Ibid., 376.

17. Francesco del Punta, "The Genre of Commentaries in the Middle Ages and Its Relationship to the Nature and Originality of Medieval Thought," *Miscellanae Mediaevalia: Was ist Philosophie im Mittelalter?* ed. Jan A. Aertsen and Andreas Speer (New York: Gruyter, 1998), 138–51, at 151 and 139. There are, of course, various genres of commentaries in the Middle Ages with various ranges of "originality." If one assumes the analysis of del Punta, Aquinas's commentaries on Aristotle would be more "original" than a simple *expositio literae* or a paraphrase of a given text but less "original" than a commentary *per modum questionis* like Aquinas's commentary on Boethius's *De trinitate* or Lombard's *Sentences*. Aquinas's commentaries on Aristotle, like his commentaries on Scripture, include an effort to come to a conceptual understanding of the text (they are therefore *Sententiae*), a treatment of the logical structure of the text, and occasional "notandum." See del Punta, "The Genre of Commentaries," 148 and following.

Joseph Owens, "Aquinas as Aristotelian Commentator," *St. Thomas Aquinas: Commemorative Studies* (Toronto: Pontifical Institute of Mediaeval Studies, 1974), 236–37.

M.-D. Chenu, OP, in his *Introduction a l'étude de saint Thomas d'Aquin* (Paris, Librairie Philosophique J. Vrin, 1950), writes: "Ainsi, à la différence de l'exégèse moderne, qui s'abstient de faire sienne la pensée de son auteur, et n'a pas à dire s'il ne l'accepte pas, le commentateur médiéval fait sien implicitement le contenu de texte, et, s'il ne l'accepte pas, le dit explicitement, tandis qu'il est présumé le faire sien s'il ne dit rien" (177). Aquinas's teacher Albert the Great does just this.

B. Carlos Bazán, "13th Century Commentaries on *De Anima*: From Peter of Spain to Thomas Aquinas," in *Il Commento Filosofico nell'Occidente Latino* (secoi XIII–XV), ed. Gianfranco Fioravanti, Claudio Leonardi, and Stefano Perfetti, (Turnhout, Belgium: Brepols, 2002), 119–84, at 176–77.

Concerning Torrell, see Kaczor, "Only an Interpretation of Aristotle?" 379, n. 58.

"From the foregoing words of Themistius, it is clear that he not only holds that the possible intellect is a part of the human soul but the agent as well, and he says that Aristotle taught this."[18]

Third, Aquinas makes various "anti-disclaimers" and additions to Aristotle that clearly express his own perspective. As B. C. Bazán notes:

The *Notanda* of previous exposition-commentaries are also present, but are introduced by more forceful words (*Sciendum, Considerandum, Ad evidentiam, Manifestum, Patet*). The choice of words is significant in itself. I have already mentioned that these "notanda" were for a master the occasion for making a doctrinal intervention in order to clarify the sense and scope of some problem arising from the text. Thomas made full use of this method to present his *personal* philosophical views on the different subjects. My remark is intended to underline the fact that Thomas's commentary is not only an exegetical work (although it excels in this genre), but also a witness to Thomas' personal philosophy, and that it should be considered as such by scholars, who otherwise would be tempted to overlook Thomas' commentary on *De anima* and on other Aristotelian treatises on the grounds that they are subordinated in the order and structure of somebody else's writings.[19]

If we turn to the *Sententia libri ethicorum* specifically, in many places Aquinas alerts readers of the truth of the views mentioned. As I have noted, Aquinas very frequently alerts the reader that the exposition reflects what he holds to be true. For instance, in his brief treatment of the happiness of the dead, he concludes: "elsewhere we have treated these matters more fully," ("alibi haec plenius disservimus"),[20] implying that the discussion in the *Sententia* does indeed reflect his views, albeit not in their fullness. In a single *lectio* from book ten, Aquinas almost redundantly affirms the truth of various views expressed in the commentary, using phrases such as they are "reasonably deduce[d]" ("rationalibiter sequitur quod");[21] "the truth of the matter" ("Et hoc quidem secundum rei veritatem");[22] "manifest" ("manifestum est quod");[23] "in harmony with our discussions on happiness in the first book and with truth itself" ("videtur esse consonum eis quae in I dicta sunt de felicitate et etian ipsi veritati");[24] and finally, "an evident fact conceded by everyone" ("sicut est manifestum et concessum ab omnibus").[25] These affirmations do not consti-

18. Aquinas, *De unitate intellectus*, chap. 2, 51–53, citation at 53; translation from Ralph McInerny, *Aquinas Against the Averroists* (West Lafayette, Ind.: Purdue University Press, 1993), 73.

19. Bazán, "13th Century Commentaries on *De Anima*," 176–77.

20. *Sent. Eth.* 1.17.212.

21. Ibid., 10.10, Spiazzi #2080 (LE 47:582.8).

22. Ibid., 10.10, Spiazzi #2080 (LE 47:583.14–15).

23. Ibid., 10.10, Spiazzi #2081 (LE 47:583.72–73).

24. Ibid., 10.10, Spiazzi #2086 (LE 47:583.77–78).

25. Ibid., 10.10, Spiazzi #2090 (LE 47:584.117–18).

tute even an exhaustive list of examples from this single lectio,[26] and it is also clear that throughout the *Sententia libri ethicorum* Aquinas often remarks on the truth of what he has written in the commentary.[27]

Fourth, given that Aquinas was deeply familiar with Albert's works on Aristotle—indeed, he had served as the secretary for one of Albert's commentaries on the *Ethics*—the contrast with Albert's explicit disclaimers raises the question why Aquinas did not make his interpretive stance explicitly evident as did Albert, if his stance toward the commentary was similar to Albert's.

Fifth, the reception of the *Sententia libri ethicorum* indicates that the commentary was viewed—by those friendly to Aquinas as well as those who opposed him—as representing his own views. As I noted, the historical reception of Aquinas's commentaries on Aristotle reinforce this conclusion. Following the condemnations of 1277, just a few years after Aquinas's death, critics of Aquinas sought to implicate him in the condemnation, while some of his Dominican brothers (as well as others) endeavored to exonerate him from these charges. It is instructive to note that although these parties often disagree about the interpretation of both the 1277 condemnations and of Aquinas, the critics and defenders alike cite Aquinas's Aristotelian commentaries in their presentation of Aquinas's views. Henricus Bate of Mechelen in his *Speculum divinorum et quorundam naturalium* cites the commentary on the *Metaphysics* in his reconstruction (and criticism) of Aquinas's treatment of the question of whether knowledge of separate substances is altogether impossible.[28] On the other hand, those more sympathetic to Aquinas include his commentaries on Aristotle in their reconstruction of Aquinas, as did Petrus a Bergomo, OP (d. 1482), *Concordantiae Textuum discortantium Divi Thomae Aquinatis.*[29] Early readers of Aquinas,

26. E.g., ibid., 10.10, Spiazzi #2090, 2095, 2096, 2097.

27. He does this also, and frequently, elsewhere; for instance, ibid., 1.6, Spiazzi #80 (LE 47:22.110); ibid., 1.2, Spiazzi #30 (LE 47:8.170); ibid., 6.2, Spiazzi #1138 (LE 47:338.231–33), "et ad hoc inducit verbum agathonis qui recte dixit: quod solo isto posse privatur deus, ut faciat ingenita, id est non facta quae sunt facta. et hoc recte dixit." In paragraph 2080, Aquinas alerts the reader that an earlier passage (2078), a passage not in itself affirmed in any unusual way, represents what he considers to be true.

28. See, for example, Henricus Bate, *Speculum divinorum et quorundam naturalium*, Tome 1, ed. E. Van de Vyver (Leuven: Leuven University Press, 1960), 73–90; Bate, *Speculum divinorum et quorundam naturalium*, Parts VI–VIII, ed. Carlos Steel (Leuven: Leuven University Press, 1994), 59–70. See too Carlos Steel, "Medieval Philosophy: An Impossible Project?" in *Miscellanea Mediaevalia: Was ist Philosophie im Mittelalter?* ed. Jan A. Aertsen and Andreas Speer (New York: De Gruyter, 1998), 152–74, at 163.

29. Petrus a Bergomo, *Concordantiae Textuum discortantium Divi Thomae Aquinatis*, Edition fototypica (Florence: Libreria Editrice Fiorentina, 1982). One can find a photographic reproduction of the *Concordantiae* placed at the end of volume 10 of the Roman edition (1773) of Aquinas's *Summa theologiae*.

indeed those who would be most sensitive to the various "genre" of medieval commentaries and what the choice of genre indicates about the views of the expositor, understood the Thomistic commentaries on Aristotle to be expressing Aquinas's view.[30]

Jordan's Response and an Evaluation of Its Adequacy

In an article appearing in the same issue, Mark Jordan responds to these criticisms,[31] focusing his remarks on three points in particular: first, generalizations about genera; secondly, the purposes and limits of Aquinas's expositions, and thirdly, the hierarchy of the sciences. I am going to argue that each of these responses fails to respond adequately to my criticisms of Jordan's views in my original article.

First, Jordan disputes the idea that scholars can make meaningful generalizations about commentaries in the Middle Ages, given that so many counterexamples spring to mind. "The risk of impossible generalizations can be justified as pedagogical necessity only if we move beyond it quickly without leaving equally misleading prejudices and mythologies behind."[32] Genres do not have essences; they cannot be affixed in grand taxonomies; so we cannot move from what Aquinas says about someone else's commentary on Aristotle to what Aquinas is doing in his own commentaries on Aristotle; nor can we suitably compare his commentaries on Scripture with his commentaries on Aristotle, as if they were in essence the same.

However, I did not, and do not need to, suppose that genres have fixed essences, or that they can all be fitted within some grand taxonomy, or that all medieval commentaries are alike. Indeed, I explicitly point out that medieval commentaries are not all alike, in noting that Aquinas chose to write "*sententia*, rather than other forms of medieval commentary—*paraphrasis*, *abbreviatio*, *summa*, commentary with questions, *tabula*, or *concordatia*."[33] Jordan's response to my objection attacks a straw man, since I do not explicitly or implicitly suppose what Jordan attributes to me.

Jordan's view proves too much, since, if it were correct, it would equally

30. Jean-Pierre Torrell, who kindly read this section, agreed with the claims made in it but suggested, quite properly, that I should also emphasize that a complete understanding of the ethical life for Aquinas must also include a treatment of grace, Christ, and the sacraments as found in the *Summa theologiae* and not the commentary on the *Ethics*. Even though the *Sententia libri ethicorum* represents Aquinas's views, it clearly does not represent the full theological treatment of ethics, which is available only outside the commentary.

31. Jordan, "Thomas as Commentator in Some Programs of Neo-Thomism: A Reply to Kaczor," *American Catholic Philosophical Quarterly* 78 (Summer 2004): 379–86.

32. Ibid., 380–81.

33. Kaczor, "Only an Interpretation of Aristotle?" 359.

undermine Jordan's own generalizations about Aquinas's commentaries on Aristotle. If we cannot make generalizations about commentaries, then of course we cannot make the generalization that Aquinas ought not to be burdened with the views expressed in his commentaries on Aristotle. If Jordan is right about the impossibility of generalizations about commentaries, then he is wrong to generalize about them as he does in so many essays. Jordan writes, for example, "The genre of literal exposition just by itself constitutes a kind of disclaimer. It need not suggest that the commentator disavows what is taught in the underlying text, but it does suggest that additional warrant will be required for attributing what is taught to the commentator.... The expositor of a text cannot in general be taxed with the views being expounded."[34] If generalizations are problematic and unsuitable save for pedagogical purposes, then Jordan's scholarly practice is inconsistent with his critique. If we suppose that generalizations about various kinds of commentaries can indeed be suitably made, then the question is whether Jordan's generalization or my own (their contradictory claims are equally general) is true. To address this question, we can look at the other dimensions of the argument.

In this section of his response, Jordan also mentions "contestations in principle of the cogency of a distinction between 'interpretation' and 'creation.'"[35] But this is not something I denied but rather something I emphasized—for example, by citing approvingly the work of Francesco del Punta and of Joseph Owens. In his article "The Genre of Commentaries in the Middle Ages and Its Relationship to the Nature and Originality of Medieval Thought," del Punta contrasts medieval and modern approaches to commentary:

When properly viewed in its historical context, therefore, the medieval notion of commentary is not antithetical to the notion of originality, but rather complementary to it. The medieval commentary is a way of receiving knowledge that leads to the development of such knowledge, even to the point of denying substantial parts or aspects of the received legacy.... In the medieval commentary a rigidly formalized structure coexists with various degrees of speculative originality. This coexistence, the first essential characteristic of the medieval commentary, manifests itself as a polarity between, on the one hand, a strictly codified and relatively standardized form, and, on the other, a remarkable capability to adapt itself to the commentator's expression of his personal views.[36]

Owens makes a similar point about medieval "originality" not coinciding with typical modern conceptions:

<hr>

34. Jordan, "Disclaimers," 104, 107. See, too, Jordan, *Alleged Aristotelianism of Thomas Aquinas*, 11.

35. Jordan, "Thomas as Commentator," 381.

36. Del Punta, "Genre of Commentaries in the Middle Ages," 151 and 139.

The medieval mind experienced no difficulty in seeing an author express as his own material taken nearly one hundred percent from other authors. Peter Lombard, for instance, could be regarded as the author of everything in his four books of the *Sentences*, even though practically all the material was taken from others. As long as the writer was asserting mastery over material used and was organizing and directing it to his own purpose, he was expressing it as his own.[37]

Obvious examples of such work include medieval commentaries on Scripture which sought fidelity in exegesis but obviously did not exclude a personal adherence to that which was written in the commentary.

Jordan offers a second critique of my position: that it misconstrues the nature of a science as a kind of building block that can be used intact, but not transformed, when brought into relationship with theology. "Kaczor seems to see philosophy as a work of self-contained building blocks that establishes certain results on top of which the results of theology can be mortared in. The building-block view is not adequate even inside the Aristotelian corpus."[38] Jordan continues:

How is one to conceive an addition to the autonomously "philosophical" but "incomplete" teaching about ethics in Aristotle? I can conceive adding supplementary terms, overlooked topics, undetermined cases, or argumentative refinements to existing teaching. Radical redefinitions, unimagined topics, miraculous cases, and new principles are not "additions." You do not "add" to Aristotelian ethics when you argue, as Thomas does, that no virtue is a virtue strictly speaking unless linked to infused charity, that the natural knowledge of the human end is both obscured by original sin and in need of grace for enactment, that our full flourishing is enabled by sacraments that have efficacy through Christ's passion. The relationship of Aristotelian ethics to Thomas's moral teaching is not part to whole or sketch to portrait, but something more like a road seen at night and then at noon, or a situation judged in despair and then in hope.[39]

On Jordan's view, Aquinas's moral teaching radically transforms Aristotelian ethics, such that to understanding Aquinas's commentary as representative of Aquinas's own mind is thoroughly misguided.

How might I respond? The "building block" metaphor is not mine, and it is misleadingly unwelcome. I never asserted that philosophy is "self-contained" and uninfluenced by the religious beliefs of those practicing philosophy. For Aquinas, whatever is true cannot contradict whatever else is true. So, a truth uncovered through natural reasoning cannot contradict a truth revealed by God, and truths revealed by God cannot contradict truths

37. Owens, "Aquinas as an Aristotelian Commentator," 236–37.
38. Jordan, "Thomas as Commentator," 383.
39. Ibid., 384.

discovered through the light of natural reason. To use the analogy suggested by Jordan, the road seen at night and the road seen during the day are not different roads but rather the same road, and any true insight about a road in the night of reason darkened by original sin will remain true in the light of Revelation.

Jordan provides no argument but merely asserts that radical redefinitions, unimagined topics, miraculous cases, and new principles are not additions. Why not? Particularly, since Aquinas is reading Aristotle in such a way as to develop the Greek's fundamental insights, it is not self-evident that distinctly Christian additions are not just that—additions.

Even if these differences between Aquinas and Aristotle—and no one is denying that there are many—are construed as transformations rather than additions, the import of this difference is not obvious. The logic of Jordan's argument remains obscure.

Finally, in the last section of Jordan's response, he reiterates his view that Aquinas has been used, abused actually, for well over a century now as part of a response to modern projects of philosophy. Jordan argues that the question about the status of the Aristotelian commentaries is part of a larger discussion of the relationship of philosophy and theology, particularly in the work of Aquinas.

Kaczor chose not to mention my most controversial remark, namely, that it is quite difficult to find a passage in which Thomas applies the term "philosopher" approvingly to someone he knows to be a Christian. I repeat the remark more loudly whenever a modern notion of the philosopher is substituted for notions with which Thomas was familiar. If more than a century of brilliant historical labor has settled anything, it is that Thomas did not conceive himself as a neo-Thomist philosopher.[40]

And so it would seem that, in Jordan's eyes, to hold that Aquinas's views are expressed in the commentary is to be part of a discredited neo-scholastic project.

This final contention, however, appears to be a circular argument. How do we know that the Aristotelian commentaries do not represent Aquinas's own view? Because Aquinas chose not to write philosophy. But how do we know that Aquinas chose not to write philosophy, especially since some works like the commentaries seem to be philosophical? Because the commentaries do not represent Aquinas's views. My position, by contrast, does not suffer this circularity, for I believe on independent grounds that Aquinas expresses his own views in the commentary, and for other reasons I reject the view that the commentary is "theological."

40. Ibid., 385–86.

Even if it were true (and I do not know whether it is) that Aquinas never speaks approvingly about any Christian as a philosopher, it does not follow that the commentaries on Aristotle cannot represent Aquinas's own philosophical perspective, since the argument from silence proves nothing. Aquinas also never spoke (approvingly) of Christians as jumping on one foot, or eating green beans, or painting with watercolors, but it hardly follows that Aquinas never did these things or that somehow these activities are suspect if done by Christians.

Jordan's charge that it is a part of the neo-Thomist program to view the commentaries as Aquinas's own is historically inaccurate. The view that the commentaries should be understood as representing—in some sense—Aquinas's view does not arise with pre-Vatican II neo-Thomism. It does not arise with Leo XIII and *Aeterni patris*. It is traced all the way back to the controversies arising from the condemnations of 1277, when Henricus Bate of Mechelen (1246–1310) cited Aquinas's commentary on the *Metaphysics* in his criticism of Aquinas on whether knowledge of separate substances is altogether impossible.[41] Defenders of Aquinas likewise include commentaries on Aristotle in their reconstruction of Aquinas, as did Petrus a Bergomo, OP (d. 1482), *Concordantiae Textuum discortantium Divi Thomae Aquinatis*.[42] Likewise, post-scholastic historians of the thought of Aquinas, like Jean-Pierre Torrell, endorse my view. [43]

Since it is not historically accurate, why plaster the "neo-Thomist" label on this interpretive position? The likely answer is that the rhetoric of "neo-Thomisim" or "neo-scholasticism" serves to prejudice readers against the position I am advocating. As Bruno Schüller noted, "In most cases, when used as an evaluative term, 'Scholasticism' stands precisely for what one must totally abandon or, better still, completely forget."[44] I think the evaluations Schüller mentions are reactionary, a product of a by-gone "spirit" of an age that uncritically accepted whatever was considered modern and just as uncritically rejected the traditional. Nevertheless, the neo-Thomist label, inaccurate as it is, serves simply to prejudice (some) readers against a fair consideration of the arguments about the *Sententia libri ethicorum*.

Jordan rightly discards two extreme answers to the question of how to

41. See for example, Bate, *Speculum divinorum et quorundam naturalium*, Tome 1, 73–90; Bate, *Speculum divinorum et quorundam naturalium*, Parts VI-VIII, 59–70. See too, Steel, "Medieval Philosophy: An Impossible Project?" 163.

42. Bergomo, *Concordantiae Textuum discortantium Divi Thomae Aquinatis*, Edition fototypica.

43. See Kaczor, "Only an Interpretation of Aristotle?," 369, n.58.

44. Bruno Schüller, *Wholly Human: Essays on the Theory and the Language of Morality*, trans. Peter Heinegg (Washington D.C.: Georgetown University Press, 1986), 1.

interpret the Aristotelian commentaries in relation to the Thomistic corpus. In relation to the *Sententia libri ethicorum*, Jordan holds that commentary is not the whole of Aquinas's thought about ethical topics, nor does it contain nothing of Aquinas's ethical thought. Obviously Thomas's thought on moral matters is expressed more fully in other works. For example, Aquinas's treatment of the nexus of acts of will and intellect in human action is much more sophisticated and differentiated in questions 6–18 of the *prima secundae* than anywhere in the *Nicomachean Ethics*. On the other hand, the commentary expresses Thomas's own thought at least in part, since Aquinas explicitly remarks that some parts of his commentary are true.[45]

Of the remaining, more moderate positions, Jordan describes the third view as holding that the commentaries contain the core of Aquinas's philosophical thought. "The exegetical practice that tends to follow upon this third view can be abbreviated as a rule: Anything added by Thomas to the Aristotelian text is to be taken as what he thought to be true in fact, unless there is explicit contextual evidence to the contrary."[46] The fourth view, "which holds that the commentaries contain at best parts of Thomas' own thought, would seem to yield a negative rule: any non-periphrastic remark in the commentaries is to be taken as true only if confirmed elsewhere in the corpus or if Thomas explicitly remarks on its truth."[47] These distinctions in reference to exegesis seem useful. However, the question of whether the commentaries contain the "core" of Aquinas's philosophy is not the same as the question whether Aquinas's own thought is represented in them. One could hold consistently that the commentaries, although not the "core" of Aquinas's philosophical thought, nevertheless can be attributed to him as his own thought, just as the scriptural commentaries might or might not be considered the "core" of Aquinas's theology vis-à-vis the *Summa theologiae*. Likewise, one could hold that Aquinas had no *complete* philosophy outside his theological writings, yet still judge that he would assent to the commentaries as representative of his own thought. After all, some, such as Harry Jaffa, have read the commentaries on Aristotle as theological works rather than philosophical. The questions of philosophy's relation to theology, Aquinas's relationship to Aristotle, the commentaries' relationship to Aquinas's philosophy, if any, and the legitimacy of using the commentaries as works to which Aquinas gave assent are interrelated, but distinct, questions. To mix them up is to make difficult questions even more difficult to answer.

---

45. *Sent. Eth.* IV, ii, 1138: "Et ad hoc inducit verbum Agathonis qui recte dixit: necesse est enim quod solo isto posse privatur Deus, ut faciat ingenita, id est non facta, quae sunt facta. Et hoc recte dixit."

46. Jordan, "Disclaimers," 111.   47. Ibid.

Remembering a Genuine Lover of Wisdom

The Impressive Legacy of Ralph McInerny

MICHAEL NOVAK

I am afraid I never think of Ralph as "gone." I am reminded of this every time I fly, when our plane climbs through thick clouds and comes out behind them where the sun is as present as ever, brilliant and blinding. Ralph is as present as the sun, even on cloudy days.

Did you hear about the female collie that gave birth to four pups along the roadside, and was arrested for littering? Ralph's presence sharpens in me every time I hear a pun. A bad pun or a good one, Ralph loved them both. Ralph called one of his mysteries *Mom and Dead*. Ralph's friends used to chide him with "Ralph McInerny, OP"—Ralph McInerny, of the Order of Puns.

Then there are the jokes he told, usually deadpan and with an uninflected voice, such as the one Gerry Bradley recalled at Ralph's funeral. Years ago, Ralph was coming out of the dining room at Notre Dame when he saw two dozen students with paper bags on their heads streaking naked down the quad from the old Rockne Hall. He was asked later if they were guys or gals. He said, deadpan, that he couldn't tell, they had bags over their heads.

Ralph is always present when I read or hear a Shakespearian sonnet.

293

Ralph wrote a whole book of them, one of them in honor of the fortieth wedding anniversary of Karen and me. He called it, ineluctably, *Quadragesimo Anno*. Here is the first part of what he wrote (I especially like one of the two ironic couplets which he threw in at the end, for good measure). His opening lines are an ironical refutation of the Cartesian split between body and mind. As when my wife used to remind me, usually in the midst of some heavy petting, "But you did marry me for my mind, didn't you?" I always replied, "Yes, dear. Your figure had nothing to do with it." Ralph had a healthy "philosophy of the body," so to speak. You can hear it in this part of his sonnet:

> *Let me not to the marriage of true minds*
> Devote these lines, as if we could, Cartesian-wise,
> Doubt away our heads and toes and all that lies
> Between, and end as thought, without behinds.
> How could minds be wed except as faculties
> Of souls so one with flesh, that only lips
> Can breathe our spirits, or in sips
> Imbibe its metaphorical lees.

The couplet he put in for me at the end was quite on target—not literally so (my life was very full before Karen came into it) but comparatively so: Compared with resting under Karen's fruitful orchard, I lived earlier rather in a desert. In Ralph's words:

> No vacuum, Michael, was more barren
> Than your heart ere you met Karen.

Karen and I loved Ralph's wife, Connie, very much because she was so down to earth she seldom bothered to lift a foot. What a wry deflating, debunking wit she had—just the right mate to prick a philosopher's self-importance and fuzzy highfalutin way of putting simple things. She and Karen together formed the AWHMH: the Association of Wives with High-Maintenance Husbands.

Both Connie and Karen kept us grounded, Ralph and me. On the other hand, when any writer dared attack us, or wrote a wounding review, both of them raised up like rattlesnakes to take a bite or two of that offender's unprotected parts. It was *their* job to criticize their husbands. They intended death for anyone else who tried to do it.

And they were both totally unforgiving wives. When they each untimely died, the last thing to give up breath in them was the grudges they nursed against Ralph's and my detractors. Our wives swore eternal retribution. Even tonight I tremble for our enemies when I think that Connie and Karen are still pursuing them.

There is one special reason I love Ralph and think of his presence oftentimes. Ralph wrote thirty books of philosophy, twelve monographs and other shorter books (such as *What Went Wrong at Vatican II*, and three books of poetry), and on top of those forty-two books, sixty-some novels, some 102 books in all. And he was always dreaming of more.

In this, Ralph reminds me of Winston Churchill, who was riding in a railway car when he read in a newspaper that the average Englishman of that time drank during one lifetime the equivalent of an entire railway car full of brandy. Thereupon, Churchill squirmed in his seat to look toward the back of the car, the ceiling, the floor, and toward the front, and muttered sadly to his companion: "So much to do, so little time."

Ralph had SO much in his imagination and his brain and his heart that he wanted to put down on paper, there was *always* so much to do, so little time.

Will there ever be a graduate thesis on the life and work of Ralph McInerny, once any graduate student looks in awe at the body of work he or she will have to read? First of all, they will discover that it requires three single-spaced pages just to list all his academic appointments, honors, and organizational offices. Then four pages just for his 102 books. Then maybe forty pages for the articles he has written in magazines and journals. If a thesis needs to be about 300 pages long, this bibliography alone will fill up fifty pages of it.

There is a kindly, jolly Lutheran layman from the Midwest—in the Midwest, even Lutherans are jolly and happy—who claims to have read every word that Richard John Neuhaus wrote. And HE says that, by his best count, Neuhaus published just over six million words. So Ralph was not the only prolific writer in the crowd he traveled in. The two of them, plus Andrew Greeley, make me feel shamefully lazy.

Moreover, Ralph had *need* to write. Before your wedding nobody tells you that for twenty years or so marriage is essentially a transportation service for little kids. Thus, while Ralph and his dear wife Connie tried to drive their six young kids from event to event at Creighton and then Notre Dame in their younger days, Ralph discovered the biting need to raise money for tuitions.

Most Americans use thirty percent of their income to pay for housing, another thirty percent to pay for the education of their children, another thirty percent for taxes—federal, state, and local taxes, income taxes, real estate taxes, gasoline taxes, telephone taxes, and sales taxes—with about ten percent left over for food, clothing, and other necessities, including dog food and a little change for beer money. To keep the wolf from the door,

Ralph decided to learn to write. Not as in "read and write." Rather, as in "write for income." He put a little sign over his desk down in the basement, to remind himself every night as he sat down before a blank piece of paper: "NO ONE OWES ME A READING." You want their money, you have to earn their attention and their desire.

And so, slowly, he learned to write for income: short stories for the few magazines that pay the rent. It took several years to learn the skill—and to see the income—and a lot of patience from a very skeptical, commonsensical Connie. (You want skepticism? You have to meet a wife married to a writer who dreams of making money. Behind every successful man, there is a lovely little woman telling him he's nuts.)

Suffice it to say that Ralph McInerny had gone to Catholic schools in Minnesota, where he was taught by puns. Among his sixty-some novels— all of them exceedingly good entertainments, all of them witty, also wise, and wonderfully informative about daily life—a high number had puns in their titles. My favorite punning titles are *Sine Qua Nun*, *And Then There Were Nun*, and *Half Past Nun*. Then there were these others: *Her Death of Cold*, *Lying Three*, *Let Us Prey*, *Loss of Patients*, *Body and Soil*, *Frigor Mortis*, *Abra-cadaver*, *Four on the Floor* (before reading this one, I thought it might be about the old dormitory visitation rule at the old Notre Dame: If a female visitor comes to the room, there must be four feet on the floor at all times). Then there were *The Nominative Case*, *Judas Priest*, and *Law and Ardor*.

My favorite series is his Notre Dame mysteries, *On This Rockne*, *The Lack of the Irish*, *The Book of Kills*, *Celt and Pepper*, *Irish Coffee*, *Irish Gilt*, and the one about two Notre Dame sophomores who registered their weddings in the Log Chapel, mistakenly, for the same day three years later and the same hour. Ralph called this story about walking down the aisle: *The Emerald Aisle*.

I have got hours of pleasure, hours of lilt, hours of fun from Ralph McInerny's mysteries, and I have been proud to see the honors he won from his peers in the world of mysteries and detective stories—a really great fraternity/sorority of smart and witty people—from whom he won prizes, honors, and awards, including the Lifetime Achievement Award of the Mystery Writers of America, an Ellery Queen Prize, and the presidency of the Mystery Writers of America. He was a real pro, and they knew it, and they praised him. And the whole world watched the wonderful national television series, *The Father Dowling Mysteries*, that flowed from his own creativity—flowed from more than a dozen delightful novels of his about a good Midwestern priest.

All that would be enough reason to honor Ralph McInerny tonight, for the tellers who tell a nation's stories direct a part of its vision and its morals, as surely as a mother's hand rocks the nation's cradle. Ralph has left a vivid record, without equal (J. F. Powers aside), of what Midwestern American Catholic life was like from about the time of World War II into the new century. He also wrote THE truly great novel about the long, slow undermining of the public reputation of the American priesthood in his 1973 bestseller—*1973*—his most serious and ambitious novel, *The Priest*. What a terrifyingly uplifting and also depressing story, about a priest living a double sexual life, for which Ralph's mother never forgave him. (Don't we all have mothers shocked by what we have written?) *The Priest* exposed the origins of a slowly building betrayal of vows—its social conditions, and its educational conditions, and its seminary conditions—long before it burst into daylight some decades later. And yet my favorite other serious novel of Ralph's is full of the scarlet robes, and watered silk, and marbled columns of Rome: *The Red Hat*. I think I am a cardinal in that one. Anyone who thought he was a friend of Ralph's who did not show up in one of his novels felt bitterly cheated.

Ralph's achievements have been staggering in fiction, even if his main ambition there was playfulness. Ralph wrote with the best of all motives for writing, as Samuel Johnson taught us, to pay his bills! "A man who writes for anything else but money is a damn fool," Johnson wrote. And also, paraphrased: "Seldom is a man so innocently engaged as in the making of money."

Then add to that Professor McInerny's very heavy lifting in the field of philosophy. He has made available as publisher and sometimes translator and always introductory commentator a dozen really key books in the history of philosophy that the English world had not had available before him: To mention only two, the most important introduction to the thought of Thomas Aquinas (Maritain's favorite) by John of St. Thomas; the long, line-by-line commentary of St. Thomas Aquinas on Aristotle's *Nichomachean Ethics*—my own all-time favorite book, a rare and breathtaking glimpse into two entirely different ethical systems, fifteen centuries apart, that of pagan Athens and the new Christian humanism of the 1200s, just at the beginning of the modern era.

In a certain sense, this commentary of Aquinas on Aristotle marked out a whole new direction for the West—for the Renaissance, for modern science, for modern humanism. It marked out a radically different path for the Christian world than for Islam. It marked the turn away from Plato and the spiritualization of almost everything, toward the world of flesh and the concrete and the immediate, toward the empirical, toward the real unity of body and soul in the human person, toward existence and the taste of sweat and the brilliant light of the noonday sun of August in the piazza of an Italian city like Orvieto or Siena.

This unexpected recovery of the works of Aristotle, lost or hidden away for a thousand years, arrived just in time to turn Christendom away from the direction in which the Islamic world was speeding ahead, in the works of such thinkers as Avicenna and Averroes. And so Ralph also had translated and published the decisive book in which Aquinas turned away the Islamic intellectual tide that was sweeping through the gate of the universities of Italy and France, *Against the Averroists*. This treasure in the history of Western civilization is too little known, and before Ralph it was almost inaccessible to English-only readers.

Ralph, a student of that renowned Thomist of Quebec, Charles De Koninck, also wrote several books on quite critical turns in the history of philosophy pioneered by Aquinas, namely, on analogy, the human soul, and especially on human action and on ethics, as well as on art and prudence. Here, too, if all the graduate student of the future had to go on were the twenty books in the history of Western philosophy brought into being by Ralph McInerny, those would alone represent a lifetime of great achievement. And this achievement was recognized by his election to present the most prestigious series in philosophy in the Anglo-American world, the Gifford Lectures in Scotland. The large humanity of his work was recognized by his appointment by the president of the United States to the National Council on the Arts and Humanities.

Ralph was also, as his fiction would suggest, a great teacher. He had a rare facility for imagining just the right vivid story, and the telling example, that grabbed hold of the listener's imagination, and allowed the *aha!* insight to transform puzzlement into the pleasure of a new light in the intelligence, a new way of seeing reality. Professor McInerny also invented as imaginary students in the same classroom as his real students, characters alternately annoying and delightful, usually coeds such as (my favorite) the sometimes obtuse, sometimes soul-cheering "Fifi LaRue."

Ralph had a genius for introducing difficult subjects. Thus, in some ways, his little introductory text for home-bound readers, *A First Glance at Thomas Aquinas, Handbook for Peeping Thomists*, is another one of my all-time favorites.

Not only was Ralph elected president of the Mystery Writers of America, then, but his recondite and imaginative work also won him one of the most distinguished chairs at Notre Dame, the Michael P. Grace Chair in Medieval Studies, and in addition to that, the directorship of the university's Medieval Institute, doubtlessly one of the two most distinguished medieval institutes in the Western hemisphere. As if that weren't enough, recognizing Ralph's interest in the arts as well as in ethics, in the work of such existentialists as Søren Kierkegaard, and in the contemporary range of reason in Christian philosophy today, the university also appointed Ralph the director of the Maritain Center, the reservoir of the books and some of the papers of one of the two greatest Thomists of our time, Jacques Maritain. And his peers in the field of Maritain studies have had no difficulty in presenting McInerny with the handsome bronze Maritain Medal.

Poor Ralph, he was weighted down with medals and awards. He was so modest, however, that he probably tried to imagine how he was to move from one chapter to another in the mystery story on his inner calendar for that part of every year while he wrote! His mind was always wandering toward sunshine on an island—in the Mediterranean, off Sicily, Capri, Sardinia, off the Florida coast. Writing for a living is not all pain and suffering, you see. But it does mean exhausting, uninterrupted work for about eight weeks of every year. And more.

This ex-Marine from Minnesota carried in his ample and well-stocked brain and imagination and creative juices an entire world of persons, events, funny scenes, good puns, sad and tragic moments, and wonderment at the glory of the human story, as it follows in the shadows of the Way of the Cross. Taught by nuns, he remained nunplussed by praise.

Ralph McInerny was a serious Christian man, a profound and crystal-clear Thomist of the Bright Observance, a cunning mystery writer, a punning philosopher, the perfect model of the humanities in our time, a pattern by which a Christian humanist, in love with the time in which God placed him, ought to be measured.

It is for that reason that we are proud to call (thank you Chris Kaczor for your book) "O! Rare Ralph McInerny" back to mind, high above the clouds in the brilliant sun, with us still, not now—not ever—"gone."

Selected Bibliography

Adler, Mortimer J. *The Difference of Man and the Difference It Makes.* Bronx, N.Y.: Fordham University Press, 1993.

Aertsen, Jan, and Andreas Speer, eds. *Miscellanae Mediaevalia: Was ist Philosophie im Mittelalter?* New York: De Gruyter, 1998.

Alexander, Irene. "*Lumen Fidei* and Contemporary Errors on Faith." *Nova et Vetera* (English ed.) 12.1 (2014): 11–23.

Aristotle. *Complete Works in the Revised Oxford Translation.* Edited by Jonathan Barnes. 2 Volumes. Princeton: Princeton University Press, 1984.

————. *Metaphysics*, A Revised Text with Introduction and Commentary by W. D. Ross. 2 Volumes. Oxford: Clarendon Press, 1958.

Ashley, Benedict, OP. *The Ashley Reader: Redeeming Reason.* Ave Maria Fla.: Sapientia Press, 2006.

————. *The Way Toward Wisdom: An Interdisciplinary and Intercultural Introduction to Metaphysics.* Notre Dame, Ind.: University of Notre Dame Press, 2006.

Augustine. *Editio critica Corpus Christianorum Series Latina.* Turnhout: Brepols.

————. *On Christian Doctrine.* Translated by D. W. Robertson. New York: Liberal Arts Press, 1958.

————. *Opera Omnia editio Patrologiae Latinae Elenchus* 31–45. Nuova Biblioteca Agostiniana. http://www.augustinus.it/latino/index.htm.

Bauckham, Richard. *Jesus and the Eyewitnesses: The Gospels as Eyewitness Testimony.* Grand Rapids, Mich.: Wm. B. Eerdmanns, 2006.

Bellamah, Timothy, O.P. *The Biblical Interpretation of William of Alton.* New York: Oxford University Press, 2011.

Benedict XVI, Pope. "Lecture of the Holy Father: Faith, Reason and the University; Memories and Reflections." "Regensburg Lecture." Libreria Editrice Vaticana, 2006.

Benestad, J. Brian. *Church, State, and Society: An Introduction to Catholic Social Doctrine.* Washington, D.C.: The Catholic University of America Press, 2011.

Beretta, Béatrice. *Ad aliquid: La relation chez Guillaume d'Occam.* Fribourg: Editions Universitaires, 1999.

Black, Deborah L. *Logic and Aristotle's Rhetoric and Poetics in Medieval Arabic Philosophy.* New York: Brill, 1990.

Blanchette, Oliva. *The Perfection of the Universe According to Aquinas: A Teleological Cosmology.* University Park, Penn.: The Pennsylvania State University Press, 1992.

Blankenhorn, Bernhard, OP. "The Good as Self-Diffusive in Thomas Aquinas." *Angelicum* 79.4 (2002): 803–37.

———. "The Instrumental Causality of the Sacraments: Thomas Aquinas and Louis-Marie Chauvet." *Nova et Vetera* 4 (English ed.) (2006): 255–94.

Bouton-Touboulic, A.-I. *L'ordre caché: La notion d'ordre chez saint Augustin.* Paris: Institut d'Études Augustiniennes, 2004.

Boyle, John F. "Thomas Aquinas and His *Lectura romana in primum Sententiarum Petri Lombardi.*" In *Mediaeval Commentaries on the Sentences of Peter Lombard*, vol. 2, 149–73. Leiden: Brill, 2010.

Boyle, Leonard. *The Setting of the* Summa Theologiae *of Saint Thomas*, Etienne Gilson Series, vol. 5. Toronto: Pontifical Institute of Mediaeval Studies, 1982.

Braine, David. *The Human Person: Animal and Spirit.* Notre Dame, Ind.: University of Notre Dame Press, 1992.

Bultmann, Rudolf. *Jesus Christ and Mythology.* New York: Charles Scribner's Sons, 1958.

Burger, Ronna. *Aristotle's Dialogue with Socrates: On the* Nicomachean Ethics. Chicago: University of Chicago Press, 2008.

Burnell, Peter. *Augustinian Person.* Washington, D.C.: The Catholic University of America Press, 2005.

Buttiglione, Rocco. *Karol Wojtyła: The Thought of the Man Who Became Pope John Paul II.* Translated by Paolo Guitti and Francesca Murphy. Grand Rapids, Mich.: Eerdmans, 1997.

Capreolus, John. *On the Virtues.* Translation with introduction and notes by Kevin White and Romanus Cessario. Washington D.C.: The Catholic University of America Press, 2001.

Cessario, Romanus, OP. *Christian Faith and the Theological Life.* Washington, D.C.: The Catholic University of America Press, 1996.

———. *Introduction to Moral Theology.* Washington, D.C. The Catholic University of America Press, 2001.

———. "The Sacraments of the Church." In *Vatican II: Renewal within Tradition*, edited by Matthew L. Lamb and Matthew Levering, 129–46. Oxford: Oxford University Press, 2008.

Chenu, M.-D., O.P. *Introduction à l'étude de saint Thomas d'Aquin.* Paris: Cerf, 1950.

Collins, Francis S. *The Language of God: A Scientist Presents Evidence for Belief.* London: Pocket Books, Simon and Schuster, 2007.

Crosby, John F. *The Selfhood of the Human Person.* Washington, D.C.: The Catholic University of America Press, 1996.

Dahan, G. *L'exégèse chrètienne de la Bible en Occident Medieval, XIIe-XIVe siècle.* Paris: Cerf, 1999.

Daley, Brian, SJ. "Boethius' Theological Tracts and Early Byzantine Scholasticism." *Mediaeval Studies* 46 (1984): 158–91.

———. *The Hope of the Early Church.* New York: Cambridge University Press, 1991.

———. "The *Nouvelle Théologie* and the Patristic Revival: Sources, Symbols, and the Science of Theology," *International Journal of Systematic Theology* 7 (2005): 362–82.

———. *Gregory of Nazianzus.* London: Routledge, 2006.

———. "Knowing God in History and in the Church: *Dei Verbum* and 'Nouvelle Théologie.'" In *Ressourcement: A Movement for Renewal in Twentieth-Century Catholic Theology*, edited by Gabriel Flynn and Paul D. Murray, 333–51. Oxford: Oxford University Press, 2012.

Dauphinais, Michael, and Matthew Levering, eds. *John Paul II and St. Thomas Aquinas.* Ave Maria, Fla.: Sapientia Press, 2006.

De Koninck, Charles. "The Unity and Diversity of Natural Science." In *The Philosophy of Physics,* edited by Vincent E. Smith, 5–24. St. John's University Studies, Philosophical Series, 2. New York: St. John's University Press, 1961.

———. "A Philosopher of Order." *The New Scholasticism* 39 (1965): 491–516.

———. "In Defense of Aquinas." *The Aquinas Review* 4.1 (1997): 171–349.

———. "On the Primacy of the Common Good: Against the Personalists." *The Aquinas Review* 4.1 (1997): 1–70.

———. *The Writings of Charles De Koninck.* 2 vols. Translated by Ralph McInerny. Notre Dame, Ind.: University of Notre Dame Press, 2008, 2009.

Denzinger, Henricus, ed. *Enchiridion symbolorum: Definitionum et declarationem de rebus fidei et morum,* Editio XXXII. Fribourg: Herder, 1963.

Dewan, Lawrence, OP. "Thomas Aquinas and Being as a Nature." *Acta Philosophica* 12 (2003): 123–35.

———. "Discussion: On Anthony Kenny's *Aquinas on Being.*" *Nova et Vetera* (English ed.) 3.2 (2005): 335–400.

———. "St. Thomas, Norman Kretzmann, and Divine Freedom in Creating." *Nova et Vetera* (English ed.) 4.3 (2006): 495–514.

———. "St. Thomas Aquinas as an Example of the Importance of the Hellenistic Legacy," pt. 1. *Doctor Communis* (2008): 88–118.

———. *Wisdom, Law, and Virtue: Essays in Thomistic Ethics.* New York: Fordham University Press, 2008.

Dulles, Avery, SJ. *The Assurance of Things Hoped for: A Theology of Christian Faith.* New York: Oxford University Press, 1997.

———. *A History of Apologetics.* San Francisco: Ignatius Press, 2005.

Échivard, Jean-Baptiste. *Une Introduction à la philosophie: Les proèmes des lectures de saint Thomas d'Aquin aux principales oeuvres d'Aristote. 1. L'esprit des disciplines philosophiques fondamentales; 2. Science rationelle et philosophie de la nature; 3. Philosophie morale et politique; 4. Métaphysique.* Paris: François-Xavier de Guibert, 2004–2006.

Emery, Gilles, OP. "La relation dans la théologie de saint Albert le Grand." In *Albertus Magnus: Zum Gedenken nach 800 Jahren,* edited by Walter Senner, 455–65. Berlin: Akademie Verlag, 2001.

———. *The Trinitarian Theology of Saint Thomas Aquinas.* Translated by Francesca A. Murphy. Oxford: Oxford University Press, 2010.

Emery, Kent, and Mark Jordan, eds. *Ad Litteram: Authoritative Texts and Their Medieval Readers.* Notre Dame, Ind.: University of Notre Dame Press, 1992.

Fabro, Cornelio. *Introduzione all'ateismo moderno, seconda edizione riveduta e aumentata.* Rome: Editrice Studium, 1969.

Faulkner, Robert. *The Case for Greatness: Honorable Ambition and Its Critics.* New Haven, Conn.: Yale University Press, 2007.

Flannery, Kevin, SJ. *Christian and Moral Action.* Washington, D.C.: The Catholic University of America Press, 2013.

Fortin, Ernest L. *Classical Christianity and the Political Order: Reflections on the Theologico-Political Problem.* Edited by J. Brian Benestad. Lanham, Md.: Rowman and Littlefield, 1996.

Frede, Michael, and David Charles, eds. *Aristotle's Metaphysics Lambda, Symposium Aristotelicum.* Oxford: Clarendon Press, 2007.

George, Robert P., and Patrick Lee. *Body-Self Dualism in Contemporary Ethics and Politics.* New York: Cambridge University Press, 2008.

Gilson, Etienne. *God and Philosophy.* New Haven, Conn.: Yale University Press, 1941.

———. *Dante the Philosopher.* London: Sheed and Ward, 1948.

———. *The Unity of Philosophical Experience.* San Francisco: Ignatius Press, 1999.

Gregory, Brad S. *The Unintended Reformation: How a Religious Revolution Secularized Society.* Cambridge: Harvard University Press, 2012.

Guerra, Marc. "Aristotle on Pleasure and Political Philosophy: A Study in Book VII of the *Nicomachean Ethics.*" *Interpretation: A Journal of Political Philosophy* 24:2 (1997).

Hadot, Pierre, ed. *Simplicius: Sa vie, son oeuvre, sa survie.* New York: Walter de Gruyter, 1987.

———. *What Is Ancient Philosophy?* Translated by Michael Chase. Cambridge, Mass.: Harvard University Press, 2002.

Halligan, Nicholas, OP. *The Administration of the Sacraments. Some Practical Guides for Priests and Seminarians.* Staten Island, N.Y.: Alba House, 1963.

Hardy, Edward R., ed. *Christology of the Later Fathers.* Translated by C. G. Browne and J. E. Swallow. Philadelphia: Westminster Press, 1954.

Harnack, Adolf von. *History of Dogma.* Translated by Neil Buchanan. London: Constable and Robinson, 1900.

———. *What Is Christianity?* Translated by Thomas Bailey Saunders. Philadelphia: Fortress Press, 1937.

Hayes, Zachary. *St. Bonaventure's On the Reduction of the Arts to Theology: Translation with Introduction and Commentary.* St. Bonaventure, N.Y.: Franciscan Institute, St. Bonaventure University, 1996.

Henninger, Mark G. *Relations: Medieval Theories 1250–1325.* Oxford: Clarendon Press, 1989.

Hütter, Reinhard. "Reflections on *Lumen Fidei.*" *Nova et Vetera* (English ed.) 12.1 (2014): 1–10.

Jaffa, Harry V. *Thomism and Aristotelianism.* Westport, Conn.: Greenwood Press, 1972.

John Damascene. "Spring of Knowledge." In *Die Schriften des Johannes von Damaskos,* vol. 1, edited by Bonifatius Kotter. Berlin: De Gruyter, 1969.

John Paul II, Pope St. *Fides et Ratio.* Libreria Editrice Vaticana, September 14, 1998.

Jordan, Mark. *The Alleged Aristotelianism of Thomas Aquinas.* Etienne Gilson Series, vol. 15. Toronto: Pontifical Institute of Mediaeval Studies, 1990.

Journet, Charles. *What Is Dogma?* Translated by Mark Pontifex. San Francisco: Ignatius Press, 2011.

Kaczor, Christopher. "Is the *Sententia libri Ethicorum* of Thomas Aquinas Only an Interpretation of Aristotle?" *American Catholic Philosophical Quarterly* 78.3 (2004): 353–78.

———, ed. *O Rare Ralph McInerny: Stories and Reflections on a Legendary Notre Dame Professor.* South Bend, Ind.: St. Augustine's Press, 2011. A complete bibliography of McInerny's work is found in Kaczor's volume, pp. 114–23.

Kane, William, OP. *Approach to Philosophy: Elements of Thomism.* Washington, D.C.: The Thomist Press, 1962.

Kant, Immanuel. *The Conflict of the Faculties (Der Streit der Fakultäten).* Translated by Mary J. Gregor. Lincoln: University of Nebraska Press, 1992.

———. *Foundation of the Metaphysics of Morals.* Translated by Lewis Whitebeck. Upper Saddle River, N.J.: Prentice-Hall, 1997.

Keys, Mary. *Aquinas, Aristotle, and the Promise of the Common Good.* New York: Cambridge University Press, 2006.

Klubertanz, George, SJ. *St. Thomas Aquinas on Analogy: A Textual Analysis and Systematic Synthesis.* Chicago: Loyola University Press, 1960.

Koterski, Joseph, SJ. *An Introduction to Medieval Philosophy.* Oxford: Wiley-Blackwell, 2008.

———. "The Status of Personalism in Catholic Moral Thinking Today." *The Dunwoodie Review* 32 (2009): 241–59.

Lamb, Matthew. *Eternity, Time, and the Life of Wisdom.* Ave Maria, Fla.: Sapientia Press, 2007.

———. "The Challenges Facing Catholic Intellectual Life." *Nova et Vetera* (English ed.) 11. 4 (2013): 969–91.

Leo XIII, Pope. *Aeterni Patris.* Libreria Editrice Vaticana, August 4, 1879.

Liptay, John, and David Liptay, eds. *The Importance of Insight.* Toronto: University of Toronto Press, 2008.

Litt, Thomas. *Les corps célestes dans l'univers de saint Thomas d'Aquin.* Paris: Publications Universitaires-Béatrice Nauwelaerts, 1963.

Lonergan, Bernard, SJ. *Insight: A Study of Human Understanding.* Toronto: University of Toronto Press, 1992.

Long, James, OP., ed. *Philosophy and the God of Abraham: Essays in Memory of James A. Weisheipl, O.P.* Toronto: Pontifical Institute of Mediaeval Studies, 1991.

Long, Steven A. "The Efficacy of God's Sacramental Presence." *Nova et Vetera* 7 (English ed.) (2009): 869–76.

———. *Natura Pura: On the Recovery of Nature in the Doctrine of Grace.* Bronx, N.Y.: Fordham University Press, 2010.

———. *Analogia Entis: On the Analogy of Being, Metaphysics, and the Act of Faith.* Notre Dame, Ind.: Notre Dame University Press, 2011.

Loux, Michael J. *Primary Ousia: An Essay on Aristotle's Metaphysics Z and H.* Ithaca, N.Y.: Cornell University Press, 1991.

Lyotard, Jean-François. *La condition postmoderne: Rapport sur le savoir.* Paris: Editions de Minuit, 1979.

MacArthur, R. "Universal *in Praedicando*, Universal *in Causando*." *Laval Théologique et Philosophique*, 18.1 (1962): 59–95.

MacIntyre, Alasdair. *Whose Justice? Which Rationality?* Notre Dame, Ind.: University of Notre Dame Press, 1988.

———. *Three Rival Versions of Moral Enquiry: Encyclopedia, Genealogy, and Tradition*, Notre Dame, Ind.: University of Notre Dame Press, 1990.

———. *God, Philosophy, Universities: A Selective History of the Catholic Philosophical Tradition.* New York: Rowman and Littlefield, 2009.

———. *After Virtue: A Study in Moral Virtue*, 3rd ed. Notre Dame, Ind.: University of Notre Dame Press, 2010.

Maritain, Jacques. *An Essay on Christian Philosophy.* Translated by Edward Flannery. New York: Philosophical Library, Inc., 1955.

———. *The Degrees of Knowledge.* Translated by Gerald Phelan. Notre Dame, Ind.: University of Notre Dame Press, 1995.

McInerny, Ralph. *Ethica Thomistica: The Moral Philosophy of Thomas Aquinas.* Washington, D.C.: The Catholic University of America Press, 1982.

———. *Aquinas on Human Action: A Theory of Practice*. Washington D.C.: The Catholic University of America Press, 1992.

———. *Aquinas against the Averroists: On There Being Only One Intellect*. West Lafayette, Ind.: Purdue University Press, 1993.

———. *Characters in Search of Their Author*. Notre Dame, Ind.: University of Notre Dame Press, 2001.

———. *Aquinas*. Cambridge, UK: Polity Press, 2004.

———. *I Alone Have Escaped to Tell You: My Life and Pastimes*. Notre Dame, Ind.: University of Notre Dame Press, 2006.

———. *Praeambula Fidei: Thomism and the God of Philosophers*. Washington, D.C.: The Catholic University of America Press, 2006.

———. "Why I Am a Thomist." *American Catholic Philosophical Quarterly* 83.3 (2009).

———. *Dante and the Blessed Virgin*. Notre Dame, Ind.: University of Notre Dame Press, 2010.

———. "The Division of Philosophy." Thomas Aquinas, *in History of Western Philosophy*, vol. 2. http://www3.nd.edu/Departments/Maritain/etext/hwp220.htm

Minnis, A. J. *Medieval Theory of Authorship*. Philadelphia: University of Pennsylvania Press, 1984.

Möhler, Johann Adam. *Unity in the Church, or, The Principle of Catholicism: Presented in the Spirit of the Church Fathers of the First Three Centuries*. Washington D.C.: The Catholic University of America Press, 1996.

Montagnes, Bernard. *The Doctrine of the Analogy of Being According to Thomas Aquinas*. Translated by E. M. Macierowski. Milwaukee: Marquette University Press, 2004.

Morerod, Charles. *Cajetan et Luther en 1518*. Edition, traduction et commentaire des opuscules d'Augsbourg de Cajetan, "Cahiers Œcuméniques" 26, 2. Fribourg: Editions Universitaires, 1994.

———. *Ecumenism and Philosophy: Philosophical Questions for a Renewal of Dialogue*. Translated by Therese C. Scarpelli. Ave Maria, Fla.: Sapientia Press, 2006.

———. *La philosophie des religions de John Hick: La continuité des principes philosophiques de la période "chrétienne orthodoxe" à la période "pluraliste."* Paris–Les Plans: Parole et silence, 2006.

———. *The Church and the Human Quest for Truth*. Washington, D.C.: The Catholic University of America Press, 2008.

Newman, John Henry. *An Essay on the Development of Christian Doctrine*. New York: Sheed and Ward, 1960.

O'Callaghan, John. "*Imago Dei*: A Test Case for St. Thomas's Augustinianism." In *Aquinas the Augustinian*, edited by M. Dauphinais, D. Barry, and M. Levering, 100–144. Washington, D.C.: The Catholic University of America Press, 2007.

Pangle, Thomas, ed. *Studies in Platonic Political Philosophy*. Chicago: University of Chicago Press, 1983.

Peghaire, J. *Intellectus et ratio selon s. Thomas d'Aquin*. Ottawa: J. Vrin–Institut d'études médiévales, 1936.

Percy, Walker. *Lost in the Cosmos: The Last Self-Help Book*. New York: Picador, 1986.

Plato. *The Collected Dialogues and Letters*. Edited by Edith Hamilton and Huntington Cairns. Princeton, N.J.: Princeton University Press, 1985.

Quay, Paul, SJ. *The Mystery Hidden for Ages in God*. New York: Peter Lang, 1995.

Rice, Joseph P. "Consciousness, Conscience, and Persons: A Reflection on Wojtyła's

'Trans-Phenomenological' Approach to Subjectivity and Intersubjectivity." Fellowship of Catholic Scholars Conference, 2012.

Rorty, Richard M. *Philosophy and the Mirror of Nature* Princeton, N.J.: Princeton University Press, 1979.

———. *Objectivity, Relativism and Truth.* New York: Cambridge University Press, 1991.

Russell, Bertrand. *Why I Am Not a Christian and Other Essays on Religion and Related Subjects.* Edited by P. Edwards. New York: Simon and Schuster, 1963.

Schall, James V., SJ. *The Order of Things.* San Francisco: Ignatius Press, 2007.

Scheeben, Matthias J. *The Mysteries of Christianity.* Translated by Cyril Vollert, SJ. St. Louis, Mo.: B. Herder Book, 1946.

Schüller, Bruno. *Wholly Human: Essays on the Theory and the Language of Morality.* Translated by Peter Heinegg. Washington D.C.: Georgetown University Press, 1986.

Smalley, B. *The Study of the Bible in the Middle Ages.* 3rd ed. Oxford: Blackwell, 1983.

Sokolowski, Robert. *Husserlian Meditations: How Words Present Things* Evanston, Ill.: Northwestern University Press, 1974.

———. *Presence and Absence: A Philosophical Investigation of Language and Being.* Bloomington, Ind.: Indiana University Press, 1978.

———. *Pictures, Quotations, and Distinctions: Fourteen Essays in Phenomenology.* Notre Dame, Ind.: University of Notre Dame Press, 1992.

———. *Eucharistic Presence: A Study in the Theology of Disclosure.* Washington, D.C.: The Catholic University of America Press, 1994.

———. *The God of Faith and Reason.* Washington, D.C.: The Catholic University of America Press, 1995.

———. *Introduction to Phenomenology.* Cambridge: Cambridge University Press, 2000.

———. *Christian Faith and Human Understanding: Studies on the Eucharist, Trinity, and the Human Person.* Washington, D.C.: The Catholic University of America Press, 2006.

———. *Phenomenology of the Human Person.* Cambridge: Cambridge University Press, 2008.

Spitzer, Robert, SJ. *New Proofs for the Existence of God: Contributions of Contemporary Physics and Philosophy.* Grand Rapids, Mich.: Wm. B. Eerdmans, 2010.

Sulavik, Andrew T. "*Principia and Introitus* in Thirteenth Century Biblical Exegesis with Related Texts." In *La Bibbia del XIII secolo, Storia del testo, storia dell'esegesi,* edited by G. Cremascoli and F. Santi, 269–87. Florence: SISMEL—Edizioni del Galluzo, 2004.

Tanner, Norman, SJ. *The Decrees of the Ecumenical Councils.* Washington D.C.: Georgetown University Press, 1990.

Tessitore, Aristide. *Reading Aristotle's* Ethics: *Virtue, Rhetoric, and Political Philosophy.* Albany: State University of New York Press, 1996.

Thomas Aquinas. *De ente et essentia.* Opera Omnia Edition Leonine. Vol. 47. Rome.

———. *De unitate intellectus contra Averroistas.*

———. *Expositio libri Posteriorum Analyticorum.*

———. *Expositio super librum Boethii De Trinitate.* Edited by B. Decker. Leiden: Brill, 1965.

———. *In Aristotelis librum De anima.*

———. *Lectura romana in primum Sententiarum Petri Lombardi.* Edited by L. E. Boyle and John F. Boyle. Toronto: Pontifical Institute of Mediaeval Studies, 2006.

———. *Opera Omnia, recognovit ac instruxit Enrique Alarcón* Pamplona: Universitas Navarrensis.

———. *Prologe zu den Aristoteles-Kommentaren* Edited by Francis Cheneval and Ruedi Imbach. Frankfurt am Main: Klostermann, 1993.

———. *Summa contra Gentiles.* Opera Omnia 13–15. Rome: Riccardi Garroni, 1918–30.

———. *Summa theologiae.* 4 vols. Ottawa: Commissio Piana, 1953.

———. *Treatise on Separate Substances.* Translated by Francis J. Lescoe. West Hartford, Conn.: St. Joseph College, 1963.

Torrell, Jean-Pierre, OP. *L'Initiation à Saint Thomas d'Aquin: Sa personne et son oeuvre.* Paris: Editions Cerf, 1993. English translation: *Saint Thomas Aquinas.* Vol. 1, *The Person and His Work.* Washington, D.C.: The Catholic University of America, 1996.

Vattimo, Gianni. *Dopo la cristianità: Per un cristianesimo non religioso.* Milan: Garzanti, 2002.

———. *Credere di credere: È possibile essere cristiani nonostante la Chiesa?* Milan: Garzanti, 2007.

Wallace, William A. *Galileo and His Sources.* Princeton, N.J.: Princeton University Press, 1984.

Weisheipl, James, OP. *Friar Thomas D'Aquino.* Garden City, N.Y.: Doubleday, 1974.

Wippel, John F. *The Metaphysical Thought of Thomas Aquinas: From Finite Being to Uncreated Being.* Washington D.C.: The Catholic University of America Press, 2000.

Wojtyła, Karol. *The Acting Person.* Translated by Andrzej Potocki. Boston: D. Reidel Publishing, 1997. German translation: *Person und Tat.* Translation by Herbert Spencer. Freiburg: Herder, 1982.

Contributors

TIMOTHY BELLAMAH, OP, teaches at the Dominican House of Studies, Washington, D.C. He received his Ph.D. with highest honors from the École Pratique des Hautes Études (Section des Sciences Religieuses), Paris, 2008. He has published Medieval Biblical Commentaries with Oxford University Press and Brepols Publishers, as well as articles in a number of Dominican publications.

JOHN BOYLE is professor of theology and Catholic studies at the University of St. Thomas in St. Paul, Minnesota, where he has taught since earning his Ph.D. in Medieval Studies from the Center for Medieval Studies at the University of Toronto. In 1995 he was named University of St. Thomas Distinguished Educator of the Year, and he was awarded the 2013 Aquinas Medal from the University of Dallas. He has authored a number of essays on the theology of St. Thomas Aquinas, as well as on his scriptural commentaries, that are published in books and such journals as *Nova et Vetera, Moreana, Annuario Filosofico, The Thomist, Pro Ecclesia*. With Leonard P. Boyle, OP, he edited the critical edition of St. Thomas's *Lectura romana in primum Sententiarum Petri Lombardi*.

ROMANUS CESSARIO, OP, is professor of systematic theology at St. John's Major Seminary in the Archdiocese of Boston, Massachusetts, and also taught for many years at the Dominican House of Studies in Washington, D.C. In 2013 the Dominican Order honored him as a "Master in Sacred Theology." He is a member of the Pontifical Academy of St. Thomas Aquinas. He has written many books, including *A Short History of Thomism, Introduction to Moral Theology, Christian Faith and Theological Life, The Moral Virtues and Theological Ethics, The Seven Last Words of Jesus, The Seven Sorrows of Mary*, and *Theology and Sanctity*. He has also authored numerous popular and scholarly articles in such journals as *The Thomist, Logos, New*

Blackfriars, Pierre d'angle, Communio, Medieval Philosophy and Theology, Catholic Historical Review, and others.

BRIAN DALEY, SJ, is the Catherine F. Huisking professor of theology at the University of Notre Dame. Among his books is *The Hope of the Early Church, Gregory of Nazianzus,* and *Light on the Mountain: Greek Patristic and Byzantine Homilies on the Transfiguration of the Lord.* His scholarly articles have been published in such journals as *Modern Theology, Pro Ecclesia,* and *Journal of Early Christian Studies.* In 2012 he received the Ratzinger Prize for Theology personally from Pope Benedict XVI.

LAWRENCE DEWAN, OP, was professor of philosophy at Dominican University College in Ottawa, Canada, and was a member of the Pontifical Academy of St. Thomas Aquinas. On February 12, 2015, he died, having enriched the fields of Thomistic metaphysics, natural philosophy, and ethics. Recent books are *Form and Being: Studies in Thomistic Metaphysics* and *Wisdom, Law, and Virtue: Essays in Thomistic Ethics.* He has written numerous articles in such journals as *Science et Esprit, Maritain Studies, Nova et Vetera, Acta Philosophica, The Review of Metaphysics, The Thomist, Gregorianum,* and *American Catholic Philosophical Quarterly.*

GILLES EMERY, OP, is professor of dogmatic theology at the University of Fribourg. In 2012 the Dominican Order honored him as a "Master in Sacred Theology." He is a member of the International Theological Commission of the Catholic Church and the Pontifical Academy of St. Thomas Aquinas. He is editor of the French edition of *Nova et Vetera,* and an associate editor of the English edition of *Nova et Vetera.* He has authored *La Trinité créatrice, The Trinity: An Introduction to Catholic Doctrine on the Triune God, The Trinitarian Theology of Saint Thomas Aquinas,* and *Trinity, Church, and the Human Person: Thomistic Essays.* He has co-edited with P. Gisel *Le Christianisme est-il un monotheisme?*; and with M. Levering, *The Oxford Handbook of the Trinity.* His articles have appeared in numerous edited books, as well as in *Nova et Vetera, Revue Thomiste, The Thomist,* and *Freiburger Zeitschrift für Philosophie und Theologie.*

KEVIN FLANNERY, SJ, is professor of the history of ancient philosophy at the Pontifical Gregorian University in Rome, Italy, where he has served as dean of the Faculty of Philosophy. He has authored many studies on the history of philosophy and logic, especially on Aristotelian logic, in journals such as *Ancient Philosophy, Journal of the History and Philosophy of Logic, American Journal of Jurisprudence, Gregorianum, International Philosophi-*

cal Quarterly, and *Heythrop Journal*. He has written, among other books, *Action and Character According to Aristotle: The Logic of the Moral Life*, *Christian and Moral Action*, and *Acts Amid Precepts: The Aristotelian Logical Structure of Thomas Aquinas's Moral Theory*.

MARC D. GUERRA is associate professor and chair of the Department of Theology at Assumption College, Worchester, Massachusetts. He previously taught and was director of graduate students at Ave Maria University in Florida. With Peter A. Lawler he was granted the prestigious University of Chicago New Science of Virtues award, and he has co-edited with Lawler *The Science of Modern Virtue: On Descartes, Darwin, and Locke*. He has authored a number of essays published in *Perspectives on Political Science*, *First Things*, *Modern Age*, *Interpretation*, *Society*, *Logos*, *Gregorianum*, and *Religious Studies and Theology*. He wrote *Christians as Political Animals: Taking the Measure of Modernity and Modern Democracy*; and he has edited *Reason, Revelation and Human Affairs: Selected Writings of James V. Schall*, and *Jerusalem, Athens, and Rome: Essays in Honor of James V. Schall, S.J.*

CHRISTOPHER KACZOR is visiting fellow in religion and public life at Princeton University's James Madison Program and is professor of philosophy at Loyola Marymount University in Los Angeles. He was a Federal Chancellor Fellow at the University of Cologne, Germany, and returned there as a Fulbright scholar. He is author of a number of books, including *Thomas Aquinas on Faith, Hope, and Love*, and *The Ethics of Abortion: Women's Rights, Human Life, and the Question of Justice*, as well as *Proportionalism and the Natural Law Tradition*. With Janet Smith he co-authored *Life Issues—Medical Choices*; and with Thomas Sherman, SJ, *Thomas Aquinas on the Cardinal Virtues*. He edited *O Rare Ralph McInerny*. He has done research on issues of ethics, philosophy, and religion that have appeared in *National Review*, *The New York Times*, *The Wall Street Journal*, etc.

JOSEPH KOTERSKI, SJ, is professor of philosophy at Fordham University, having served as chair of the Philosophy Department. He is editor-in-chief of the *International Philosophical Quarterly*, and he continues to serve as president of the Fellowship of Catholic Scholars. He was awarded the Maritain Medal for Scholarly Excellence in 2008. He wrote *An Introduction to Medieval Philosophy: Basic Concepts*, and has co-edited a number of books, including, with Ron Begley, *Medieval Education*; with John Conley, SJ, *Culture and Creed*; and with David R. Foster, *The Two Wings of Catholic Thought: Essays on Fides et Ratio*. He has authored numerous articles that have appeared in books and in journals such as *Nova et Vetera*, *Dunwoodie Review*,

Fellowship of Catholic Scholars Quarterly, Thomas More Studies, Journal of Catholic Legal Studies, Jahrbuch der Österreichischen Karl Jaspers Gesellschaft, The Heythrop Journal, Augustinian Studies, and *The New Scholasticism.*

STEVEN A. LONG is professor of theology at Ave Maria University, having previously taught at St. Thomas University in St. Paul, Minnesota, Christendom College, and the Catholic University of America. He is a corresponding member of the Pontifical Academy of St. Thomas Aquinas. He has authored the books *Analogia Entis: On the Analogy of Being, Metaphysics, and the Act of Faith; Natura Pura: On the Recovery of Nature in the Doctrine of Grace;* and *The Teleological Grammar of the Moral Act.* With Christopher Thompson he has co-edited *Reason and the Rule of Faith: Conversations in the Tradition with John Paul II.* He has written many scholarly articles published in books and in journals such as *The Thomist, Communio, International Philosophical Quarterly, National Catholic Bioethics Quarterly, Revue Thomiste, Nova et Vetera, New Blackfriars,* and *Studies in Christian Ethics.*

GUY MANSINI, OSB, is professor of systematic theology at Saint Meinrad School of Theology and has served as a visiting professor at the Pontifical Gregorian University. He has authored many scholarly articles in journals such as *First Things, The Thomist, Nova et Vetera,* and *Gregorianum.* Among his recent books are *Promising and the Good,* and *The Word Has Dwelt Among Us: Explorations in Theology.* He has co-edited with James Hart, *Ethics and Theological Disclosures: The Thought of Robert Sokolowski.*

CHARLES MOREROD, OP, is bishop of the Diocese of Lausanne, Geneva, and Fribourg, Switzerland. He was professor of dogmatic theology and rector of the Pontifical University of St. Thomas Aquinas in Rome. He serves as secretary general of the International Theological Commission and consultor of the Congregation for the Doctrine of the Faith, and as a member of the Congregation for Catholic Education. He has authored many studies for edited books and in journals such as *Nova et Vetera* (French and English editions), *Cahiers Oecuméniques, Sources, Freiburger Zeitschrift für Philosophie und Theologie, Greek Orthodox Theological Review, Parole et silence, L'Osservatore Romano, Anglicum, Divus Thomas, Lumen Veritatis, Revue Thomiste,* and *Camillianum.* Among his recently authored books are *Ecumenism and Philosophy: Philosophical Questions for the Renewal of Dialogue; The Church and the Human Quest for Truth;* and *Tradition et unité des chrétiens: Le dogme comme condition de possibilité de l'oecuménisme.*

MICHAEL NOVAK is the retired George F. Jewett Scholar in Religion, Philosophy, and Public Policy at the American Enterprise Institute, and he is now trustee and visiting professor at Ave Maria University. He was awarded the prestigious Templeton Prize in 1994 and was appointed U.S. ambassador to the United Nations Commission on Human Rights. He has authored numerous essays, both scholarly and popular, that have appeared in many languages. Among the more than forty-five books he has written, *The Spirit of Democratic Capitalism* enjoyed international acclaim, especially in the Solidarity movement in Poland and in other Eastern European countries. Prime Minister Margaret Thatcher stated his was the most important book she read while in office. Recently he has authored *Writing from Left to Right: My Journey from Liberal to Conservative; All Nature Is a Sacramental Fire: Moments of Beauty, Sorrow, and Joy;* and *No One Sees God: The Dark Night of Atheists and Believers.*

ROGER NUTT is associate professor of theology and director of graduate students in the Theology Department at Ave Maria University. He previously taught at Aquinas College in Nashville, after receiving his doctorate in sacred theology from the Pontifical University of St. Thomas Aquinas in Rome. His dissertation was awarded the Aquinas Prize by the Aquinas Center for Theological Renewal. He is managing editor of *Thomistica.net.* His scholarly articles have appeared in *Nova et Vetera, Louvain Studies, Gregorian, The Josephinum Journal of Theology, Angelicum,* and *Antiphon.* His translation and introduction to Thomas Aquinas's *De Unione Verbi Incarnati* will soon appear in the Dallas Medieval Texts and Translations Series. He edited and introduced Charles Journet's *What Is Dogma?*

JOHN P. O'CALLAGHAN is associate professor of philosophy at the University of Notre Dame and a member of the Pontifical Academy of St. Thomas Aquinas, and has been president of the American Catholic Philosophical Association. He has authored many scholarly articles on metaphysics, ethics, and Thomism in books and journals such as *The Thomist, The Review of Metaphysics, American Catholic Philosopical Quarterly,* and *Nova et Vetera.* His books include *Thomistic Realism and the Linguistic Turn: Toward a More Perfect Form of Existence;* with Thomas Hibbs he co-edited *Recovering Nature: Essays in Honor of Ralph McInerny.*

SEBASTIAN WALSHE, O PRAEM, is professor of philosophy in the seminary program of the Norbertine Abbey of St. Michael in California, since receiving his Ph.D. from the Pontifical University of St. Thomas Aquinas in Rome. He was also a visiting professor of philosophy for several years at the

Angelicum. His responsibilities as a much-sought-after retreat master have directed his research and writing toward spiritual direction. At the same time he has written scholarly articles on Trinitarian theology, Christology, predestination, the common good and causality in Aquinas, publishing them in *The Aquinas Review, The Angelicum Review, The Thomist,* and *Folia Theologica.*

KEVIN WHITE is associate professor of philosophy in the School of Philosophy at the Catholic University of America. After receiving his Ph.D. from the University of Ottawa, he was a postdoctoral fellow in the Social Sciences and Humanities Research Council of Canada, and became a member of the Leonine Commission. He is editor of *Hispanic Philosophy in the Age of Discovery* and co-editor and co-translator with Romanus Cessario of *John Capreolus on the Virtues.* He has authored many scholarly articles that appeared in books and in the following journals: *Dialogue, La Parola, Documenti e studi sulla tradizione filosofica medievale, Medieval Studies, The Thomist, American Catholic Philosophical Quarterly, Studies in Thomistic Theology, Achivum Franciscanum Historicum, The Review of Metaphysics,* and *Nova et Vetera.*

Index

Abelard, Peter, 165

abortion, 65, 66

Abraham, 97, 169n47

abstraction, 61, 113, 255, 276

Ackrill, J. L. 176n3

act: human, xviii, 21, 94, 138–39, 148, 150, 151, 152, 292, 298; pure, xvii, 78, 277

Actus Purus, 85, 233

Adler, Mortimer J. 56n3, 231

adoption, 67–68

Aetius, 102

Albert the Great, 52, 145, 156n7, 165, 176, 188, 193, 232, 235, 280, 284n17, 286

Alcibiades, 24, 258, 263

Alexander of Alexandria, Bishop, 99–100

Alexander the Great, 144

Alexander, Irene, xi

Alighieri, Dante, xx, 240–49

al-Kindi, Abu Yusuf Ya'qub ibn Ishaq, 155, 157

Amann, E., 168n44

analogy, xvii, xix, 70, 92, 176, 203, 205–8, 210, 242, 276, 298; of being, 82–85; of participation, 74, 83–85; of proper proportionality, xvii, 82, 85

anamnesis, 35

angels, 33, 35, 61, 103n31, 249, 271, 277

Anselm of Canterbury, 93, 176

anthropocentrism, 7

anthropology, 37, 154; philosophical, 56, 166; theological, xvi, 37, 62–63, 67, 128

Apologists, 98n23

appetite, 63, 264

Aristotle, xv, 28, 31, 33, 37, 39, 50n23, 106, 107, 109, 132n65, 155, 241, 298; and Aquinas, xvii, xix, 40, 44, 51, 74–82, 85–7, 136–46, 175, 177–78, 181–82, 185, 187, 190–91, 201, 230–31, 238, 243–44, 253–54, 275, 279–92, 297; anthropology of, 166; on the beautiful, 256, 260; on being, 51n26, 52, 75, 81–82, 86; on the human body, 255–56; on the four causes, xviii, 44, 51, 52, 75, 76, 78–80, 85, 142, 159, 160, 162, 164, 171, 230, 235, 276n24; distinction of essence and existence, xvii, 77–8, 86; on form, 25, 29, 59, 143; on the good, 256, 275–76; on happiness, 263; on human nature, 33, 59, 65, 138, 254n3; on human acts, 138; on imagination, 166; on the intellect, 26, 166, 285; on knowledge, 166; on magnanimity, 253–66; on matter, 59, 143; natural theology of, xvii, 31, 49, 74–82, 85–6, 100, 211n7, 244–46; on *nous*, 25–26; on order, 146–47, 150, 176; philosophy of, xii, 75, 18, 150, 152; on potency and act, 82, 85; on first principles, 150, 152, 156, 212n8; proper proportionality, xvii; on reason, 150, 182, 187, 201; on relative predicates, 176, 178–79, 187, 180n15, 186, 191, 193–94, 201; on relations, 176, 182, 185, 187, 190, 194–95, 201; on the senses, 166; on the soul, 25, 29, 166, 253, 285; on substance, 59, 75–7, 86, 144, 280; on *telos*, 33; on truth, xx, 51n26; on the universe, 52, 74–8, 80, 82, 144–45; on the virtues, xx, 212, 257–58, 263, 281; on wisdom, 21, 39, 146, 154, 276n24. *See also* Aquinas's commentaries on Aristotle; causes, *individual writings of*; magnanimity

Coffey, Brian, 138n8, 142n15
Collins, Francis, 11
Commentary on the Book of Causes
(Thomas Aquinas). *See Super librum De
causis* (Thomas Aquinas)
Commentary on the Epistle to the Hebrews
(Thomas Aquinas). *See Super Epistolam
ad Hebraeos* (Thomas Aquinas)
Commentary on the Metaphysics (Thomas
Aquinas). *See Sententia libri Metaphysi-
cae* (Thomas Aquinas)
Commentary on the Nicomachean Ethics
(Thomas Aquinas). *See Sententia libri
Ethicorum* (Thomas Aquinas)
Commentary on the Physics (Thomas Aqui-
nas). *See In libros Physicorum* (Thomas
Aquinas)
Commentary on the Politics (Thomas
Aquinas). *See Sententia libri Politicorum*
(Thomas Aquinas)
common good, xxi, 267–78
communitarianism, 10, 235
Congar, Yves, 239
connaturality, xvii, 131, 132, 133
Conrad, Joseph, 242, 246
consciousness, xi, xiii, 9, 16, 17, 62, 63, 215;
historial, 35, 36
Constantinople, Second Council of, 106, 168
Constantius II, Emperor, 101
contemplation, 49n23, 53, 95, 110, 113, 119,
127, 262
contingency, 36, 51–52, 113, 169, 171, 211n7
contradiction, principle of, xv, 13, 195, 199,
289
Copernicus, 36
cosmology, 229, 232. *See also* philosophy
cosmos, xxi, 57, 97, 99, 126, 229, 257, 265
Cottier, Georges M.–M., 138n8
councils, Church, 68. *See also individual
councils*
creationism, 11
creeds, 8, 50, 67, 100, 132–33, 211, 225
Crosby, John F., 56n4
Cynicism, 94, 218

D'Ancona Costa, C., 155n4, 156n6, 157n7
Dahan, G., 158n11, 159n14, 165n33, 167n41,
169n47

Dalton, John, 36
Danneels, Godfried, 237
Dante. *See* Alighieri
Darwin, Charles, 36, 270
De aeternitate mundi (Thomas Aquinas), 52
De anima (Aristotle), 25–6, 29, 154, 166,
284, 285
De caelo (Aristotle), xviii, 137, 142–47
De ente et essentia (Thomas Aquinas),
14n39
De Koninck, Charles, xx, xxi, 116–17, 123,
134, 228–29, 232–35, 236, 239, 267–78, 298
de Lubac, Henri, 245n13
de Margerie, B., 168n44, 168n45
De principiis naturae (Thomas Aquinas),
283
de Soto, Domingo, 232
De substantiis separatis (Thomas Aquinas),
51n27, 52n29, 76n5, 76, 77
De unitate intellectus contra Averroistas
(Thomas Aquinas), 26, 283, 285n18
deism, 57
Del Punta, Francesco, 284, 288
deliberation, xii–xiii, 57
democracy, 10
Descartes, René, xvi, 14–16, 18, 31, 32, 35, 36,
37, 59, 119, 137, 245n13, 294
desire, xiii, 39, 61, 69, 103n31, 126n40, 127,
244, 245, 248, 269, 273, 274, 296
Dewan, Lawrence, 130, 131
dialectics, xxi, 104, 106, 112, 140–41, 150
dignity, xx, 56, 105, 263; human, 46n11, 65–
67, 226, 234; natural, 57, 213; moral, 57
Dionysius, 165n35, 281
dogma, 8, 10, 98n23, 106, 112, 120, 131, 228,
236
Dondaine, Hyacinthe, 183n31
Droge, Arthur J., 95n8, 96n13
Dronke, P., 159n14
dualism, xiv, xvi, 37, 58, 64
Dulles, Avery, xi n2, 119n11, 120, 132
Duns Scotus, John, xviii, 27, 81, 196n93,
198–99, 233
duty, 65, 67–68

Échivard, Jean-Baptiste, 136
economics, 65, 66, 113, 149, 151n32
Eddington, Arthur Stanley, 229

education, xiv, xxii, 40, 43, 54, 55, 60, 65, 94,
104, 135, 203, 209, 210, 215, 295, 297
Einstein, Albert, 36, 229
emotion, 58, 62, 63, 64, 269, 299
Empedocles, 244, 270
empiricism, 119–20, 145n21. *See also* science
Endress, G., 155n4
ends. *See* teleology
Enlightenment, xiii, xvii, 3, 92n2, 94, 111,
112, 117–18, 120, 122, 231, 236, 237
epistemology, 5n5, 35, 37–38, 55, 66, 119–20,
122, 123, 125n37, 126, 132
eschatology, 114
essence, xvii, 26–27, 29, 44, 77–78, 85–86,
93, 101, 103, 113, 142, 146, 178–80, 182, 196,
197n99, 198–200, 219, 244, 271–72, 277, 287
eternal life, 38n24, 52–3. *See also* beatitude
eternity, 6, 68–69, 283–84; of the world,
44n5, 76–77, 80
Eudemian Ethics (Aristotle), 256n14
Eudoxius, 101, 102
Eunomius of Cyzicus, 102–3, 104
Eusebius of Nicomedia, 100–101
euthanasia, 65, 66
exegesis, 5, 7, 38, 158–72, 231, 284n17, 285,
289, 292
Expositio libri Posteriorum Analyticorum
(Thomas Aquinas), xviii, 22, 137–42,
146, 148
Expositio super librum Boethii De Trinitate
(Thomas Aquinas), 45n9, 49n22, 125,
130n57, 130n58, 131n61, 133n67, 133n68,
134, 284n17

Fabro, Cornelio, 5, 14–16
family, 62, 65, 149; of God, 67
Faulkner, Robert, 260
Fernández Alonso, Aniceto, 232
fideism, 10–11
filiation, 192, 193n74
filioque, 68n18
forgiveness, 68, 71
Fortin, Ernest, 264, 265n65
Francis, Pope, xi
fundamentalism, xiv, 10–11

Gauthier, René-Antoine, 146
Geach, Peter, 53

genetics, 60, 64, 65
George, Robert P., 59n11
Gerard of Cremona, 156
Gide, André, 241
gift, xix, 13, 63, 68–69, 71–72, 84, 131, 133,
153, 207, 235, 238, 256, 264
Gilbert of Poitiers, 176
Gilson, Etienne, xiv, 52, 238, 241–42, 243,
245n13
glory, 60, 69–70, 96, 99n24, 115, 168n46,
172, 215, 216, 220n36, 221, 249, 299
Gnosticism, 38
goals. *See* teleology
Godfrey of St. Victor, 151
grammar, 141
Greeley, Andrew, 241, 247, 295
Gregory Nazianzen, xvii, 102–6, 114
Gregory of Nyssa, 102, 217n22
Gregory the Great, Pope, 166
Gregory, Brad S., xiv n6
Guerric of Saint-Quentin, 165

habit, xiii, xix, 50n24, 53n36, 62, 63, 77, 94,
123, 124, 148, 157n9, 178, 186, 195
Hadot, Pierre, 94
happiness, 49, 50, 63, 95, 96, 129, 243, 263,
281, 285
Harnack, Adolf von, 92, 93n2, 98, 112
Havel, Vaclav, 254n3
heaven, xx, 8, 21, 38n24, 46n11, 60, 103n31,
243, 245n14, 246, 249
Heidegger, Martin, 9n21, 245n13
hell, xx, 244, 246, 278
Hemming, Laurence Paul, 78
Henninger, Mark G., 175n1
Henry of Ghent, 27, 196n93
Heraclitus, 97
hermeneutics, 101, 284
heteronomy, 63
Hick, John, 5n5
historicism, xiv, 214n14
Hobbes, Thomas, 39, 272n9
holiness. *See* sanctification
holocaust, xix
Holy Spirit, xvii, xix, xx, 18, 56, 69, 70–72,
105, 114, 133, 161–62, 167n40, 169, 170,
195, 202–8
Homer, 243, 246, 260

Raffray, Matthieu, 176n4

Rahner, Karl, 237

rationalism, xvii, 6, 10–11, 49, 112, 116, 134,
158, 214n14, 245n13

rationalization, 6

Ratner, Herbert, 231n15

Ratzinger, Joseph, xii, 5n5, 245n13. *See also*
Benedict XVI

reason: practical, xviii–xix, 63, 142–43, 147;
speculative, xviii–xix, 120, 132, 142–43,
145, 147, 263, 275–76. *See also* intellect;
science

recapitulation in Christ, xvi, 56, 57, 67,
72–73

receptivity, 69–70, 197, 238

redemption, xiv, xvi, xx, xxi, 52, 70–71, 99,
113, 153, 167, 226, 234–35, 243

reincarnation, 95

relation between beings, xii, xiv, xviii,
25–27, 44n5, 49, 58, 68–69, 81, 83–85, 99,
111, 114, 122, 158, 175–201, 207, 211, 215,
223, 229, 258–59, 266, 274

relativism, xiv, 5n5, 10–11, 17, 18, 202

Remigio de Girolomi, 268n1

resurrection: of body, 38, 58–60, 114; of
Christ, 6, 8, 60, 218, 224

rhetoric, xviii, 103, 140–41, 150, 151n32, 281,
283, 291

Rhetoric (Aristotle), 140–41

Rice, Joseph P., xii n3

Ricoeur, Paul, 224

rights, 17, 65–68

Rorty, Richard, 9–10, 55n1

Rosen, Stanley, 282

Rupert of Deutz, 166

Rushd, Ibn. *See* Averroes

Russell, Bertrand, xvii, 118, 120–22, 123, 125,
131, 134

sacra doctrina, 19–22, 27, 29, 32, 34, 35–40,
45, 46n15, 111

salvation, xi, 9, 32, 38, 45, 47n17, 55, 71, 114,
126, 128–30, 217, 224, 233, 236, 243–44,
278

sanctification, 55, 68, 71–72, 95, 105, 228

Sartre, Jean-Paul, 15–16

Schall, James V., xiii n6, 153

Schillebeeckx, Edward, 237

scholasticism, 17, 34, 58, 106, 107, 112, 136,
146, 213, 291; neo- 69n20, 245n13, 290–91

Schönberger, Rolf, 175n1

Schüller, Bruno, 291

Science, 148; empirical, xv, 55, 112, 229, 236;
natural, xii, xviii, 143–46, 229, 231, 270;
practical, 21–2, 34, 39–40; speculative,
21–2, 34, 39–40, 103–4, 120, 202, 214

Scott, A., 155n3

Scriptum super Sententiis (Thomas Aquinas), 44n3, 50n25, 59n25, 78n7, 84,
142n15, 179n11, 179n13, 180n16, 180n18,
180n20, 181n22, 181n23, 181n24, 181n25,
182n26, 182n27, 182n29, 182n30, 183n32,
185n39, 185n40, 186n47, 187n50, 188n58,
189n60, 190n65, 190n66, 191n69, 192n72,
192n73, 193n77, 194n80, 194n81, 194n82,
194n84, 195n88, 196n92, 196n94, 197n96,
197n98, 197n99, 271n5, 273n12, 275n22

Scripture: allegorical sense, 159, 166, 167,
171, 229, 232; anagogical sense, 169, 171;
literal sense, xviii, 155, 159–60, 163–71;
spiritual sense, xviii, 159, 164, 166, 169,
171; tropological sense, 159, 169, 171

secularism, xv, 49

self-determination, 61–63, 171

Sententia libri De anima (Thomas Aquinas),
26, 285

Sententia libri De sensu et sensato (Thomas
Aquinas), 108

Sententia libri Ethicorum (Thomas Aquinas), xviii, xx–xxi, 137, 138n10, 146–49,
151, 254, 261–63, 279–86, 287n30, 289–92,
297

Sententia libri Metaphysicae (Thomas
Aquinas), 25n8, 82n12, 137n6, 147n25,
175, 177n6, 177n7, 178n10, 179n13, 185n42,
185n43, 186, 194n84, 195n86, 286, 291

Sententia libri Politicorum (Thomas Aquinas), 265n64, 137n6

sentience, 62

Sherwin, Michael, xi n2

Siger of Brabant, 58

similitude, 131, 186

Simon, M. Raphael, 231n15

Simplicius, 144, 187n51

sin, xiv, 4, 247, 248; original, 38, 57, 68–62,
128, 159, 218, 289–90

Virgil, xx, 243, 246

virtue, xiv, xx, xxi, xxii, xxiv, xx–xxi, 50,
53, 55, 63, 69, 70, 103, 124, 132, 133, 209,
212, 213, 245, 248, 253–66, 277, 281, 284,
289; fortitude, xx, 63, 120, 247, 254, 264;
generosity, 69–70, 241; justice, xx, 63, 159,
254, 257; 260; prudence, 21, 222n45, 257,
265, 298; religion, 50, 264–65; temperance, 63n16, 213. *See also specific virtues*

voluntarism, xi, xiii, 18, 92, 157–58

Wallace, William A., 232

Weinandy, Thomas, xi n2

Weisheipl, James, 51n27, 145n19, 149n27,
150n28, 230

Weisheipl, James A., 51n27, 145n19, 149n24,
150n28, 230

will to power, xiii, xvi

William of Alton, 159–62, 165, 167, 172n54

William of Luxi, 162n24, 165

William of Moerbeke, 154n1, 156, 157n7,
180n15

William of Ockham, xiii, xvi, 27, 188

Wippel, John F., 28n12, 178n10, 212n8

wisdom, xv, xx, 18, 20–22, 39, 45n7, 49n23,
84, 94, 96, 97, 147, 154, 235, 269, 276n24,
277n26, 281; Book of, 160, 161, 221, 223,
232, 234; Christ is, 100, 108–10, 113, 114,
161, 221, 234; divine, 13, 46n14, 49n23, 96,
98, 103, 110, 114; Mary as, 233–34

Wojtyła, Karol, xii–xiii, 214n15. *See also*
John Paul II

Wolter, Allan, 58n9

Xanthippe, 24

Theology Needs Philosophy: Acting Against Reason Is Contrary to the Nature of God was designed in Minion with Requiem display type and composed by Kachergis Book Design of Pittsboro, North Carolina. It was printed on 60-pound Natures Book Natural and bound by Thomson-Shore of Dexter, Michigan.